SAMS *Teach Yourself*

Networking

in 24 Hours

Matt Hayden

SECOND EDITION

 **SAMS** *201 West 103rd St., Indianapolis, Indiana, 46290 USA*

Sams Teach Yourself Networking in 24 Hours, Second Edition

Copyright © 2001 by Sams Publishing

International Standard Book Number: 0-672-32002-9

Library of Congress Catalog Card Number: 00-105611

Printed in the United States of America

First Printing: December 2000

05   04   03   02   7   6   5   4

Trademarks

Warning and Disclaimer

ACQUISITIONS EDITOR
Betsy Brown

DEVELOPMENT EDITOR
Susan Hobbs

MANAGING EDITOR
Charlotte Clapp

PROJECT EDITOR
Carol Bowers

COPY EDITOR
Susan Hobbs

INDEXER
Eric Schroeder

PROOFREADER
Katherin Bidwell

TECHNICAL EDITOR
Dallas Releford

TEAM COORDINATOR
Amy Patton

INTERIOR DESIGNER
Gary Adair

COVER DESIGNER
Aren Howell

PRODUCTION
Darin Crone

Contents at a Glance

Contents

About the Author

Matt Hayden is a systems engineer for a Silicon Valley technical firm. His primary expertise is operating systems and networking, and his background includes a stint as a technologist for a merchant banking firm. Matt holds a bachelor's degree in History and a master's degree in English.

When he's not networking or traveling, he spends his time playing music, reading, and cycling.

Dedication

For Beth

Acknowledgements

To everyone who has helped with this: Thank you!

Books don't just appear out of thin air! I'd like to thank Valda Hilley, Betsy Brown, Susan Hobbs, and Dallas Releford, all of whom worked very hard to make this book as good as it could be. To paraphrase my management mentor, Tony the Tiger, "You're great!"

Thanks to the relatives and friends who waited patiently for this to be done, with special thanks to my parents, Doug, Andy, Jenny, and Dan.

Thanks to you, the reader. I hope that this book helps you learn networking fundamentals.

Last, a meditation on starting to read a technical book:

"Here let us breathe and haply institute
A course of learning and ingenious studies."

Shakespeare, The Taming of the Shrew I:i

Tell Us What You Think!

As the reader of this book, *you* are our most important critic and commentator. We value your opinion and want to know what we're doing right, what we could do better, what areas you'd like to see us publish in, and any other words of wisdom you're willing to pass our way.

You can email or write me directly to let me know what you did or didn't like about this book—as well as what we can do to make our books stronger.

Please note that I cannot help you with technical problems related to the topic of this book, and that due to the high volume of mail I receive, I might not be able to reply to every message.

When you write, please be sure to include this book's title and author as well as your name and phone or fax number. I will carefully review your comments and share them with the author and editors who worked on the book.

Email: consumer@samspublishing.com

Mail: Mark Taber
            Associate Publisher
            Sams Publishing
            201 West 103rd Street
            Indianapolis, IN 46290 USA

Introduction

Throughout this book (as you will find when you start reading), the emphasis is placed on theory rather than practice. The reason for this focus: It's easy to figure out how to connect network equipment. The difficult part of networking is understanding theory and being able to put it to use.

Networking is, first and foremost, a process. It's not a static body of knowledge that you can assimilate and then go out to work with. Instead, it's a dynamic field in which change is the only constant. A firm grasp of the fundamentals makes it possible to stay abreast of the changes in networking.

Part I of this book, "A Networking Primer," provides an introduction to networking that explains what a network is (and, indeed, what a computer is). The hours (or chapters) in this part of the book provide a basis for understanding the tightly-bound relationships between hardware and software and an understanding of how those relationships work.

Part II of the book, "The Basics," is dedicated to the basic concepts underlying modern data networking—primarily packet-switched data. If there is one idea that is central to this book, it is packet-switched data. It is my goal that at the end of reading this part of the book, you will have an understanding of packet-switched data, since it's the underlying mechanism for all data networking.

Part III, "Building a Network," walks you through the process of building a network from conception through delivery. The most important idea in Part III is interoperability, an idea that simply means that the parts of a network must all work in concert according to open standards. Capacity planning, security, and so forth are also discussed in this section.

Part IV, "Network Operating Systems," deals with network operating system software. This part of the book is necessarily Microsoft heavy, not because of any bias but because of the depth of Microsoft's market presence. Any of the operating systems discussed in these hours can adequately serve your needs, but the guidelines set forth in Part III of the book should help you select the network operating system and client operating system that best suit your needs.

Part V, "Introduction to Network Administration," deals with the aftermath of building a network. Building a network affects your day-to-day life: There is always something to be fixed or upgraded, and there's a lot of training going on all the time. Administering a network is not for everyone; some people enjoy building networks, some enjoy administering them, and some people enjoy both.

Part VI, "The Future of Networking," talks about where things are in the networking world, where they're going, and what you can do to prepare yourself for them.

If you have any suggestions about what you would like to see in subsequent editions of this book, please send them to www.mcp.com. This book is intended to serve the reader—if we can make changes that will enable this book to work better for you, let us know.

Matt Hayden
Fremont, CA
September 22, 2000

PART I
A Networking Primer

Hour

HOUR 1

An Overview of Networking

Networks are ubiquitous. If you use a credit card or a debit card to make phone calls, or if you use a computer to access the Internet, you're directly relying on a computer network.

Because networks control just about everything, and because networks are made up of computers (which people always seem to consider complex), it's easy to assume that networking is too complex for the average person.

Here's a secret: *Networking isn't really that complicated.*

Networking is no more difficult to learn than is anything else having to do with computers. By spending a little time learning the basics, getting some practice, and having some patience, networking is relatively simple.

There's a lot of technical terminology in this book—what many would call *networking jargon*. Don't be put off by this. Networking is a specialized skill; like any other specialized skill, it has its own vernacular. You aren't expected to know everything about networking, but try to familiarize yourself with many of the concepts and terms presented here. (The glossary at the end of this book can help if you forget a term or two.) A good knowledge base is one of your best assets for successful networking.

In this hour, you'll have the opportunity to learn about the following topics:

- What a network is
- Why you should build a network
- How networks are put together
- The varieties of computer networks
- How the Internet relates to your network

What Is a Network?

If you've ever used a telephone, tracked a package with an overnight shipper, or purchased a new car from a dealership, you've used a network. Of course, they weren't computer networks—they were, respectively, the phone company's switching network, the overnight shipper's package-tracking network, and the car manufacturer's distribution network. And although these networks move phone calls, packages, and cars instead of computer data, they are examples that explain the fundamental purpose of a network. The single most important purpose of any network—computer or otherwise—is to link similar items together using a set of rules that ensures reliable service.

In the telephone network's case, the rules have to do with what happens when you dial a phone number based on how many digits you dial: If you dial seven digits, it's a local call; eleven digits is a long-distance call. For the overnight shipper's network, the rule is that your package is assigned a tracking number that must be recorded each time the package goes through a weigh station or transfer point. And for the car dealership, the rule is that there's only one reseller within a given geographical area; all new cars are delivered to that dealer, and that dealership has a direct link to the manufacturer.

Like other networks, computer networks have basic rules that ensure the safe delivery of information instead of telephone calls, overnight packages, or new cars. A basic set of rules for how a computer network should do its job might look something like this:

- Information must be delivered reliably without any corruption of data.

- Information must be delivered consistently—the network should be capable of determining where its information is going.

- Multiple computers must be able to identify each other across the network.

- There must be a standard way of naming and identifying the parts of the network.

These rules are simple, but they're the core of what a computer network does. Networks can be as simple as a file-transfer program that runs between two computers on a printer-port cable; networks can be as complex as the high-end banking systems that transfer data on pulses of light in fiber-optic cables. Despite this variety, all networks have the same basic goal: to ensure that data is shared quickly, reliably, and accurately.

Why Build a Network?

Why build a network at all? There are a lot of reasons for building networks, whether they're computer networks or car-dealer networks. However diverse the reasons, they ultimately boil down to a few basic points:

- Networks enable communications in ways that fundamentally change the way we view and interact with the work around.

- They increase efficiency.

- They help standardize policies, procedures, and practices among network users.

- Networks can bring together diverse ideas and issues into a common forum, where they can be addressed in a global fashion rather than in a haphazard, case-by-case fashion.

- Networks help ensure that information is redundant—in other words, that it exists in more than one mind (or computer) at a time.

These points made, there are as many different reasons for building computer networks as there are computer networkers. One person may have a bunch of computers at home—one for her, one for her kids, another for her husband. She wants to hook all the computers together so that they can have a common calendar and email—which (trust me) kids will read much more readily than they will a note on the fridge. So she networks the computers. Another person may have a small office with a couple of computers and a single dial-up Internet account. He wants to provide Internet access to all users with a single account…so he networks the computers. And then we have computer hobbyists who want to join together computers just because they can be joined together. Basically, if you have a need to communicate, to share data, to share applications, and want to avoid running from machine to machine with floppy disks, networking offers a lot of benefits.

How Networks Are Put Together

If you were to break a network down into its simplest components, you'd have two pieces. One is the physical network—the wiring, network cards, computers, and other equipment the network uses to transmit data. The other is the logical arrangement of these physical pieces—the rules that allow the physical pieces to work together. We will look at both of these broad subdivisions in this hour. Remember—all this is covered in more detail in the coming hours.

Physical Networking—the Hardware

The *physical network* is easy to understand because it's easy to see—it's hardware! It's the wiring and network cards and computers and hubs and all the other stuff that allows the network to function. If you don't know what those things are, don't worry. It will be explained in the next few pages and throughout the rest of this book. The important thing to remember is that the physical part of networking is all hardware. It's tangible—you can hold it in your hands.

Physical Layout—What Are the Wires Like?

The physical side of the network is, at its simplest, made of wires strung between computers and other network devices. The wires connect to network interface cards, or NICs, installed in computers; NICs handle the computer's interaction with the rest of the network. With these two items, you can create a simple network.

For all practical purposes, there are only two types of physical layout that matter from a copper-wire "how do I wire it?" perspective: bus and star. Most of the equipment you'll find will be for a *star topology*. You'll hear about ring and mesh topologies as well, but from a wiring perspective, a *ring topology* is essentially identical to a star topology. It's the way the network functions that differentiates star and ring.

At its base, a *physical topology* is simply the arrangement of the wires in a network. A network laid out along a physical bus is (essentially) a long cable with taps along its length to which computers connect. If any of the links between computers are broken, the network is down. This design isn't particularly robust, which is why Ethernet 10BASE-2 and 10BASE-5 (forms of Ethernet that used a bus topology) have more or less died out—the topology design just isn't capable of supporting a network where additions, moves, and changes take place on an ongoing and unpredictable basis.

If, by contrast, all of the wires are run from a central area directly to computer locations, with one wire per computer, the network is laid out like a star. Ethernet, Token Ring, FDDI, and ATM all currently run some variation of a star wire layout.

The main differences between *Ethernet, Token Ring, FDDI,* and *ATM* topologies stem from how they allow computers to communicate with each other. For the purposes of this example, however, all you need to know is that none of these topologies can directly communicate with each other—that is, they don't coexist on the same network wire. Also, Ethernet, Token Ring, and FDDI are referred to as logical topologies. Unlike physical topologies, which you can touch and pick up, logical topologies are not concerned with wires, cabling, and hardware; logical topologies are the rules of the road for networks.

Physical Bus Topologies

The advantage of a 10BASE-2 bus-topology network is its simplicity—networking doesn't get much simpler than this (refer to Figure 1.1). Once the computers are physically connected to the wire, all you have to do is install the network software on each computer. In general, all the computers will be capable of seeing each other without difficulty. The downside of a bus network is that it has a lot of points of failure. If one of the links between any of the computers is broken, the network is down. And as of this writing (second edition, mid-2000), bus topologies are old tech—bus technology, while simple, just doesn't scale to large network installations, given the ease with which it can be broken.

FIGURE 1.1

A diagram of a simple Ethernet 10BASE-2 bus-topology network, showing how computers are connected together.

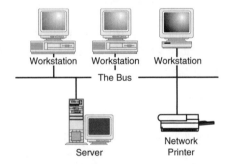

Physical Star Topologies

More complex networks are built on a physical star topology, as this design is more robust and less prone to interruptions than a physical bus topology. In contrast to the bus topology in which the wire runs serially from computer to computer, a star-topology network uses a junction box called a *hub* or a *concentrator* to connect computers to one another. All the computers connect to the hub/concentrator that manages intercomputer communications. The example in Figure 1.2 is based on a star topology called 10BASE-T.

FIGURE 1.2

*A simple Ethernet
10BASE-T star
topology network.*

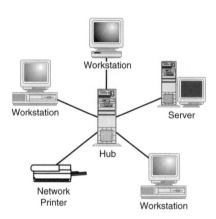

Do not confuse a 10BASE-T network (shown in Figure 1.2) with a 10BASE-2 network (shown in Figure 1.1). The names, and even the way they send data, are similar, but from a wiring perspective they are as different as night and day.

10BASE-2 is the older standard; it uses coaxial cable and looks sort of like a cable-TV wire. 10BASE-T looks like an oversize phone jack with too many connections. They don't work together without special equipment called *transceivers*.

Networks built on physical star topologies have a couple advantages over bus topologies. First and foremost is reliability. In a bus-topology network, disconnecting one computer is enough to crash the whole network; in a star-topology network, you can connect computers on-the-fly without causing network failures. Star-topology networks do cost a bit more—after all, they require a hub, which is additional hardware—but the increase in reliability inherent in this design is worth the cost.

Physical Ring Topologies

The physical layout of ring topologies, such as Token Ring and FDDI, uses the same wiring and physical arrangement as star networks. The wiring in the wall between a Token Ring MAU and an Ethernet hub is the same. The difference between an Ethernet network and a ring topology network lies in the way the device at the center of the network works—just because they use the same arrangement of wire doesn't mean they'll talk to each other!!

In contrast to Ethernet, which uses a device called a hub to bring all the wires together, ring topologies use a device called a *Multistation Access Unit*, or *MAU* (see Figure 1.3). The MAU does the same thing a hub does, but it works with Token Ring networks instead of Ethernet networks and handles communications between computers in a different fashion. We'll explore these differences in coming chapters.

FIGURE 1.3

A diagram of a simple Token Ring network.

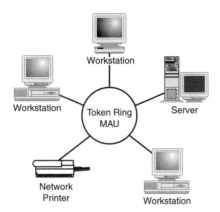

In contrast to the other topologies shown here, FDDI networks run on optical fiber cables instead of copper cabling. FDDI's topology is very similar to that of Token Ring with one exception: A single computer can be connected to two concentrators/MAUs so that if one network connection fails, the other can automatically pick up the slack. Systems connected to more than one concentrator are called *dual homed* (see Figure 1.4), and are effectively connected to two rings simultaneously. FDDI is very fast. However, it is also very expensive to install and operate, and so it is normally used only for high-end applications such as stock traders' terminals and other applications that demand the capability to push a lot of data over a wire.

FIGURE 1.4

A diagram of a FDDI network, showing how dual-homed computers can be connected to multiple concentrators.

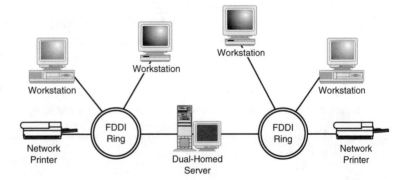

Network Devices

Earlier in this hour, we mentioned some of the reasons why you'd want a computer network. To get this functionality from your network, you need a host of *network devices* to connect to each other in specific ways. Without getting into the specifics of how to hook these things together, let's take a look at the basic network devices you'll encounter throughout this book. The first devices are computers and printers, neither of which require a network to function.

- A workstation is the computer on which a user does his or her work—hence workstation. Simple, no?
- A server is a computer whose resources are shared with other computers.
- A network printer is a printer connected to the network so that more than one user can print to it.

Figures 1.5 and 1.6, found later in this chapter, are schematic representations of these three different types of devices connected to network wires.

Other devices that can be connected to a network were mentioned in the sections on physical topologies; these devices are specific to networks—without a network, these devices have no function. They're absolutely central to the process of networking:

- A **Hub** or **MAU** is a device that provides the network with a single point of contact for all other devices.
- **Routers and bridges** are devices that move data between networks to create larger networks. You'll learn more about them later in this hour and in Hours 3 through 5.
- Although **wiring and cabling** don't strictly sound like devices, they actually are— they are pretty important to the process. Wire has to meet very stringent standards for networking to work, so it's included in the list of devices, although only peripherally.

By the way, if the number of terms you've encountered so far has been daunting, don't worry. Like any other specialized field of study, networking has a terminology all its own—just as the fields of medicine and law do. The jargon comes with the territory— attorneys talk about *habeus corpus* and *writs of certiorari*; doctors talk about *biopsies* and *etiologies*; and accountants talk about the *tax code*. Likewise, networking has its own shorthand. Understanding it doesn't automatically make you want to wear a pocket protector, bad glasses, and high-waters (though the Dark Side is strong, Luke).

To make certain that you're familiar with the jargon of networking, we'll revisit all these terms in much greater depth in the hours ahead.

The Logical Network

We have learned that the physical network is the collection of wires, computers, and other hardware that can be picked up and held. It's the stuff that you can point to and say "that's the network." But all that hardware isn't a network by itself. There's another layer based on the function of that hardware, and that's what we call the *logical network*. The logical network is what users see and use when they're working at their computers on the

1

network. Logical networks are collections of resources, such as hard drive space, printers, and applications, that workstations wouldn't have access to if they weren't connected to a network. Logical networks are not physical—they result from the organization of the physical network. In other words, the logical network is the organization of the hardware that results from networking software.

Examples of logical networks include things like *network protocols*. Network protocols (which we'll discuss in upcoming chapters) are special ways that computers have to communicate with each other—they're a lot like a language. If you speak only English and you're talking to someone who speaks only French, chances are you won't be able to communicate as well as if both of you were speaking the same language. For all their complexity, computer networks work the same way—they have to talk the same language, which in networking jargon is called a network protocol.

The logical network can include other things as well—in fact, it includes anything that isn't hardware. Novell's NetWare offers a logical network service called NetWare Directory Services (NDS) that organizes networked computers and printers; Microsoft's method for organizing the same things is called a Domain (or the Active Directory in Windows 2000). These services offer ways to organize your network so that the resources are neatly grouped according to their function—printers, servers, and so on.

A tremendous number of network-related services and software packages fit on the logical side of a network. Listing them all here would be both boring and confusing. Just remember this: If it's not part of the physical network, it's part of the logical network.

The Varieties of Networks

The hardware and topologies that networks run on are only the beginning of networking. Once you understand the basic technical concepts, it's time to become familiar with the basic organizational concepts of networking: LAN (Local Area Network) and WAN (Wide Area Network).

It is important to remember that all the networks mentioned in the preceding sections and in the following sections are private networks. That is, they are used by one organization, even though the networks may be in more than one location. This is an important distinction, as detailed in the section on the Internet, later in this hour.

LANs

A *Local Area Network*, or *LAN*, is the least complex organizational distinction of computer networks. A LAN is nothing more than a group of computers linked through a network all located at a single site. LANs often come very close to fitting the descriptions shown in Figures 1.1 through 1.4, earlier in this chapter. LANs have the following parameters:

- They occupy one physical location, and one physical location only—hence the word local in the title.
- They have high-speed data transfer rates, typically 10 or 100 megabits per second.
- All data travels on the local network wiring.

Part of what makes a LAN a LAN is high-speed data transfer. Ethernet LANs usually transmit data at 10 megabits per second. For comparison, Token Ring operates at 4 and 16 megabits per second, and FDDI and Fast Ethernet operate at a blistering 100 megabits per second or more. The fastest LANs run ATM; these can run at 155 mbps. These data transmission speeds are not expensive when they are part of the local network.

Although LANs are the simplest networks, that does not mean they are either necessarily small or simple. LANs can become quite large and complex; it is not uncommon in trade press magazines to read about LANs with hundreds or thousands of users.

WANs

When a series of LANs are too geographically scattered to make linking them at full LAN speeds impractical due to cost constraints, it's time to build a *Wide Area Network*, or *WAN*. Wide Area Networks are geographically scattered LANs joined together using high-speed phone lines and *routers*. A router is a device that manages data flows between networks.

How do you know how to get where you're going when you're driving in unfamiliar country? Chances are that you'll stop and ask for directions from the locals who know how to get *thay-uh* from *heah*, as we say in New England.

In a network, a router functions like the direction-providing people you find along your route. Routers know the best ways for data to travel to get from point A to B—and they're always learning new routes.

Access to resources across a WAN is often limited by the speed of the phone line (some of the most popular digital phone lines have speeds of only 56 kilobits per second). Even full-blown phone company trunk lines, called T-1s, can carry only 1.5 megabits per second, and they're very expensive—it's not unusual to pay several thousand dollars a month to a phone company to use a T-1. When you contrast the speed of a 56-kilobits-per-second phone line or a 1.5-megabits-per-second T-1 with the speed of a local LAN or MAN running at 10 megabits per second, the slowness of digital phone lines is readily apparent. These speed restrictions are also called *bandwidth* issues. Of course, if you've got deep pockets, it's possible to run data over a T-3 line, which provides 45 megabits per second...which is faster than many networks.

Bandwidth is a term used to describe the maximum speed at which a given device (such as a network card or modem) can transfer data. In other words, measuring bandwidth is like measuring how much air a fan can move: A fan that can move 100 cubic feet of air per minute has a lower bandwidth than a fan that can move 1,000 cubic feet of air per minute. Bandwidth is measured in kilobits per second (kbps) or megabits per second. Comparing megabits per second with kilobits per second is a lot like comparing a running person and a fast car: The car (which compares to megabits-per-second data speeds) is much faster than the runner (who compares to kilobits-per-second speeds).

WANs are often built when it is important that all users have the ability to access a common pool of information such as product databases or Automatic Teller Machine bank records. As long as the purpose of the WAN is well defined and limited, the speed restrictions imposed by phone lines are not an issue for network designers. If the quantity of data to be transmitted is less than or equal to the capacity of the line, the WAN works fine.

Unlike LANs, WANs always require routers. Because most of the traffic in a WAN takes place inside the LANs that make up the WAN, routers provide an important function—traffic control. Routers must be set up with information called routes (more on that in the TCP/IP chapter) that tell the router how to send data between networks. It's not very difficult to set up a router to do this; Cisco System's IOS (Internetworking Operating System) requires about a week of training, and you might not even need that if you can read a manual and know a bit about TCP/IP (more on that later).

Figure 1.5 shows a WAN configuration. Note that the main difference between a LAN and a WAN is that a WAN is essentially a series of LANs connected by routers.

FIGURE 1.5

A typical WAN configuration.

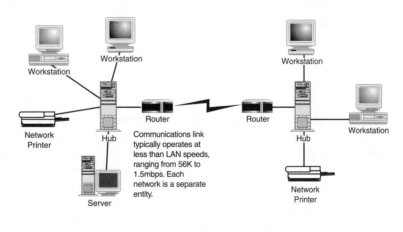

How the Internet Relates to Your Network

The last 10 years have seen an explosion of publicity for the Internet. Unless you've been in a cave somewhere, you've seen the explosion of Web addresses, email addresses, and references to cyberspace that have pervaded the public consciousness. Dot-com mania has invaded, and everything from billboards to trucks to t-shirts are emblazoned with logos proclaiming the virtues of one or another dot-com business venture.

The publicity has been difficult to ignore. Unfortunately, with mass-media publicity comes the maundering pronouncements of pundits who don't really understand what the Internet is, what it does, or (and most importantly for those building networks) how it works. The goal of this section is to explain in very basic terms what the Internet is and what ramifications the Internet has for your local network. Ultimately, this section exists as a foil to the preceding material because it helps you understand how your network exists *vis-à-vis* the Internet, which is sort of the ur-network from which all other networks have descended.

What Is the Internet?

The standard answer to this question has been the following pithy quote:

The Internet is a network of networks.

Although no one really knows who first said this, it is probably fair to note that the speaker hadn't thought too much about his or her audience's level of familiarity with technology. A network of networks is a useful definition only if your audience already has some idea what a network is; otherwise it's simply a synecdoche. Needless to say, most people don't have more than a terribly limited understanding of what a network is. With that in mind, here's a less recursive description of the Internet:

> The Internet is a series of private computer networks (LANs and WANs) connected to each other. Each individual private network (called an Autonomous System in networking-ese) is composed of a series of connected computers within an organization. Each organization takes responsibility for only the computers in its sphere of influence. Typically, the individual networks are connected by special devices called *routers* that are responsible for figuring out what data should stay inside the local network and what data should be passed on to other networks. Each private network also takes on the responsibility of telling the rest of the world which systems they have on their network (but only if they want the rest of the world to be able to find them—more on that in the network security chapter).

What does this have to do with your network? Quite a bit, actually. If you build a small network, you have a private network. If you connect a router to your network and you're connected through an Internet Service Provider (aka ISP), some part of your network will wind up on the Internet.

Figure 1.6 shows how local networks connect to each other to make up the Internet.

FIGURE 1.6

The connections between local networks are what makes the Internet the Internet.

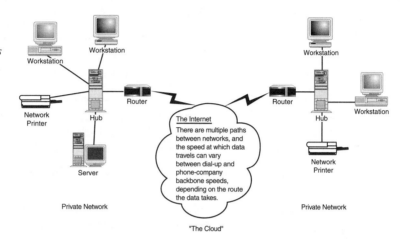

Understanding Bandwidth

As an astute reader, you're probably looking at Figure 1.6 and wondering what makes it different from the WAN in Figure 1.5. The two figures are almost the same. The important distinction is that, in Figure 1.5, the WAN is all part of a single network and is under one organization's control. By contrast, the only parts of the Internet that can be identified as *strictly dedicated to the Internet* are the extremely fast (also called *high-bandwidth*) phone lines that make up what's called the *backbone* of the Internet.

The backbone—is a series of very high-speed phone lines (ranging from 155 to 622 megabits per second—*really* fast!) that phone companies use to transmit high volumes of traffic. Compare this speed to the speed of your LAN (where data moves at 10 megabits per second), and you begin to see why it's called the backbone. By contrast, the Internet is under no single organization's control. Even the high-speed phone lines that make up the backbone of the Internet aren't under one organization's control.

Understanding Different Kinds of Internet Connections

Here's an easier way to think of the various speeds of connection on the Internet. Because the Internet is always being compared to a highway, the following analogy is based on that metaphor.

The dial-up connection most users use to traverse the Internet is like a dirt trail. At best, it's a country road. It's still fun to travel, but you have to be prepared for the bumps. Dial-up connections aren't terribly expensive, but they're not something you're going to race your Lamborghini on, either. They're also not very reliable, so you've got to deal with regular interruptions in service.

The next step up in this metaphor are dedicated connections using 56 kbps phone lines. They are faster than dial-up phone lines, but not by much. These are equivalent to two-lane state highways—better paved, more reliable, but you still can't go too fast on them.

Next in the lineup are trunk connections—T1s, E1s, and T3s (these lines may also be called OS1s, DS1s, DS3s, and other names, depending on which phone company you're dealing with). Using the road metaphor, these are the limited-access highways (interstate highways): They have two lanes in each direction, and you can travel as fast as you require.

Between 56k and T1 or faster access lies a new form of superhighway: high-speed data access provided over Digital Subscriber Lines (DSL) or cable modems. Typically, this access is at least as fast and sometimes faster than T1 access, but instead of being delivered to a place of business and costing huge amounts of money, it's delivered to your home and costs $50 a month or so. Essentially, if we continue to use the old, tired Infobahn metaphor, this is an exit at your house. DSL and cable modems represent the next generation of Internet access: digital dial tone. With DSL or cable modems, your internet connection is up 24/7/365 (or as close as your service provider can come to that ideal), it's fast enough to do anything on the Internet that most users require, and it's part of your home. For those of us who have this access, giving it up just isn't a possibility; stories are legendary about home-buyers who rule out buying houses because DSL and cable modems aren't available.

Sometimes, however, traveling on the road just isn't fast enough. So we'll expand our highway metaphor into a travel metaphor. If you have to move a lot of people between New York and Los Angeles overnight, you don't drive them—you use a plane. The phone companies are like the airline companies because they have to move a high volume of something—in the airlines' case, it's people and cargo; in the phone companies' case, it's data. Both have to ensure that they have the hardware to move the volume of stuff they have to move. Another similarity between the phone companies and the airlines is that other forms of transportation (in the airlines' case, roads, trains, and buses; in the phone companies' case, lower-speed Internet connections) converge on a common location (an airport or a phone company's network center) and dump a bunch of their contents on the high-volume carrier.

To meet this challenge, the phone companies have created extremely high-speed networking lines—the *backbone* previously mentioned—based on optical fiber that can carry data at up to about 1500 megabits per second (that's one and a half gigabytes per second). It's like the airline model in that it has a variety of locations at which you can get into the system (just as the airports are to the airline system), and it's redundant.

1

(If your flight from New York to California isn't direct—and that's very expensive in both networking and flying—you may be routed through Atlanta, Dallas, Chicago, or some other large-volume hub.) The beauty of the Internet is that you generally don't have to worry how your data is routed; the backbone routers largely automate the process with help from ISPs who monitor traffic.

If you reconsider Figure 1.6, it's possible to see that the Internet is not all one network; it is a series of connected private LANs. Data travels among them and, depending on a given private network's degree of involvement in the Internet, each network can take responsibility for sending data on towards its intended destination.

Why Does the Internet Matter for Your Network?

As the Internet has increased in visibility, it's become a beacon for network designers everywhere. The Internet, unlike many smaller networks, is based on standards established by committee and common consent. These standards all exist in the public domain; none of the standards are proprietary, or the sole property of any single manufacturer. The result is that Internet-standard–based software is easy for software manufacturers to write because Internet standards are very well defined. (Their specifications are covered in exhaustive detail in a series of documents called *RFCs*, or *Requests for Comment*, which are readily available on the Internet.) Because these standards are in the public domain, software developed using these standards is also cheaper to manufacture—there's no need for software manufacturers to pay royalties on patented or copyrighted ideas.

The best thing about Internet standards, however, is just that—they are *standards*. If you use Internet-standard software on your network, it will be much easier to ensure that your computers and applications will be able to interact. In fact, many products from wholly different manufacturers can work with one another if they're standards-compliant. When software products adhere to Internet standards, the resulting application cooperation is called interoperability, which essentially means that Part A works with Part B without undue difficulty. And interoperability means a local network that functions more smoothly and less expensively than one whose parts don't interoperate.

Intranets, Extranets, and the Internet

Typically, if you build a LAN or WAN—that is, a private network—using Internet standards, you've created an internal Internet, or an *intranet*. Intranets offer a great deal of promise for simplifying the networking of different manufacturers' components; used properly, intranets can reduce costs and simplify life for your end-users as well. An example might be a company Web site that distributes company news—it's much cheaper and environmentally responsible to put the newsletter on a company intranet than to create a separate paper copy for each reader.

If you connect your intranet to the Internet and make provisions for your customers and business partners to use pieces of your intranet to do business with you, you've gone a step beyond an intranet and created an *extranet*. Extranets, which fall under the current rubric "B2B" for business-to-business, are essentially intranets that use the Internet as a vehicle to interact with their customers, suppliers, and business partners. With the proper security precautions, extranets offer tremendous value; they reduce the costs of tying your computer systems to your various business partners' systems and potentially expose your products to a huge audience.

Summary

In this hour, you've learned what a network is, how a network works, the varieties of networks available, and how the Internet relates to your network. In the next hour, you'll learn about the benefits of networking—why networked computers are better than non-networked computers.

Q&A

Q What is a network?

A A network is any collection of items linked together to pass on information or physical goods.

Q What are some of the varieties of computer networks?

A Some of the most common types of computer networks are Local Area Networks (LANs) and Wide Area Networks (WANs).

Q What is the relationship between an intranet and the Internet?

A An intranet is a private network that makes use of the same software and protocols used for the Internet.

HOUR 2

The Benefits of Networking

Have you ever thought about what life would be like if human beings did not have what Alexis de Tocqueville, the French observer of early America, called a natural propensity to organize things at the drop of a hat? Just think about it—everything would be local. There would be no national brands and very little standardization. There might not be a post office. There would not be a standard currency.

Why? Because all these things rely on networks—the postal service, sales distribution networks, and even the set of national currency-issuing banks. Without networks, many of the things we take for granted in our daily lives, from the measures we use to the mediums of exchange, could not exist.

A network is first and foremost a system that enables communications among multiple locations and people. A network also creates synergy, where the sum of the whole is potentially greater than the sum of the parts. In this hour, you learn how computer networking can benefit users.

In this hour, you have the opportunity to learn about the following topics:

- Computing before computer networks
- The first computer networks
- How resources were shared before networking
- Downsides of *not* networking your computers
- The benefits of networking

Computing Before Computer Networks

Assume that you have a time machine and can go back in time 30 or 40 years to examine the computers that existed then. Chances are that you wouldn't recognize much about them. The computers that businesses and the government were using then were huge water-cooled behemoths the size of rooms. In spite of their bulk, they weren't powerful by today's standards; they could process only very small programs, and they usually lacked sufficient memory—that is, the physical part of the computer where the computer stores the 1s and 0s of software and data—to hold a whole program at one time. That's why, in old movies, computers are always shown spinning huge reels of magnetic tape— the tapes held the data that the computer wasn't using right at that moment. This model of computing now seems antiquated, but 30 to 40 years ago, it was state of the art.

In those days, computers offered very little interaction between the user and the system. Few computers had video display screens and keyboards that allowed users direct access to a session. Initially, computers had NO display screens—instead of sitting at a terminal typing characters and using a mouse, users submitted the work they needed the computer to do to the computer operator, who was the only person allowed to directly interact with the computer. Usually, the work was submitted on punched paper tape or punchcards.

A great deal of the time, computers were kept in climate-controlled rooms with glass walls—hence the slang name *glass house* for a data center. In any case, users submitted their jobs on punch cards that were then run in batches on the computer—one or two batches per shift—from which we derive the term batch processing. Batch processing was a situation common in early mainframe environments in which many tasks were scheduled to run at a specific time late in the evening. The user never directly interacted with the computer in batch processing.

Given the lack of interaction between users and computers, it's not at all difficult to believe that computers at that time couldn't interact well at all. A large IBM computer simply couldn't talk to a Honeywell or Burroughs computer. Even if they had been able to connect, they couldn't have shared data—the computers used entirely different data formats; the only standard at that time was ASCII. ASCII is the American Standard Code for Information Interchange, a way that computers format 1s and 0s (binary code, which it can understand) into the alphabet, numerals, and other characters that humans can understand. The computers would have had to convert the data before they could use it… which, in those prestandard days, could have taken as long as re-entering the data.

Even if the computers had been capable of understanding each other's data formats, the data transfers would have been relatively slow, because at that time there was no way to link computers together. Even between computers made by the same manufacturer, the only way to transfer data was to send a tape or a large hard disk to the recipient of the data. This meant physical delivery of disks to each new location that needed a copy of data, which was certainly not fast when compared to modern networks.

Fortunately, the U. S. Government's Advanced Research Products Agency had funded a small program operated by Bolt, Beranek, and Newman (BBN), a computer and technology firm in Cambridge, MA. BBN's job was to figure out how to allow computers to interact with each other. BBN figured out how to tie computers together using phone lines and *modems* (devices that can convert the 1s and 0s of digital data into sound waves that can be transmitted over phone lines) to transmit data that had been packaged into small fi XEd-length pieces called *datagrams*, or *packets*. The technology of converting data into packets was called *packet-switching*, and it is the single most important development in the history of computer networking.

Networking's Breakthrough: Packet-Switched Data

In this section, you learn how packet-switching works, which will help you understand how networks work; packet-switching is how all computer networks—from your network to the mighty Internet—move data around.

Packet-switched data is important for a variety of reasons:

- It allows more than one stream of data to travel over a wire at a time.
- It inherently ensures error-correction, meaning that data transmitted over a wire is free of errors.
- It allows data to be sent from one computer to another over multiple routes, depending on which routes are currently open.

It can be difficult to conceptualize packet-switching the first time around—but if you want to understand how networks work, packet-switching is something you have to understand. Here's a brief thought-experiment to help explain how packet-switching works.

Assume that you are an author writing a manuscript that must be delivered to an editor who lives a thousand miles away from you. Also assume (for the purposes of this thought-experiment) that the postal service limits the weight of packages it carries, and that your entire manuscript is heavier than the limit. Clearly, you're going to have to break up the manuscript in a way that ensures that your editor can reassemble it in the correct order without difficulty. How are you going to accomplish this?

First, you're going to break up the manuscript into standard sizes. Let's say that a 50-page section of manuscript plus an envelope is the maximum weight that the postal service will carry. After ensuring that your manuscript pages are numbered, you break the manuscript into 50-page chunks. It doesn't matter whether or not the chunks break on chapter lines, or even in the middle of a sentence—the pages are numbered, so they can be reassembled easily. If any pages are lost because of a torn envelope, the page numbers help determine what's missing.

Breaking up the manuscript into equal-sized chunks with a method of verifying the correctness of the data (through the use of the page numbers) is the first part of *packetizing* data. Packetizing is the process by which a computer breaks a single large chunk of data into smaller pieces so it can be transmitted over a network. The page numbers, which are a property of the data, are used to determine whether or not all the data has arrived; in networking terms, this is called a *checksum*. When data is packetized, the computer checks the values of the 1s and 0s in the data and comes up with a number that it includes in the packet of data. We'll see how checksums are used a little later.

Second, you put the 50-page manuscript chunks into envelopes numbered sequentially— the first 50 pages go into envelope number 1, the second 50 pages go into envelope number 2, and so forth until you've reached the end of the manuscript. The number of pages in each envelope is also written on the outside of the envelope; that is equivalent to a data packet's checksum. Finally, you write your editor's address as the destination and your address as the return address on the outsides of the envelopes and send them using the postal service. Figure 2.1 diagrams our hypothetical envelope and the relationship each element has to a data packet in a computer network situation.

FIGURE 2.1

The various parts of the envelope and how they correspond to the parts of a data packet.

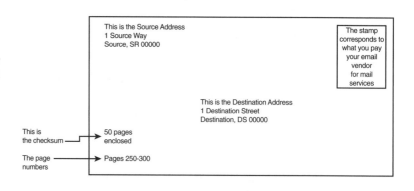

The route the envelopes take while in transit between your mailbox and your editor's desk is unimportant. Your editor gets mail from a different post office, but uses the same service, so the envelopes go through out-of-town mail. Some of the envelopes might be routed through Chicago, others might be routed through Dallas—it's not important as long as all the envelopes get to the editor (see Figure 2.2). If the number of pages your editor receives does not match the number of pages written on the outside of the envelope, the editor knows something's wrong—the envelope came unsealed and pages fell out, or someone tampered with the contents. If you had sent your editor something over the Internet, the process would work the same way—the packets could have been routed through many different machines before arriving at your editor's computer.

FIGURE 2.2

Data packets can follow several paths across the Internet.

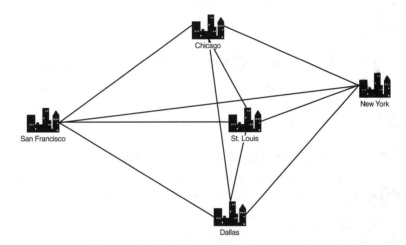

Mail can travel from New York to San Francisco across any combination of these routes.

In networking terms, each finished envelope is a packet of data. The order in which your editor—or a computer—receives them doesn't matter because the editor (or the computer) can reassemble the data from the envelope numbers (which were sequential), the checksum (the number on the outside of the envelope detailing how many pages to expect in this envelope), and the page numbers of the manuscript itself. If one envelope is lost in transit, after an agreed upon length of time, your editor can request that you send another copy of that specific envelope so that the editor has the entire manuscript.

Packet-switched data doesn't correspond perfectly with this example, but it's close enough to give you a reasonable idea of the process.

Any data you send over a computer network is packetized—from the smallest email message to the largest files transferred across a wire. The beauty of packet-switching networks is that more than one computer can transmit data over one wire at a time. You can have lots of packets of data from multiple machines without confusion because each data packet (like each envelope in the preceding example) has the following elements:

- A *source address*—this is the return address, or where the packet came from.
- A *destination address*—this is where the packet is headed.
- A *sequence number*—this explains where this packet fits in with the remainder of the packets.
- A *checksum*—this ensures that the data is free of errors.

Because each computer has a different address (called a MAC address, as explained in the next hour), transmitting data is essentially a process of sending mail from one piece of hardware to another electronically.

Life Without Computer Networks

Transferring data between computers before networks was clearly difficult, but in those days, there was no alternative. Now networks are ubiquitous. But what would your computing life be like without a network?

Inefficient Resource Sharing

If you didn't have a network, you wouldn't be able to share the resources on your computer with others—or use their resources either. What are the ramifications of this?

Sneakernet

Back when Ethernet networking was invented, computer users who were networked came up with a clever name for sharing files from files stored on computers that were not connected to the network. They called it *sneakernet*. What it meant was that if a user wanted to move files between nonconnected computers, he or she had to copy the file to a floppy disk, walk to the other machine (hence the *sneaker* in *sneakernet*), and copy the file to the other computer.

Needless to say, sneakernet is not an efficient way to move or manage files. It is time-consuming and unreliable to begin with, and it works easily only for files small enough to fit on a floppy disk. The worst thing about it is that data is decentralized, meaning that every user can conceivably have a different version of a particular file stored on their nonnetwork-connected computer. The chaos that ensues when users need the same version of a file and don't have it (usually because the file changes as users copy it to their machines and work with it before copying it to the next machine) can be truly horrific.

No Shared Software Applications

Disconnected computers also suffer from another malady: They can't share software applications. When computers are not networked, every application must be installed on every computer if data passed by sneakernet is to be effective. If a user doesn't have the application that created a file stored on his or her computer, the user can't read the file, period.

Of course, if you can't share applications, that means no one can share their calendars or contact lists with other users, let alone send them email. Not being networked can hinder communications.

No Shared Printer Resources

If computers aren't networked, the only way they can share devices like a printer is by using manual switch boxes that select which computer's printer port connects to the printer at any time. This is not simply an inconvenience; it can be harmful to your pocketbook. Some printer manufacturers do not warranty a printer that has been connected to a switch box; switch boxes can damage printer electronics.

No Shared Internet Access

Nonnetworked computers can't share a common connection to the Internet. The increasing popularity of the Internet combined with a desire to reduce Internet-account costs has provided a reason for many people to build small networks—just so that they can connect all their users to the Internet through one connection.

Slo-o-ow Data

Suppose that the only way you could get some commodity you use frequently—say, gasoline—was by mail order. Also suppose that you could get it only in bucket-sized increments. It would take forever to get your gasoline—and even longer to fill the tank on your car.

That's what networking by floppy disks is like. Floppies hold very little data and trying to do useful work while exchanging disks is an exercise in frustration. The recent advent of high-capacity removable-media drives, such as Iomega's Zip and Jaz drives, partially ameliorates this situation, but it does not solve the underlying problem: the lack of real-time connectivity a network provides.

No Centralized Data Management

When computers are not networked, there is no way to manage them collectively and ensure that they share common configurations and access to data. This means that administration is costly and time-consuming. Configurations cannot be standardized unless the person in charge of the computers repeats installations and configurations on each system, which at best is redundant and wasteful of effort and resources.

Expense

Nonnetworked computing is expensive because of the labor costs, the cost of lost-worker productivity, and the capital costs of multiplying the cost of resources by the number of computers. In other words, if your computers aren't networked and all your users have to print, you may have to purchase a separate printer for each user.

Contrast this with networked situations in which a single printer can serve 15 or 20 users. The cost savings are huge.

Benefits of Networking

The preceding paragraphs pointed out the downsides of computing in a non-networked environment, but they did not enumerate the benefits...

Simplified Resource Sharing

Resource sharing is easier over a network; whether the network uses a peer or client/ server configuration is immaterial.

Shared Disk Space

Networked computers can share their hard disk space with each other. At first glance, this doesn't seem momentous; after all, many computers have large hard drives. But it's not the file-storage capabilities that are important here—it's sharing applications and files. It is satisfying to be able to find a copy of a file you require, copy it to your desktop computer, and work on it without leaving your chair.

Shared Applications

Although sharing files is an important reason for networking, sharing applications is another, equally important reason. Shared applications can be as prosaic as using a copy of Microsoft Word stored on another user's drive or as elaborate as a *groupware application* that routes data from user to user according to complex preset rules.

A groupware application (also called *groupware* or *collaborative software*) is an application that enables multiple users to work together using the network to connect them. Such applications can work serially, where (for instance) a document is automatically routed from person A to person B when person A is finished with it, or it can be software to enable real-time collaboration. IBM's Lotus Notes software is an example of the former, and Microsoft's Office 2000 has some real-time collaborative features.

Examples of shared applications include *group calendaring*, which allows your staff to plan meetings and tasks using a centralized schedule instead of 20 different ones, and email, or electronic mail, which is widely called the *killer app* of networking. Email and other network applications are discussed in more depth in Hour 12, "Network Applications."

The term *killer app* is not pejorative. In spite of what might be a sensible conjecture about its meaning, it does not refer to viruses or other malicious software. Instead, a killer app is an application that is so useful that it increases the demand for computer resources. Email is the killer app of networking because when it was introduced, it allowed users to hold serial conversations in a common workspace that didn't require paper files and running around with memos. Email is a great way to send off quick messages that aren't meaningful enough to merit a memo. For example, email is great for project tracking: Workers can send a two-line message to their boss telling him or her what the status is on a project, and the boss can assign work and send out group messages quickly and efficiently without wasting paper.

Shared Printers

A third aspect of resource sharing is shared printers. As noted earlier in the discussion of the disadvantages of nonnetworked computers, standalone printers—that is, printers attached to computers that aren't networked—represent a significant capital expense. Printers typically also cost a lot to run—they consume ink or toner when they print, and inkjet and toner cartridges are typically expensive.

A visual example of resource sharing can be seen in Figure 2.3.

FIGURE 2.3

Resource sharing with a computer network.

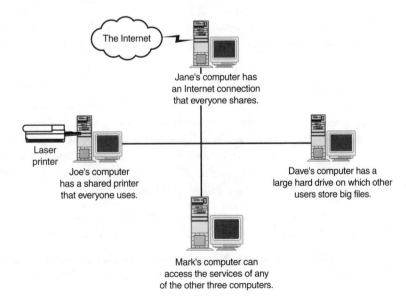

Networking Is Faster

Given everything else that has been said in this hour, it seems obvious that networking is faster than not networking. And, in fact, it is faster. Just think about it:

- No more printing memos—use email!
- No more running from desk to desk to check everyone's availability for a meeting—use the group calendar!
- No more wondering whose Rolodex has the name of the person you need to call— you can get it from the contact database.
- No more racing around from computer to computer to get the file you need—just copy or open it from the network drive.

Centralized Management

If you were a preschool teacher with a bevy of three-year-olds, you wouldn't try to manage them all individually. Instead, you'd try to do activities in groups. Imagine trying to fill the needs of 25 three-year-olds, each engaged in a different activity—the mind boggles at the management strategies you'd need. Most reasonable people agree that this is the case; they also agree that managing children as a group works better.

Yet a great many of these same people, faced with a computer network, continue to treat network users' needs totally outside the context of the network. All too often, system administrators wind up running from desktop to desktop, installing, fixing, and managing idiosyncratic software installations. This is extremely inefficient—and it wears down the patience of the network users and the technical person whose job it is to support them.

A better solution to managing networks is to centralize management functions. Once computers are networked, there are a host of software utilities (Microsoft's Systems Management Server, McAfee's Saber LAN Manager, Tivoli's TME10, and Symantec's Norton Administrator for Networks, among others) that enable the administrator to diagnose and fix problems and install and configure software. These utility suites allow a network administrator to collect and standardize computer configurations from across a network—and very often, to install software on users' computers without leaving his or her desk (bad for personal fitness, good for the network).

To find out more about managing networks, look at the network administration chapters in Part V of this book, "Introduction to Network Administration."

The initial installation and learning curves are a lot of work for the administrator, but once the initial installation is finished, the administrator's life gets easier. Centralized management saves time and money (two things accountants appreciate) as well as the goodwill of the users and the credibility of the administrator (two things the users and administrators appreciate). Networking is worth the investment and time.

Summary

Clearly, when computer resources are shared through a network, you reap a variety of benefits ranging from reduced costs to ease of use to simpler administration. The cost savings and per-worker productivity gains represented by networks will be appreciated by companies trying to economize; from the worker's viewpoint, he or she has received a bonus because he or she doesn't have to chase down information anymore. If applications such as email, calendaring, and contact management are added to the mix, the network begins to establish synergistic relationships (that is, relationships that produce more value than the sum of their parts would suggest) between users and data. A well-designed and functional network allows groups of people to interact in ways that extend their natural capabilities and enables them to accomplish a great deal more than they could without the network.

2

Q&A

Q What is the name of the technology that enables computer networks to exist?

A Packet-switching makes computer networks possible.

Q What sorts of computer resources can be shared on a network?

A Networks enable the sharing of all sorts of things—drives, printers, and even connections to the Internet.

Q What are some of the reasons that centralized management is useful for networks?

A Centralized management of a network enables more efficient administration, the automated installation of software on network users' desktop computers, and easier desktop computer configuration management.

PART II
The Basics

Hour

Hour 3

Getting Data from Here to There: How Computers Share Data

In the preceding hour, you read a brief definition of packet switching and an explanation of why packet switching is so important to data networking. In this hour, you learn more about how networks pass data between computers. This process will be discussed from two separate vantage points: logical topologies, such as Ethernet, Token Ring, and ATM; and network protocols, which we have not yet discussed.

Why is packet switching so important? Recall that it allows multiple computers to send multiple messages down a single piece of wire, a move that is both efficient and an elegant solution. Packet switching is intrinsic to computer networking; without packet switching, no hay nada network.

In the first hour, you learned about physical topologies, such as 10BASE-2 and fiber optics, which create the highways over which data travels. In the next hour, you learn about these topologies in more depth. But before we get to physical topologies, you have to know the rules of the road that determine how data travels over a network. In this hour, you'll learn about

- Logical Topologies
- Network Protocols

Logical Topologies

Before discussing topologies again, let's revisit the definition of a topology. In networking terms, a topology is nothing more than the arrangement of a network. The topology can refer to the physical layout of the network (which we discussed in Hour 1, "An Overview of Networking," and really deals with the wiring, more or less) or the logical layout of the network.

Logical topologies lay out the rules of the road for data transmission. As you already know, in data networking, only one computer can transmit on one wire segment at any given time. Life would be wonderful if computers could take turns transmitting data, but unfortunately, life isn't that simple. Computers transmitting data have all the patience of a four-year-old waiting in line at an ice-cream parlor on a hot summer day. As a result, there must be rules if the network is to avoid becoming completely anarchic.

In contrast to physical topologies, logical topologies are largely abstract. Physical topologies can be expressed through concrete pieces of equipment, such as network cards and wiring types; logical networks are essentially rules of the road.

In this hour, we will first discuss four common logical topologies, starting with the most common and ending with the most esoteric:

- Ethernet
- Token Ring
- FDDI
- ATM

Although the preceding list of logical topologies isn't complete, it contains most of the topologies that run on personal computers. If you ran a mainframe or a minicomputer, such as an IBM AS/400 or a Digital VAX, you might see IBM's Advanced Peer to Peer Networking (APPN) or Systems Network Architecture (SNA) or Digital's DECnet. But it's not likely that you'll be working with any of these at the outset—these are advanced networks.

Ethernet

When packet switching was young, it didn't work very efficiently. Computers didn't know how to avoid sending data over the wire at the same time other systems were sending data, making early networking a rather ineffective technology. Just think about it—it was similar to two people talking on the phone at the same time, but really understanding each other.

Ethernet, invented in 1973 by Bob Metcalfe (who went on to found 3Com, one of the most successful networking companies), was a way to circumvent the limitations of earlier networks. It was based on an IEEE (Institute of Electronic and Electrical Engineers) standard called 802.3 CSMA/CD, and it provided ways to manage the crazy situation that occurred when many computers tried to transmit on one wire simultaneously.

CSMA/CD Explained

The foundation of Ethernet is *CSMA/CD*, or *Carrier Sense Multiple Access/Collision Detection*. Although this sounds complicated, it's actually quite simple. In an Ethernet network, all the computers share a single network segment, called a *collision domain*. A collision domain is the group of computers that communicate on a single network wire. Each computer in a collision domain listens to every other computer in the collision domain; each computer can transmit data only when no other computer is currently transmitting. The segment is called a collision domain because if there's more than one computer in it, it's a cinch that at some point those computers are going to try to transmit data simultaneously, which is a big no-no. When two computers transmit packets at the same time, a condition called a *collision* occurs. In terms of networking, a collision is what happens when two computers attempt to transmit data on the same network wire at the same time. This creates a conflict; both computers sense the collision, stop transmitting, and wait a random amount of time before retransmitting. The larger the collision domain, the more likely it is that collisions will occur, which is why Ethernet designers try to keep the number of computers in a segment as low as possible.

In CSMA/CD, each computer listens for a quiet time on the wire. When the network wire is quiet (which is measured in nanoseconds—network quiet has no relationship to human quiet), a computer that has packets of data to transmit sends them out over the network wire. If no other computers are sending, the packet will be routed on its merry way.

Take a look at Figure 3.1 to see a diagram of an Ethernet topology.

FIGURE 3.1

An Ethernet topology: Only one computer can transmit data at a time.

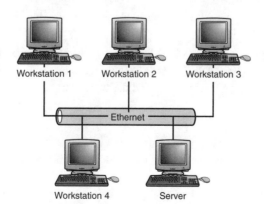

If a second computer tries to transmit data over the wire at the same time as the first computer, a condition called a *collision* occurs. Both then cease transmitting data, wait a random number of milliseconds for a quiet period, and transmit again; usually this solves the collision problem. It is really that simple. Sometimes a network card goes into a mode where it fails to obey CSMA/CD and transmits all the time—this is called *jabber*, and it's caused either by faulty software or a defective network card.

Ethernet's Nuclear Family

Ethernet is broadly used to describe both the logical topology that uses CSMA/CD and the physical topologies on which CSMA/CD networks run. All the basic Ethernet topologies are described in IEEE standard 802.3. The members of the nuclear family are listed here:

- 10BASE-2, or coaxial networking. The maximum segment length of 10BASE-2 is 185 meters. This is an OLD technology, and is not used for new installations.

- 10BASE-5, or thicknet. Thicknet is also called *AUI*, short for *Attachment User Interface*. AUI networks are an intermediate step between 10BASE-2 and 10BASE-T. 10BASE-5 is a bus interface with slightly more redundancy than 10BASE-2. The maximum length of a 10BASE-5 segment is 500 meters. Like 10BASE-2, this is an old technology and is not typically used for new installations.

- 10BASE-T, which runs over two of the four pairs of unshielded twisted-pair wire. In 10BASE-T, the maximum cable length from the hub to a workstation is 100 meters.

However, the Ethernet standard has grown to include faster networks and fiber-optic media. The newer members of the Ethernet family are described in IEEE Standard 802.3u, and include these:

- 100BASE-T, also called Fast Ethernet, in which data travels at 100 megabits per second over two pairs of unshielded twisted-pair copper wire. The maximum cable length between the concentrator and the workstation for Fast Ethernet is 20 meters.

- 100BASE-FX, which is Fast Ethernet running on optical fibers. Because optical fibers can carry data much further than copper wire, 100BASE-FX does not have a maximum cable length.

- 100BASE-T4, which is 100BASE-T running over four pairs of unshielded twisted-pair wire. Like 100BASE-T, 100BASE-T4 has a maximum cable length of 20 meters between the concentrator and the workstation.

Token Ring and FDDI

Ethernet CSMA/CD networks provide a relatively simple way of passing data. However, many industry observers correctly note that CSMA/CD breaks down under the pressure exerted by many computers on a network segment. These observers are correct; the squabbling and contention for bandwidth that is part and parcel of Ethernet does not always scale efficiently.

In an attempt to circumvent this problem (does anyone see a pattern here? Every new invention is built to rectify the older standard's shortcomings), IBM and the IEEE created another networking standard called 802.5. IEEE 802.5 is more commonly identified with Token Ring, although FDDI also uses the 802.5 method of moving data around networks.

Token Ring works very differently from Ethernet. In Ethernet, any computer on a given network segment can transmit until it senses a collision with another computer. In Token Ring and FDDI networks, by contrast, a single special packet called a *token* is generated when the network starts and is passed around the network. When a computer has data to transmit, it waits until the token is available. The computer then takes control of the token and transmits a data packet. When it's done, it releases the token to the network. Then the next computer grabs the token if it has data to transmit (see Figure 3.2).

FIGURE 3.2

A Token Ring topology (FDDI works in the same fashion): The only computer that can transmit is the computer holding the token.

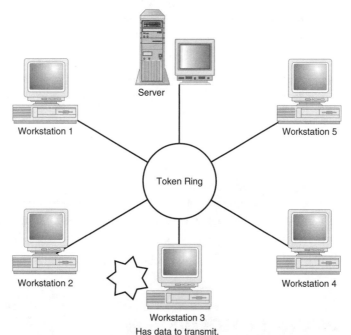

Server

Workstation 1   Workstation 5

Token Ring

Workstation 2   Workstation 4

Workstation 3
Has data to transmit.
It has taken the Token (an electronic message that's passed around the network)
and only it can transmit. When it's done transmitting data, it returns the Token to the ring,
where the next computer that needs to transmit will pick it up.
FDDI works basically the same as Token Ring.

In comparison to the contentious nature of Ethernet, Token Ring and FDDI appear quite civilized. These two logical topologies do not have collisions in which multiple stations try to send data; instead, every computer waits its turn.

Token Ring suffers slightly fewer bandwidth-contention issues than Ethernet; it holds up under load fairly well, although it too can be slowed down if too many computers need to transmit data at the same time. Ultimately, this situation results in network slowdowns.

Asynchronous Transfer Mode (ATM)

ATM networking is the newest topology available at this time. It is a wholly new topology; unlike Ethernet, Token Ring, or FDDI, it can carry both voice and data over network wire or fiber. ATM transmits all packets as 53-byte *cells* that have a variety of identifiers on them to determine such things as *Quality of Service*.

Quality of Service in packet data is very similar to quality of service in regular mail. In regular mail, you have a choice of services: first class, second class, third class, bulk mail, overnight, and so forth. When you send an overnight message, it receives priority over first-class mail, so it gets to its destination first.

A few bits of data in a packet of data indicate the quality of service required for that data. When the Quality of Service feature is implemented—as it is in ATM and will be in Internet Protocol version 6 (Ipv6)—you can send packets based on their need for bandwidth. For example, email is relatively low priority and might be given third-class service; video or audio content, which has to run constantly, gets a higher priority.

ATM is fast. At its slowest, it runs at 25 megabits per second; at its fastest, it can run up to 1.5 gigabits per second (which is why phone companies use it for some of the huge trunk lines that carry data for long distances). In addition to its speed, ATM is exponentially more complex than either Ethernet or Token Ring. Most commonly, the 155 megabit per second speed of ATM is used for applications where quality of service and extraordinary speed are required.

Currently, ATM equipment is both esoteric and expensive. Fore Systems and IBM have both invested heavily in ATM-to-the-desktop technology (that is, they use ATM to link servers and workstations) and are banking on the need for multimedia networks over the next several years. ATM standards and interoperability are still touch-and-go, however.

That just about wraps up the discussion of logical topologies. Now it's time to discuss protocols.

Network Protocols

At the base of a network system is the physical topology. On top of that is the logical topology. And on top of the logical topology are *protocols*. If the idea of "on top of" or "beneath" doesn't make sense, don't worry; it's based on a system for describing how networks work called the OSI model, which is described in the following section.

Just as a logical topology is, a protocol is a set of rules for sending and receiving data across a physical network. Logical topologies instruct the hardware on how to packetize and transmit data across the physical topology; protocols handle the translation of data from applications (that is, software) to the logical topology.

If that all sounds confusing, don't worry. The next couple of pages discuss how protocols work, what some of the most popular protocols are, and how they're organized. Here is a list of the protocols you are most likely to run across:

- TCP/IP
- IPX
- NetBIOS/NetBEUI

To understand what network protocols are, you have to understand what they do and their function in relation to the rest of the network. To begin, let's examine the most popular theoretical model of networking: the OSI model.

The OSI Model (And Why You Should Be Familiar with It)

During the 1980s, a group called *Open Systems Interconnect*, or *OSI* for short, attempted to create a logical arrangement for the various parts that make up a network. In the long term, their efforts were futile (practically no one runs OSI protocols), but they did create a great model to explain how a network should work. The model is called the OSI seven-layer model, and it's a stalwart of networking theory (see Figure 3.3). The OSI model is useful to know, but it's not necessary to memorize—it simply provides a theoretical model you can use for network problems ranging from design issues to connection problems.

3

FIGURE 3.3

The OSI model shows how data is moved in a network.

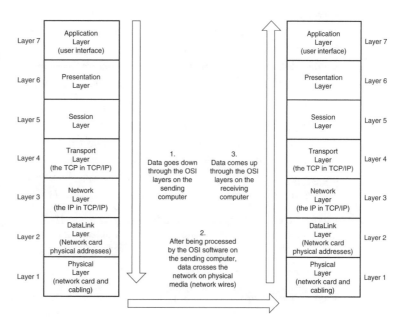

The OSI model is not particularly complicated. The trick is to remember that as the OSI layer numbers increase from 1 to 7, so does the *level of abstraction*. The lower the layer, the less abstract and more concrete it is. Each layer communicates only with the layer directly above or below it while moving data from electrical impulses on a wire into data on your screen. If we return to the postal metaphor from Hour 2, "The Benefits of Networking," as an analogy, OSI becomes even easier to understand:

Layer 7 (Application) deals with the software applications that you use on your screen. Layer 7 is concerned with file access and file transfer. If you have ever used applications such as FTP or Telnet, you have interacted with an example of Layer 7. In the postal model, the Application layer corresponds to writing a letter.

Layer 6 (Presentation) deals with the way different systems represent data. For example, Layer 6 defines what happens when it tries to display Unix-style data on an MS-DOS screen.

Layer 6 doesn't really have an analogue in the postal model, but if it did, it would be like rewriting the letter so that anyone could read it (which, as you can see, doesn't make much sense in a physical context). Probably the best analogy is to a translator; using the postal model again, assume that your letter is being sent to Mexico. A translator (equivalent to Presentation-layer software) can translate the data in your envelope into the local *lingua mexicana*. Like the letter in the example, data is mutable and protean and can be rearranged to fit the kind of computer on which it needs to run.

Layer 5 (Session) handles the actual connections between systems. Layer 5 handles the order of data packets and bidirectional (two-way) communications. In a postal metaphor, the Session layer is similar to breaking a single large document into several smaller documents, packaging them, and labeling the order in which the packages should be opened. This is where streams of data get turned into packets.

Layer 4 (Transport) is like the registered-mail system. Layer 4 is concerned with ensuring that mail gets to its destination. If a packet fails to get to its destination, Layer 4 handles the process of notifying the sender and requesting that another packet be sent. In effect, Layer 4 ensures that the three layers below it (that is, Layers 1, 2, and 3) are doing their jobs properly. If they are not, Layer 4 software can step in and handle error correction. For what it's worth, this is where the *TCP* in *TCP/IP* does its work.

Layer 3 (Network) provides an addressing scheme. If you send someone a letter, you use a street address that contains a ZIP code because that's what the post office understands. When a computer sends a data packet, it sends the packet to a logical address, which is like a street address.

Layer 3 works with Layer 2 to translate data packets' logical network addresses (these are similar to IP addresses, about which you'll learn in a few pages) into hardware-based MAC addresses (which are similar to ZIP codes) and move the packets toward their destination. Layer 3 is similar to the mail-sorting clerks at the post office who aren't concerned with ensuring that mail gets to its destination, per se. Instead, the clerks' concern is to sort mail so that it keeps getting closer to its destination. Layer 3 is also the lowest layer that isn't concerned with the hardware. Layer 3 is where the term *protocol* really comes into play; the *IP* in *TCP/IP* stands for Internet Protocol.

Layer 2 (Data-Link), by contrast, isn't physical. In our postal model, this layer represents a set of rules governing the actual delivery of physical mail—pick up here, drop off there, and so forth. This is where the rules for Ethernet, Token Ring, FDDI, ATM, and so on are stored. It's concerned with finding a way for Layer-1 stuff (the cards and hubs and wire and so forth) to talk to Layer 3. Layer 2 is where network card addresses become important.

Layer 1 (Physical) is similar to the trucks and trains and planes and rails and whatnot that move the mail. From a network perspective, this layer is concerned only with the physical aspects of the network—the cards, wire, and concentrators that move data packets. Layer 1 specifies what the physical aspects are, what they must be capable of doing, and (basically) how they accomplish those things.

If you refer back to the description of packet data in Hour 2, you'll realize that if data packets are to pass over the network, the network (like the postal service) has to accomplish several tasks successfully:

- It has to be capable of transmitting data across a physical medium (copper wire, optical fiber, or—in the case of wireless networks—air).
- It must route data to the correct location by MAC address.
- It must be capable of recognizing the data when it arrives at the destination.
- It must be capable of checking the correctness of the transmitted data.
- It must be capable of sending messages to acknowledge that a particular packet has been received.
- It must be capable of interacting with users through an interface that displays the data.

As you can see, the various layers of the OSI model accomplish these goals admirably. OSI, however, was never actually implemented as a network protocol; instead, the existing protocols—mostly TCP/IP—were refined using the powerful OSI reference model.

TCP/IP

If you've read anything about the Internet that's deeper than a newsweekly's puff piece, you've probably heard of *TCP/IP*, or *Transmission Control Protocol/Internet Protocol*. TCP/IP is the protocol that carries data traffic over the Internet. Of all the network protocols in the marketplace, TCP/IP is far and away the most popular.

The reasons for TCP/IP's success, however, do not stem from the popularity of the Internet. Even before the current Internet boom, TCP/IP was gaining popularity among business networkers, college computer-science majors, and scientific organizations. The reason why TCP/IP has gained popularity is because it is an *open standard*—no single company controls it. Instead, TCP/IP is part of a set of standards created by a body called the *Internet Engineering Task Force (IETF)*. IETF standards are created by committees and are submitted to the networking community through a set of documents called *Requests for Comment (RFCs)*.

RFCs are draft documents freely available on the Internet that explain a standard to the networking community. All RFCs are considered "draft" documents because any document can be superseded by a newer RFC. The reason for this focus on RFCs is that they form a large part of the basis for the various standards that make up Internet networking today, including TCP/IP.

TCP/IP Defined

But what exactly is TCP/IP? It is many things. For one thing, the name TCP/IP is a bit misleading—TCP/IP is just shorthand notation for a full *protocol suite*, or set of protocols that have standard ways of interacting with each other. TCP and IP share the name of the whole protocol suite because they form the bedrock of the whole protocol suite; they are respectively the transport (OSI Layer 4, which regulates traffic) and the network (OSI Layer 3, which handles addressing) layers of the TCP/IP protocol suite. The suite includes, but is by no means limited to, the ways of transmitting data across networks listed in Table 3.1.

TABLE 3.1 Some TCP/IP Suite Members and Their Functions

Name	Function
TCP	Transmission Control Protocol. Ensures that connections are made and maintained between computers.
IP	Internet Protocol. Handles software computer addresses.
ARP	Address Resolution Protocol. Relates IP addresses with hardware (MAC) addresses.
RIP	Routing Information Protocol. Finds the quickest route between two computers.
OSPF	Open Shortest Path First. A descendant of RIP that increases its speed and reliability.
ICMP	Internet Control Message Protocol. Handles errors and sends error messages for TCP/IP.
BGP/EGP	Border Gateway Protocol/Exterior Gateway Protocol. Handles how data is passed between networks.

TABLE 3.1 continued

Name	Function
SNMP	Simple Network Management Protocol. Allows network administrators to connect to and manage network devices.
PPP	Point-to-Point Protocol. Provides for dial-up networked connections to networks. PPP is commonly used by Internet Service Providers to allow customers to connect to their services.
SMTP	Simple Mail Transport Protocol. How email is passed between servers on a TCP/IP network.
POP3/IMAP4	Post Office Protocol version 3/Internet Message Advertising Protocol version 4. Both set up ways for clients to connect to servers and collect email.

As you can see, there are quite a few pieces in the TCP/IP protocol suite, and this is just the beginning—there are a whole bunch more that we're not going to discuss here. All these pieces are necessary at some point or another to ensure that data gets where it's supposed to be going. The pieces listed in Table 3.1 are standards at this point, but the process of defining standards is far from over.

In contrast to the OSI reference model's seven layers, TCP/IP uses only four layers, some of which amalgamate several OSI layer functions into one TCP/IP layer. Table 3.2 compares OSI and TCP/IP layers.

TABLE 3.2   Contrast Between TCP/IP and the OSI Model

OSI Layer	TCP/IP Layer	TCP/IP Applications and Protocols Running at This Level
7 (Application)	TCP Layer 4 (Application)	FTP (File Transfer Program)
6 (Presentation) 5 (Session)		Telnet (terminal program), SMTP (mail transfer), POP3, and IMAP4 (mail clients)
4 (Transport)	TCP Layer 3 (also called Host-to-Host; a host is any system running TCP/IP)	TCP (Transmission Control Protocol), UDP (User Datagram Protocol)
3 (Network)	TCP Layer 2 (Internet)	IP (Internet Protocol)
2 (Data Link) 1 (Physical)	TCP Layer 1 (Network Interface)	Hardware (network cards, cables, concentrators, and so on)

From this table, you can see that TCP/IP accomplishes the functions required in the OSI reference model.

IP Addresses

TCP/IP got its start as part of the Unix operating system in the mid-1970s. Networkers who had previously relied on *UUCP* (*Unix to Unix Copy Program*) to copy files and mail between computers decided that there had to be a better, more interactive way to network, and TCP/IP was born. Given the academic heritage of placing material in front of the academic community for critical review and discussion, it was a natural progression to include TCP/IP in the RFC process, where its standards have been set ever since.

The original specification for TCP/IP was open ended—or so the designers thought. They created an address space, or standard way of writing addresses, which set up 2 to the 32nd power addresses (4,294,967,296 separate addresses). In the days when TCP/IP was still young, the thought that four billion computers could exist was a bit of a stretch, especially because computers—even cheap ones—cost $5,000–10,000 each. However, with the increased popularity of the Internet, these IP addresses have been disappearing at a tremendous clip.

Why are IP addresses so important? Well, in the postal-mail metaphor we've been using for our network, every person has a unique name and address. The Internet likewise requires unique names and addresses; and once the current IP address space of four billion-plus addresses are used up, there won't be any more addresses. That's why the next generation of Internet Protocol, called IPv6, is so important—it increases the number of addresses to such a great number that it will be a while before we're in danger of running out of addresses again.

The reason why IP addresses have disappeared so fast is because of the way the addressing scheme is designed. All IP addresses are written in *dotted decimal notation*, with one byte (eight bits) between each dot. A dotted decimal IP address looks like this:

```
192.168.100.25
```

Because each number is described by one byte, and because each byte is 8 bits (or binary 1s and 0s), each number can have a value of anything from 0 to 255. Because there are 4 numbers with 8 bits each, the total *address space* is said to be 32 bits long (4×8 = 32).

With a 32-bit address space that can handle four billion addresses, you might think that the Internet would never run out of IP addresses (or that it would take a while at any rate). Unfortunately, that's not the case. IP addresses are allocated to organizations that request them in what are called *address blocks*. Address blocks come in three sizes, based on the *class* of address. And once you've read about IP address allocation in the following sections, you'll agree that the present method of allocating IP addresses is inefficient given the way the Internet has grown.

Class A Addresses

Class A addresses, of which there are very few (if any) left unused, have up to 16,777,216 addresses. It uses 24 of the 32 bits in the address space read left to right. A Class A address looks like this:

`X.0.0.0`

The number represented by the `X` is one fixed number from `0` to `126` and always begins with binary `0`. This number is used as the first number before the leftmost dot by all the IP addresses in a Class A address space.

All the numbers represented by the `0`s can range from `0` to `255`. Because three of the four available numbers are used to create unique IP addresses, and three-quarters of 32 is 24, a Class A network has a *24-bit address space*. Collectively, Class A addresses use up 50% of the available addresses of the IPv4 address space, or 2,147,483,648 of the 4,294,967,296 total available addresses.

Class B Addresses

Class A addresses provide 16 million IP addresses per network. The next increment, Class B, has a total of 65,536 IP addresses per network. A Class B address looks like this:

`X.X.0.0`

All Class B addresses begin with a binary `10`. Class B addresses compose 25% of the available IP address space. This means that Class B addresses account for 1,073,741,824 of the 4,294,967,296 available IP addresses.

The numbers represented by the `X`s are fixed numbers ranging from `0` to `255`. The numbers represented by the `0`s can range from `0` to `255`. Because the two rightmost dotted numbers are used to create unique IP addresses, and because one-half of 32 is 16, a Class B network has a *16-bit address space*.

Class C Addresses

The smallest increment of IP addresses available to an organization is Class C. In a Class C network, only the rightmost dotted decimal number can be used for a total of 256 IP addresses.

All Class C addresses begin with a binary `110`. Class C addresses compose 12.5% of the available IP address space. This means that Class C addresses account for 536,870,912 of the 4,294,967,296 available IP addresses.

Here's an example of a Class C address:

`X.X.X.0`

As with the Class A and B examples just presented, the numbers represented by the `X`s are fixed numbers that range from `0` to `255`; the number represented by the `0` can range from `0` to `255`.

Other Network Classes

In addition to Classes A, B, and C, there are two other network classes:

- Class D. The leftmost address always begins with binary 1110. Class D addresses are used for multicasting, or sending messages to many systems at once. This isn't commonly used, but there are applications where many computers need to receive the same data in order to provide redundant systems.

- Class E. The leftmost address always begins with binary 1111. Class E addresses are reserved for experimental purposes.

Why IP Address Allocation Is Wasteful

Under the current 32-bit Internet address scheme, organizations must select a network class that will provide enough IP addresses for their needs.

The few remaining Class A addresses could potentially be assigned to organizations that need more than 65,536 (Class B-size) IP addresses, even if the organization doesn't require anywhere close to 16 million addresses.

Class B addresses are likewise assigned to organizations that require more than 256 IP addresses, whether or not they require anywhere near 65,536 addresses.

Class C addresses are, fortunately, available for small networks. However, keep in mind that if you take a full Class C, you have 256 addresses, even if you require only 20 addresses.

Fortunately, several solutions are on the horizon. The first is *CIDR*, or *Classless Inter Domain Routing*, which allows several Class C addresses to be combined. As an example, using CIDR, if you need a thousand network addresses, you can get four 256-address Class Cs and combine them for a total of 1024 addresses (256×4=1024), rather than tying up a whole Class B address of 65,536 addresses. CIDR, or *supernetting*, as it's been called, has become a means of efficiently allocating network addresses without wasting large chunks of class B address space.

Also on the horizon (and getting closer, but not as fast as we'd like) is IPv6, or the next generation of IP. IPv6, in contrast to current IP (IPv4), has a 128-bit address space (versus a 32-bit address space for IPv4) and is laid out in a slightly different way than IPv4. The following listing compares an IPv4 address with an IPv6 address:

IPv4 Address:	x.x.x.x	Each X represents 8 bits in dotted decimal notation (1 through 255).
IPv6 Address:	x:x:x:x:x:x:x:x	Each x represents 16 bits, written in hex notation (0 through F).

IPv6 addresses are written in hexadecimal, or base-16, numbers. The reason hex is used is that if each 16-bit number between the colons were written out in decimal, the address would be huge (remember that 16 bits can represent any number from 0 to 65,536).

If you're not familiar with hex notation, don't worry. There's an old conundrum that will mnemonically help you remember how it works:

How does a programmer count to 16? Zero, One, Two, Three, Four, Five, Six, Seven, Eight, Nine, A, B, C, D, E, F.

By using hex notation, it's possible to represent an IPv6 number in something approaching comprehensibility: FEDC:BA98:7654:3210: FEDC:BA98:7654:3210. Fortunately, IPv6 will also do a lot of self-configuration, so you won't have to worry about this.

IPv6 will essentially eradicate the address-space problem with IPv4. Recall that 32 bits represent an address space of over 4 billion different addresses. Now, let's extrapolate. If 32 bits is equal to 4,294,967,296 different addresses, we add one more bit (to make a total of 33 bits) and we have 8,589,934,592 addresses. Make it 34 bits, and you have 17,179,869,184 addresses…. Now keep doubling that number with each additional bit until you get to 128 bits, and you'll see that the number gets larger very quickly. To kill the suspense, I'll tell you that if you continue doubling the quantity represented by a string of bits until you hit 128 bits, you'll wind up with 340 billion billion billion billion (340 times 10 to the 38th power). This means that there would be 67 billion billion addresses for every square centimeter on the earth's surface. In other words, we're not going to run out of addresses anytime soon if we use IPv6.

IPv4 is currently the world's most popular protocol. It's the backbone of the Internet, and most large networks rely on its standardization, interoperability, and reliability. If you elect to run your network on it, there will initially be an added dimension of complexity. However, once your network is set up to use IP, it will be capable of talking to any other computer of any type—from a personal computer to a mainframe—that can speak TCP/IP. It's the universal solvent of networking.

IPX

Internetworking Packet Exchange, or *IPX*, is Novell's answer to the complexity of IP. Novell designed IPX in the early 1980s before the current furor over IP and the Internet, and it shows. IPX is a relatively efficient protocol that does several things for which network administrators are duly grateful:

- Unlike IP, IPX can configure its own address. This is very useful, particularly when there are a lot of systems to install.

- IPX is a "chatty" protocol. That is, it advertises its presence on the network. This characteristic is okay on networks with finite boundaries because the bandwidth it uses is not too bad. On a huge network (a WAN, for example), the chatty nature of IPX can become quite troublesome because it can overwhelm low-bandwidth WAN connections.

On the whole, IPX is easy to install and simple to use. Unfortunately, it's not an open standard; it's controlled by Novell. In spite of its ease of use, even Novell has acknowledged that IPX will eventually bow out in favor of IP.

IPX has lost in the face of the IP onslaught. The only network operating system that continues to use IPX is Novell's NetWare, and even NetWare currently uses IP.

NetBIOS and NetBEUI

Network Basic Input/Output System (*NetBIOS*) and *NetBIOS Extended User Interface* (*NetBEUI*) are single-site network protocols. NetBEUI is based on a way of passing data called *Server Message Block* (*SMB*), which relies on computer names to resolve destination addresses.

Of the three protocols we have covered in the last hour, NetBIOS and NetBEUI are far and away the simplest to implement. Most often used for small peer-to-peer LANs, the NetBIOS and NetBEUI protocols are part of the networking suite that comes with every version of Windows (from Windows for Workgroups to the present), OS/2 Warp, and several third-party networking software packages such as Artisoft's Lantastic.

Summary

Whew! You covered a lot of ground in this hour to ensure that you have a grasp of network topologies and protocols. You should have a good foundation for the next several chapters in which you'll learn the specifics of computer and network hardware and software. With the theory presented in this hour and the knowledge of network hardware that's coming up, you'll have the basic knowledge to design your network.

Q&A

Q What are the actual breakdowns of Class A, B, and C addresses?

A There are actually limitations on which numbers can be assigned to each address class. These limitations are specified in RFC 796 and later related RFC documents. The breakdowns are as follows:

- Class A addresses range from roughly 1.X.X.X to 126.X.X.X, where the Xs represent any number from 0 to 255.

- Class B addresses range from 128.0.X.X to 191.255.X.X.
- Class C addresses range from 192.0.0.X to 223.255.255.X.

IP address numbers are assigned through the Internet Assigned Numbers Authority (IANA) through Network Solutions, Inc., in Virginia.

Q What happens if I need a Class C address, but have to use the addresses in a WAN in which routers pass data between networks at different locations?

A Believe it or not, this is not a problem. In an attempt to allocate IP addresses as efficiently as possible, the designers of IP made provisions for subnetting, which means breaking a given address space (such as a full Class C address of 256 IP addresses) into smaller units. Data is routed between the subnets according to the way the network is divided.

For example, consider a Class C network with the network number 192.168.10.0. This network has 256 IP addresses ranging from 192.168.10.0 to 192.168.10.255. Suppose that you have 25 users in separate locations. The first subnet covers addresses 192.168.10.1 through 192.168.10.26 (remember that the 0 address is usually reserved for the network address itself). The next network's rightmost number ranges from 26 to 51, and so forth. This arrangement enables a network to appear to be one network—192.168.10.0—to anyone outside the network (in other words, on the Internet) but actually to be many smaller networks.

3

HOUR 4

Computer Concepts

Networks are made of computers in the same way a band is made of musicians. Each computer—and each band member—is unique, and in the right circumstances, they all work together. If they don't, then all you get is chaos.

Similarly, networks require that certain conventions be observed when computers are networked. Although each computer is unique, it nonetheless works in the same fashion as the other computers on the network. If you understand how a computer works, you'll be better prepared to understand how networks work.

So here goes…a primer on basic computer concepts. In this hour, you'll learn the following:

- How computers work
- The varieties of computer hardware
- What software is and what it does

Computer Hardware

When you get right down to it, computers have two components: *hardware* and *software*. Hardware, as you have probably guessed, are the physical components that make up a computer. It includes, but is not limited to, the following items:

- The CPU (Central Processing Unit)
- Memory
- Disks
- Add-in adapters
- Printer and communications ports

In the next few pages, you'll get a very high-level virtual tour of a PC. Although the descriptions will most correctly describe an IBM-compatible PC (the most common kind of personal computer), the concepts presented here also hold for Macintoshes and Unix boxes and any other computer designed with a modular, expandable architecture. Don't get hung up on the type of computer; the basic concepts are what is important.

The CPU

When you remove the cover from a personal computer, the first thing you should see (after you have cleared away the tangle of cables that seem to run everywhere like jungle foliage) is a large square section of metal and ceramic, attached to the electronics, that dwarfs everything else completely. That's the *Central Processing Unit* (the *CPU*, or "the chip" as people familiar with computers call it). A CPU is, in principle, nothing more than a chip of silicon that's had several layers of microscopic transistors etched and doped into it using extremely delicate and complex processes.

The CPU is the *sine non qua* of personal computing—without it, there would be no computer. The CPU is the device that takes all of the 1s and 0s that make up the input from the keyboard and the mouse and the disks and whatever else you have in your system and processes it so that you can accomplish whatever it is you want to accomplish—see a display on a video screen, type a letter, create a spreadsheet...whatever.

But don't get the idea that CPUs operate entirely on their own; CPUs are usually mounted in a *motherboard*, which is a large printed circuit board that has several systems on it to enable data to be sent to and received from the chip. Motherboards come in a dizzying array of varieties and are available from many different manufacturers.

Typically, CPUs are *microprocessors*, that is, they have multiple microscopic transistors in logical arrays. The earliest microprocessors had only a few hundred transistors per chip; modern microprocessors such as Intel's Pentium II chip, Sun Microsystem's SPARC chip, Motorola's PowerPC chip, and Digital Equipment Corporation's Alpha chip may have more than five million transistors on a square the size of your thumbnail. And the next generation of chips are projected to have up to fifteen million transistors—an astronomical increase in power.

Memory

A CPU is a microprocessor, but all chips are not microprocessors. Some chips are built as arrays that can hold the 1s and 0s that the CPU is processing; these are memory chips. When these chips are arranged into groups, the resulting memory devices are called *Single Inline Memory Modules* (*SIMMs*) or *Dual Inline Memory Modules* (*DIMMs*). SIMMs and DIMMs are the most common way to add memory to computers; when you buy memory from a retailer, you're buying memory modules instead of individual memory chips. You'll also hear about *DRAM* (*dynamic RAM*) and *SDRAM*, let alone *RamBus* and other memory architectures. In spite of the difference in nomenclature, all memory works in essentially the same fashion. Just make certain that the memory you purchase is the same sort that your computer requires.

The purpose of memory chips is not solely (as some people have said) to provide a work-space for the CPU. Memory is also used to provide CPU-speed access to data. If the computer had to read data from tapes or disks each time it needed the next batch of data or instructions, computers would be terribly slow—far too slow to be useful. But the use of memory, specifically *Random Access Memory* (*RAM*), has led to computers being fast and useful for most users.

Here's an example that may help. Suppose that you are following a complicated recipe. It has 50 ingredients (it's a very complicated recipe) and 39 steps. Imagine what would happen if you had no counter space and no table space to store your instructions and ingredients? Here's what might happen: Each time you were ready to perform the next step, you would have to leave the kitchen, go to the bookcase, find the book, open it to the correct page, figure out where you are, read the next step, replace the book, and then remember the next step. That by itself would slow you down pretty significantly.

To complicate matters further, suppose that you had a bunch of ingredients stored in cupboards, refrigerators, and freezers. Each time the instructions said you needed a new ingredient, you would have to go to the appropriate storage location, find the ingredient, measure out the correct amount, close the package, replace the ingredient, and then bring the ingredient back to the kitchen. This organizational nightmare would pretty well guarantee that even if you could cook, the process wouldn't be too useful.

It's the same way for computers. The CPU is the kitchen, where the work gets done. The bookcase is one piece of local storage (such as a hard drive), where the *program*, or cookbook, is stored. The cupboards, fridge, and freezer are where data is stored, and the counter is your memory.

4

Just think about it; if you had enough counter space, you could load up all the pieces you need to follow your recipe—the directions and the ingredients—and the cooking process would go much faster. You could conceivably still cook without the counter space, but without it, you would have to go to storage for each item, and that makes the whole process less efficient.

> That's why analysts from think-tanks like the Gartner Group and the Meta Group say that memory is often more important than CPU power: Memory is fast storage. Typically, a computer can access memory chips very fast; memory access speeds are measured in nanoseconds (millionths of a second). Contrast this with the fastest hard drives, which have millisecond access times, which are an order of magnitude or three slower—a thousand times slower. Kinda makes you want to fill your computer with as much memory as you can afford, doesn't it? Even if a computer has a very powerful processor, if it is short of memory, it will run slowly. By contrast, a less powerful CPU armed with a lot of memory can outrun a more powerful but memory-starved CPU.

Memory is great for ensuring that computers run fast. However, there's one thing memory can't do, and the next section explains what.

Disks

Memory makes a computer run faster. This is good. However, RAM is *volatile*, which means that it only works when the computer is turned on. Because RAM is made of chips that depend on an electrical power source to store data, when the power is cut, it can no longer store anything. And because you don't want to retype everything every time you turn on the computer—that was, after all, one of the reasons you bought a computer in the first place, to replace the typewriter that made you do that—there ought to be a way to store data so that it can be retrieved next time you turn on the computer.

That's why disks were invented. Hard disks fulfill two of the most common needs of the computer: Disks store data in a *nonvolatile* state (that is, the data stored on disks doesn't disappear when the power is cut), and they act as additional (very slow) memory when the computer needs more memory than is physically installed.

The technology behind disks is not new. A Sony Walkman uses basically the same technology to read (or write to) a cassette tape. Almost all tapes and disks are members of the *magnetic media* family, which simply means that these devices store data—whether that data is Pink Floyd on MP3 or your presentation to the boss on a floppy disk—by manipulating the position of the north-south poles of tiny magnetic particles.

How, exactly, do disks work? Here's how: Magnets have two poles, north and south. Remember that computers only use 1s and 0s? Well, 1s and 0s are binary—that is, they are either 1 or 0; there's nothing in between. Fortunately for those of us who need to store data, north and south on magnetic particles are also binary, and the computer can use the orientation of microscopic magnetic particles to correspond to the 1s and 0s it needs to function. A magnetic particle with the north pole facing up might be a 0, and a particle with the south pole facing up might be a 1—just what we need to store data.

For a long time, disks did not have very large capacities—a drive that could store a *megabyte* (a million characters) was a huge drive 30 years ago and cost half a million dollars. Today, we can store twice that much data on a floppy disk that sells for 30 cents, and it's possible to get hard disks that store several *gigabytes* (a billion characters) of data for a couple hundred dollars. The trend has been that, over time, storage capacities have gotten larger and the cost per unit of disk storage has gotten cheaper.

Modern disks for personal computers generally come in one of two varieties: IDE and SCSI. These are simply different methods by which hard drives connect to computers. Because devices of one type are not compatible with devices of the other type, it's important to know a bit about them.

Integrated Drive Electronics, or *IDE* (pronounced "eye-dee-eee," just like the letters that make up the acronym), is a standard for hard drives that places the electronics that control the drive directly on the drive itself. IDE supports up to two drives connected to a single cable, and disk sizes up to 528 megabytes. A more recent version of the IDE standard, called *Extended IDE* (*EIDE*), can support larger disks; it's now common to see EIDE disks with capacities of to five or six gigabytes. EIDE is now often called *Ultra DMA*.

Small Computer Serial Interface, or *SCSI*, is a standard for connecting all sorts of devices to a computer. SCSI (pronounced "skuzzy;" in the early days, salespeople tried to get people to pronounce it "sec-see" but that pronunciation flew like a lead balloon) allows up to seven devices to be connected to the computer in a chain (see Figure 4.1).

Newer SCSI devices allow up to fifteen devices to be connected to a computer on one chain of devices. Each device on a *SCSI chain* (that's what a series of connected devices is called) has a number called (not surprisingly) a SCSI ID that enables the computer to locate that device when needed. Each end of the SCSI chain must be terminated, which means that a special device called a *terminating resistor* must be plugged into the end of the cable. The terminating resistor essentially ensures that the impedance of the cable remains consistent along its length.

FIGURE 4.1

A typical SCSI device chain with a hard drive, a scanner, and a tape drive connected.

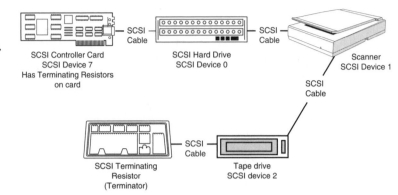

Of the two standards, IDE is usually simpler to set up because it supports only hard drives and only two hard drives per cable. It's also generally less expensive than SCSI equipment, which is good to know if you're on a budget. On the other hand, SCSI is faster and more versatile; if you're setting up a server computer, SCSI drives are almost always a better choice than IDE drives. And for some computers (notably Macintoshes and most commercial Unix systems), you don't have a choice—you have a choice of SCSI, SCSI, or SCSI (shades of Monty Python's Spam skit...)

Of course, drives don't operate on their own; they have to connect to something. What drives connect to is part of the next section.

Add-In Adapter Cards

At the beginning of this hour, you learned that the CPU fits into a socket on the motherboard. In addition to the socket for the CPU, the motherboard has sockets for aftermarket devices that handle several of the computer's functions. These devices, which fit into sockets called expansion slots on the motherboard, are called *adapter cards*. These cards are part of an electronic assembly that connects to a computer through a standard interface (see the following section, "Slot Interfaces") called a *card slot*. Adapter cards can provide a variety of services to the computer, including video, network, modem, and other functions as required.

It is safe to make the claim that without IBM's decision to adopt a modular design for their initial personal computer, and the computer industry's following suit, modern personal computers wouldn't have become the powerful and adaptable machines that they are today. The modularity and adaptability of the IBM PC drove the personal computer's explosion of popularity in the early 1980s. In fact, the computer industry's rapid growth can be attributed to the adapter-card standards promulgated by IBM for the early PC.

Adapter cards handle a wide array of functions, including the following:

- Network adapters connect computers to the network.
- Video adapters provide a way for the computer to display images on a video monitor.

- Drive controllers connect floppy drives and hard drives to the system.
- SCSI controllers connect any devices that use the SCSI interface to the computer.
- Sound and video cards enable a variety of multimedia types—from CD to MP3— to be played on your system.

This list is not comprehensive; it does not include all the different types of adapter cards. Nonetheless, it does cover all the devices you are likely to encounter in a common computer.

Slot Interfaces

Although most motherboards have expansion slots, the expansion slots on all motherboards are not the same. Various computer manufacturers have devised different interfaces for cards used in their systems; in general, the interfaces are not compatible with each other.

For Intel-compatible computers, the most common slot designs are, in order of age from oldest to youngest, ISA, EISA, and PCI. ISA stands for *Industry Standard Architecture*, which was what IBM called this interface when it initially created it in the early 1980s. ISA has a 16-bit data path (which means that it can move only 16 bits of data simultaneously), and it runs at 8 megahertz, even if the rest of your computer is blazing along at 300 megahertz. EISA, or *Extended ISA*, was an attempt to extend the ISA interface by increasing the data path to 32 bits and increasing the speed to 32 megahertz. One good side benefit of EISA is its *backward compatibility*, or its capability to be used with older equipment. ISA cards can be used in EISA slots (but not the other way around!)—they just don't get the speed and performance benefits of EISA.

PCI, or *Peripheral Component Interconnect*, was the result of an initiative by Intel, the microprocessor manufacturer, to allow add-in adapters to run almost as fast as the system in which they are installed. PCI is blazingly fast, offering data transfer rates of up to 128 megabits per second.

Most Pentium-level and newer Intel-compatible servers have a mixture of EISA and PCI slots to ensure good performance. Older systems based on 386 and 486 microprocessors usually have only an ISA bus. Occasionally, it's possible to find a 486 motherboard with what are called *VESA-Local-Bus slots* (VLB); VLB is a dead standard initially introduced before PCI in an attempt to speed up adapter card access to the CPU. Unfortunately, it was closely tied to the 486 and never gained wide acceptance; now it's more of a curiosity than a performance enhancer. Broken VLB equipment is becoming increasingly difficult to replace, so if you have mission-critical systems that use this standard, you may want to upgrade the motherboard to a design that makes it easier to get replacement parts. Fortunately, VLB slots are, like EISA, backward compatible with ISA.

For Macintosh computers, there are two slot types: Nubus and PCI. The Nubus interface is found on older computers such as Mac II series machines that use various levels of the Motorola 68000 microprocessor. The PCI interface is found on the newer Power Macintosh computers that use the Motorola PowerPC chip. Interestingly, the PCI slots used on Power Macs are the same as the slots used on IBM compatibles—it might be possible to use PCI adapter cards interchangeably.

UNIX-based systems, such as Sun's SPARC-chip computers or Digital's Alpha-based systems (the Alpha also runs Microsoft Windows NT), use either PCI or proprietary slot types.

Intel-compatible computers have the largest market segment and the widest selection of add-in cards. As a result, the following sections primarily focus on cards designed to fit into Intel-compatible PCs.

Network Adapter Cards

If you want to connect a computer to a printer, you use a printer port. If you want to connect a computer to a network, you use a *Network Adapter Card* or *Network Interface Card* (the terms are synonymous), usually called either a *network card* or *NIC*, respectively. Network cards are available from a wide variety of manufacturers and in a variety of interfaces including Ethernet, Token Ring, and FDDI, which you'll remember from Hour 1, "An Overview of Networking," and 3, "Getting Data from Here to There: How Computers Share Data."

Network cards are seldom difficult to install. Typically, you turn off the power to the computer, open the case, find a slot that matches the card's interface (it'll usually be ISA, EISA, or PCI), center the card above the slot, and press the card firmly into the slot to seat it. Once you have done that, turn the computer back on. When the computer is fully running, you can install the *device drivers*, or software that allows the computer to talk to the network card. Once the device driver software is installed, you usually have to reboot your computer one more time to load the driver and be able to connect to the network.

One important thing to remember about network adapters is that every card is assigned a unique 48-bit number (that is, a 6-byte number; remember that 8 bits equals 1 byte, so 48 bits equals 6 bytes) called a *MAC address*. MAC is an acronym for *Media Access Control*. The network wire and network cards and concentrators are also collectively called *network media*, which is where the *media* in *Media Access Control* comes from.

Video Adapter Cards

If you asked most people to point to "the computer," they would point to the monitor on their desks. Although they'd be incorrect in defining a monitor as the computer (the box that holds the CPU and motherboard and power supply and adapter cards is, strictly speaking, the computer), they'd be making a powerful point that you'd do well to heed. Human beings are, by and large, visually oriented creatures. In general, things that are visually catchy get higher priority and garner more attention than things that aren't visually catchy. The computer box beside your desk just doesn't create visual interest. This would explain why Compaq and Apple (among others) now offer the CPU in bright colors, since it adds visual interest and emphasis to the computer itself.

By contrast, the monitor *is* visually interesting because it's colorful and full of motion. Computer monitors get attention out of proportion to the amount of actual work they do. The keyboard and mouse are where the user's part of the work is done, and the system box actually does the computing, but the monitor is what we see, and therefore is what we respond to.

Because what we see on a video monitor screen is such an important part of how we interact with computers, the *Video Adapter Card*, or *video card*, is obviously an important part of the system. Video cards take the digital information the computer uses internally and converts it to an analog, or waveform, format that can be displayed on a computer monitor.

The minimum standard for video displays on modern Intel-compatible computers is called *VGA*, or *Video Graphics Array*. In order to meet the VGA standard, a video card must be able to display an image that is 640 pixels wide by 480 pixels tall, in at least 16 colors. (A *pixel* is a picture element; just picture one square in a grid and you've got the basic idea of a pixel.) VGA is a useful standard because so many manufacturers adhere to it as a baseline for their video adapters; almost all Intel-compatible video adapters have a VGA mode.

However, VGA is limited—640 by 480 with 16 colors does not provide particularly good screen resolution; it can't display images and colors very accurately. In an attempt to get around the limitations of VGA, video adapter manufacturers created several standards that extend VGA and make it more useful for computer users who actually have to spend time working at a screen: *Super VGA* (800 pixels wide by 600 pixels tall by 16 colors) and *Extended VGA* (usually 1024 pixels wide by 768 pixels tall). Additional display settings for some adapters offer increased *color depth*, or the number of colors on the screen, that range from 256 colors up to 16.7 million colors, which is photograph quality.

4

Color depth can get a bit confusing, especially if you do not need high-end video or graphics editing capability. But there's a very simple way to understand all the terms that surround video adapter color depths; it's common sense once you know how to interpret it.

Sometimes 256 color screens are called 8-bit color. This is because 8 bits (or eight 1s and 0s) are required to tell the computer what color to display in each pixel. Because 8 bits can be combined into 256 different combinations, that gives us 256 colors.

The next step up from 8-bit color is 16-bit color, which simply uses 16 bits to describe each pixel—but what a change! With 16 bits, you can have up to 65,536 simultaneous colors on screen. You might hear 16-bit color referred to as *high color*.

Beyond 16-bit color is 32-bit color, also called *true color*. Using 32 bits to describe the color of a pixel, you have up to 16.7 million color possibilities. In many cases, using 32-bit color in conjunction with a very high-quality monitor and video card, you cannot see the difference between a monitor screen and a photograph.

Drive Controllers

Floppy drives, hard drives, and tape drives have to connect to the system to be useful. Drive controllers provide that connection. As noted earlier in this hour, most common drive controllers operate in the IDE, EIDE, or SCSI standard. The rule of thumb is to use SCSI drive controllers for servers and IDE drive controllers for desktops because SCSI is fast and expandable and IDE is simple. Drive controllers are available in ISA, EISA, and PCI interfaces; if your motherboard has PCI slots, use a PCI controller no matter what kind of drive you use because the PCI interface will increase performance.

SCSI Cards

Although SCSI cards were mentioned in the preceding "Drive Controllers" section, it's only fair to give them their own section because they allow a broad array of devices to connect to computers. In addition to hard drives, SCSI adapters can connect to scanners, removable-media drives from companies like Iomega and Pinnacle Micro, sensor test equipment, and other devices. If you're faced with a limited budget and the probability that you'll need to expand a computer system, put a SCSI card in your system. It enables you to connect a range of peripherals using only one adapter card, thus reducing cost and complexity.

Client Operating System Software

Computer hardware is great, but it doesn't get you anywhere by itself. Hardware requires software, usually *operating system software*, to do anything useful. An *operating system*, or *OS*, is the software that enables users and applications to interact with the computer hardware. An OS is essentially a set of baseline functions for the computer. There's no reason why each program couldn't essentially contain an OS and boot the system, but an OS essentially frees application designers from having to redesign the world each time they write software. The OS also offers consistent user and programming interfaces and standard ways of doing simple tasks such as copying data between applications.

There are a variety of operating system types:

- **Single-tasking systems** such as MS-DOS—These can do only one task at a time.
- **Multitasking systems**—These can run several tasks simultaneously.
- **Single-user systems**—These are intended for use by one user at a time on one machine at a time.
- **Multiuser systems**—These are intended to support many simultaneous user sessions on one computer.

These distinctions are important when you select the various components of your network, so remember these terms.

Multitasking Versus Single-Tasking Systems

Just as with everything else, there's more than one type of multitasking. This probably sounds a bit disingenuous—if an operating system can do more than one thing at a time, it can do more than one thing at a time, right?—but it bears a bit more explanation.

First, let's talk about what *multitasking* means. An MS-DOS system (which isn't common any longer) can, for all practical purposes, run one program at a time. DOS does not offer multiple sessions, so what you see on your screen is basically all that the computer can do.

DOS also doesn't have a windowing system. This means that each program in DOS fills up the whole screen. If you use DOS' task switcher, you can switch between different full-screen instances of programs, but when a program isn't in the foreground filling the screen, it's inactive.

Some operating systems are multiuser—which means that they can support multiple users, each user having a unique session. Unix is probably the best example of a multi-user system, although Digital's VMS and Linux also fit into this category. In a multiuser system, one computer runs one or more sessions simultaneously, and each user has a device called a terminal. Terminals are devices which look like a monitor but offer some additional connectivity services. ASCII terminals are generally connected via a serial port (a COM port, for PC users). ASCII terminals work at the command line—they don't have a graphical interface. X Terminals, by contrast, are usually network-connected devices that use Ethernet or Token Ring, and they offer a graphical user interface (GUI) called X Windows that appears in many forms (GNOME, KDE, CDE, OpenLook) and works in ways similar to Microsoft's Windows or the Mac's interface.

4

Multitasking systems are systems that can do more than one task at a time. Almost all multiuser systems are multitasking, but not all multitasking systems are multiuser. Unix supports terminals to its command-line interface and it can multitask. By contrast, Windows 98/Me and Windows 2000 are multitasking but not multiuser.

There are two types of multitasking: *cooperative* and *preemptive*. Rather than go through all the technical jargon about how the OS kernel handles task switching and so forth, we'll use an analogy to illustrate the difference between these two methods: Multitasking can be likened to managing preschool children.

Cooperative multitasking, performed by Microsoft's Windows 3.x products and the backward-compatible parts of Windows Me, is like having one toy (the operating system resources) that must be shared by several preschoolers (the software applications). Further, in the cooperative multitasking model, the teacher (or task-switcher, or scheduler), who ideally should be ensuring that the toy is passed equitably, sits in the corner not doing much. In this model, the preschoolers are responsible for cooperatively relinquishing the toy when they're done with it and gracefully passing it on to the next child in line.

Clearly, this is not a recipe for successful multitasking. To return to the analogy, pre-schoolers are not known for their ability to cooperate when sharing resources. Invariably, one child will refuse to relinquish the toy and the whole system comes to an abrupt, screeching (and crying) halt. In the computer model, when one application hogs all the resources and the system "locks up," it's called a *system crash*. This is when preemptive multitasking becomes a more desirable model.

Preemptive multitasking is what happens when we have several preschoolers and only one toy, but with one major difference: The teacher is actively involved in governing the sharing of the toy. When one child has had the toy for a fixed period of time, the teacher takes it away, whether or not the child protests, and passes it on to the next child, and so forth. In other words, the teacher preempts the child's request to hang onto the toy, and so the toy, or resource, is successfully shared, even if one child protests. Preemptive multitasking is the model used in Unix, Microsoft's Windows NT/2000, and the 32-bit sections of Windows 98/Me, IBM's OS/2, and Novell's NetWare 4.

If you're using a server, you almost certainly want to ensure that the server operating system preemptively multitasks. Preemptive multitasking is also desirable from a client applications perspective. It offers the user the ability to recover from a crashed application without being forced to restart the operating system.

In spite of the superiority of preemptive multitasking operating systems, there is still room for Microsoft's venerable single-tasking MS-DOS. Although MS-DOS has serious memory limitations, it is still a useful platform for terminal applications as well as for making use of older computers. Even if your company has standardized on Windows Me, Windows NT, or OS/2, it is useful to know a bit about the DOS (or Unix) command line because it's tremendously powerful (see Figure 4.2).

FIGURE 4.2
A DOS command-line screen.

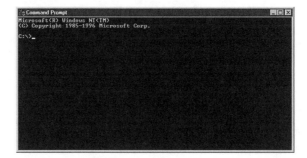

MS-DOS to Windows

During the late 1980s, Microsoft bowed to market pressure and developed a Graphical User Interface, or GUI, for their computers and called it Windows. Windows 3.X operated as an extension of the single-tasking MS-DOS and offered only cooperative multitasking. The advent of Windows for Workgroups in the early 1990s provided native networking capabilities in Windows, which simplified networking for a great many users (see Figure 4.3).

FIGURE 4.3

A Windows for Workgroups 3.11 screen.

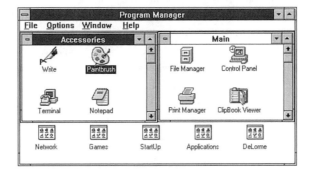

As a network client, the combination of DOS and Windows 3.x left a great deal to be desired. DOS/Windows lacked preemptive multitasking, for one thing, and its use of memory was inefficient and clumsy. Nonetheless, it provided millions of users with their first taste of a graphical user interface (GUI) and basic networking.

Although Windows 3.x was a commercial success and established Microsoft's dominant market position in personal computer operating systems, it was not the most advanced system available at the time. Instead, it was a GUI grafted onto the single-tasking DOS, which made it a bit of a compromise. Cooperative multitasking and the limitations of DOS dogged Windows while users complained.

MacOS

In fact, many Macintosh users complained that Microsoft Windows had "stolen" the look and feel of the Macintosh. Apple invented the Macintosh OS, also called *the System*, in 1984. It was a clean and spare interface, well-suited to nontechnical users; this, combined with the Macintosh's reputation for never making the user worry about the computer hardware (Macintosh operating systems software ran only on Macintosh computers), led users to develop a near-fanatical devotion to Apple.

MacOS initially came with a proprietary network called LocalTalk, which eventually turned into AppleTalk. With the rise of the Internet, MacTCP arrived and enabled Mac users to connect to the Internet and use TCP/IP standards.

Windows 98

In an attempt to better address the needs of their customers, Microsoft began to develop a pair of operating systems that would offer true multitasking and greater stability than Windows 3.x. The initial results of these efforts were Windows 95 and Windows NT, which have evolved into Windows 98/Me, the descendant of Windows Me, and Windows 2000, the descendant of NT.

Windows 95 and its descendants Windows 98 and Windows Me were designed as network-aware client operating systems intended for use only on Intel-compatible computers. They preemptively multitask when they run 32-bit applications, such as Microsoft's Office97 or Lotus' SmartSuite 97, but cooperatively multitask when running Windows 3.x applications, such as Word 6 or Lotus 1-2-3 version 5. The major difference between Windows 3.x and later versions of Windows, however, is a radical change in the way the screen looks. Windows 3.x relies on the Program Manager to organize the screen real estate; in Windows 95, Windows Me, Windows 98, Windows NT4, and Windows 2000, there is no Program Manager, just the Taskbar that resides at the bottom of the screen (see Figure 4.4). To access your applications in recent versions of Windows, you click the Start button or create a shortcut to the item that's placed directly on the desktop.

FIGURE 4.4

A Windows 95 screen.

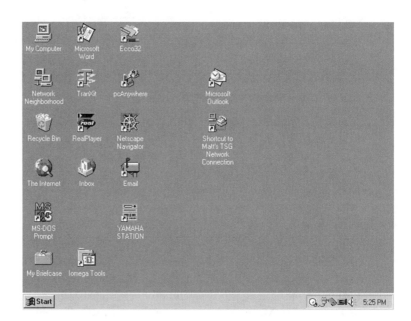

From here on out, we're going to refer to the Windows 95/98/Me hierarchy collectively as Windows Me, since Windows Me is the lineal descendant of these earlier operating systems.

As a network client, Windows Me is an astronomical improvement over Windows 3.x. Its networking components are much better integrated with the operating system than Windows 3.x's, and those components are much more stable and configurable. The interface is also much improved, which makes for better user interaction with the system. It also includes TCP/IP, the world's most widespread network protocol, which means that it can connect to the Internet quite easily.

We'll take a closer look at Windows Me in Hour 14, "Microsoft Windows Peer Networking."

OS/2

In the late 1980s and early 1990s, just before the time Microsoft was rolling out Windows and ramping up to Windows NT and 95, IBM, in conjunction with Microsoft, was selling their own Intel-compatible operating system. Operating System/2, or OS/2 as it is commonly called, is a truly preemptive 32-bit operating system designed to run on Intel-compatible hardware. OS/2 is a highly customizable system that supports multiple simultaneous logins into different resources on remote computers. OS/2 is a competent, capable operating system available in a server version as well as a workstation version.

However, Microsoft and IBM's partnership on OS/2 floundered after version 1.3 of the product, with Microsoft focusing on its Windows NT and Windows95/98/Me development efforts. Unfortunately, Microsoft's dominance in the personal systems market has placed OS/2 at a distinct disadvantage. Because Microsoft held and continues to hold a very high percentage of the personal operating systems market, application developers gravitated toward developing products for Microsoft's Windows platform to the detriment of other operating systems. IBM's market share with OS/2 was sufficiently low that very few OS/2-native (written to run on OS/2) business applications (word processors, spreadsheets, presentation graphics programs, and the like) were created. From an application developer's perspective, there wasn't much profit in writing OS/2 applications. Also, because OS/2 can run 16-bit Windows applications in what's called the *Win-OS/2 subsystem*, developers reasoned that users would just run Windows apps on OS/2.

In spite of its commercial lack of success, OS/2 is a quality operating system that is stable, fast, and easy to use. Currently in its 4.0 release, Merlin, as OS/2 4.0 is known, offers a great user interface and great stability (see Figure 4.5). As a network client, it is quite good because it can support multiple simultaneous logins to multiple systems. In other words, in one window you can be logged in to server JOE, and in another window be logged in to server JAME, and with a third window be logged in to an Internet server or what-have-you. OS/2 is the only PC-based commercial operating system that supports this sort of login, which makes it very useful from an administrator's point of view.

4

FIGURE **4.5**

An OS/2 screen.

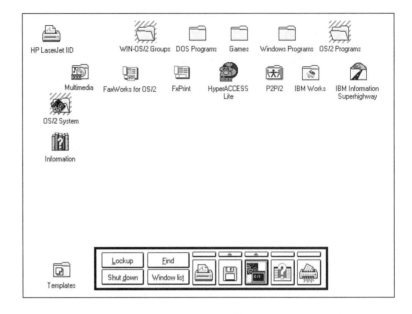

Windows 2000

As mentioned in the preceding section, Microsoft planned to co-develop OS/2 with IBM, and in fact did share development efforts until version 1.3. However, in the early 1990s, Microsoft's plans changed, and Microsoft moved away from the OS/2 model to create an enterprise-class workstation and server operating system that could run on more than just Intel-compatible computers. Microsoft's name for this system was *Windows NT*.

> The derivation of the name Windows NT is unknown. However, there's a lot of speculation. Windows NT was initially assumed to mean Windows New Technology. Later, it became known that the Windows NT development team had several key people who had been involved in the development of Digital Equipment Corporation's VMS operating system—and WNT is VMS with one letter moved forward. Conspiracy buffs, take note!

Windows NT was created from the ground up to serve two functions. One was to be an *enterprise-class server operating system*, which means that businesses could run their systems on it and be confident that it would work well for them.

The other function was to be a workstation-class operating system. In this context, the word *workstation* takes on a slightly different meaning from the way we've been using it. Up until now, workstation has meant a client system on a network. In the Unix parlance that

Microsoft appropriated, a workstation is a machine that has a great deal of processing power and a powerful, flexible, fast operating system that can run huge applications, such as engineering apps, digital video or audio editing, or financial data calculations.

In any case, Microsoft succeeded with NT. As a server operating system, it is reasonably fast, and it's easy to administer. The workstation client OS, Windows NT Workstation, is a fully preemptive 32-bit operating system that can run on Intel-compatible processors.

After the first several releases of Windows NT, Microsoft changed the name to Windows 2000. The look and feel have changed a bit, but Windows 2000 is still easy to network and is, in the author's opinion, a great deal more stable than older versions of NT.

As a network client, Windows 2000 Professional, the workstation version of the OS, is unparalleled in terms of its options. It can natively connect to almost any network without third-party software and its connectivity is reliable. Its interface is almost the same as Windows Me's, which means that users have a simpler learning curve (see Figure 4.6). Windows 2000 also has secure logins and entirely separate security for each user. We'll take a closer look at Windows 2000 server in Hour 15, "Microsoft Windows 2000 Server."

FIGURE 4.6

A Windows NT Workstation 4.0 screen. Note that the interface is very similar to that of Windows Me.

Unix

The last operating system we'll deal with for network client personal computers is Unix. Unix began as an experiment in a Bell Labs computer lab about 30 years ago and is now the preeminent workstation operating system in the sense that Windows NT Workstation is a workstation operating system. Unix runs on almost every type of computer ranging from Intel compatibles to high-end multiprocessor transaction servers used by banks and other institutions.

Unix, like its younger sibling Windows NT, is a fully preemptive operating system. Unlike every other operating system we've discussed, it's often shipped with the source code (the set of instructions written in a computer language such as C) that runs the system. Most commercial operating system vendors do not provide source code because they believe it is proprietary. With Unix, you often get the source code, which means that if you can program a computer, you can customize the operating system. In fact, it's pretty much necessary to customize the OS to do what you want—it's standard operating procedure!

Since the mid-1990s, a new variant of Unix called Linux has sprung up and received a lot of media attention. Essentially, Linux IS Unix—but it's entirely unencumbered by the copyright restrictions on commercial Unixes and the source code is always there for the taking. At the moment Linux is probably the best operating system on the planet from a cost/benefit perspective; for the cost of a CD from a Linux distributor (some of the most popular are Red Hat, Debian, SuSE, Slackware, and Yggdrasil), and a bit of time spent on the learning curve, it's possible to have the capabilities of a high-end Unix workstation on an Intel-compatible PC. We'll discuss Linux more in Hour 17, "Unix and Linux."

Unix is very complex. At its heart is a command-line interface much like DOS's, but with a great deal more power and flexibility than DOS offers. The standard graphical interface for Unix is called X Windows; there are several slightly different versions of X graphical interfaces (in Unix, they're called window managers) including Motif, fvwm, and Open Look. The varieties of X window managers provide slightly different visual schemes, but all work in ways similar to Microsoft's Windows or the Macintosh's graphical interfaces.

As a network client, Unix works extraordinarily well. Its default network protocol is TCP/IP, which is the protocol of the Internet, and Unix (or, more properly in this case, Linux) servers are the foundation of most of the Web servers on the planet.

We'll take a closer look at Unix in Hour 17.

That pretty well wraps up client operating systems. The next topic you have to understand is network applications, which are (as noted earlier) the raison d'etre of many a network.

Summary

At the beginning of this hour, we noted that it's necessary to know the parts in order to really know the whole. This chapter was written to assist you in doing just that.

By understanding something about computer hardware and operating system software, you have hopefully gained a global understanding of how a computer works and what client operating systems are.

These are important, material concepts. If you don't know how a computer works, what the parts of a computer are, or what an operating system is, you really can't understand a network at the build-it-yourself level. So make certain that you've assimilated these concepts—not doing so can make networking more difficult than it needs to be.

Q&A

Q Why are there different types of adapter-card slots?

A The primary reason is that newer slot designs are faster.

When IBM first released the IBM PC in 1981, it had seven adapter card slots that ran at 8 megahertz and passed data 8 bits (1 byte) at a time. Over time, this became too slow, so the slots were expanded to handle 16 bits (2 bytes) at a time.

Even this proved too slow, so EISA, VLB, and the newest standard, PCI, were invented to speed up the movement of data between adapter cards and the CPU.

Q What are some of the criteria that are useful for selecting an operating system?

A First and foremost, compatibility with the applications you'll be using on the network is desirable. An operating system can be great—but if it doesn't support your application, you're up a creek.

Next, look for the features that do the most for you. If you need an operating system that supports multiple user IDs logged into different servers, OS/2 works. If you need to ensure that each application runs in its own memory space and can't crash other applications, try Windows NT. For computers that are connected to a network sporadically, such as laptops, try Windows Me.

4

HOUR 5

Network Concepts

By this point, you have had the opportunity to learn some basic computer concepts and how they relate to networking. This hour introduces and explains basic network concepts in some depth. Some of the concepts covered in this hour have been mentioned earlier but are discussed here in greater depth.

To ease the process of assimilating these concepts, this chapter is arranged in the same way as the preceding chapter on computer concepts:

- What networks are made of
- Network-specific hardware
- Network-specific software

What Networks Are Made Of

In Hour 4, "Computer Concepts," you learned about the hardware and software that comprise computers. In this hour, you're going to revisit both hardware and software from a network-specific perspective. The preceding discussion of computers looked at them as standalone devices, not connected to anything else. Now, we're going to see how to take that hardware and software (and some other devices mentioned only in passing, such as hubs and MAUs) and discuss how they fit together to create a coherent whole.

Network-Specific Hardware

Network-specific hardware comes in two varieties. The first variety is computers that have been specifically built for networking but that could function without a network. The second variety is hardware such as network hubs, switches, cables, and routers that have no function outside a network context.

Servers

In the first two hours, you heard the term "server" used to describe a computer that shares its resources with other computers over a network. In the following sections, you learn more about servers—what they are, how they are different from regular computers, and what they're used for.

What Is a Server?

A server is a powerful computer that shares its resources with other computers on a network. In brief terms, that's what a server is and what it does. But a server is a great deal more—and, surprisingly, often a great deal less—than your desktop computer. Server hardware is usually built around two primary needs: moving data quickly and ensuring the safety and integrity of data.

For starters, a server is usually a great deal more powerful than your desktop computer. Even if your desktop computer has a ten-zillion-Hertz Perfectium processor, chances are that it lacks the *I/O,* or *throughput* (generally, a loose measure of the speed at which a particular piece of hardware can move data), to adequately service other computers' needs. No matter how fast your desktop computer is, if it can't move data off disks and onto a network wire quickly enough, it is not much use as a server. It's like a car's doughnut spare tire—a desktop computer can function as a server computer in a pinch, but you don't want to make a regular practice of using it as your mission-critical system.

In basic terms, a server has as powerful a processor—sometimes even more than one—and as much memory as you can afford to put into it. Typically, a server is more powerful than your desktop systems. Although important, processor speed and memory are not the best measure of a server's usefulness, as you are about to discover.

A server usually provides some form of insurance against disaster; most desktop computers don't. To return to the motor-vehicle metaphor, servers have systems to deal with disasters for the same reason that 18-wheeler highway trucks have dual tires. If one of the dual tires blows, the other one can keep supporting the load, and the truck doesn't crash. In server terms, the "backup tire" is called *redundancy* or *fault tolerance* and is a cornerstone of server architecture. Ultimately, fault tolerance simply means that your system is less likely to completely crash as a result of hardware failure. In the subsequent pages, you'll learn about I/O and fault tolerance as they apply to servers.

We'll cover redundancy in more detail later in this hour.

The Need for Speed

Server speed can be measured any number of ways. Most server speed measurements are processor-based and thereby largely meaningless to you. The only speed tests that are worthwhile for servers measure the real-world performance of the server.

> As a rule, the large-format computer weeklies such as *InfoWorld*, *Network World*, and *CommunicationsWeek,* offer real-world testing that applies to the average network. It is well worth your while to search their archives on the Web; their reviews generally offer a worthwhile perspective on hardware.

Because pure speed testing does not offer much value, the most important items to consider when purchasing an Intel-compatible server is processor speed. The type of card that fits into the server has largely ceased to matter, since almost all servers made have only a *PCI bus*. Maximum available disk space or maximum available drive bays are the next consideration—how much disk can the system handle?

No matter how fast a server operates, other computers on a network see only how fast it transmits data. A server that can't pass data to multiple clients efficiently is perceived as slow, even if it actually runs tremendously fast. As a result, server I/O is extremely important. Typically, servers have two potential I/O bottlenecks: limitations on the speed of a network card and limitations on the time it takes to read and write to the server's hard drive.

Network Card Speed

The speed of the network card is determined by two things: the *bus* of the card and the *speed* of the card. For servers, PCI-bus network cards are the best choice right now because the PCI bus allows data to flow between the computer and adapter cards much faster than any alternative.

The speed at which the card transmits data is determined by the network type. If your network topology is 10BASE-T Ethernet, you can't transmit data faster than 10 megabits per second; if your topology is 100BASE-T or ATM, you may be capable of transmitting data at 100 or 155 megabits per second.

If you're having trouble rationalizing these network speeds, consider the following: At 10 megabits per second (standard Ethernet speed), it's possible to copy a 1-megabyte file in significantly less than fifteen seconds. At 100 megabits per second, you can copy a 10-megabyte file in about the same time as the 1-meg file on the 10BASE-T network.

At really high speeds (ATM or Gigabit Ethernet, which move data at 1,000 megabits per second), the same transaction would fly past so fast it wouldn't even register.

Hard Drive Speed

The speed of a server's hard drive is determined by two things. As with network cards, the first is the bus type of the hard drive controller card. All things being equal, the faster the bus of the hard drive controller card is, the faster the computer can read and write to and from the disk. The second limitation on the speed of the hard drive is the interface. Even though IDE drives have become much faster in recent years, they are still not as fast as SCSI drives, so SCSI has become a server standard. When purchasing hard drives, look at the drive's speed in revolutions per minute (RPM) and its access time in milliseconds. Look for 10,000 RPMs or faster and the lowest possible access time to get the fastest drive.

Redundancy

If your data is on one disk, that's good. If your data can be copied across two disks, so that either disk can break and you don't lose data, that's better. If you can chain three or more drives together so that if you lose one drive, the remaining drives can reconstruct the data on the broken drive, that's better still. Remember that redundancy increases reliability. That's why it's used so often in servers, where no one can afford to lose data.

SCSI cards, as you may recall from Hour 4, can have up to seven devices per SCSI chain. What this means is that you can use some special SCSI controllers (Adaptec makes the best-known devices, but there are lots of manufacturers) to set up multiple hard drives on one chain that is very resistant to data loss. This type of setup is called *RAID*, for *Redundant Arrays of Inexpensive Disks*; the special SCSI controllers that handle RAID are called (what else?) *RAID controllers*. RAID operates in a variety of levels ranging from 0 to 5, but most people only need to know about levels 0, 1, and 5, since they're the ones that seem to get used the most.

RAID 0

RAID 0 is best described as several hard drives connected to a computer with no redundancy. The purpose of RAID 0 is simply to increase throughput—if data is spread over several drives, it can be read from and written to the drive more rapidly. But servers need redundancy, so RAID levels 1 through 5 are commonly used for that purpose.

RAID 1

RAID 1 is *disk mirroring* or *duplexing*. In disk mirroring, two SCSI drives of the same size connect to the RAID controller card, but the computer sees them as one drive. For example, in a RAID 1 configuration, if you connect two 4-gigabyte drives to the computer, the computer sees only 4 gigabytes of disk space rather than 8 gigabytes. This happens because the RAID controller arranges the disks so that all data is written identically to both disks. In a RAID 1 configuration, one drive can fail and the other drive continues working—

the users never know the network is down. In some systems, it's possible to connect each drive to a separate SCSI controller so that there is no single point of failure—either disk or either controller in a mirrored set can break and no data or function will be lost.

RAID 1 is useful for a variety of reasons. It provides reasonable disk security and prevents downtime. Nonetheless, it's got several failings: It does nothing to accelerate reading data from disks, it cannot reconstruct missing data, and it is expensive.

RAID 1 is expensive because all hardware is redundant and set up in a fault-tolerant configuration. This means that the server would have to have two drives for each logical unit of disk space. Here's how it works: To provide 4 gigabytes of storage, it would be necessary to purchase two 4-gigabyte disks and mirror them so that each disk had exactly the same information.

Despite its expense, mirroring is often the easiest means of providing redundant disk space. When a disk drive goes bad, replacing the blown disk and mirroring the good disk to the new disk will often suffice to put a computer system back on track.

The performance of RAID 1 is quite good, because each time the computer reads from disk, it reads from two disks at once. The speed of writing data to disk is slightly slower because data is written to two drives, which the computer must keep in sync.

RAID 5

RAID 5 addresses the shortcomings of RAID 1 admirably. RAID 5 typically requires three disks of equal capacity (compared to RAID 1, which requires two disks), but the net improvement is worth the cost. In a RAID 5 configuration, all data is spread across multiple disks in a process called *striping,* which is the process by which a RAID drive controller card writes data across multiple disks. Additionally, information about the file called *parity data* is also saved on all three disks. What this means is that any single drive in a RAID 5 set can fail, and the parity data on the other two drives can be used to reconstruct the data on the failed drive.

RAID 5 offers another advantage: raw speed. Because any given file is divided into smaller pieces and stored on multiple disks, any time a user requests a file from the server, three disks read it simultaneously. This means that the file is read into memory and out to the network more rapidly, which keeps your users happy.

RAID controller capabilities vary widely. Some require a tremendous amount of human configuration, and some (such as HP's AutoRAID units) can largely manage themselves after being given some basic parameters.

RAID 7 and Hot Swapping

Beyond RAID 5, there's a proto-standard called *RAID 7* or *JBOD* (*Just a Bunch Of Disks*—we're not making that up), in which data is striped with parity data to more than three physical disk. (Raid 5 uses three disks; JBOD uses more than three disks.) It's not entirely standard, but it can provide even greater data security in the event of a disk crash.

RAID is good and well, but it still doesn't finish the topic of redundancy. If a drive fails when it's in service, it must be fixed. However, network administrators are sometimes caught in a bind when a drive fails; in many cases, networks simply cannot go down except for extremely rare scheduled maintenance. So how does a network administrator replace a failed drive in a production server?

Fortunately, many RAID controllers also function in a "real-time" mode that allows drives to be pulled out of the system and replaced while the computer is on. This process is called *hot swapping* (see Figure 5.1). Hot swapping is commonly used on RAID systems; when a drive is removed and replaced, many RAID controllers can automatically copy data to the new drive. For users, there's no effect other than a slight slowdown.

FIGURE 5.1

A server with hot-swappable drives and drive bays on the right side of the case.

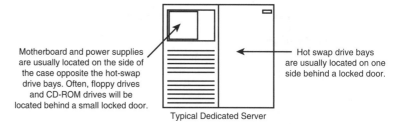

Motherboard and power supplies are usually located on the side of the case opposite the hot-swap drive bays. Often, floppy drives and CD-ROM drives will be located behind a small locked door.

Hot swap drive bays are usually located on one side behind a locked door.

Typical Dedicated Server

Hot swapping is not something you can do with your average desktop system. First, most desktop systems don't have RAID controllers. Second, most desktop systems don't have *hot-swappable drive bays*, special drive bays in the case from which a drive can be installed and removed in real time. Typically, server manufacturers such as Digital, Hewlett-Packard, and Compaq offer hot-swap bays in their workgroup (mid-line) and enterprise (high-end) servers. Most manufacturers require that you mount a hard drive in a special cradle that protects the drive and connects it to the hot-swap drive bays.

Hard drives are not the only devices that can be fault tolerant. Typically, servers offer options for redundant hard drives, power supplies, and sometimes even motherboards. The rule to remember is that as you increase the redundancy and fault tolerance of your system, you increase the price of the system.

Concentrators: Hubs, Switches, and MAUs

In Hour 1, "An Overview of Networking," you first became acquainted with hubs, switches, and MAUs. In the following pages, you will learn how they work, starting with the simplest networks and going to the most complex.

Typically, when you purchase a server for business application, it's a good idea to go with an established brand such as IBM, Hewlett-Packard, AST, Compaq, or any of the other first-tier manufacturers. This reasoning is not based on blind brand loyalty; instead, it stems from the major manufacturers' capability and commitment to design, build, and troubleshoot their own systems. Servers are too important to slap together from parts; if a home-built server fails, it's up to the person who built it to get it fixed—and he or she may not have the knowledge or resources to do so. By contrast, first-tier manufacturers' technical support and service personnel often have exceptional knowledge of their products as well as access to the system designers. In the main, first-tier manufacturers discover bugs sooner and issue patches faster than do smaller or no-name manufacturers, which means that your server is more reliable.

Ethernet 10BASE-2

As you may recall, one network topology didn't use hubs, switches, or MAUs: *Ethernet 10BASE-2*, also called *thinnet*, uses coaxial cable that runs from computer to computer. In spite of the fact that Ethernet 10BASE-2 doesn't use hubs, an explanation of how Ethernet 10BASE-2 works is helpful in understanding the role of hubs in topologies such as 10BASE-T, Token Ring, and FDDI.

Ethernet 10BASE-2 runs on coaxial cable from computer to computer (see Figure 5.2). All data travels along this single wire whether its destination is the next computer on the wire or 20 computers down the wire. This wire is called a *segment*. Each segment functions for all practical purposes as though it were a single piece of wire. Here's a list of the conditions that must be met for 10BASE-2 to work:

- All the data must travel on this wire between all destinations.
- All computers must be attached to this wire so that they can "listen" to the network wire to see whether any other computers are transmitting data.
- Only one computer on a segment can transmit data at any given time. Computers can transmit data only when no other station is transmitting data.

In Figure 5.2, the wire that connects all the computers is called a segment. A segment is not one piece of wire; it's actually composed of a series of shorter wires that each begin and end at a computer. At each end of the segment is a device called a *terminator* that essentially marks the end of the network. (There's a bunch of electronic theory behind termination that involves using resistors to stop electrical bounce, and so on, but that's outside the scope of this book.)

If any one of the pieces of wire that runs from computer to computer in an Ethernet 10BASE-2 segment breaks or (in some cases) if a computer crashes, the network crashes. Why?

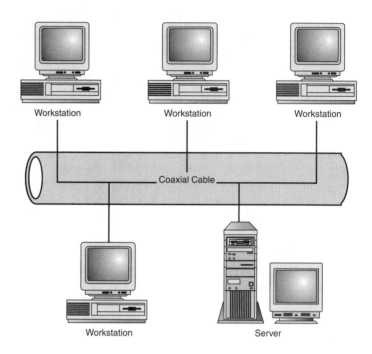

FIGURE 5.2

An Ethernet 10BASE-2 network.

Well, because the termination on the segment will be missing. Because the termination will be gone, computers will lose the capability to determine whether any other computers are transmitting data on the wire. Because the computers can't communicate, they will drop any connections they have with other systems on the network.

Clearly, Ethernet 10BASE-2 is a fragile technology if it can crash when one wire breaks. Even though Ethernet 10BASE-2 is fragile, the three conditions listed earlier in this section must be met for effective networking. So the challenge is to figure out how to create a *logical segment*—that is, a network segment that mimics the effect of a single wire without being so fragile and temperamental that a single disconnection brings down the whole net.

10BASE-2 has been superseded by versions of Ethernet that use unshielded twisted-pair (UTP) wiring such as 10BASE-T and 100BASE-T. It's unusual to find 10BASE-2 networks anywhere any longer. At this point, you may be asking why we're discussing it at all, since it's an outdated technology. Here's why: The basic functions of Ethernet (a bus topology in which all computers listen on one wire properly terminated to kill off electrical bounce, CSMA/CD) is more easily pictured using a 10BASE-2 network than a 10BASE-T network. Fundamentally, both networks operate the same way, but 10BASE-2's physical layout makes it easier to associate with the characteristics of Ethernet than later networks. This is why in network diagrams, Ethernet is shown as a bus, whether or not it uses 10BASE-2, to remind us of the fundamentals of Ethernet.

In Search of a Logical Segment: Concentrators and Switches

Enter the concentrator or the switch, which, depending on the network topology, can be called a hub, a switch, or a MAU. All these devices share a single function—to create logical network segments. In networks that use concentrators, the individual pieces of wire that connect computers together no longer run from machine to machine. Instead, they run from the concentrator to the workstation in a star configuration. This point-to-point wiring is also called "home running" wire, since each wire goes from a central point (home base) to the field (offices, desks, cubes, and so on) (see Figure 5.3).

FIGURE 5.3

A star configuration with a hub (a.k.a. concentrator) at the center.

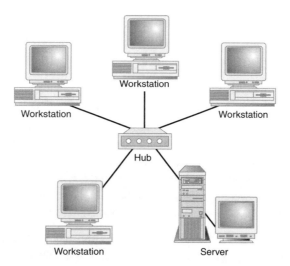

The presence of a concentrator ensures that no single network wire can break and bring down the network. A concentrator essentially is a complete segment in a box. If a wire from Data Terminal Equipment, or DTE (anything that can connect to the network—computers, printers, routers, and so on), is connected to a port on the concentrator, the concentrator can communicate with that port. If nothing is connected to a port, the concentrator bypasses that port and does not (unlike Ethernet 10BASE-2) see the lack of a connected port as a break in the network wire.

Given how complicated this arrangement is, another analogy is in order. Imagine a trucker whose truck is loaded in such a way that all the packages he carries must be unloaded in a particular order. He has to stop at John's house first, then Mary's, then Angela's, then Beth's, and then Mark's. If he gets to Mary's house and she's not there, he can't unload her package—and he's stuck. He can't go to the next station (Angela's) because he must deliver Mary's package first. He can't bypass this "break" in the system. The break in the system is equivalent to a break in the bus on a 10BASE-2 network

Another (more sensible!) trucker has packed his truck so that he can get to any package at any time without difficulty. If he gets to Mary's house and she's not there, he just doesn't deliver the package and proceeds to the next delivery. He can bypass "breaks" in the system, which is what a concentrator helps a network do.

Concentrators increase the reliability of a network by ensuring that the segment is not interrupted or broken. In general, concentrators are "intelligent" enough to know when a device is connected and when it is not. In this way, concentrators have increased the reliability of networking adequately to make networking a mass-market technology.

The reliability of concentrators, however, is only the beginning of the story. The third condition we set forth—that only one computer on a segment can transmit data at any given time and computers can transmit data only when no other station is transmitting data—opens up several new issues.

Device Contention

If only one computer on any given segment can transmit data packets at any given time, the possibility that any single computer can grab hold of the network segment long enough to transmit data packets decreases as the number of computers on that network segment increases. When more than one computer or other network device has to transmit data packets at the same time, there are conflicts, and the network slows down. This process is called *device contention*, and it means that a single shared resource—in this case, the network segment—cannot service all the requests it receives in an efficient manner.

Most small-to-medium sized networks operate with a single logical segment, or only one wire, so that only one computer can transmit data at any time. At the same time, computers have become much faster and have developed ever-more-rapacious appetites for *network bandwidth*, or the time during which they can transmit data packets. As a result, many networks have excessive amounts of device contention and operate slower than users would like.

The solution to device contention demands that two additional conditions be met:

- Any equipment that can decrease device contention must be directly *backward compatible* with existing equipment.
- Any standard that can be applied to reduce device contention must work with current standards.

Network equipment manufacturers, faced with a steadily increasing demand for network bandwidth and the need to retain compatibility with the existing installed base of network adapters and concentrators, were in a conundrum. They had to reduce the number of stations contending for bandwidth on a given segment and at the same time increase connection speed.

To accomplish these goals, network manufacturers invented *switching technologies*. A network switch (which is available for all topologies, from Ethernet to Token Ring to FDDI to ATM) essentially creates a separate segment for each port on a switch (see Figure 5.4). Because only one computer per segment can transmit data at any given time, this clearly frees up computers to establish connections to other computers connected to the switch and transmit data with much less contention for bandwidth.

Another use for switches is to segment networks by connecting switch ports to older shared-media (single-segment) concentrators to create several smaller network segments, thereby increasing the per-computer bandwidth and increasing the response time of the network.

FIGURE 5.4

A network segmented through the use of a switch.

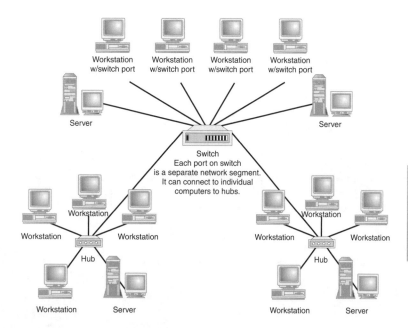

Premise Wiring: Cabling

No matter how well a network is designed, no matter the quality of its individual components, if the wire that joins the computers together isn't installed properly, the network will not work well. Network cabling is the invisible yeoman of the network. When it works well, it goes unnoticed; when it doesn't work, it can be very difficult to diagnose without very sophisticated tools.

In general, there are three types of network wiring: coaxial, twisted-pair, and fiber. Each type of cabling has different requirements if it is to meet network standards and work properly. The next sections list those requirements and explain what they mean.

Coaxial

Coaxial, used for Ethernet 10BASE-2 networking, has simplicity on its side. For internetworking two or three computers in a single space, Ethernet 10BASE-2 is hard to beat. Because no concentrator is needed, it is less expensive than Ethernet 10BASE-T, Token Ring, FDDI, or ATM. However, for reasons cited earlier in this hour, Ethernet 10BASE-2 is not advisable for networks in which reliability is a strong requirement.

With Ethernet 10BASE-2, up to 255 devices can be attached to a single segment, although once again, that maximum is not advisable. The maximum total length of a segment is 185 meters.

The wire used for coaxial networking is usually industry-standard RG-58 cable, which closely resembles the wire used to bring cable television into your home. RG-58 cable has a solid copper center conductor and a braided outer conductor (see Figure 5.5). RG-58 is 50 ohm cable and requires termination at both ends of each segment using a 50 ohm terminating resistor (usually just called a *terminator*). Each computer attaches to the segment with a T-connector, which fits into the back of the network card in the computer (see Figure 5.6).

FIGURE 5.5

A simplified represen-
tation of a section of
coaxial cable.

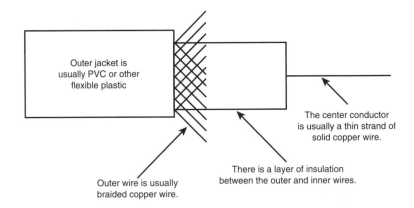

Diagram of Coaxial Cable.

Unshielded Twisted-Pair

The next step up from coaxial cable is *Unshielded Twisted-Pair*, or *UTP*. UTP is far and away the most common wire used for networking.

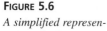

FIGURE 5.6

*A simplified represen-
tation of a T-connector
and a terminator.*

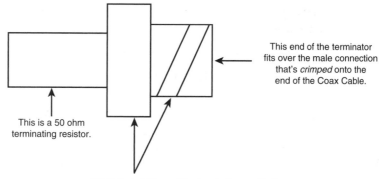

This end of the terminator
fits over the male connection
that's *crimped* onto the
end of the Coax Cable.

This is a 50 ohm
terminating resistor.

These two sections of the terminator provide the
connection to the end of the 10Base-2 Coax Cable.
It twists on with a very coarse thread;
the connector is called a *BNC connector*.

The UTP wires used for networking are eight copper-conductor, four-pair wires very
similar to the wire the phone company uses when it wires a home. The main difference
between phone wire and UTP is that phone wiring generally has only two pairs of wire
(four wires) and UTP has four pairs (eight wires). The wire must be terminated at each
end of a point-to-point wire run according to very strict standards set forth in EIA 568B.
EIA 568B specifies the order of the wires in the female jack (or the male patch cord)
when viewed from above. Here is the order in which wires must be terminated (when
viewed from the top) according to the 568B scheme:

Pin	Wire Color
1	White and Orange
2	Orange
3	White and Green
4	Blue
5	White and Blue
6	Green
7	White and Brown
8	Brown

If the cables are not terminated in this order, they won't transmit data properly. Odd pin
numbers are always white combined with another color.

Additionally, twisted-pair wiring comes in several levels, ranging from Level 1 (or
Category 1), often used for telephone applications, to Level 5 (or Category 5), which is
certified for data transmission up to 155 megabits per second. Twisted-pair cables come

5

in five categories; the following list provides you with an understanding of the various cable applications:

- Category 1 is not rated for performance.
- Category 2 is used for telephone wiring and is rated to a maximum data rate of 1 megabit per second.
- Category 3 is the lowest level that can be used for networking. It is used for Ethernet 10BASE-T and has a maximum data rate of 16 megabits per second. Although Category 3 is rated for 10BASE-T, Category 5 is now much more common because it supports both 10BASE-T and faster speeds such as 100BASE-T.
- Category 4 is used for Token Ring and Ethernet 10BASE-T. Its maximum data rate is 20 megabits per second.
- Category 5 is used for Ethernet 100BASE-T and has a maximum data rate of 155 megabits per second. This is currently the most common cable; in fact, many companies are wiring everything in their offices (both phone and data) with Category 5 cable because it can be used for everything from basic two-wire phone services to ATM.

To maintain the maximum data rate, the wires must be handled and terminated, or connected, according to EIA 568B standards. If the wires are not correctly handled and terminated, much of their potential data rate can be jeopardized.

> If you're building a copper-wire-based network, it does not make sense to install cable less than Category 5 because installing Category 5 wire can extend the life of your network. Category 5 standards specify that the wires in twisted-pair cabling maintain their twist, or the braiding that leads to the name twisted pair, within $1/2$ inch of the final termination point. Category 5 also has strict standards for the radius of bends in Category 5 wire and so forth.
>
> Another reason to install the best cable you can is that the cost of the cable itself is negligible—it's about 10 cents a foot. The installation is what's expensive, so don't skimp on the cable; drive a good bargain on the installation. And always always always always install two cables instead of one. The cost of doing so is not much higher than installing one cable, and it provides tremendous expandability.

The maximum distance for Ethernet 10BASE-T using twisted-pair wires is 200 meters between the concentrator and the computer. For Ethernet 100BASE-T, the maximum distance is 20 meters between stations—quite a reduction in length!

Unshielded twisted-pair is currently the cable standard for most networks. It is relatively inexpensive, easy to install, very reliable, and easy to maintain and expand. If you elect to use twisted-pair cable for your network, find a professional cable installer if you must run wire through the walls and ceilings of your location. Fire regulations typically require that your installer follow building codes when installing cable. Cable run through open ceilings must be plenum rated, or capable of withstanding certain environmental and fire conditions without giving off toxic gases in a fire. Cable run through walls is often different than cable run through ceilings, and only your installer will know the local fire codes well enough to install the correct cable types in the correct locations.

Optical Fiber

The last type of network cabling is *optical fiber*. Optical fiber has taken on a mystique within the networking community over the last several years. Initially, the expense of fiber was such that it was used only for creating high-speed links between concentrators and other esoteric applications. However, the advent of Ethernet 100BASE-FX, which runs over fiber, as well as FDDI and ATM topologies, has brought fiber closer to the mainstream. The "fiber-to-the-desktop" mantra chanted by technology pundits at the beginning of this decade is finally beginning to see to fruition.

Rather than using electrical impulses transmitted over copper wire, optical fiber transmits network data using pulses of light. In spite of its increased acceptance, optical fiber remains extremely expensive to install and maintain. The average network administrator lacks the skills to run fiber and terminate it properly at each end.

Termination of optical fiber is both difficult and chancy. Unlike copper wire, the finished end of a piece of optical fiber must be polished and capped with a special tip that fits into special receptacles on network cards and concentrators. If the polishing and grinding of the end of the cable is off in any way, the cable will not work.

Despite the care that must be lavished on optical fiber infrastructures, fiber has certain advantages because of its unique way of passing data. First, fiber is secure. Copper wire gives off electrical impulses that can be recorded through inductive sensors; optical fiber does not. Optical fiber can carry data at very high bit rates—in some cases, over a gigabit per second.

Ultimately, the cabling type you select depends on your needs. If you're just starting to network and you want to become familiar with basic software and hardware, try coaxial networking with two or three machines. If you're installing a network that must be reliable yet cost-effective, try twisted pair. And if you've got to provide your users with huge amounts of high-speed real-time data, install fiber.

Software: Network Operating Systems

Just as network clients must have operating systems loaded for the client machines to function, a network server must have an operating system (refer to Hour 4 for explanations of the most popular client OSes). The chief differences between desktop operating systems and Network Operating Systems (or NOSes) are, not surprisingly, scale and resources.

Typically, network operating systems are optimized differently than desktop operating systems. A desktop operating system is designed to provide the user at his or her desktop workstation with the best possible performance for the application currently being used. By contrast, a network operating system's charge is to balance the needs of all users accessing the server rather than giving priority to any one of them.

In the following sections, you will learn about three network operating systems and one peer configuration. Because this book is devoted to beginning networkers, the network operating systems listed here are all primarily used on Intel-compatible systems.

Novell NetWare

Novell NetWare (now called IntranetWare) is the oldest PC-based product in the Network Operating System category. In the early 1980s, it was Novell, founded by Raymond Noorda, who led the charge into personal-computer networking.

NetWare is an intense and complex product. By contrast with other, newer network operating systems such as Microsoft Windows 2000, it is difficult and contentious. Its system console is a command line similar to DOS or Unix.

In the file, print, and directory services arena, NetWare is a formidable contender. For file and print services, it remains the standard at a great many companies. With the advent of *NetWare Directory Services*, or *NDS*, in NetWare version 4, it has cornered the *directory services* market.

As networks have grown more complex and require management of greater numbers of users, directory services have become a saving grace for network administrators trying to manage access across thousand-plus-user, multisite networks.

In Figure 5.7, the image is not the NetWare command prompt; instead, it shows Monitor, the application most commonly in the foreground on NetWare server screens. Monitor allows the administrator to access a variety of information about the current state of the server ranging from available memory to disk space.

FIGURE 5.7

A Novell NetWare console Monitor screen.

Unlike many newer PC-based network operating systems, NetWare was not designed with the Internet in mind. A great many of the design choices Novell made appear to have been an attempt to simplify networking enough to make it palatable for PC users.

In the first place, Novell did not build native support for TCP/IP, the language, that computers use to communicate across the Internet. Novell had good reason for this: When NetWare was developed, TCP/IP was a relatively new and immature protocol standard; it required a great deal of manual configuration, and maintaining it was difficult.

Given the complexity of TCP/IP and the technical skills of its target market group, Novell decided to develop a simpler protocol. Novell's proprietary network protocol was called *Internetworking Packet Exchange/Sequenced Packet Exchange* (*IPX/SPX*); in many ways, it was ideal for PC networking. IPX was and is largely self-configuring, easy to install, and simple to maintain.

> Recall the discussion of protocols at the end of Hour 3, "Getting Data from Here to There: How Computers Share Data." Protocols are the languages that computers use to speak to one another.

Unfortunately, as the Internet revolution picked up steam (and TCP/IP with it), Novell's position deteriorated because NetWare is fundamentally founded on IPX networking. Newer versions of NetWare can speak IP and this has helped bring back NetWare's popularity.

If you want a more detailed look at NetWare, read Hour 16, "Novell NetWare."

Microsoft Windows 2000 Advanced Server

Beginning in the late 1980s, Microsoft decided that it needed a high-end network operating system to compete with NetWare and Unix. After a ferocious three-to-four-year struggle (aptly described in Pascal Zachary's book *Showstopper*), Microsoft had what it had set out to create: Windows NT. Initially, Windows NT version 3.1 (the first version, but renumbered to match the existing version of 16-bit Windows) was all one product—there was initially little if any differentiation between versions used for servers and versions used for workstations.

By the time Microsoft released Windows NT 3.5 in 1995, Microsoft had created two different versions of the operating system: Windows NT Workstation (profiled in Hour 4) and Windows NT Server. To date, these have evolved into Windows 2000 Professional for the workstation market and Windows 2000 Advanced Server for the server market. For all intents and purposes, both OSes are built on the same basic platform, but Windows 2000 Server has a rich set of utilities and tools the Workstation product lacks.

5

The capability to connect to all sorts of networks was built in to Windows 2000 from the start. Additionally, it can handle the server portion of network application work, which makes it an ideal application server platform from the start. It uses the familiar Windows interface that simplifies administration—Windows 2000 is admirably well-suited to small organizations because of its point-and-click administration (see Figure 5.8).

FIGURE 5.8

A Microsoft Windows 2000 Server 4.0 screen.

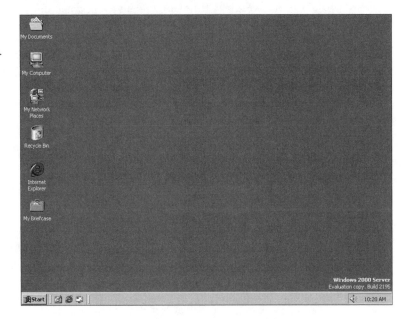

For the vast majority of beginning networkers, Windows 2000 Server is probably the easiest enterprise-class network OS to install and maintain. Do not construe that statement to mean that Windows 2000 is simple; it is not. But in comparison to other network operating systems, Windows 2000 has a certain amount of familiarity because it uses the ubiquitous Windows interface.

Unix

As mentioned in the Unix client workstation section in Hour 4, Unix is the result of Bell Labs' innovations some 30 years ago. It is a fully preemptive network operating system with a rich interface unmatched by any other operating system. Unfortunately, with Unix's richness comes a tremendous degree of complexity. Unix can accomplish almost any task a computer can do, but the complexity of the interface has unfortunately led to Unix being maligned as user-hostile. In spite of a much-undeserved reputation for difficulty, Unix makes a fast file and print server and offers perhaps the best application services of any network OS presented here.

As with Windows 2000 Server, Unix can operate as either a client or a server on a network. For the most part, there's little or no difference between a client Unix system and a server Unix system except for the power of the hardware—the server should be more powerful than the workstation—and the tightness of the security. Unix comes with such a rich feature set that it seldom needs third-party software to administer its users. It's possible to create shell scripts, Perl scripts, and compiled C programs to take care of mundane tasks on most Unix systems.

Because of its age, Unix is a very stable platform. However, Unix is not produced by any single vendor; instead, a host of vendors purvey Unix, and each version is slightly different. As a result, there is a lack of shrink-wrapped applications, or applications ready to install right out of the shrink-wrapped box. In recent years, Unix vendors have tried repeatedly to create a standard for Unix to ensure binary compatibility, which simply means that an application, once compiled, can run on a variety of different operating systems. Unfortunately, this has met with only limited success; hopefully, the threat of Microsoft's Windows 2000 will make the Unix vendors rally around a standard.

Unix is best suited to networks in which an experienced system administrator is in charge. Its complexity makes it unsuitable for the casual user or part-time system administrator, but in the hands of a truly knowledgeable system administrator, Unix can accomplish almost any task reliably and fast.

Client/Server Versus Peer Network Configurations: A Quick Guide

So far in this book, we have mentioned the terms *client/server* and *peer networking* several times. In the following brief sections, you learn what client/server and peer really are, and what ramifications they have on you.

Client/server and *peer* are terms that describe the logical relationship between computers on a network. Remember that a logical relationship is not the same thing as a physical relationship—computers can operate in either client/server or peer on any network topology, from 10BASE-2 to FDDI.

Client/Server Networks

In a client/server network, the computers are divided into servers and clients. The *server* is usually a dedicated, powerful machine bearing all the hallmarks of servers as described earlier in this hour; the *clients* are usually less powerful than the server and connect only to the server through the network. Figure 5.9 shows an example of a client/server network.

5

FIGURE 5.9

A client/server network.

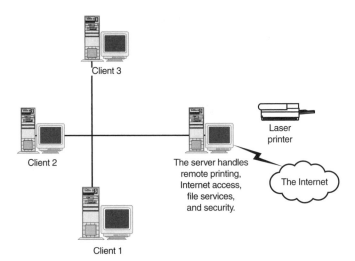

The benefits of a client/server configuration (or *architecture*, as it is sometimes called) are mostly of interest to people who rely heavily on the network's reliability. They include the following benefits:

- Centralized management of network resources
- The capability to set stringent and rigorous controls on security, file access, and other potentially sensitive material
- A significant reduction in management at the client
- The capability to secure and back up data from the server
- The capability to "scale"—that is, to increase in size gracefully

In the client/server relationship, clients can see only the server; they cannot see each other. This arrangement results in greater security and increased "replaceability"—if a client workstation fails, it is possible in a client/server architecture to simply replace the client workstation with a comparable machine. If the applications are run from the server's hard drive, once the new computer is connected to the network, the user will have access to most of what he or she had before the workstation failed.

The downsides of client/server are less apparent:

- Client/server networks cost more to implement than peer configurations because of the cost of the server—a dedicated machine that no one uses as a workstation.
- The server becomes a single point of failure. If it breaks, the network is down. Many servers have fault-tolerant features (as do RAID servers, described earlier in this hour)—fault tolerance is truly necessary for client/server networks.

Client/server is almost always the architecture on which large enterprise networks are built. Reliability and scalability are almost always the stated reasons behind this choice, but make no mistake about it—data security and centralized management, which are big dollar-savers, are also a large factor in the choice of the client/server network.

Peer Networks

At the other end of the spectrum is the peer network. In a peer configuration, all user workstations also handle some server functions. For example, one machine with a large hard drive may be used to store some of the users' files. Another system, connected to a printer, may share that printer with other workstations. The chief fact about peer networking, though, is this: In a peer network, there is no server, and all computers can be used as user workstations (see Figure 5.10).

FIGURE **5.10**

A peer network.

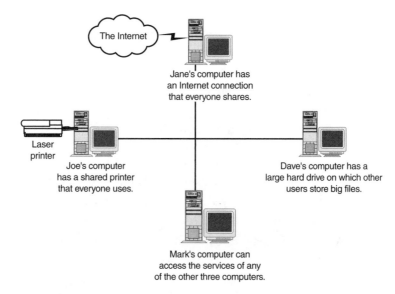

A peer network has some distinct advantages:

- Ease of installation and configuration
- Inexpensive compared to client/server networks

However, peer networking has several downsides that (in the author's opinion) outweigh its benefits:

- It has a total lack of centralized control, which means that a peer network is basically unmanageable.
- It is tremendously insecure—security on a peer network is almost nonexistent.
- It is unreliable. Peer networking relies on the vicissitudes of user workstations, which means that the network can be seriously disturbed if (for example) the workstation to which the printer is connected is rebooted or locks up.

Peer networking is suitable only for the very smallest networks—those people build to teach themselves networking or those in an office with no more than three or four computers.

This winds up the discussion on what makes up a network. In the next hour, we'll revisit the ways in which networks pass data between computers and look at how networks pass data to other networks.

Summary

In this hour, you had the opportunity to learn about the hardware used to connect computers together, as well as some basic concepts about network layout. In the preceding hours, you learned about basic computer concepts and how networks pass data; in subsequent hours, you'll learn how to extend your network beyond the confines of the local office.

Q&A

Q What are some compelling reasons why you might want to use fault-tolerant hardware?

A Fault-tolerant hardware is worth the cost whenever you need a computer to be up and running 24/7/365 because the hardware can partially fail without ceasing to work altogether. For this reason, banks, insurance companies, hospitals, and other round-the-clock businesses use highly fault-tolerant systems.

Q What are some of the reasons that could drive the decision to use a switch rather than a shared-media hub?

A There are many reasons, but these are some of the most common situations in which switches are better choices than hubs:

- Networks that have a lot of traffic and tend to slow down because of bandwidth contention
- A local network that has grown to too many users to comfortably share one collision domain or Token Ring
- Networks that must be segmented for security or performance reasons

Q What are the circumstances in which a peer network might be more useful or appropriate than a client/server network?

A Here are several situations in which a peer network may be more appropriate than a client/server network:

- When the network consists of only two or three computers
- When resources are extremely scarce and a separate computer can't be allocated as the server
- For small home networks

Hour **6**

Extending Your LAN: Wide Area Networks

How often do you send overnight-delivery packages? If the answer is "often," you understand the need to be able to move information over long distances rapidly. It's not a new problem.

Sending information over long distances has traditionally been a struggle for humankind. Before the advent of electricity, people moved information quickly by using smoke signals or fast and lean modes of transportation such as the Pony Express or the railroad. With the coming of electricity, telegraphs suddenly could send messages much faster—a message sent from New York could conceivably be in San Francisco almost instantly.

Despite its speed, the telegraph still had drawbacks. The information it transmitted was encoded, and therefore required a specially trained person to decipher the data; in addition, it could carry only limited amounts of data.

Early networks suffered the same problem as earlier technologies: They were slow, too. Over time, however, networking companies have invented ways to hook together networks that allow users spread out across the world to have access to the same data in real time. That's what this chapter will discuss.

In this hour, you'll have the opportunity to learn about the following aspects of networking:

- What a Wide Area Network (WAN) is
- How WANs are put together
- What the digital phone service is and why WANs need to use it
- How you can use the Internet to help you assemble your WAN

What Is a WAN?

As you learned in Hour 1, "An Overview of Networking," sometimes networks are distributed over too great a geographical area to make networking feasible using regular network cards, concentrators, and wiring. When multiple Local Area Networks (explained in Hour 3, "Getting Data from Here to There: How Computers Share Data") in different locations need to be connected, the result is a WAN.

As you remember from Chapter 1, a Wide Area Network (WAN) is so named because it is a network that links together geographically dispersed computer networks. A WAN is basically two or more LANs tied together using high-speed phone lines (such as *T1s* or *56K frame relay*). Beyond that, it is difficult to make generalizations about WANs, other than saying they link many sites into common resources. What matters is that there are LANs at either end of the WAN (or, if it's a large WAN, that it ties together two or more LANs).

Because WANs serve many purposes, it is sometimes difficult to precisely define the term. Should the systems connected to a WAN all be interactive desktop computers? If a network is linked only for internal email and other communications tasks, is it a WAN or just an expensive private Internet (also called an *intranet*)? Is an *extranet* (a system linking your system with your suppliers' and customers' systems) a WAN?

Here are several examples that explain the astonishing versatility (and bewildering elusiveness) of WANs:

- If you've recently purchased anything at a retail outlet with a credit card, chances are good that your card's credit was examined over a very slow WAN connection to the cashier's computer. The cashier's computer is certainly not a computer in the sense that we usually think of a computer—it has only a limited set of functions and an extremely limited purpose—but it does data lookups in corporate databases across leased phone lines. Is this a WAN? It certainly is, according to the working definition given above.

- Your international company has installed groupware at all its remote locations around the world. To ensure that email and groupware messages and data replication work reliably, the company builds a private network using leased lines instead of using the Internet as a backbone. The users at one site do not directly access the resources of users at another site. Is this a WAN? The answer, again, is yes.

- Your international company has installed groupware at all its remote locations around the world. To ensure that email and groupware messages and data replication work reliably, the company builds a *Virtual Private Network* (a method for connecting networks that uses the Internet to carry data; referred to as a *VPN*) using the Internet as a data conduit. The users at one site can access the resources of users at another site. Is this a WAN? Yep.

- A small company with a regional presence (like the Northeast or Northern California) has to provide its traveling sales representatives with access to the central network resources. The company does so by using a private dial-up link into its network; the company also uses the Internet (for the more far-afield reps) as a way to carry traffic in and out of its LAN from distant locations. Is this a WAN? Yes.

All of these kinds of networks have been considered WANs; the concept has expanded to include all of them. In the final analysis, a WAN is just a way to extend your network resources beyond the local area. In the age of the Internet, there are a host of ways to do so, ranging from expensive digital phone lines to VPNs, from dial-up network access to other ways that haven't been invented yet.

However, the basic WAN configuration (in which computer users on multiple LANs share resources) is the focus of this hour (see Figure 6.1). WANs built for special purposes are not applicable strictly to this discussion; simply being aware that they exist as viable alternatives is quite enough.

WANs, more than LANs, require a great deal of planning on the front end if they are to function effectively. They require that a company's Information Systems staff develop a variety of competencies ranging from the relative simplicity of data networking to the arcane voodoo of the public telephone network. But more than anything else, WANs need a purpose. WANs built without a specific, articulated, clear, and broadly accepted purpose are nothing more than money pits. Before you build a WAN, ask yourself the following questions to ensure that you need one:

- Do users in multiple locations need to have real-time access to a common database, such as a transactional system?

- Do your remote locations already have LANs, or are they mostly home offices or one-person offices?

6

- What are the services you want to share across a WAN? Database? File services? Email? Something else?
- Are your remote sites capable of administering their end of a WAN, or are you going to have to hire traveling system administrators?
- Are you willing to pay the costs of high-speed digital phone lines?

FIGURE 6.1

A basic WAN configuration.

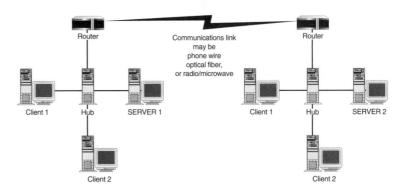

If you have users who need real-time access to a common database, a WAN can offer real value. But if you're dealing with small offices or home offices, it is likely that you will require significant system administration to ensure that your end users (who are probably not computer gurus) can actually get their work done. System administration costs are often relatively hidden, but they often make up the greater part of the *total cost of ownership* (*TCO*) of a WAN (or even of a large and complex LAN). Administration costs can and will increase the overall operating costs of the WAN if you don't plan for them. Make certain that the return is greater than the cost. It is very easy to spend several tens of thousands of dollars a month on a WAN, and if you don't recoup it through increased services or productivity, it will become a drain instead of a help.

WAN Hardware

Several pieces of hardware can be used to link LANs. Of these, the most common devices are bridges, gateways, and routers.

Bridges

A *bridge* is a network device that essentially does what its name describes: bridges two LANs together. The difference between a bridge and a router is based on the way they link networks. In a telecommunications network, a bridge is a hardware device or software that copies Layer 2 packets (see the following note) from one network to another network. For example, two LANs can be connected with a bridge, a digital phone line, and another bridge at the other end. A bridge connects networks at the hardware level. If you connect two networks by bridging them, they'll essentially be one segment with a very slow link. Bridging is not the best way to handle WAN connections unless it's absolutely necessary because bridging passes broadcast traffic—messages sent to every machine on a particular network—which can waste quite a bit of WAN-link bandwidth.

> If you want to brush up on your networking theory and the seven layers of the OSI model, Hour 3 has a description of the OSI model and a discussion of protocols. A good understanding of the OSI model is very useful when learning the functions of a network.

In general, a bridge is a *router* that's been configured to bridge networks at OSI layer 2 rather than OSI layer 3, which is where routers work. When a bridge links networks, for all practical purposes, users see a larger version of their current network—they can access remote resources using the same methods they use in their local LAN. Bridges, however, are slow and resource intensive, which is why most interLAN networking today is routed, not bridged. The "Routers" section a bit later in the hour will help you understand the differences between routers and bridges.

Bridges are often used for networks that use protocols that cannot be routed (for example, NetBIOS or NetBEUI). However, these protocols can be carried over a bridge because the bridge works at the Data-Link layer (which is still concerned with hardware) rather than the Network layer (where data packet routing depends on software).

Gateways: Protocol Translators

The term *gateway* can refer to a variety of different devices. At its most basic, a gateway is a device that acts as a two-way path between networks. For example, in an Internet-connected network, a proxy server can be a gateway between the internal network and the external Internet (see Figure 6.2).

FIGURE 6.2
These proxy servers are acting as gateways.

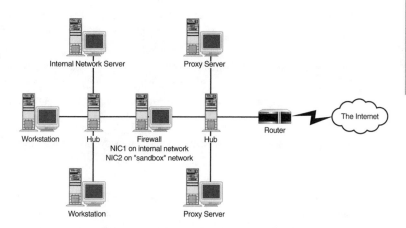

6

Another common use of the term *gateway* is any device that passes IP packets from one network to another network around the Internet. Routers and bridges loosely belong to the global group called gateways, but the gateways discussed in this section have specific purposes other than routing packets between networks or bridging networks.

Gateways link networks together. As noted earlier, gateways are different from bridges in that they can create junctions between dissimilar networks; this can come in very useful for networks that do not run TCP/IP. Gateways that can translate one protocol to another are called *protocol translators,* devices that can translate between two network protocols. Typically, protocol translators translate NetWare IPX to TCP/IP so that users on an IPX network can access the Internet or IP resources.

Protocol translators are not commonly used to link LANs into WANs; these days, protocol translators are often used to translate between NetWare's IPX protocol and the TCP/IP protocol so that an IPX-based network can connect to the Internet. If you have chosen to build (or have inherited) a NetWare LAN, protocol translation may be the best way to provide Internet access to your users. However, NetWare's main protocol, IPX, is routable, so a router is probably a better choice if you want to join two LANs into a WAN.

Routers

A *router* is a device that handles the traffic flow for data packets that are not addressed inside the local network. In other words, a router is the long-distance post office sorting machine that passes data between multiple networks. It works at the OSI Network layer (Layer 3), which means that it must be able to understand the data packets so that it can route them to their destinations. Routers are essentially computers optimized for handling packets that have to be transferred between separate networks. Not surprisingly, routers attempt to send packets from their source to their destination in the fastest way possible, which (as you'll see) is not always the absolute shortest path.

On a network, packets with destinations on the local network go directly from the sending machine to the destination machine without any intermediaries. However, if the destination address of a packet is outside the local network, the sending machine sends it to the router (which the sending machine knows as the default gateway) and has no further interaction with that packet. When the router receives a packet destined for a point outside the local network, it looks to see if it has a route to get the packet to that destination network; if it does (or if it has a default gateway of its own), it will send the packet to the next stop.

Routing between LANs, as you recall from Hour 2, "The Benefits of Networking," is like a postal system or a courier network. A package traveling from New York to San Francisco might travel through a hub in Memphis or Chicago and be resorted in Reno before heading to its final destination. If the package had to be hand-delivered quickly, you could do that, but the cost would increase significantly. And hopefully, the package won't get routed the long way around because that tends to be inefficient and difficult to trace.

In the same fashion, routers send packets according to the available routes between networks and try to determine the shortest possible route at any given time. How does a router do this? Well, inside a router (which is actually a very powerful computer—you'll see why in a moment), there's a set of data called *routing tables*. Routing tables are dynamic—they are updated by routing protocols called *Routing Information Protocol* (*RIP*) or *Open Shortest Path First* (*OSPF*) that constantly pass messages between routers. Routing tables contain all the possible routes the router is aware of; the router consults them to determine whether or not it has a route to a particular destination address. A router is sort of a combination travel agent and personal assistant—it is always looking for the best possible route at the least possible cost. The process of sending a packet closer to its destination is called *routing*.

Explanation of Routing

When a router takes a packet and sends it closer to its final destination, we say it has *forwarded* a packet. In the simplest terms, that's what a router does: It forwards packets toward their destinations. And it tries to do so at the least possible *cost*—which is a tricky concept that has to be explained next.

Cost, for a router, is not measured in dollars and cents. Instead, it is measured in hops. Every time a packet is routed between one router and another, a number in the data packet called the hop count increases by 1 (this is usually called "incrementing the counter"). If the hop count reaches certain preset limits (for example, the Routing Information Protocol, RIP, allows a maximum of 16 hops between the source and the destination), the packet may be discarded as undeliverable since in 16 hops, the routers have not been able to deliver the packet to the destination address.

For routers, however, cost is not the absolute variable it is in the physical world because it's not terribly more expensive to go "the long way" from an origin to a destination when dealing with the Internet. Note these two facts:

- Data (which is basically just pulses of electricity) moves at the speed of light (or very close to it over copper wires), so it would take a pretty serious out-of-the-way, round-about route before the additional distance made a truly significant difference in speed.

- The Internet was designed to be redundant. (Remember, it was created for military use during the Cold War.) The planners of the Internet had to deal with military demands for a network that could still find a way to get data from point A to point C when point B (which was on the route from A to C) had failed (ostensibly because an ICBM had wiped out a city or something like that). The planners had to figure out a way to route data redundantly: If the first route fails, try the second, and so forth.

Fortunately, we've never seen the redundancy of the Internet tested—at least not because of Cold War atomic weaponry. Nonetheless, the design is solid because the network reroutes data packets all the time as a result of events like natural disasters and power failures.

6

How Routers Route Data: Gateway Protocols

Routers variously use one or more of four pieces of the TCP/IP protocol suite to determine which route a packet should take to a given destination at any time. These four pieces are collectively referred to as *gateway protocols*, a needlessly confusing term. Gateway protocols are members of the TCP/IP protocol suite that routers use to determine the best route for data packets. Rather than gateway protocols, a more descriptive and accurate term would be *router protocols* because routers use them to determine the proper way to forward data packets.

These four pieces are called *Routing Information Protocol (RIP)*, *Open Shortest Path First (OSPF)*, *Border Gateway Protocol (BGP)*, and *Exterior Gateway Protocol (EGP)*. Don't be scared off by the names; they're really very easy to understand.

Two of these four protocols (RIP and OSPF) are called interior gateway protocols; they deal with routing data only within a self-contained network such as a LAN or WAN. The other two protocols (BGP and EGP) are called (not surprisingly) exterior gateway protocols and are used to route data outside a LAN or WAN.

Interior Gateway Protocols: RIP and OSPF

In Hour 3, you learned the names of two of the protocols that TCP/IP uses to figure out the best way to send packets: RIP (Routing Information Protocol) and OSPF (Open Shortest Path First). Of the two, RIP is the older routing standard and has limitations on how well it can route data when the network is changing constantly. RIP is *static*; that is, it has rigid settings that allow for a maximum of 16 hops, which means that it doesn't work very well in large network settings (like, not surprisingly, the Internet). OSPF, on the other hand, is *dynamic*. It can change its routing strategy according to the current conditions on the network—so if your main router has gone down for some reason, OSPF can adapt and send data packets through your other router (if you have one).

These protocols are used in private networks, or what technical types call *Autonomous Systems (AS)*. An AS is a collection of routers that are all related and that all route data using the same gateway protocol (RIP or OSPF).

For a great many WANs, RIP suffices to handle interoffice data routing. The rise of the Internet has made router manufacturers simplify the basic configuration of their routers so that users don't often have to worry about RIP and OSPF directly. Instead, when the router is set up, the administrative user adds some static routes to the routing table in one or more routers.

Network providers ranging from your local phone company to Internet service providers have realized that they have to be responsible for configuring routers that connect to their networks, so they've developed significant competencies in installing, configuring, and troubleshooting routers. Even so, try to have a reasonably technically literate person on staff (even if that person is you!). Even if that person isn't directly managing the system, he or she will be able to translate the technology issues into business issues that executives can understand.

Cisco Systems is arguably the largest manufacturer of routers and routing technology products today. They sponsor a broad range of educational programs designed to help budding system administrators and network administrators get up the curve on the *IOS* (*Internetwork Operating System*) software that runs on their routers. Further, their classes provide an excellent base in practical TCP/IP. Such programs are well worth investigating.

Exterior Gateway Protocols: EGP and BGP

Sometimes, however, you have to send packets out to the wide world. That means your packets have to be sent over...the Internet. To do this with something approaching effectiveness, you have to use BGP or EGP, your exterior gateway protocols.

Remember the acronym AS (for Autonomous System or private network) that was just introduced? Well, BGP and EGP are what routers use to send data packets between ASes. In other words, if you route within your own private network, you only need RIP and OSPF. However, when you start sending data to other people's networks (for example, an extranet), you need BGP or EGP.

Border Gateway Protocol (*BGP*) is a newer version of EGP, which is largely out of date these days. Where RIP and OSPF look at packets and try to route them to a destination inside the network, BGP and EGP look at packets and route them to the outside world. BGP is newer and is preferred to EGP because of its increased flexibility and configurability.

BGP relies on TCP to ensure that packets get delivered—another example of the tremendous degree of integration and efficiency in the TCP/IP protocol suite. BGP has an optimized routing table procedure that means it doesn't waste network bandwidth. It also detects when a particular route has failed, which, given the size of Internet routing tables, is no small feat.

One thing to keep in mind: More than one router running BGP can be used inside a single private network (or AS), but this requires that the private network must have a router running RIP or OSPF as well. If RIP or OSPF isn't running inside the network while several routers inside the network are running BGP, the BGP routers start routing packets to each other, each expecting the other to forward the packets to an external network. This creates an infinite loop and crashes the system. Once again, careful planning can help avoid this kind of mistake.

In summary, Table 6.1 offers a breakout of the basic TCP/IP routing protocols. With this chart, you can see the various functions that interior and exterior gateway protocols accomplish.

6

TABLE 6.1   Routing Protocols

Type of Protocol	Protocols Included in This Heading	Explanation	Notes
Routing protocols used to route packets inside a local network.	RIP (Routing Information Protocol)	RIP allows packets to be routed a maximum of 16 times.	RIP is used, but is being superseded by OSPF.
	OSPF (Open Shortest Path First)	OSPF uses a link-state algorithm to determine the current best route. No maximum number of hops during routing.	
Gateway protocols used to route packets to networks outside the local networks.	EGP (Exterior Gateway Protocol)	Sends packets to destinations outside the local network.	Is being super-seded by BGP.
	BGP (Border Gateway Protocol)	Sends packets to destinations outside the local network.	

Using Routers to Make the Internet Efficient: Classless Inter-Domain Routing (CIDR)

Although the current IP supports several billion hosts, that's simply not enough anymore. More and more, enterprises are getting a whole Class B (65,536 IP addresses) or a whole Class C (256 IP addresses) when they actually require significantly fewer IP addresses than are allocated under the current domain rules. This process is rapidly leading to a shortage of available Class B and Class C addresses—even though many of those host IP addresses are unused. Also, the size of the *routing tables* in routers is exploding, which means the Internet runs slower. This is bad all around.

Hour 3 discussed the network and broadcast addresses of TCP/IP networks. Remember that the network address is the section of the address that iden-tifies which network the computer is on, rather than the specific computer. For example, 192.68.1.X is a network address for computers where X can range from 0 to 255. The broadcast address is the address that can be used to send messages to all machines on the network. Traditionally, the broad-cast address is the highest number in the local network; in the preceding example, 192.68.1.255 is the broadcast address.

Classless Inter-Domain Routing (CIDR, pronounced "cider") provides a method for circumventing the limitations of standard IP address allocation. Essentially, it enables multiple Class C addresses to be combined, circumventing the "16 million or 65,536 or 256 host addresses and nothing in between" Class A, B, or C allocation method (that's why it's called *classless*). This technique is generally called *supernetting* because instead of taking a large network and breaking it down into smaller component networks, it's combining smaller component networks into one larger network.

The authors of RFC 1519, which describes CIDR, explained the reason why they invented this protocol: With CIDR, a business that would have taken a whole Class B address and left most of it unused—remember that a Class B network has 65,536 addresses—would now be capable of combining as many 256 IP address Class C networks as they required. In other words, CIDR makes more efficient use of IP addresses than standard Class A, B, or C address allocations, which respectively provide 16 million, 65,000, and 256 addresses per class.

Why is this important for your network? There are three reasons:

- CIDR makes more efficient use of a shrinking pool of IP addresses than standard Class A, B, or C IP address allocation. Because modern networks commonly connect to the Internet, they require IP addresses. The more efficiently we use IP addresses, the longer we'll be able to add new networks to the Internet.

- CIDR potentially represents an additional layer of complexity to the routing tables. As CIDR becomes more common, your network is going to require either more or faster routers because the size of routing tables is primed to explode.

- If one of your suppliers or customers uses CIDR, your equipment has to be capable of supporting it. It's better to be prepared for it by ensuring that your routers can support CIDR (ask the manufacturer), as well as the various gateway protocols. By ensuring that your routers have support for CIDR at the outset, you will avoid a whole series of headaches. Until IPv6 (with its 128-bit address space and nearly unlimited number of IP addresses) is widely implemented, CIDR is going to be an essential, if not central, part of IP routing.

Other Router and Packet-Routing Functions: Authentication and Encryption

Now you know how routers function in general terms. What else can they do? Fortunately, the answer is that routers can add security to your WAN. If your WAN is accessed by many users, or if it passes over high-speed digital phone lines or the Internet, your WAN is a potential target for a *cracker* (a person who maliciously breaks into data networks to steal, damage, or otherwise compromise data). How can you avoid this?

6

Well, you can begin by using the features built in to your routers. A lot of modern routers can strengthen network security while they route packets. Although routers are not *firewalls* (computers dedicated to security), they have a limited capability to verify that data has come from where it claims to have come from (the process of *authentication*). Routers can also encrypt data so that it can't be read without the appropriate key; this is called *encryption*.

> Strictly speaking, authentication and security aren't router features; they're firewall features. But increasingly, router manufacturers are including security functions, so we've written about them. Cisco provides Ipsec firewall/routers, as do Nortel and other networking vendors.

Authentication

Authentication is simply the process of ensuring that data comes from the place it claims to come from. Let's go back to our postal metaphor: Generally, you trust that the return address on a letter is accurate. However, if the return address on your VISA bill were suddenly different and your bill told you to send your payment to a different company name and address, you would be suspicious that someone was trying to defraud you.

In the same fashion, firewalls that run in tandem with routers can check whether a data packet came from the computer it claims to have come from. This technology is not perfect, but it is becoming increasingly popular as *spammers*, or junk-emailers, have taken to routinely appropriating other people's Internet addresses to send their junk mail. If the packet contents don't match where the packet says it is from (as is the case with some spam, or junk email), routers can be instructed to discard the packets and send an alarm to an administrator.

Encryption

Encryption is simply taking one string of data and using a system to render it into a form that can't be read directly. For example, solve the following encryption. Hint: It's a famous "question"…

```
up cf ps opu up cf
```

In this example, a simple phrase is rendered unreadable by simply taking the *plaintext*, or unencrypted phrase ("to be or not to be") and changing it to *ciphertext* by changing each letter to the letter immediately following it in the alphabet ("t" becomes "u," "o" becomes "p," and so on). When firewalls and other such devices perform encryption, it is similar, although the encryption schemes are much more complex than the one used in this example.

To explain the terms used above a bit better, plaintext indicates text of a message in human-readable format. In other words, "*to be or not to be*" is an example of a plain text message.

By contrast, *ciphertext* is the text of a message that has been encoded so that it's not readable without decrypting it into plaintext. In other words, "*up cf ps opu up cf*" is an example of a ciphertext message.

> If you're going to encrypt data that you send over the Internet, try to use Diffie-Hellman data exchange. In this system, encryption keys are exchanged; the software uses those keys to generate a third key, called a session key. The session key is used to encrypt data before it is transmitted. With Diffie-Hellman, the encryption keys themselves are never passed over the network, which makes stealing them more difficult.

Public-Key Encryption

Public-key encryption is one of those neat things that you wish you knew when you were a kid. It's the ultimate way to encrypt stuff. If you'd had this when you were a kid, you could have hidden the secrets of your club and no one would ever have decrypted them.

Public-key encryption is based on esoteric mathematics that deal with factoring really big prime numbers. The only thing you have to know is that public-key encryption offers the potential for great security.

Encryption key is a series of letters and numbers used to make plaintext messages into ciphertexts. An encryption key's security depends on how long it is. For example, a 40-bit key can be broken with today's powerful computers; this level of encryption (often called "weak encryption") may lawfully be exported from the United States. However, 128-bit encryption is much more difficult to break (as of yet, 128-bit encryption hasn't been broken) and cannot be lawfully exported from the United States.

In public-key encryption, each person who sends and receives messages has two keys: a public key and a private key. Public keys are widely distributed and anyone can know them; private keys are (not surprisingly) kept private. Messages encrypted with a user's public key can only be decrypted with that user's private key, and vice versa.

If Fred wants to send Ginger a message, he encrypts it using Ginger's public key (which she's given to him or made freely available). When Ginger gets the message, she decrypts it using her private key, which she alone knows. When Ginger replies to Fred, she encrypts the message using Fred's public key and Fred reads it with his private key.

6

At this time, encryption and authentication are not part of any standards. IPv6, the next generation Internet Protocol, will have encryption and authentication built into the protocol, which will make it much easier to have secure data routing over the Internet.

High-Speed Data Access

WANs typically link to each other using high-speed *digital phone lines*. Although most digital phone services do not run as fast as the local LAN, they do provide sufficient bandwidth to allow users to access resources with reasonable performance. Digital phone services are available in a dizzying array of speeds, services, and prices; the following sections give you an opportunity to learn about some of them.

Digital phone lines convert the sound of your voice into digital data. Digital phone lines work better for computers because computers transmit information digitally. Digital phone lines are often used for WANs where data is transmitted at high speeds over long distances.

Analog phone lines transmit the sound of your voice as a waveform (like a radio wave). Analog phone lines are common (chances are that analog phone lines are what you have your home phone plugged into). To transmit data over an analog phone line, you must convert it from digital data to sound—that's why modems (devices that convert data to sound) make funny-sounding squawks and hisses. That's digital data being converted to sound.

> There are also alternatives to local phone lines. Some companies link their networks together into WANs using satellite links, which are tremendously expensive. Nonetheless, this type of networking is rapidly becoming more popular, particularly in parts of the world where the telecommunications infrastructure is limited.

Trunk Lines: T1 and T3

Trunk lines are the backbone of long-distance packet-switched networks. With speeds as low as 128 kilobits per second and as high as 45 megabits per second, they cover a broad range of networking needs. At the low end, they can provide Internet services to LANs or can link LANs together at speeds just fast enough to be useful for long-distance networking. At the high end, they have enough bandwidth so that a user might never suspect that the computer he or she is accessing is hundreds or thousands of miles away.

Types of Trunks

The trunk lines system, dating to the 1960s, was the first digital phone line system. The original transmission rate (1.544 megabits per second) is the T1 line, often used to interconnect WANs. Another level, the T3 line with a bandwidth of 44.736 megabits per second, is also available. T3 lines are commonly used by large corporate WANs and Internet service providers—they're tremendously expensive and outside the realm of most networking budgets.

Trunk lines are entirely digital. T1s use four wires and provide full-duplex (two-way simultaneous transmission) capability. The T1 digital stream consists of 24 64-kilobits-per-second channels bonded together to create the 1.544 megabits-per-second rate. The four wires on which T1 circuits were originally carried were usually copper twisted-pair wiring. Modern T1s can operate over coaxial cable, optical fiber, digital microwave, and other media. You can use the T1 service in a variety of ways; almost anything is possible. The plethora of options available for T1 service can make deciding what you want a daunting task. The next few paragraphs help explain the possible selections.

Possible Uses for Trunks

Although all trunk lines are digital phone service, all trunks do not carry data. A T1 line, for example, can carry up to 24 separate voice phone lines. Alternatively, it can carry up to 1.544 megabits per second of data. A third possibility is that it can use 12 voice channels (half the available channels) and use the remaining bandwidth (about 768 kilobits per second) to carry data. A fourth possibility is that it can use only a small percentage of the bandwidth for a *fractional T1*. A final possibility is that you can use a T1 line to carry ISDN Primary Rate Interface, which is yet another variety of digital phone service.

All these possibilities are available through your local phone service. The difference between the kinds of trunks listed here is based on their use, not from any inherent difference. All the aforementioned services can be carried over exactly the same type of trunk line. This is why knowing a bit about trunks is useful before you begin to order digital phone service for your WAN.

Provisioning Trunks

When you order a trunk line from your local phone company, the phone company is going to ask you how you want to *provision* it. What that means is that you have to explain how you are going to use the *circuit*, which is the phone company's term for any line they drag into your space. Depending on your application, you may want the trunk for voice traffic, for data traffic, or some combination of the two. For small-to-medium-sized WANs, you usually will be using either a fractional or full T1. Large WANs sometimes use fractional or full T3 lines, which can carry up to 45 megabits per second. Chances are that you won't encounter a T3 unless you have a connection to a major corporate data center, or work for either an Internet service provider or a local phone company.

Leased Lines

Trunk lines are often called *leased lines*. When you purchase fractional or full T1 data services from a telephone company, you get what is called a *point-to-point line*, which means that it is a circuit that carries data only between two specific points. Those two points can be two of your offices (in which case you'd have a WAN), or one end could be your office and the other could be an Internet service provider's location that would connect you to the Internet. Because these lines go between two points and are used by only one entity (one company or organization), they are called leased lines.

Frame Relay

Frame relay is one of the methods used to carry data over digital phone lines such as T1s and 56Ks. Frame relay is commonly used to connect to the Internet, as well as being used to link multiple sites together.

Frame relay is easy to use but makes less efficient use of the available bandwidth than does a clear channel line. Why? There are two reasons:

- Committed Information Rate (CIR) from your vendor. A CIR is a measurement of the worst possible performance you'll get over your frame line; typically, it is half the bandwidth of the line. In other words, if you order a 128 kilobits-per-second frame line, you usually get a 64 kilobits-per-second CIR. This means that during periods of heavy traffic, your connection could drop to a maximum speed of 64 kilobits per second, rather than the 128K maximum speed the line is rated for.

- Your computers have to packetize their data to send it through your local LAN. For packetized data to travel across *frame relay*, the router has to repacketize the data into specially formatted data packets called *frames* that can be routed over frame relay lines.

  Frames, like data packets inside a LAN, have source and destination addresses, checksums, and the rest of the features of packets. This means that frame relay effectively puts packets into packets and sends them off. This process is like putting a completely addressed envelope into a larger envelope when it is sent to an out-of-town location. Clearly, this is wasteful: The weight of the extra envelope (packet) makes the postage heavier, so it costs more to send. Likewise, the extra data in each frame (used for labeling and controlling data) reduces the amount of data that can be sent.

Clear Channel

The alternative to frame's inherent inefficiencies is clear channel. Clear Channel Signaling (CCS, which also stands for Common Channel Signaling, a term that means exactly the same as Clear Channel Signaling) is a way of sending all the instructions on how to move data (also called *signaling*) over a separate channel than the data. This means that there is less overhead for data—there isn't a need for the phone company to frame your data packets in their data frames—so you get a higher throughput. CCS is expensive, however. Be prepared to pay as much as one and a half times the price of frame relay for clear channel.

Trunk Line Speeds

The vast majority of trunk lines sold are T1s and various fractional permutations thereof. Table 6.2 lists the most common T1 speeds available, from 1.544 megabits per second (MBPS) to 128 kilobits per second (KBPS).

TABLE 6.2   T1 Speeds

Full T1	Fractional T1
1.544 MBPS	128 KBPS
	256 KBPS
	384 KBPS
	512 KBPS
	768 KBPS
	896 KBPS
	1.024 MBPS
	1.152 MBPS
	1.280 MBPS
	1.408 MBPS

This is not a complete list; instead, it lists the most common speeds. Remember that a T1 line has 24 channels—when you purchase and provision your T1, you will be able to join, or bond, the channels in 64K increments all the way up to a full T1.

T1 lines offer tremendous flexibility. They are not inexpensive—some telephone companies routinely charge $3,000 or more a month for a full T1—but if you need to connect a WAN, a T1 is one of the premier methods.

Phone companies have a bewildering array of methods to calculate digital phone line charges, and these charges differ from phone company to phone company. Before you purchase, shop around. More important than name recognition is the CIR and the reliability of the carrier.

6

Integrated Services Digital Network (ISDN)

Integrated Services Digital Network, or *ISDN*, is the biggest party that never happened for the phone companies. During the late 1970s and 1980s, the telephone companies attempted to prepare themselves for an onslaught of demand for *switched digital services*, or digital phone lines that could connect in the same way your regular phone line connects.

Any switched phone service, whether it is ISDN or your plain old phone line, establishes a temporary dedicated two-way connection between two locations. When the call is finished, the call is disconnected, and the line is available for another call.

The phone company expected a huge demand for switched digital services and created ISDN. Unfortunately, the demand never materialized—or, rather, did not materialize until almost 10 years after the phone companies expected it. There are at least three factors in the early market failure of ISDN:

- Complicated and nonstandard ordering
- Lack of demand
- Complete lack of marketing

SPID Settings

The first and foremost problem with ISDN until recently was getting the *Service Provider ID* (*SPID*) settings correct. The SPID (rhymes with "kid") specifies the particular features of the ISDN line: the speed of the connection, the phone number, and a host of other variables. Unfortunately, until the Internet boom, most phone company sales representatives were either unaware of ISDN or so unfamiliar with its convoluted ordering procedures that they could not get it configured properly. Complicating matters was the fact that each ISDN *terminal device* (a device similar to a modem, but using digital technology) required specific SPID settings in order to connect—and the phone company often wasn't aware of the correct settings. Also, one phone company's ISDN did not always match another company's ISDN, which had the potential to seriously hinder communications.

Types of ISDN

Happily, most of the difficulty of getting ISDN is now history. Phone companies, eager to ride the Internet wave, have realized that there is finally a viable demand for ISDN and have shaped up their ordering processes to simplify ISDN setup. They have also begun aggressively marketing ISDN as an alternative connection for smaller businesses that require high-speed digital phone access. Because a *Basic Rate Interface* (or *BRI*, roughly equivalent to a single line) ISDN can carry up to 128 kilobits-per-second of data, it is certainly fast enough. Add in a relatively low monthly fee (it can be as low as $50 per month in some states and as high as $250 per month elsewhere; either price is relatively inexpensive for 128K access) and a low per-minute charge (as with long distance), and ISDN becomes an attractive alternative.

For larger businesses and enterprises that want the benefits of switched digital service without the high cost of a T1, there is *Primary Rate ISDN*, or PRI. PRI is a *switched multimegabit data service* and is just shy of 12 BRIs rolled into one interface. PRI has approximately the same bandwidth as a T1 but is handled differently by the phone system. PRI is also often much less expensive.

Each BRI has three subchannels: There are two 64 kilobits-per-second B ("Bearer") channels, which carry the data, and one 16 kilobits-per-second D ("Delta," or change) channel, which controls the circuit. The two 64K channels can be *bonded* into a single 128K channel; in a PRI, multiple 64K channels can be bonded to provide higher speed for WANs that require videoconferencing or other high-speed data applications.

Table 6.3 presents the major differences between Basic Rate Interface (BRI) and Primary Rate ISDN (PRI). Note that this only holds for ISDN in the United States; it's provisioned differently in Europe and other places. If you're working outside the United States, check with your local telephone company for details.

TABLE 6.3   BRI Versus PRI

	Total Bandwidth	# of B channels	# of D channels
BRI	128 KBPS	2, each 64 KBPS	1 at 16 KBPS
PRI (US)	1.472 KBPS	23, each 64 KBPS	1 at 64 KBPS

ISDN is an inexpensive and powerful solution for smaller businesses and home-office use. It is still not perfect, but the phone companies have made ordering and installing ISDN service no more difficult than a T1 installation—and it is often much less expensive.

Digital Subscriber Lines (DSL)

The telephone companies' latest entry into the digital phone line market is *Digital Subscriber Line (DSL)* service. DSL is at least as fast as a T1, but unlike a T1, DSL runs over standard two-wire telephone wire. DSL service used to be very expensive, and phone company expertise in provisioning and installing it was inexact. However, the phone companies responded to the challenge posed by cable modems and have made DSL both affordable and easy to provision. These days, it's possible to get DSL service for fifty dollars a month or so, and it can be sold by ISPs, not just the phone company. DSLs also provide an excellent means of connecting to the Internet.

Benefits of DSL

DSL services have tremendous promise. They can carry lots of data at very high speeds, and prices are being reduced at a breakneck rate to provide incentives for consumers to invest in this technology. Another distinct plus is that DSL services can run over the same copper wire that your regular phone lines use—*unconditioned two-wire copper*. This means that the installation costs for DSL services will be much less than for ISDN or T1 service.

6

The Downside of DSL

In spite of its upsides, DSL has a potentially deadly downside. In most cases, the maximum distance for DSL circuits is less than six miles. In other words, if the distance between your office and the telephone company's central office is more than six miles, you can't use the service. This is not an issue for metropolitan WAN builders, who are very likely to be within easy walking distance of their phone company's central office, but it represents a potential problem for adding DSL capability to suburban phone networks.

DSL Configurations

DSL is available in a variety of configurations:

- For Internet access, Asymmetric Digital Subscriber Line (ASDL) is usually requested because the data flow coming into the network operates much faster than the data routing out of the network. This is not as useful for WANs as it is for Internet access, where data coming into the network is more important than data going out. A lot of home-based DSL users use this particular flavor, since most users will download a great deal more than they'll upload.

- More useful for WANs are High-speed Digital Subscriber Lines (HDSL). HDSL transmits data at symmetrical speeds at T1 data rates (1.544 megabits per second) over distances of 12,000 feet or less. Telephone companies have used HDSL lines to provision T1 lines for ages because HDSL can be installed much faster than regular T1 or T3 wiring.

- Rate Adaptive DSL (RADSL) is a useful tool for WANs that are more spread out. RADSL can change its speed in response to line conditions. It can work farther from central offices than the rest of its siblings, but it still has trouble beyond six miles. This isn't used much any longer.

- The fastest member of the family is VDSL (Very high bit-rate Digital Subscriber Line). These lines go as little as 1,000 feet, but they can operate at LAN speeds (10 megabits per second) or faster. If you have to build a campus WAN, VDSL is a great solution. VDSL is very expensive, but it still costs less than a fractional T3. This is also not used much any longer, because increases in fiber-optics and WAN technology have rendered it unnecessary.

Service Level Agreements and Quality of Service Agreements

When you order digital phone lines, make certain that you write out and contract a Service Level Agreement (SLA) or a Quality of Service (QoS) guarantee. These are powerful tools to hold WAN downtime to a minimum.

As a network builder, you will necessarily be responsible for the network under your control. Unfortunately, once you have a WAN, you are also responsible for one item that is not totally under your control—the digital services that tie your WAN together.

Given the phone companies' propensity to accidentally disconnect lines and the like, it is well worth your while to hammer out an agreement that defines the percentage of uptime your digital lines will have. This agreement is usually called an SLA. Typically, SLAs provide for fiscal relief or refunds if you suffer network downtime in excess of what is specified in the agreement and is an incentive for the carrier or service provider to keep the lines up and running as much as possible.

QoS agreements, on the other hand, are concerned with ensuring that you get the service you pay for. If you have a 128 kilobits-per-second fractional T1 line with a CIR of 64K, get a guarantee that your slowest data rate (the CIR) will be 64K, and that if it drops below that, you receive proportionate dollar relief from the carrier or service provider.

Given that a WAN is an organizational tool, SLAs and QoS agreements provide you, the network builder/designer/administrator with a powerful tool to ensure uptime. That is more important than anything else on a WAN—because if the WAN goes down, there is no WAN, just a lot of unhappy users.

Can the Internet Help You Build Your WAN?

Given the high costs of digital phone service, building a network with a lot of remote sites linked together with digital lines can get very expensive very quickly. Part of the expense is inescapable; to connect networks together on a reliable ongoing basis, digital phone service is necessary. However, there are additional, incremental costs of developing a private WAN, such as the cost of one or more system administrator's salaries and the overhead that comes with the management of a private network.

One of the ways to reduce the administration costs of your WAN is to *outsource* it, or hire someone else to handle the interLAN networking for you. Initially, the businesses that accepted WAN outsourcing jobs came from the pool of computer systems integration and administration firms; often, they were large consultant groups trying to use WAN management as a new source of revenue. These firms operated on a consultative basis, and the costs of their service reflected it. The cost of hiring a computer consultant to manage a WAN was inefficient because consultants typically charge on an hourly basis, and the clock was always ticking.

As the Internet has grown, however, Internet service providers such as AT&T, Network/MCI, SprintNet, Netcom, and Digex have gotten involved in the business of providing WAN services. Their business model differs from the consultants' in one major

6

fashion: They view their connection services instead of their expertise as the service being sold. The ISPs elect to absorb a large chunk of the cost of integrating digital phone lines and WAN technology, choosing instead to make their money on the network service being provided. Of the two models, the consultative is more lucrative, but the ISP model is more likely to survive because it is following in the phone system's footprints by providing a for-cost service and inexpensive integration.

In any case, the ISP model has another net positive: ISPs essentially are nothing more than computer-based routing networks. Because the ISP has a computer-based network, it is a cinch to set up reliable, relatively secure WANs for their clients. How do they do it? Well, they already have networking expertise; more importantly, they have a networking infrastructure already in place. The ISPs' networking infrastructure is designed solely for the purpose of specifying how data routes from point A to point B and back again. If they set up their routers to route packets coming from certain networks only to certain other networks and use the Internet as a transport between ISP service locations, they have set up a type of WAN called a Virtual Private Network (VPN). For all practical purposes, a VPN accomplishes the same tasks as a totally dedicated point-to-point digital phone line-based WAN, but in general it costs less and requires less end-user maintenance. As long as the ISP is doing its job, the costs of maintaining internetwork links should be included in your monthly ISP fee.

There are a few important caveats about VPNs. First, a VPN uses the Internet to route some or all of its data. Clearly, the Internet as it currently exists is not a terribly secure place. There are ways to capture a lot of network traffic if someone knows how (trust me, someone does know how to capture data traffic). If that person captures traffic that contains your unencrypted credit card information or sensitive memos, you could be in serious trouble. If you decide that a VPN sounds like a good idea, spend some time learning about computer security (discussed in Hour 19, "Security") and take the time to implement it properly. VPNs are a great solution to the age-old battle between cost and features, but only if they're put together correctly. If you do it right, you can leverage the power of the Internet for your needs—which is not an inconsiderable accomplishment.

So Who Needs a WAN, Anyway?

WANs are usually set up by large companies or organizations that want to establish significant network presence in multiple offices around the nation or the world. They are not inexpensive, but the benefits can—if correctly designed and configured—outweigh their costs many times over. If data on a server can be replicated to a group of users who need it to serve clients adequately (and thereby retain the clients), the WAN has done its job. If the WAN can be turned to proactive uses such as tracking packages for clients or (my all-time favorite example) managing flight data at airports, it has become a *Value-Added Network* (*VAN*), where its services become the product that clients purchase.

Summary

In this hour, you learned some basic concepts about what constitutes a WAN and some of the hardware that WANs use. You also learned something about digital phone service, which lies at the core of WAN architecture.

In the next hour, you'll learn about the other outside-the-local-LAN network—remote access.

Q&A

Q What is a WAN?

A Any situation in which computers are networked can be a WAN if it also fits the following conditions:

- It connects to private networks.
- It transmits data over telephone lines in general; microwave transmission is the one obvious exception.
- Users can be authenticated at both ends.

Q What kind of phone lines can WANs use?

A There are two basic types of lines that can be implemented for a WAN:

- Standard dial-up lines
- Digital phone lines such as ISDN, frame relay, or T1 service

Q What are the upsides and downsides of VPNs?

A A Virtual Private Network (VPN) has the following pros and cons:

- Upsides: VPNs are relatively inexpensive and use Internet-standard protocols.
- Downsides: VPNs aren't as secure as "private" WANs.

6

Hour 7

Remote Networking

How many times has this happened to you?

You're in a hotel three thousand miles from home, and you have to get a copy of a file for a meeting in the morning but you have no way to get that file other than hoping your assistant has stayed late so that he or she can print it and then fax it to you.

You'd like to go home for the evening, but you have to finish up some work because once you leave, you're cut off from the corporate network.

You'd like to work from home but can't because you have no network access.

If one of these scenarios hasn't happened to you, rest assured that it *has* happened to someone in your organization. The demand for remote access is going through the roof, and network professionals are scrambling to catch up.

What do these users want? To be able to get their network resources from anywhere. Getting access used to be synonymous with "computer-and-modem," and about as sophisticated. But the rise of the Internet, cable modems, DSL, and virtual private networks (VPNs) have changed the layout of the playing field. Now, having a computer and a modem is only one way to gain *remote access* to your network.

Clearly, there is a demand for remote access to the resources of computer networks. But only in the last couple of years has remote access begun to mature.

In this hour, you have the opportunity to learn about the following aspects of remote networking:

- What remote networking is
- The history of remote access
- Why remote networking is becoming more important
- Remote access requirements
- How remote access works using PPP and SLIP
- Using VPNs and the Internet for remote access
- Remote networking security
- Using the Internet for remote access
- Remote networking hardware

A Brief History of Remote Access: Remote Control and Remote Node

Before the explosion of the Internet, users who needed remote access to their network resources did not have many options....

Remote Control

The first remote access was really Unix's Telnet program. Unix users needed to be able to connect to their Unix host system when they were not directly connected to the system's main character-mode terminal. The result of this need was and remains Telnet. Telnet is a program used by Unix (and eventually by many other operating systems) that offers a user the capability to open a command-line session across a network. In a Telnet session, all the user sees are a few characters that make up a screen image, while all of the processing is being done on the remote system. For the user, there's no difference between a Telnet session 1,000 miles away and a Telnet session from another computer right next to the Unix machine.

The first PC remote access solutions were built using Telnet's remote-control behavior. It's not surprising that remote control was the first method of remote access used for personal computers since initially, personal computers weren't considered sufficiently powerful to do any processing locally.

Consequently, in the early days of PC remote access, when users requested a way to get to their applications and files from on the road, an Information System (IS) person would arrive at their desk with floppy disks in tow and install remote control software, such as Symantec's pcAnywhere, Stac's ReachOut, or Traveling Software's LapLink, on both the user's desktop computer and the laptop computer. The IS person would then instruct the user to put the desktop system into a mode in which the computer waited for a call while the user was out of the office. The user would take their trusty eight-pound laptop on the road, and if they needed to read email, check a schedule, or gain access for any other reason, they would dial into the desktop computer. The screen of the desktop computer would appear on the laptop, and the user could slo-o-o-owly read email or work with other applications. When the session was over, the user disconnected the laptop's modem, and that would be the end of data access for that session.

The use of remote control stemmed from the use of applications that depended on a server to operate—these applications had to be spawned across a network, and even if the remote computers had been connected by some sort of dial-up networking, a phone line's bandwidth would have been insufficient to run them. So in early remote access, users only got to see a remote desktop screen on their laptop screens. They couldn't save data from a remote control session to their laptops' hard disks, and thus they couldn't do any real work unless they were connected to their network. This model was inefficient, but it was all that was available at the time.

Remote control applications are still used for certain applications where sending an image of the desktop screen is more efficient than sending actual data over the phone wire. For example, a firm that has a huge database would not want users to try to run reports and queries across a phone line masquerading as a network wire; it would be too slow. So they run the queries on the server, and the client laptop sees only screen data. It's not a perfect solution, but in certain potentially bandwidth-wasteful applications, remote control is more efficient than its competition, remote node, discussed in the next section.

In recent years, Microsoft, Citrix, and Sun have breathed new life into the remote control paradigm with their introduction of terminal-based networks. In Microsoft's Terminal Server and Citrix's WinFrame, Windows applications run on a central server, and only a picture of the screen (a bitmap) gets transmitted over the network. In Sun's model, the same thing happens, except that Unix applications are distributed—that is, they're set up so that one piece of the application runs on the server and another piece runs on the client computer.

7

This model offers compelling advantages for some networks. If a network has a high proportion of workers who move from space to space, terminal servers using distributed applications in a remote-control configuration makes sense, since the users' session settings can move from position to position.

There *is* one area where remote control has increased and in fact has become one of the preferred methods for remote access to computers: system administration. Some organizations have elected to avoid phone support for their workers, preferring instead to simply install a system management remote control agent on each end-user PC. With the agent in place, a user can report a problem with their computer and an administrator can use the agent to temporarily take over the user's desktop across a network. Note that most of the time, dial-up remote control is too slow for this sort of administration, so it's used over a network such as Ethernet or Token Ring, both with 10 megabits per second or more. The administrator sees what the user sees at their desktop and can interact with the user to either teach them or diagnose (and fix) symptoms. This significantly reduces administrations costs for PCs, since the system administrator only needs to actually go to a user's desk if the user's computer is so broken that it can't support the remote control agent software. Microsoft, IBM, HP, and a host of others have built excellent client systems.

However, for systems where users need to have significant local storage and processing, this model fails. This leads into the next discussion: remote node networking.

Remote Node

Over the last several years, a variety of items have come together to enable many more computers to join networks from remote locations as opposed to remote-controlling a remote computer on a network. These factors include the following:

- An increase in the processing power of laptop computers
- The exponential increase of Internet use
- An increase in the installed base of reasonably good quality analog phone lines and in consumer software to use them for network (as opposed to remote control) access
- The increase in high-speed data access provided by cable modems and DSL
- Increased numbers of TCP/IP implementations designed to work over phone lines
- The introduction of IP Security (IPSec) and implementations that enable VPNs to work using the Internet as a medium

These changes in the computer and networking arena allowed remote node networking to become preeminent. *Remote node* means that the computer in the field connects to the central network over one of a variety of media (dial-up phone lines, the Internet via high speed cable or DSL, radio networks) using a network protocol, such as TCP/IP. Once connected, the remote computer becomes a network client just like any other client on the network.

Actually, what you just read is not quite true for analog phone lines, radio networks, and other low-bandwidth connections. They will use the same protocols as faster networks, but they tend to run much more slowly, which places limits on what services are realistically available to them. For instance, a network client located on a LAN has a 10 megabits per second connection (or faster), but low-bandwidth remote-node connections usually max out at between 9600 and 33.6 kilobits-per-second. A low-bandwidth remote node connection is therefore an order of magnitude or two slower than the LAN connection.

Remote node is important because it allows a variety of changes to the remote access model. Essentially, the model changes: In remote control, you have a highly graphical dumb terminal session (in which you see a picture of the server computer's screen but can't copy data to your local hard drive) but in remote node, your computer is part of the network. This means that even though the overall connection speed doesn't change, the user gets benefits, such as being able to compose mail and schedule meetings offline, and then sending them when they connect using a phone line.

Being a part of the network has other benefits as well. Since a computer connected as a remote node is part of the network, it can use standard network services, such as Telnet, FTP, ping, and (far more important) email and Web services such as POP3 for mail and HTTP for the Web.

If you have ever used a dial-up connection to the Internet, you have used a remote node session. The protocols used for Internet dial-up access are coincident with the protocols used for remote node access.

The importance of remote node is in what it can do for disconnected users. Because the connection over a phone line (or in some cases, an ISDN connection) mimics being connected to the LAN while using the modem as a network card, the user simply has slower access to all the same resources that he or she has when connected to the network in the office. So far, this is not an improvement over remote control.

However, in a remote node network connection, the software the user requires to get a job done is stored on the local laptop drive. The application isn't passed down the wire in remote node; only data, such as email or Web pages, are transferred across the network.

Because data is passed over the phone wire just as if it were an in-office network connection, the user can save the data locally. Why is this important? Because if a user needs a file, they only have to dial into the network, change to the network drive, and FTP or copy the

7

file to their hard disk. Although the transfer will be slower than a full-bandwidth LAN connection, when the user is finished copying the files, they can disconnect from the network and still be able to work on the copy of the file made on the laptop's hard drive. That by itself is enough to justify remote node access, but it can do more. (This is starting to sound like a TV ad—"It chops, it slices, it dices!"—except that this one really *does* do it all.)

Remote users face one dilemma not shared by their desktop-using compatriots: the accuracy of their data. Because remote users are not constantly connected to their home networks, they have to worry about the quality, accuracy, and timeliness of the data they are working with.

For example, if there's a file to which several users are contributing, and the changes are time sensitive, the remote user is clearly at a disadvantage. However, some groupware manufacturers such as Lotus and Microsoft have tried to address this problem by creating software that can replicate data from the remote user to the host network, and vice versa. Replication technology is closely tied to business rules that govern the movement of data and establish which document becomes the reference document. It's pretty complex and is outside the scope of this book—but if you're going to support remote users who work as part of groups, it's something to research in depth.

In addition to providing the ability to work offline, typical remote node email and calendaring software allows a remote laptop user to compose email messages and schedule appointments while he or she is not connected to the network. The next time the user connects, they can send the prepared email and schedule data, and receive their email on the laptop's hard drive; then the user can go offline and read it while not connected.

Clearly, remote node is more desirable for most applications than remote control. And that's a good thing, because remote node is remote networking. Remote node connections are based on Internet standards that ensure that you can dial your client laptop into any host server that runs the same group of Internet-standard protocols.

Remote node connections are not necessarily based on Internet standards. However, the use of TCP/IP-based Point-to-Point Protocol (PPP) is so ubiquitous that IPX and NetBEUI-only solutions are out of date and crippled in comparison to PPP. PPP is discussed in "Protocols," later in this chapter.

Clearly, remote node offers benefits to the end user. However, that's not the only reason it is becoming more popular.

Different Organizations Need Different RAS Solutions

Imagine this scenario: You're at home (an hour's commute) after a hectic week at work. You are looking forward to a bit of well-deserved relaxation.

Then the phone rings. It's your boss, who needs something done by Monday. He knows it's a last-minute assignment, and he's sorry, but he needs you to get this done. It's not a major project—you can knock it out in a couple of hours—but there's the drive in to the office that adds a couple of hours at either end of the work.

If this scenario sounds familiar, it's because it's an increasing part of life for many workers. Work hours have gotten longer, and the flattening of the organization has led to a greater degree of responsibility and accountability for the individual worker. Some workers are now expected to be available around the clock. These workers have to have access to networks from offsite if they are to be effective (as well as to keep up morale). If an employee goes home from work and still has more work to do from home, their reasoning would probably be, "At least I'm home and comfortable, rather than still at work." For the modern worker, being able to access corporate data from remote sites is a big help.

There are two other factors that come into play:

- The first is the rise of the virtual office. Many workers don't even have desks in a regular office, *per se*. Instead, they work from home or on the road, as corporations try to meet government regulations that seek to reduce pollution by increasing the number of at-home workers. These workers are part of an organization, but if they don't have some common center—in this case, a network with common email and resources—there's no real way to keep them in the company loop. A worker who's out of the loop is a worker who's worried about their job and will be looking for another one soon.

- The second issue is the Americans with Disabilities Act (ADA). There are a lot of very capable people who lack mobility and consequently find it difficult to get around in a very mobile world. These people represent a significant chunk of brainpower, and under ADA, they're getting a chance to let that brainpower shine through. ADA has had another effect that is also good: Once managers realized that allowing people to work at home once or twice a week was good for morale and (believe it or not) productivity, they realized that they had a powerful tool to increase worker satisfaction, which has, in some organizations, resulted in lower employee turnover.

Organizations no longer have a choice: With the rise of the virtual office, the virtual corporation, and the ADA, organizations must take steps to be in compliance with the law as well as provide the data access their workers need to succeed in an offline environment.

7

At this point, you may be wondering what you need to get started with remote networking. The following sections enumerate a fairly common remote networking setup.

Remote Access Requirements

Unlike LANs, which tend to require a whole pile of special cable, wire, and other equipment, remote networking using phone lines is refreshingly simple. In the main, all you need are two computers, two modems or other telephony devices, a standard phone line, and some industry-standard software.

You know about the computer; we discussed that in Hour 3, "Getting Data from Here to There: How Computers Share Data." As long as the computers at both ends of a modem connection can share files and so forth, the type of computer does not matter. The main thing to remember is that there must be a computer at each end of the connection.

Modems or other telephony devices, on the other hand, have not been discussed yet. The following sections acquaint you with modems and ISDN terminal adapters, which form the basis of many remote networking solutions.

Modems

The term *modem* stands for *mo*dulate-*dem*odulate. What this means is that a modem takes digital data sent from your computer's serial ports and modulates it into an analog, or sound, form that can travel over the regular phone lines. At the other end of a modem connection, another modem translates the analog signal back into digital so that the computer on the other end can read it (see Figure 7.1).

FIGURE 7.1

A modem connects to a computer and changes the data from digital to analog.

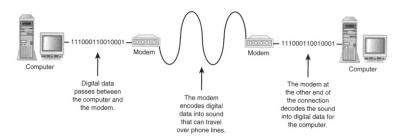

Computer — 111000110010001 — Modem

Digital data passes between the computer and the modem.

The modem encodes digital data into sound that can travel over phone lines.

Modem — 111000110010001 — Computer

The modem at the other end of the connection decodes the sound into digital data for the computer.

"Why are modems necessary at all?" you ask. "Why not just transmit the data digitally? We've just learned about digital phone lines."

Modems are, unfortunately, still necessary for the vast majority of users who need to access networks. The reason is because most current telephone installations are standard two-pair (that is, four wire) copper cables that are designed to carry only analog signals. In fact, the regular phone wires running into your house have more in common with the wires connecting speakers to a stereo than to a T1 or a LAN wire. So we're stuck with modems, at least until the phone company starts making home phone service digital. And that's not going to happen very soon.

> Modems were invented to circumvent the need for expensive digital phone lines. Initially, modems ran at 300 bits per second or slower—it could take a couple of minutes for a whole page to show up on your screen at that speed—and gradually got faster until they reached the current ceiling of approximately 53 kilobits per second (which is asymmetric, or nonsymmetric—that is, in one direction; there's a 53 kilobits-per-second download speed but the maximum speed in the other direction is 33.6 kilobits per second). Modems are not terribly efficient devices because a very high proportion of the data they transmit is dedicated to catching and correcting data transmission errors. Nonetheless, modems are the most common way for a remote user to tie into a network.

With a modem, the user has a significant degree of involvement in the connection process. The user has to dial the modem when he or she wants to connect to the corporate network; there is no *dial-on-demand*, or automatic connection, when they select a resource not stored on the laptop. Also, modems are usually sensitive to the quality of the phone line. If our user is calling from Outer Mongolia and trying to get a fast connection, he'd better forget it—there will be too much distortion in the phone lines to get a good connection (if he can get connected at all). Poor phone line quality is not limited to out-of-the-way locations, however; because of increasing pressure on the phone companies to service increasing numbers of users, line quality can be iffy even in major metropolitan areas. Make certain that your users know that a bad connection can often be rectified by disconnecting and redialing—it's a simple fix.

The user's involvement in the connection process also involves a certain amount of patience. With current modem technology, it can take up to two or three minutes to establish a reliable network connection, and users have to be taught that this is normal—the laptop has not locked up.

> Read Part V, "Introduction to Network Administration," for more information on managing your users' interaction with networks and technology.

7

Modems can be purchased as standalone units or (if you have lots of users who need to connect) in special boxes called *modem racks*, which you'll learn more about in a few pages. All things considered, modems represent a cost-effective, technically acceptable solution for remote users.

ISDN Terminal Adapters

ISDN terminal adapters are devices that connect to BRI (128K) ISDN digital phone lines. Unlike modems, ISDN terminal adapters do not connect directly to a computer's serial port. Instead, they connect using Ethernet. In an ISDN terminal configuration, your remote computer has a network adapter installed in it. The network adapter connects to the ISDN device using a special cable called a *crossover cable*, which negates the need for a hub or switch between two systems.

When your computer needs network resources, it sends out data packets onto the little tiny LAN. When the packets reach the ISDN device, the device dials the ISDN phone number of the host network, and (if all is working properly) the user should be connected in as little as two or three seconds at a fairly high data rate (see Figure 7.2).

FIGURE 7.2

An ISDN remote access configuration.

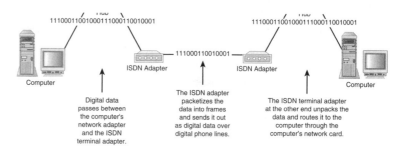

ISDN is currently primarily useful for home-office networking. Why? Because at this time, ISDN is not widely available as a consumer service, the way the regular telephone network is. Think about it: No matter where you go, you can get analog dial tone, and therefore, you can connect with a modem. With ISDN, you must have ISDN installed at both ends of the line if you want a full-speed digital connection. So don't start thinking about equipping your road warriors' laptops with ISDN terminal equipment. Sure, it will be fast…*if* they have lines over which they can connect.

If you have the opportunity to offer ISDN service to your home office users, do so. The ease of connection to the network and the speed of the connection make ISDN a no-brainer. This is the case from an ease-of-use perspective, which results in greater peace of mind for managers who have to work with offsite users and network administrators who have to manage the connections, the users, and managers' demands all at once.

Protocols

Once the hardware is in place, it is time to begin considering the network protocols that will connect remote users' computers to the main network. Ninety-nine percent of the time, the protocols used to connect remote users will be members of a special subset of the TCP/IP protocol suite that handle transferring data over phone lines. These special protocols are *PPP* and *SLIP*.

> For additional information on protocols, refer to the protocol section in Hour 3.

PPP

Of all of the protocols used to control and manage the transfer of data over telephone lines, *Point-to-Point Protocol* (*PPP*) is far and away the most popular. PPP was developed to provide a way to network computers that did not have network cards and required a modem or ISDN terminal adapter to make an effective network connection. PPP is an Internet standard.

PPP has several requirements that remain the same from system to system. First, PPP needs to know several parameters:

- The phone number of the system to which it will connect.
- A Domain Name Server (DNS) address. DNS services are very important to networks because DNS servers provide a lookup table that enables a computer to reconcile a numeric IP address (such as 192.168.207.124) to a name such as foo.bar.com.
- Whether the remote computer has a fixed IP address or if it will be assigned an address when it connects with the server. Server-assigned IP addresses are assigned by a server running the Dynamic Host Configuration Protocol (DHCP), yet another subset of TCP/IP. DHCP is used when you have a finite pool of IP addresses—for example, from address 192.168.1.1 to 192.168.1.254 (that's 255 addresses)—and a larger pool of users—for example, a thousand users vying for those 255 addresses). DHCP allows IP addresses to be assigned as required; when they're not used, the addresses return to the common pool, from which they are drawn as required.
- If the computer will be connecting to the Internet, it needs a default gateway setting (the IP address of the router or gateway that connects to the Internet). In many PPP implementations, you can tell the dialing computer to acquire this information from the server into which it dials.

7

Once these parameters are set up, it's time to dial. (Each operating system has slightly different procedures for setting up parameters. It's part of Microsoft Windows NT and Windows 95's Dial-Up Networking).

> More information on network operating systems can be found in Part IV, "Network Operating Systems."

Depending on which software you use, your computer may ask you for a user ID and password. Once you have keyed them in, the system authenticates your login and switches to PPP data handling. After the system has switched into PPP data handling, it is possible to access the host network via TCP/IP.

> For a dial-up protocol, PPP offers a rich feature set. It can carry multiple pro-tocols (TCP/IP, IPX, and NetBEUI) at the same time, and it can use a variety of methods for authentication including the vaunted Kerberos system where passwords never pass across the wire. There's more about authentication and security in the network administration chapters in Part V of this book.

PPP is remarkably reliable for a dial-up protocol. If the line is clean, PPP usually does not spontaneously disconnect unless no one has used the connection for a while. It's a great, elegant solution to a vexing problem (see Figure 7.3).

FIGURE 7.3

A typical remote-node dial-up connection configuration using PPP.

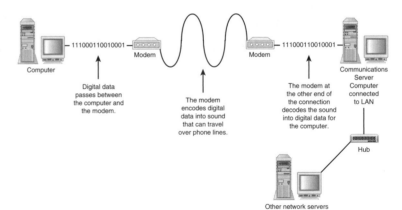

SLIP

Serial Line Internet Protocol (SLIP) is an older cousin of PPP. It requires that you specify even more parameters than PPP, and there is little guarantee that it will connect; SLIP must negotiate the size of the largest data packets that both ends can handle before it begins transmitting user data.

Essentially, SLIP is out of date. However, you may run across it on older systems. If you have the opportunity to upgrade it to PPP, do so—PPP is faster and better. SLIP unfortunately requires a great deal more from the user than does PPP, and it's less efficient— every remote user must have a unique IP address.

Authentication and Security

A modem waiting for a call is a gateway to the world just waiting to be cracked. If a modem is left waiting for a call and there is no security in place, the server computer cannot verify that users who dial in are actually who they say they are. Even simple network passwords are better than nothing.

Passwords alone, however, do not ensure that all users who connect are authorized to access the internal network. This is because passwords are sometimes passed in plain text (that is, unencrypted text) over a PPP network connection, so any user who can "listen in" on a successful login session can capture that user ID and password for use at a later date. Although this particular situation is not common by any means, it illustrates some possible weaknesses in security.

To ensure dial-in security, there are several measures you can take:

- Ensure that the system logs all incoming calls and login attempts. This can help locate users who are trying to guess passwords.

- Limit login attempts to three or less, and lock out any user who has not produced a correct password for a given user ID after three unsuccessful attempts to log in.

- Use *access tokens* (small calculator-like cards that produce numbers that constantly change) in addition to user IDs and passwords. Access tokens are particularly difficult to crack because anyone logging in must have access to a known and trusted user token in addition to a valid user ID and password.

- Change the PPP settings so that the remote user has a secure login. New security protocols such as *Challenge Handshake Authentication Protocol* (*CHAP*) and *Password Authentication Protocol* (*PAP*) can help secure the login process.

- Force users to change their passwords frequently.

No matter how secure you make your network, don't ever stop trying to make it more secure. Security is a process, not a destination. Hour 19, "Security," discusses security in more depth and can help you establish behaviors to make your network more secure.

7

Using the Internet for Remote Access

VPNs

In the previous section, you learned that remote node networking can run over a variety of media, ranging from analog phone lines and radio waves (low-bandwidth connections) to cable modems and DSL. Keep in mind that a lot of organizations don't want to have their users dialing into a central modem pool because the cost is so high, or don't want to pay for leased lines for their remote workers who need fast access to their networks. In many cases, an organization will have users who need dial-up access as well as remote users who will require higher-speed connections.

When an organization is faced with these requirements, it has two choices:

- Invest in a dedicated set of phone lines and a dial-up server to handle dial-up remote users, and invest in dedicated high-speed data links to each remote user that requires high-speed access.

OR

- Use the Internet as the media of choice. To do this, the organization needs to do the following:
    - Invest in a contract with a national or international dial-up Internet Service Provider (ISP) to provide local dial-up phone numbers.
    - Provide cable modem or DSL service to users who require high-speed remote access.
    - Set up a server between the organization's network and the Internet to authenticate users using VPN software.

The upside of the first choice (that is, the use of dedicated phone circuits) allows the organization to have complete control over all aspects of remote access. The downside of the first choice is that it allows the organization to have complete control—and responsibility, and debugging, and support—of remote access. This gets expensive very quickly, and it's not the best way to spend money.

The second choice (that is, using the Internet as a conduit between different locations), although it's more complicated, is cheaper and lower-maintenance. Although the initial setup is a headache, there are several advantages of sourcing remote access to a third-party provider, such as AT&T, and then using VPN clients to enable all remote clients (low- and high-bandwidth) to connect to the network.

- There's only one pathway into the network (via the internet), and ideally the VPN server is sufficiently well-secured to discourage or limit break-ins.

- There's no need to manage many high-speed data circuits, such as T1s.
- A dedicated provider, whose sole business is competently providing network access, provides the service. Contrast this with your business—do you want to provide network access, or concentrate on core business issues?

If your organization is wedded to doing everything locally, dial-in servers that manage PPP connections and authentication are a great way to ensure good security on your network. But if you have users who are far away—from Boston to San Francisco, for example—you might want to try using the Internet as the media to connect your remote offices.

Remember Virtual Private Networks (VPNs), discussed in the previous hour? Well, VPNs are not limited to digital phone lines. If necessary, you can outsource your dial-up remote access as well as your high-speed office interconnections. In fact, you can do it in such a way that your users won't have to dial a long-distance number or an 800 number—they can dial a local phone number almost all the time.

Does this sound too good to be true? It's not. Many Internet Service Providers and large national network providers have built networks that enable users to connect via a local phone call from almost anywhere. At the same time, ISPs have aggressively built a network of cable modems and DSL lines that give high-speed data access to home users.

These increases in network availability offer organizations the capability to set up a VPN server. One side of a VPN server is connected to the organization's network and the other side is connected to the Internet. The VPN server has software that talks to VPN clients stored on remote systems. If the key that the remote client VPN software provides matches the one in the VPN server, the user will get access. The protocol the user will use once they are connected is IP Security, or IPSec—which encrypts the contents of each data packet so it's not readable as it passes over the Internet.

Cisco Systems, Microsoft, and a host of others provide VPN software that uses IPSec for authentication and security. In the long term, this may prove to be the most efficient method for providing remote users access to secured networks.

Remote Access Hardware: Build or Buy?

Even though Internet-based remote access is becoming increasingly common, some organizations are going to build their own remote access solutions. The following discussion deals with the ramifications of doing so, and provides some insight into what's involved in building a robust remote-access architecture.

Remote access hardware comes in a variety of permutations from a huge number of manufacturers; it would be pointless to attempt to list them all here. Instead, this section focuses on the build or buy question that faces people who have to purchase and deploy remote access solutions.

7

Whether to build or buy a remote access solution is a difficult question. The answer depends on a variety of variables, including your company's size, how fast your company is growing, how many people will be using the remote access system at any given point in time, and how easily upgradeable it should be.

The process of selecting hardware for a heavy user-interactive application growing by leaps and bounds has been compared to buying clothes for a child. By the time you get the clothes home and get the child dressed, more often than not, the kid has outgrown them. Alternatively, if the clothes do fit, the child doesn't like them and won't wear them. It's a damned-if-you-do, damned-if-you-don't situation. But over time, a rule of thumb has emerged for remote access equipment: Figure out how many simultaneous users you will have and then at least double that capacity. That way, your first-year expansion is manageable.

Building a Remote Access Solution

If you have only a few users, it is possible to create a remote access solution based on connecting two or more modems to a server computer. Most server operating systems offer solutions for remote node access, including Microsoft's Remote Access Service (RAS), Novell's NetWare Connect, OS/2's LAN Distance, and the various communications server daemon programs that come with most versions of Unix. This is usually the "build" option in the build-or-buy conundrum.

Typically, a remote access server built entirely on Intel-compatible computer architecture has only one piece of hardware that is not on other computers: a *multiport serial board*. Because most Intel-compatible computers have only two serial ports to connect to modems, multiport serial boards that allow the addition of up to 16 additional modems per card offer much-needed expandability.

Systems built on a computer architecture have a variety of positives, including the capability to use an operating system's built-in security and login handling. Typically, home-built remote access systems provide very good performance at a reasonable cost. The downside of building your own remote access server solution is that it can be difficult to support if you have a problem. All too often, the operating system vendor blames a problem on the multiport card vendor, and vice versa, which gets you nowhere.

Buying Turnkey Remote Access Solutions

The alternative to building a remote access system from standard hardware and parts is to purchase a *dedicated system*. Dedicated systems usually do not follow standard Intel-compatible architecture and may or may not interface directly with your network operating system. In spite of their proprietary architecture, or nonstandard vendor-dependent designs, many of the dedicated remote access solutions available in the market offer great value for what they do. Shiva's LANrover and CUBIX's communications server solutions are two of the most popular dedicated remote access systems; both interface seamlessly with Windows NT, and both are upgradeable to faster modems as time goes by. Shiva offers a special authentication package with its products. Other manufacturers, such as MultiTech, offer network-login-based remote access solutions that handle the network connection as part of the login software.

Summary

In this hour, you learned what remote access is and why it has become so important over the last several years. You also learned about some of the alternative ways of deploying a remote access system.

This is the end of Part II of this book, "The Basics"—hopefully you are now fluent in basic network concepts. Part III, "Building a Network," talks about building a network, starting at the planning stages, and winding up with the products that enable you to accomplish what you require.

Q&A

Q What are some of the factors driving the growth of remote access?

A Government regulations, employee morale, and the ADA are some of the reasons for the growth of remote access.

Q What is remote control?

A Remote control is a method of remote access in which a user at a remote computer sees a picture of the screen of the dial-up host computer. ReachOut, pcAnywhere, Remotely Possible, and LapLink are examples of remote control software.

Q What is remote node?

A For all practical purposes, remote node is a network connection made across a phone line rather than across a network wire.

Q Which dial-up protocols are commonly used for remote node?

A Point-to-Point Protocol (PPP) and the older Serial Line Internet Protocol (SLIP) are commonly used for dial-up connections.

Q Which protocols can run simultaneously over a remote node connection?

A TCP/IP, IPX, and NetBEUI can all run together over a remote node connection. Doing so, however, is relatively inefficient because multiple protocols can generate more traffic than the network topology can carry. In other words, running multiple protocols simultaneously can cause network traffic jams, which are sometimes called *broadcast storms*.

7

PART III

Building a Network

Hour

HOUR **8**

The Criteria for Building Your Network

There are two kinds of people in this world: the kind who think about what they're doing and learn from their mistakes, and the kind who don't. We all know some of the latter type: They're the people who stumble through life making costly mistake after costly mistake and never seem to grasp the basic premise of success. They don't learn from their mistakes and don't think things through. As a result, they find it difficult to avoid mistakes.

Needless to say, building a network requires planning and foresight. It's not a task to undertake haphazardly; it requires some cogitation to work right. But the networking neophyte lacks experience, which makes avoiding mistakes difficult.

This hour aims to rectify a beginner's lack of experience by presenting a variety of practices that collectively cover most of the dilemmas and unforeseen crises that crop up. It doesn't provide pat answers; instead, it provides some context so that your inherent critical thinking skills have a basis for decision making in a network situation. This chapter is about methodology, pure and simple. Its aim is to provide a global framework for the upcoming design chapters. Once you have a methodology, you have a map; even if you get lost, you can retrace your steps and figure out where you are.

The things discussed in this and following hours will steer away from the basic networking theory presented in the first part of the book and will focus on management of the network. The information presented ranges from preventive maintenance to establishing organizational behaviors regarding the network.

In this hour, you will learn about the following topics:

- What "best practices" are
- The steps to successful implementations: plan, design, implement, and tune
- Security best practices: passwords and disaster recovery
- A list of best practices

What Are Best Practices?

If your job requires that you master a variety of tasks, it's a safe bet that you will figure out a regular way to accomplish them. For example, if you own a retail store, you will develop a routine for cashing out after the close of the business day:

1. Check to make certain that all customers have left.
2. Lock the doors.
3. Count the cash and checks in the register and reconcile that total against the register tape.
4. Put the cash in a bank-bag and seal it in a safe so that it can be picked up the following day by an armored car service and brought to your bank for deposit.

While you're doing this, you might also be supervising others who are preparing the store for the next day's business. And at the very end of the night, you turn out the lights.

Such behaviors are not random; they are the result of applied experience. If you're closing a retail store, you check very thoroughly to make certain that customers are out of the store because you don't want to have unknown people wandering around inside after business hours. You lock the doors before you count the cash because to some extent, that's security against being held up. You reconcile the register tape because it ensures that your cashiers are doing their jobs honestly. And you lock the cash in a safe until armored security picks it up so that it's hard to get to without a combination.

These behaviors may not be written down because they seem like common sense. However, they are an example of best practices at work. *Best practices* is a term coined by consultants in the 1980s to describe the institutional behaviors that had become ingrained and codified into standard operating procedures. Healthy organizational use of best practices can provide an organization with a sensible, flexible set of rules that provide conceptual guidelines for decision-making.

Best practices exist for networking as well as business consulting. They transcend operating systems, hardware platforms, network topologies, and every other fast-changing component of networking. Instead of dealing with specifics, they're a set of abstract concepts to which you can apply flexibly depending on the situation in which you find yourself.

Because networking technology changes so rapidly, focusing on immediate product details to the detriment of the big picture draws attention away from the core infrastructural issues faced by modern networks. This is where best practices provide their value to the networking process. Note the benefits of best practices:

- Best practices offer a perspective that enables network planners to step out of the upgrade cycle long enough to take a long hard look at their current practices. Rather than focusing on today's problems, best practices provide a perspective with which to examine the infrastructure and procedures of the underlying pieces and determine whether or not they are working together in productive fashions.

- Best practices offer a way to assess policies and procedures, codify those policies and procedures that work, and discard those that are nonproductive or counterproductive. As you assess your organization in preparation for a network or network upgrade, remember that there is no one single set of best practices for everyone. What is best for one organization is not necessarily best for another. Every organization is different from every other organization; as a result, best practices cannot be slavishly copied from a successful organization—your organization must define them for itself.

- Best practices must be tested to produce good results; they must be assessed, discovered, written, refined, and applied systematically. After this process, they must be reassessed to ensure that they reflect real concerns and can reliably ensure superior performance when implemented. After this, they can be deployed.

- Codifying and instituting best practices often results in cost savings. Cost savings are not an automatic corollary of the institution of best practices; in fact, best practices may actually increase spending if that increase is necessary. However, in many cases, best practices save money by increasing efficiency.

With respect to networking, best practices are not an option if the goal is a robust, flexible, highly functional architecture. No one would ask an architect to build a small house only later to ask that it "evolve" into a skyscraper—but that's what routinely happens in networking. Nightmare tales of ad hoc networking are legion in the consulting world.

An example that keeps rearing its ugly head is the company where several well-meaning department heads each independently build their own network, leaving the internal networking staff to Frankenstein-stitch everything together at extraordinary cost and difficulty.

The complexity of data networks at even the small-LAN level has made it imperative that network managers review the way they do their jobs to attempt to stem the flood of user-initiated requests, desktop configuration management problems, large-scale network management issues, and change requests. It is not uncommon for a network manager to find their time focused almost entirely on crises, leaving little time to deal with tactical and strategic organizational issues. Naturally, this crisis-focus does little good, but instead accomplishes much that is bad. First, constant crises burn out network managers at an alarming rate; and second, crisis management creates an adversarial relationship between management and users. Most burnout and adversarial network admin versus user conflicts, let alone cost nightmares, can be avoided, though.

Instituting best practices when a network is first being built is far and away the best way to ensure that the network will function properly, be manageable, and will meet the goals set for it. Although networking is not yet as codified as management, there are still some global truths that can assist in the development of a healthy network and a healthy culture. As this author sees them, networking best practices are listed here:

- Capacity planning
- Ensuring interoperability and adherence to industry and open standards
- Establishing strong security architecture
- Setting clear goals

Each of these practices is detailed following the brief overview of the process in the next section.

Planning Best Practices: Plan, Design, Implement, and Tune

There is an old saying that "Change is the only constant." If you've ever doubted that, look at the change in networking from month to month, even week to week. The rate of change is so rapid that it's difficult to plan. The rise of the Internet and the pace of the dot-com economy only accelerates the development of The New Cool Thing, with which networking folks are expected to keep pace.

But just because it's difficult to keep up with the pace of change doesn't mean you shouldn't try. Change happens, and you have to deal with it.

Dealing with Change

If you were building a house, would you start nailing boards together willy-nilly, or would you work from plans? You'd probably work from plans. If you didn't, you might get a house…or you might not. You might create art, but you can't always live in art. You might create a frame with a roof and sides, but there's no guarantee that it will keep out the rain and snow. And you can bet that a house built without a plan won't be square and level.

But even if you did make a plan for your house, what would happen if every week a new building material came out that provided compelling advantages over its older counter-parts? Suppose that your wife/husband/significant other demanded that you always use the latest, most efficient furnace, even if it meant ripping out huge portions of the existing architecture. You'd be in a constant state of building—never quite finished.

That's what building a network can be like, even if you have a plan. Change really is the only constant. And in the network technology world, where the pace of change is break-neck, change is more than a constant; it's an annoying, cost- and morale-draining force that knocks on your door all the time. It's difficult to plan for 30, 60, or 90 days out, let alone the next year or two, when the technology you plan to use could be obsolete by then.

Building a network is much the same as building a house. Change may be a constant, but we can try to manage it with planning and adherence to some very simple processes. When you're building a house, the process is called having plans and adhering to the design. When you're building a network, because of the rapid steps in technology, it's especially important to ensure that you follow a reasonably logical process. Otherwise, you'll wind up with a heap o' technology that no one can make sense of. The process is, simply stated, plan, design, implement, and tune:

- **Plan.** Plan your network from a user perspective. Know what your network is for! It sounds facile, but if you don't know why you're building it, you're not likely to reap much benefit from it.

- **Design.** Design your network. What is design? A good definition is that it's taking a perfectly beautiful idea and proving why it won't work. Good engineers don't look for successes during the design process; they look for potential points of failure. That's a good way to look at designing a network. It must be able to do what you need it to do without breaking down at every turn.

  Network design includes a variety of tasks, which we'll examine in more depth in the next hour. The chief task is *capacity planning*, or figuring how much your net-work will grow and trying to ensure that you have enough capacity to deal with network requirements. But the main trick to successful design (of any type) is to look for what *doesn't* work and to solve problems before you implement the design. Network design also includes *compatibility issues* in which you determine that all the pieces of the puzzle can work together.

- **Implement.** This is the point at which you take a perfectly good design and prove that the people who designed it didn't know what they were talking about. Implemen- tation is the process of physically realizing the design. Inevitably, the design process has missed something, and the implementation stage is where it pays to be flexible, knowledgeable, and creative.

- **Tune.** Implementations always leave some loose ends, just like the first time you sewed on a button. Tuning is the part of the process in which you try to rectify the small flaws in your creation. Note that tuning is not intended to compensate for fundamental design flaws. Don't try to patch a network with a fundamentally flawed design, or you'll find yourself face to face with Douglas Adams's dictum from *The Hitchhiker's Guide to the Galaxy*: "The fundamental design flaws are completely hidden by the superficial design flaws."

Applying the Best Practices

To arrive at a passable standard that adheres to the best practices set forth, you need... a crystal ball. Because crystal balls are in short supply, you have to think hard about the future of your business, your organization, and technology—and extrapolate what you'll need a year from now to remain competitive, serve your users, and not break the bank in the process. If you're going to be responsible for capacity planning for a network (and if you're the person building the network, this is almost certainly the case), answer the following questions. They represent a starting point for your reflections. As you work through these questions, take notes and add questions of your own; remember, you know your business and your network better than anyone else.

1. How many workstations does your network have?

   If your network has 5 or 10 workstations, planning should be relatively simple. If, on the other hand, you have to support 500 workstations, you'll need to structure and plan in more depth. Large networks are a challenge because they require the delivery of high-quality services to a wide variety of users, most of whom can't be supported in a constant, one-on-one personal basis. This requires network manage- ment solutions, mass software distribution solutions, and finding a way to do open- ended capacity planning.

2. How many workstations will your network have a year from now?

   This question follows on the heels of the first question. The degree of growth can help determine what equipment you initially roll out. A 5-workstation network that will have 10 workstations the following year requires less overall power and flexi- bility than a 5-workstation network that will grow to 25 or 50 workstations. Clearly, if your network is growing at a rate that outstrips the capability of existing staff to service each user and each request manually, there'll be a strong need for the ser- vices mentioned under point 1.

3. Do you or will you provide file services for your users?

   If you do, you have to make provision for a file server. Discussed in earlier hours, file servers tend to be overbuilt; if you can afford more power than you need now, get it. If you centralize data storage, you need to plan to back up that data adequately—otherwise, your users will lose confidence in the shared network storage and will not use it.

4. Will you provide Internet email services for your users?

   If you do, you require a mail gateway. It's usually best to assign a single computer to accomplish this task. You'll need to contract with an ISP to handle your bulk mail, and you'll probably need to register a domain on the Internet.

5. Will you provide Internet access (the Web, FTP, Telnet services) to your users?

   If you're going to provide Internet access for your users, you need a router, proxy server, and firewall. You can also roll the email server into this system. Chances are, you'll also need to go to the ISP marketplace and select an Internet Service Provider who can provide you access across some sort of high-speed phone line (a T1, DSL, @Work cable, or other high-speed access).

6. Do you currently provide centrally administered remote access for your users? Will you ever have to provide centrally administered remote access for your users?

   Remote access is generally best provided by computers dedicated to the task of providing remote access. If not that, then review the section on VPNs in Hour 7, "Remote Networking."

One of the benefits of going through a question-everything process is that if you do it right, the results are stellar, and people will hail you as an IS sage.

However, asking questions is only the first part of the process. You have to answer the questions. Write the answers down; you'll need these objectives as you work through the design of your network in the next hour.

What you want to create by answering these and other questions is a document that specifies what you want the network to be capable of doing.

However, even if you feel pretty confident about what your answers to the preceding questions are, you're not finished answering questions quite yet. You still have to deal with interoperability and standards-based networking and security.

Interoperability and Standards-Based Networking

Networking changes quickly. However, you don't always have to bear the brunt of that change if you plan your system according to certain guidelines.

When designing a network, it's a good idea to ensure that the network is as *future-proof*, or immune to abrupt technology shifts, as possible. Given that networking changes as rapidly as it does, you might be led to think that future-proofing is impossible, or improbable at the very least.

Fortunately, that's not the case. As you may recall from Hour 3, "Getting Data from Here to There: How Computers Share Data," a group called the IETF sets standards for TCP/IP networking and publishes those standards in documents called Requests for Comment (RFCs). The standards set forth in the RFCs are available to any and all manufacturers who want to use them, but there is no coercive effort to enforce compliance. It's simply understood in the networking world that products that adhere to RFC-based standards will *interoperate*, or work with one another, regardless of computer architecture, topology, and platform.

What does this mean in terms of best practices? First, it means that you should be aware of the various IETF and TCP/IP standards. You don't have to know them in detail, but you should at least know what is standard, what is pending standardization, and what is not. Being aware of standards and deciding to use standards-adherent products enables your network to stay open-ended because new products that are open-standards-compliant tend to interoperate well with earlier versions.

The other benefit of deciding to use standards-compliant products is that it simplifies your purchasing decisions. If a vendor's products are *proprietary* (that is, they do not conform to open standards), they are automatically out of the running.

As a result, you should ask yourself whether or not you want to make your network standards compliant. In most cases, the answer is yes—it's a no-brainer—and you should note that you've elected to do that. You'll take that into account when you select hardware and software in the next hour.

Security

Best practices are required to ensure security as well. A network might work well and provide all its users with everything they need, but if one user takes one copy of data out of the building illicitly and gives it to a competitor, you're up the creek without a paddle.

Security is more of an issue for data files than it is for paper files because data files can be duplicated exactly—there is no change in data copied from a network server to a floppy disk. It's impossible to determine whether a file has been copied unless some security is present to track the movement of files. As a result, you must institute best practices for security that do the following:

- Enunciate a set of rules
- Define secure behaviors

Enunciating Usage Policies and Procedures

When you set up your network, you must clearly define how users are and are not allowed to use data. Any violation of these rules, whether it be using floppy disks, zip disks, laptops, email, Web pages, unauthorized Internet access, or other parts of the network, *must* be punishable by sanctions up to and including dismissal and legal action.

These rules should be incorporated into an employee handbook (after all, data is just like any other company property) and should be acknowledged with a written and signed statement by the employee.

These rules should also be added to your growing list of information regarding what the network should do.

Defining Secure Behaviors

Because each company's business is different, we have not defined an exact set of rules. However, the following questions can help you figure out where your potential security holes are:

1. Do you have your servers physically secured?
2. Is each server's operating system "hardened" against common intrusions?
3. Does each user have his or her own password?
4. Are passwords regularly changed according to a schedule?
5. Is there a clearinghouse for passwords?
6. Are all logins and logouts and all file activity logged at the server?
7. Are all file-copy actions to removable media logged?

These questions represent only the beginning of the security questions you have to ask. Think about how your users work: Do they have read/write access to a corporate database? Do they have physical access to the variety of servers that make up the network? Just as with capacity planning, security is a subject that gets bigger the deeper into it you get. Go there anyhow—you'll be glad you did.

The purpose of these questions is to help you determine how you want your network to work. This material comes in useful in the chapters ahead, when you design and administer your network.

If you want to read more about security, go to Hour 19, "Security," which deals with these issues in more depth.

Collating What You've Learned

At this point, you've answered (or thought about) a lot of questions regarding what your network should do and how you want it to work. This information can help guide you in the hours ahead, when you design, build, and administer your network. If you can, assemble the information you've gathered into a document so that you will have the questions and answers available for later review. You'll find it useful for helping you stay on track as you go through the process.

Summary

During the last hour, you learned about the policies and procedures you have to establish to appropriately select the pieces of your network. The following chapters expand on all these ideas. As you design your network, be aware of the issues raised here: planning, interoperability, and security.

In the next hour, you'll go through the process of designing your network, step by step. You'll bring all you've learned in the book so far to bear on the process—so reviewing what you've read up to this point would be wise.

Q&A

Q How far into the future should you plan?

A You can never plan too far ahead! If you know that your network is slated to grow, and you know how fast, your planning can accommodate the planned growth so that your design won't limit the possibility of expansion.

Q Why is interoperability so important to network planning?

A In basic terms, the need for interoperability affects everything else when you are planning a network. Software or hardware that does not work with other software or hardware (or that does so only under certain conditions) limits the capability of your network to grow.

HOUR 9

Designing Your Network

Those readers in their mid-30s may recall an early episode of PBS's *Sesame Street* in which a couple of the characters (probably Bert and Ernie) tried to make a peanut butter and jelly sandwich from a set of instructions. They began by carefully spreading peanut butter on one slice of bread and jelly on the other. Then they commenced to join the slices and finish. The details are fuzzy now after 25 years or so, but somehow, they always managed to wind up with the peanut butter and jelly on the outside of the sandwich, and the clean side of the bread inside. The best part (from a child's vantage) was that they always seemed confused about just why their sandwiches didn't come together correctly.

Even at six years old, we knew full well what their problem was: They just didn't know that stuff in a sandwich went *between* the bread, not *outside* it.

And, of course, we laughed; who didn't know how to make a sandwich? We would roll our eyes as we watched the characters read the instructions to ensure that they used the correct materials ("Peanut butter...*check*! Jelly...*check*! Bread...*check*! Another piece of bread...*check*! Spreader knife...*check*!) and followed the right process ("Spread the peanut butter on one piece of bread...*check*! Spread jelly on the other bread...*check*!), only to muff the last part ("Now bring the two pieces together...um, Bert? Something's wrong here...").

Clearly, we knew they were missing a very important part of their instructions: Put the bread together *with the peanut butter and jelly between the slices*. And because they kept following the directions without thinking about them, they muffed it up time and again.

For a six-year-old, watching someone do the same thing over and over again and continue to miss the obviousness of his error was hilarious. At that age, there's nothing funnier than someone being dumb.

However, when you get to be an adult, this kind of thinking becomes a problem. A very wise man once said that insanity consists of doing the same thing over and over again and expecting different results. It's all well and good to read the instructions—after all, they're there for a reason—but it's quite another thing to follow them so slavishly that common sense is neglected.

Given the recent surge in networking, it might be possible to believe that you could build a network simply by purchasing the parts and following the instructions that explain how to insert tab A into slot B and so forth. To a certain extent, such a perception is merited. It is possible to purchase the parts and assemble them into a network. However, if you are working with a business or organizational network, and you want to get started on the right foot, it's necessary to approach the various sets of instructions you'll receive—with products, in books, advice from friends, what-have-you—with a healthy skepticism. As noted in the preceding hour, you are the person who knows what your networking needs are, not the rest of the world. One-size-fits-all network prescriptions from consultants and manufacturers sound wonderful, but what you really learn from them is that the consultant's competency is in network A and that manufacturer B really wants you to purchase its products...neither of which has any regard for the unique requirements of your network. It's a classic case of "If you want a thing done right, do it yourself." Otherwise, you'll end up wondering how the peanut butter and jelly wound up on the outside of the sandwich....

That's what this hour is about: learning to design a network based on your needs, goals, and expectations. This hour also tries to codify some of the more common pitfalls of network design, which, unlike most other pursuits, do not always share a one-to-one correlation with common sense.

Of the best practices discussed in the previous hour, the two most important are capacity planning and interoperability. Here's why: Capacity planning includes a multitude of tasks, among them a willingness to consider that designing anything is a process. While you're in the process of designing a network, it's very easy to fall prey to a common trap: thinking that the network will be finished. As an artist acquaintance of mine says, everything is a process. Nothing is finished until you arbitrarily decide you've put enough time into it for the return you'll derive. Networks are like anything else in that regard—they grow, evolve, and change during the design process in response to a variety of factors. If you're going to plan a network successfully, you have to try to build as many open-ended solutions as possible. Keeping your options open is tremendously valuable, particularly when technology changes as fast as it does.

Interoperability, or the capability of components to work together, is what keeps your options open. If your components work together according to networking standards, there's much less to go awry.

Finally, try to keep a mental picture of what you're building in your head. If you remain vigilant and aware of the factors that affect your network, you're less likely to overlook a news item that affects your network planning or a fact that can have an impact on what you're doing. If you consciously try to remain aware of the events on the periphery of networking, you're less likely to misstep when you design your network. And with the cost and complexity of networking, that is no small accomplishment.

In this hour, you'll have the opportunity to learn the process of designing a network. It's a seven-step process (at least the way it's organized here):

- Identifying the global uses of the network
- Listing what tasks have to happen at which systems
- Determining whether client/server or peer-to-peer is what you need
- Diagramming the network
- Reviewing your plans
- Writing a specification
- Building the network

Step 1: Identifying the Uses of Your Network

Every network is different. That point, as simple as it is, cannot be overemphasized. Just as every human being is different, or every snowflake is different, every network is different. Networking is one of the few nonartistic human endeavors in which every system, once created, grows in its own way.

Why? Because every network has a collection of individual users who, being human, bring their own baggage to the use of the network. It is the users working in productive concert with the network designers who collectively make a network usable and functional (or conversely, dysfunctional and counterproductive). So at the very beginning of the process, you have to define the purpose (and hence, the goals) for the network.

Defining the Organizational Purpose

What does your organization do? Are you a writer who works from home and has to network to ensure that the rest of the family has access to much-constrained computer resources? Are you a member of a small consulting firm that uses computers to handle job requests, client tracking, and billing? Are you in a department of a large corporation that has been given the mandate to automate its job processes? Or do you perform one of the zillion other jobs out there?

No matter what your organization does, its network has to accomplish only one task to be considered successful. It has to ensure that what your organization does, it can do better, faster, more efficiently, and more reliably with the assistance of a network. If the network doesn't do that, it will be a failure, regardless of the quantity of premium technology and quality of service. Keep this in mind as you progress through this chapter; it's probably the single most important fact here. The network is not about technology, no matter how much a techno-fanatic may want it to be. Networks are about getting things done, primarily by people who could not care less whether they do their work on a network or not.

Informational Interviews

The first order of business is determining the reason why you or your organization requires a network. This process can be likened to a journey of a thousand miles starting with a single step; like all journeys, it has the potential for peril or chaos because you have to reconcile management's reasons for networking with users' needs. The first steps on your journey lead to the desk of the most senior manager to whom you can get access. Make an appointment to meet with him or her and talk about two things: what the organization's core business is now, and how he or she wants to change or improve the business processes that support the core business. Make certain that the senior executive knows why you want this information; chances are that this will open a venerable floodgate you'll be hard pressed to fully document.

This meeting should *not* involve opining, blue-skying, or other discussion of what a network can do. In the main, this meeting has nothing whatsoever to do with networking. Instead, it's an informational interview. Your task during this initial period is to listen with great acuity to the senior manager's perception of the core business and his or her ideas on how it might work better. Take lots of notes. Rewrite them. You'll find that the clarity of your notes increases with time, as does your memory of the interview's high and low points.

Any questions you pose should be open ended. Leading the witness gets objections in courts for a reason: Doing so tends to lead to preconceived or preordained conclusions, from which you will learn nothing. Instead, try to see whether the manager has a vision, and try to understand what that vision is and what its ramifications are. As much as they are maligned in popular culture, senior management often displays a pleasantly surprising ability to succinctly capture and enumerate multiple concepts, often in a pithy (but occasionally management-jargon-laden) fashion. As well, they tend to be people of few words—the higher up in the organization you go, the more people make each word work for them. So listen hard because this is the closest you're likely to get to a mission statement.

> For what it's worth, note the suggestion that you interview a real person instead of reading a mission statement. Mission statements are fine, but they tend to be written by committee and subsequently lose a lot of passion and fire. To get a buy-in to your network proposal, you have to be able to bring some fire to the process. You'll get that fire if, after interviewing people, you can clearly see the organizational issues and how networking can help move the organization to where it wants to be, doing what it needs to be doing.

Once you've interviewed the senior executive and documented his or her responses, start talking to the rank and file or the folks on the production floor. Sit with them and find out what they do. Be up-front about the purpose of your visit; it will help break down suspicion that you're there to increase their workload. If you can, try to work with several employees over the course of a couple of days to see what it is that they do and how they do it.

Once you understand some of the various tasks necessary to ensure that the organization fulfills its purpose, it's time to ask the employee what, specifically, would make their jobs easier. Don't fish for computer-related improvements; instead, get concrete, productivity-enhancing, job-life-improving answers like "If I could find a way to track all the phone conversations everyone has with Mr. X, I would be better prepared when he calls me." Clearly, whatever gives rise to this kind of response doesn't necessarily require a computer to rectify (a public notebook could also work quite well in this example), but it offers an insight into a deeper question: *How can we all have the same information so that our clients don't think we're clueless?* Such a question can be parlayed into a piece of a *specification*, which is discussed later in this hour.

The ultimate goal of these informational interviews is to derive a set of visions, current behaviors, desired results, and desired processes. Once you have these, you can attempt to distill the deeper organizational issues out of the mash of answers. Typically, you will wind up with a couple of commonplace wants and desires, such as the following:

- Increased responsiveness to customers
- Increased ease of access to customer data
- More up-to-date information
- Capability to handle an increase in business
- Increased flexibility in order handling

These are typical goals of an organization, but they are generic. It's very likely that the responses you receive will be more specific than these, and will strictly address the issues your management and your users face every day.

Quantifying the Network

Once you have interviewed people about what the organization does, you're ready to take your first list—the core issues that management and workers want to address—and bring it to the people you interviewed the first time. Allow your interviewees to look at the list and see whether they have anything to add. If they do, ensure that it hasn't already been addressed in the global set of criteria you've created; if it hasn't, add it. Once they sign off on the list, you're ready to begin quantifying the network parameters.

First, *determine how many users your network will have*. Do not mistake this number for the number of computers on the network; that's the next question, and the two are emphatically not the same thing. One computer can adequately serve multiple users if they don't have to interact with it on a constant, real-time daily basis. The one-computer-per-desktop model works for many offices, but it doesn't hold true everywhere. For example, in a factory floor shop, one computer used for laser-wand barcode inventory control may serve 20 or 30 users. A healthcare practice may have a few public computers so that doctors can key their patient reports, but they would probably not be dedicated systems. Instead, each doctor would log on, briefly enter a report, and then go on to the next patient.

In any case, determine how many users the network will require. It's usually safe to add a couple of users if the organization is growing, but the main point of this exercise is to get the count of users who will be on the network when it is rolled out.

After you have figured out how many users you have, look at who those users are. Are they management who will use the computer primarily for administrative purposes such as memo-writing and messaging, will they be office workers, or will they be people on a production floor? This is a very important part of the process because it leads to the next question: *How many computers will the network have initially?* Actually, the question is really this: *How many computers will have only one user, and how many will be shared by many users?*

Users who need word processing and spreadsheet software have a very different relationship with computers than workers on a shop floor. Typically, the office users who do word-processing and spreadsheets work with the computer constantly and dynamically, one user to a computer. Workers on a shop floor interact with computers in other ways— many users need to interact with a single computer according to a few preordained, highly limited routines.

Once you have determined how your users will interact with the network, it is possible to *determine how many computers your network will have*. It's a simple matter: Look at how your users will interact with the network and determine whether the ratio of computers to users is one-to-one or whether it will be one-to-many. If you have a one-to-one ratio, your user count equals (or, in client/server networks, is just shy of) the number of computers. If you have a one-to-many ratio, it's quite likely that you will have to allocate computers according to job function. In other words, if you have a group of users that has a computer only for checking work in and out with a barcoding system (common in some manufacturing settings) or for checking in parts picked in a warehouse, you'll have only as many computers for that group as will concurrently use them. If you have one user queuing up at a time, one computer will do. If you have ten users queuing up and their tasks aren't fast (say, more than half-a-minute each), you may want several computers. Once again, the number of computers you allocate to user groups will depend on your organizational needs; they are the final arbiter. As with anything else, think it through and try to *rightsize* (that is, design enough capacity but not too much or too little) your design.

Step 2: Listing Which Tasks Happen at Which Computers

The second step in the network-design process seems terribly obvious: Know which applications and tasks have to be performed at each of the computers on your network. Unfortunately, it's not quite as straightforward as that; this step is less about following the workflow trail than it is about continuing the rightsizing process.

If you had to go out and cut down a giant sequoia tree (and I hope you won't; they're pretty rare), would you go out with an ax and a rope and expect to do the job adequately? Probably not. A giant sequoia is a couple hundred feet tall, 30 or 40 feet around, and probably weighs a whole lot more than your rope's breaking point. Not to mention that it would take a huge amount of time to cut down with an ax alone. In this case, your resources would be too small.

Likewise, if you had to eliminate a mosquito buzzing around your bedroom at night, would you use a laser-tracking, high-speed, deck-mounted gun system like the Phalanx guns the Navy uses to shoot down incoming missiles? Of course, you wouldn't. (Mosquitoes are annoying, but not that annoying.) The Phalanx would be far more firepower than you need, and with its weight, it wouldn't pass the local building code unless it were mounted on the foundation.

Clearly, in both cases, you have to *rightsize* the tools to match the task at hand. In networking, rightsizing is a process that starts early on and continues well after the initial rollout of the system. It starts with knowing the physical limits of your network (how many users, how many computers), but it certainly doesn't end there. It's not enough to know how many systems are out there; you also have to know how powerful each computer should be, and what each computer should be capable of.

For example, the barcoding computers mentioned at the end of step 1 generally don't have to be very powerful; they're doing one task that does not require much processing horsepower or memory. Neither do they need soundcards (add-in adapters needed for a computer to process and play back sound through external speakers) or particularly high-end video adapters.

On the other hand, some users will need all these things and more. Let's look at a couple of hypothetical cases that illustrate how to determine the quantity of horsepower and the range of features a given network system will require.

The Many-User Computer

Computers used by many users can be built minimally, as in the warehouse barcode example, or with all the bells and whistles. As with any other system, the amount of power and features depends on the application.

Simple Needs—Simple Computer

In the warehouse example, the purpose of the computer is to handle inventory recording for items picked off warehouse shelves for shipping. Typically, this task is accomplished through the use of a barcode scanner of some sort—you may be familiar with these scanners from the grocery checkout or a library counter where books are checked out with a laser barcode wand. Each time a barcoded item passes the scanner, the computer registers a transaction and records the transaction in a centralized transaction server. In this model, the *server* computer must be very powerful, but the computers out on the floor can be inexpensive, low-powered systems. Why? Because they run only one application (the barcode-scanning application) and do not have to interact with users on any basis other than that application. Typically, the barcode situation can be handled (in late 1997 terms) with a 486 or low-end Pentium system with very little memory or disk space. This specification is appropriate to the application; you don't need a high-end Pentium III running Windows NT for the client. Instead, you need something minimal and reliable with the capacity to connect to the network.

Considerable On-Site Needs—Powerful Computer

Fast forward to a bank's customer information kiosk in a mall. This system is also multiuser—but it operates with an entirely different purpose. The warehouse system is designed to allow warehouse item-pickers to check in what they've picked for inventory purposes and is deliberately kept as simple as possible to ensure its use and reliability. Information kiosks, on the other hand, are sales tools. Like most sales tools, they have to be fast, somewhat flashy, and capable of interacting with the user according to the user's desire.

In a retail information kiosk, a user could tap a button on a graphical user interface touch-screen that allows him or her to select from a menu containing several items: information about accounts, mortgage services, home equity loans, business services, and so forth. The user is likely to be greeted with video and sound that entices him or her to continue using the system. Once the user has made a selection and found some of the information he or she needs, the user might want to print out that information—so a kiosk might also have a printer.

Such a kiosk might also allow online banking for users with the correct bank-debit-card and password ID. This means that the system must be secure—in other words, it has to be capable of encrypting the user's data before the data is sent out over the network back to the bank's central transaction-processing computers.

In this scenario, the computer inside the kiosk is no minimal system. It has to be a powerful computer, possibly workstation-class: a Pentium II or faster with a lot of memory (64 megabytes or more) and *multimedia* (video and sound) capabilities. Speed is also necessary for the on-the-fly encryption required for secure transactions. Finally, the computer has to be hooked up to a printer so that it can print the user's receipts and datasheets.

Low On-Site Needs—Considerable Network Needs

Another multiuser system might be a computer in a healthcare clinic. After a patient visit, a doctor logs on briefly, records the clinical data about the patient's visit in a database application, and logs out. The computer used for this application, unlike the other two examples, must support multiple user network logins and a proprietary database interface at the workstation. It does not have to be hugely powerful, nor does it require multimedia capabilities. It simply has to be a network workstation with a screen, monitor, main box, and keyboard (and perhaps a mouse).

Clearly, systems that support multiple users at a single console (keyboard, touch-screen, keypad, barcode, or other mode of interaction) depend entirely on their application to determine the amount of power and features they require. In general, there are several rules of thumb when determining how powerful a system must be:

- You must determine whether the system will do one preset task with little user interactivity or if it will cater to multiple users.
- You must figure out how much power you need to accomplish the task. Do you need a high-end computer or will an older (and more cost-effective) system with only a few megabytes of memory do the job adequately?
- You must determine whether the system needs any multimedia capabilities.

Single-User Computers

Single-user computers generally occur in offices. Whether an office is physical or virtual, an increasing number of office workers use computers on a day-to-day basis. This shift in computer use has created a new class of office workers called *knowledge workers* because their currency is dealing with information and formatting, managing, and analyzing data.

Given the increasing focus on high-tech jobs and high-tech workforces, it's easy to lose sight of the fact that knowledge workers are not a homogeneous mass. Depending on the nature of their jobs, they tend to require higher-end computers to begin with, but they also have widely varying connectivity requirements. For example, some workers may be able to leave their work behind at the end of the day and require no remote access; other users may require two or more computers to be able to do their jobs.

Naturally, this is a rightsizing issue—if you have to provide more than one computer for some users, it's going to affect your capacity planning to a great degree. The following hypothetical examples should provide you with some idea of what is involved in the single-user computer office worker/knowledge worker sphere.

Average User—Average Power

Let's start with the simplest configuration: a user with one desktop computer permanently attached to the network. Let's call this user Sonia and say she's in Accounting. She does all her work in the office, connected to the company network. What are her computing requirements?

Well, first, she'll be running an accounting package, which generally requires a reasonable amount of computational horsepower—but not a huge amount. Her computer should have a mid-to-high-end processor with a lot of memory (processor and memory are not quantified here because they change so quickly—but the principle of rightsizing and adapting to the situation still holds). Sonia needs enough power to run the accounting application locally, but she has to be connected to the network so that her data files can be stored on a server's disk volume from which they can be easily backed up.

Power User—Powerful Computer(s)

Now let's consider the next user: Karen, the financial analyst. Financial analysts typically require tremendous amounts of power because they tend to design enormous spreadsheet models that are recalculated on a regular basis. As a result, her desktop computer will be as powerful as current technology allows, with a powerful processor and a great deal of memory. Also, because analysts generally tend to require advanced technology, Karen will have a multimedia setup that can support sound and video.

All her applications (spreadsheet, word processor, and so forth) are stored on her local hard drive, and all her data (documents, spreadsheets, investment memoranda, and so on) are stored on the network. This arrangement is relatively common on networks in which users have a lot of autonomy because it provides maximum performance at the desktop and maximum security for data.

That sounds like a lot, but it's only the beginning. Analysts also travel on business a lot. When they're traveling, they need a second computer, which is almost always a laptop. Ideally, the laptop replicates all the applications installed on the desktop machine, albeit with a few important contrasts. First, the laptop has to be capable of connecting to the network in two ways: directly through a LAN cable and indirectly through phone-line-based remote access. Second, files may be stored on the laptop while a user is offsite and disconnected from the network; this is not desirable for any other systems, and is only used in this configuration for convenience.

Laptops do not generally fit neatly into overall network schemes. It's not because they are not standard desktop computers; instead, laptops are an oddity because of the way they connect and disconnect from the network using *PC card* network cards and modems. From a network administration perspective, laptops represent a difficult tension between convenience for the user and manageability for the network administrator. Whether or not you centralize administration—and how—is one of the chief decisions to make in administering a network, and is dealt with in the next section.

This isn't to say that it isn't possible to integrate laptops into a network plan. Just be aware that doing so requires a great deal of planning. Expect to deploy docking stations with each laptop, and expect to spend time educating your mobile users.

Step 3: Determining the Degree of Centralization

There are times to centralize administration and security, and there are times not to. There are times when it is worthwhile to go the whole nine yards toward establishing a central administrative authority, and times when the return from doing so isn't worth the effort or expense. When you're designing a network, you must determine whether or not you want the ability to administer your network from a central point.

Clearly, you won't necessarily want to administer every system if your network consists of only a few computers (less than 10 or so) in the same location. The cost of network management software (software that can handle configuration management and software distribution, among other tasks) is altogether too high to justify on a small, local network. On the other hand, even for a small network, you may want to find some way of centralizing some functions such as file services, security, and backup. See Hour 21, "Network Admin Tips and Tricks," for help.

Once the design for your network grows beyond the small-network model (maybe you've got a small WAN or a LAN that has more than 15 or so computers), you really have to begin considering whether or not you want a central authority. But what is a central authority? In really basic terms, it means that you've decided to build a client/server network rather than a peer network. Generally, a simple small-network authority is a server that stores files—handles user accounts, login authentication, and security—and in general acts as a clearinghouse for the activity and work generated on the network.

Overall, peer networks lack security. Files are usually stored in a haphazard manner, users can easily get access to things they shouldn't have access to, and the files are usually poorly backed up.

Review Hour 2, "The Benefits of Networking," and Hour 5, "Network Concepts," for more information about peer-style security concerns.

9

Client/server networks, by contrast, are secure. Their files are usually stored in a central location and are backed up on a regular basis. User access tends to be controllable. As a result, there are myriad upsides of even basic centralization:

- Easier access to files
- Stronger security
- Easier backup
- Easier configuration management and standardization of workstations

Easier Access to Files

Imagine that you've popped a button from a shirt. You have to sew it back on. Simple enough, right? But suppose that the needles are stored in a drawer in the kitchen, the thread is in a basket in the den, and the thimbles are someplace in the kids' junk drawer. Clearly, you'll have to jump some hurdles before you even start to do the work of sewing on the button.

In the same fashion, files stored across multiple workstations can present a problem for network users. If the user has to put together a contract, he or she might have to find a contract file stored on Jennifer's machine, a form letter stored on Jeannine's, and a financial statement stored on Mark's system. This also presumes that our user knows where the files are stored (which is not likely in a decentralized system). This scenario is not unlike the button example, in which the work of locating the pieces needed to accomplish the task is equal to the work to be done in the first place.

To centralize access to files, you have to build a *file server*, or a server dedicated to sharing its disk space with a collection of users for file storage. Typically, a file server requires a powerful processor, a lot of memory, and as much disk space as you can afford.

Notice that no processor or amount of memory is specified for a file server. This is because technology changes so rapidly that any recommendations made here would be out of date by the time you read this. So be aware of the current power standards when you're selecting a file server.

There are some baselines, though: If you're using Windows NT Server or NetWare, you'll need a Pentium 200 or so and at least 64M of RAM. Unix requirements are similar, but because of the variance in requirements among different Unix vendors, you'll have to consult the vendor for specifics.

Stronger Security

File servers usually have some security built in so that they can ensure that access to files is limited to those users who *should* have access to them. Typically, file server security for PC-based operating systems follow some fairly simple rules:

- **Inheritance**. Security inheritance works similarly to financial inheritance; what a parent has can be inherited by a child unless it is blocked by third parties. In security inheritance, a user gets access to a particular directory (for example, F:\DIRECTRY). Whatever access a user has to F:\DIRECTRY is inherited by any and all subdirectories of F:\DIRECTRY (for example, F:\DIRECTRY\ONE, F:\DIRECTRY\TWO, and so forth). Inheritance is a useful tool to ensure that a user has as much access as he or she requires to a given part of the server's disk.

- **Access rules**. In general, users are limited to three levels of access to a given file or directory on a file server:

  - No Access, which often means that users cannot even see the file or directory
  - Read-Only Access, which means that users can view the contents of a file or directory but cannot modify it
  - Read-Write Access, which means that a user has the access rights to view and modify files and directories

Various network operating systems allow for additions to these three basic access rights, but by and large it should be possible to ensure reasonably good security using only these three rules.

Access Rules: A Simple Example

Here is a structure that is well tested and simple for designing user access to a file server's drive. This structure allows the user security for his own files and provides reasonable security for any application data installed on the network as well. Every user has a private directory that no other user can see (except the administrator), a directory that provides read-only access to other users, and a directory that provides full access to other users.

The general rule when figuring out how to set up access is to follow the same rules you'd use to set up physical security: Provide the least degree of access users require to get their jobs done. If they need additional access, it can be provided as long as the powers-that-be approve it. Otherwise, user access is limited to the least necessary set of options.

In this example, the file server has a \programs directory in which all network applications are stored and an \administrative directory in which software installation packages and administrative utilities are stored. Both of these directories are read-only to network users; they are read-write only for users who have administrative rights.

The \users directory, on the other hand, is a curious melange of access rights. Each user has three subdirectories: open, private, and share. The open subdirectory is read-write to the world. The share subdirectory is read-only, and private isn't even visible to other users. To ensure that rights to these directories are properly doled out, it's advantageous to create groups of users (if your network OS supports it), assign appropriate base rights to the group (in this case, read-write access to everyone's open subdirectory and read-only access to everyone's share subdirectory). Then simply add users to the group to give them the assigned rights. This approach prevents you from accidentally giving any single user too many rights to data.

Table 9.1 shows this sample directory structure graphically. It's based on the tree-structure that you see when you open Windows File Manager, the Macintosh Finder, or Unix X-Window file manager, xfm.

TABLE 9.1   Directory Structure for Access Rights in a Windows or Netware Network

\ (root of network drive)	\users	\joe\open (read-write access for other users)
		\joe\share (read-only access for other users)
		\joe\private (no access for other users)
	\programs	\wordprocessor (read-write access for all users)
		\groupcalendar (read-write access for all users)
	\administrative	\installs (read-write access for administrator, read-only access for other users; used to install software)
		\utilities (read-write access for administrator, read-only access for other users; used to manage the network)

Setting up a system such as this before putting the file server out for general consumption provides a great way to contain chaos. If you provide a simple directory structure and a rigorous set of access rules that are clearly enunciated and well enforced, then the groundwork for strong network security is already laid.

Unix Permissions

The permissions that are cited above are the ones that are used on PC-based operating systems. Unix works the same, for all practical purposes, but is (in the author's opinion) much easier to understand and maintain.

Every file in a Unix system is owned by a specific user and group. By doing a "long listing" (equivalent to typing *dir* in a Windows or NetWare OS), the permissions are on display and very easy to see, as the following example shows:

```
-rwxrwxrw   1 root        sys        15872 Jun 16  1997 bigfile
```

All the way to the left, there's one character. That character displays the type of file. If it's just a dash ("-"), it means that the file is a regular plain old file, the kind in which we store text and stuff. If it's a "d", then it's a directory. If it's a "b" or "c," it's a block or character device file, which means that it's a special file that the system uses to access disks and tapes and other assorted input/output (usually called i/o). The next nine characters are used to determine which users have read, write, and execute permission on the file. The first three are the permissions for the owner of the file (in the example, root is the user in the sys group), who can read, write, and execute the file. The second set of three characters determines what the rights of the users in the owning group are (in this case, members of the sys group who are NOT the user root, who owns the file). The last three are the permissions for the "world," which is to say any user who is neither the user of the file nor a member of the owning group.

Although all of this is done at the command line, it's easy to understand in principle. And it's certainly much easier to figure out and set the permissions of files using this method than in a graphical environment where determining file permissions can take several mouse-clicks.

Easier Backup

If all network users' files are stored on a centralized server, they can be backed up simply by duplicating the server's hard drive to tape. If that doesn't sound like a compelling advantage, here's an example that will explain why it is.

Assume that your network has 50 user workstations. If all the users store their files on their workstations, you'll have to back up all or part of their hard drives to ensure that no data is lost if a system crashes. Further suppose that each user has 25 megabytes of files on their workstations' hard drives (for many users, a very conservative estimate). Backing up this quantity of files across the network for this many users could take 10 or 12 hours and be a nightmare to manage.

By contrast, backing up a server's hard drive with an attached tape drive can take as little as an hour or so (assuming that you have the same quantity of data as in the preceding example: 25M × 50 users = 1.25 gigabytes). Clearly, backing up files from a single server to a tape drive takes less time and is more controllable.

There are many varieties of tape drives:

- 4mm digital audio tape (DAT) drives that handle up to 8 gigabytes of storage
- Digital linear tape (DLT) that handles 20 to 40 gigabytes of storage
- Advanced intelligent tape (AIT) that backs up as much as 50 gigabytes per tape

Most tape drives handle only one tape at a time. However, devices called *tape changers* can handle whole libraries of hundreds or thousands of tapes. The kind of tape drive you select depends on what your needs are today and what you expect them to be in the foreseeable future. Remember that the amount of data that seems huge today will seem a pittance tomorrow.

Easier Configuration Management

Storing files on a server offers compelling advantages. However, there is more to centralized management of a network than simply storing files on a server. As a guideline, if you have more than 15 workstations, it's necessary to find a way to inventory the hardware, audit the software on the hard drive, install new software, and ensure that the workstation adheres to configuration standards.

Configuration management is the art (or science) of using a central console to ensure that user workstations have the correct hardware and software installed, and that the software and hardware are set up according to consensus and preset standards. Configuration management software is complex, make no mistake about it. It's usually composed of a hugely complex database with a proprietary front end that allows a network administrator to view and modify the configurations of users' workstations. Most management software requires that each system have an *agent* (a piece of software that interacts with the administrative database) installed on the workstation; often, agents can be installed automatically as a user logs on to the network.

There is a payoff, however, for mastering the intricacies of configuration management software. Network administrators who install and rigorously use configuration management software report that they have better control over their users' workstations. They can inventory the network very quickly, and install and upgrade software for many users simultaneously. In addition, they can set up alarms that register unauthorized tampering, which helps keep the theft of hardware and unauthorized employee-installed software under control.

Even if you do not elect to have an in-house network administrator, you can still benefit from configuration management software. Many third-party consultants sell network troubleshooting services. If the consultant is authorized to access your network to perform upgrades and fixes, you can successfully outsource your network management.

The Ramifications of Centralization

Once you decide whether or not your network is going to be large enough to merit centralizing some functions, it's time to assess the ramifications of centralization.

Acquiring Additional Servers

If you decide it's important to have a central system to store files, you'll need least one other machine added to the quantity of systems you'll have on your network. If you have multiple sites in a WAN, you'll have to multiply the number of server systems by at least the number of sites the WAN connects; if any of those sites are large, you may require several servers, based on usage and performance requirements.

Choosing Operating Systems

Having a server implies a server's network operating system. The three current leaders in the PC world are Novell NetWare, Microsoft Windows NT Server, and various flavors of Unix (Sun's Solaris and the Santa Cruz Operation's SCO Unix/SCO Open Desktop are common). Of the three, Windows NT is the simplest to install and administer and Unix is the most complex; NetWare sits right between them. Before you choose, read the chapter on each network operating system (see Hours 15, 16, and 17) to help you make an informed choice.

Choosing a Topology

Whether your network is going to be client/server or peer, you have to select a topology. For all but the very smallest networks, some variety of star-configuration Ethernet (10BASE-T, 100BASE-T) is probably the simplest and least expensive choice. Only the very smallest networks should use a bus topology (10BASE-2); it's useful for learning and limited application, but it doesn't scale up well.

Choosing Network Management Software

If your network is going to be large, you'll have to find a way to manage it. A variety of manufacturers, including McAfee, Microsoft, Tivoli, IBM, Digital, Hewlett-Packard, and others, make high-quality network management tools. Many packages are modular, so you don't have to purchase the whole package to get the modules you need.

Opting for No Centralization

If you've decided not to centralize your network, make certain that you have sufficient resources to support as many workstations as you will have. Also, if you're not going to centralize the network, it makes exceptionally good sense to locate and retain a full-time or part-time network administrator; peer networks periodically present problems beyond the capability of the local user to solve.

Step 4: Making It Real—Drawing the Network

By the time you get to this step, you should know the following:

- The organizational purpose of the network
- The specifics of the network's use (which users do which tasks)
- The quantity of both users and computers
- Whether or not the network will be centralized or decentralized
- The network topology you plan to use (Ethernet, Token Ring, FDDI, and so on)

Of all the steps in this process, this is the most fun. Once you know the basics of your network, you're ready to go to the whiteboard (or easel). Get a set of markers in at least four or five colors, go to the whiteboard, and then start drawing your network.

> For what it's worth, a whiteboard is much more valuable than paper for this process because it allows you to make revisions on-the-fly without starting from scratch each time.

Drawing the Logical Network Diagram

The first drawing you make is the *logical diagram*. It details the applications that have to run on workstations and which resources workstations have to be able to access.

1. Start by drawing a workstation for each type of user (for example, one warehouse floor computer, one analyst's computer, one accounting computer, one secretary's computer, and so on). Just make a circle for each computer; draw them in a line across the top of the whiteboard or page (see Figure 9.1).

FIGURE 9.1
The first stage of the logical network diagram.

2. Below each computer, list the applications it has to run (see Figure 9.2). This could include word processing, spreadsheets, email, scheduling, and more for a user's desktop computer, or a single application for a dedicated machine, such as a factory or warehouse inventory computer or an in-office computer dedicated to routing email.

FIGURE 9.2
The second stage of the logical network diagram, showing the applications needed.

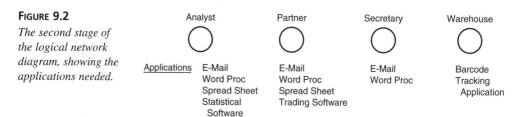

3. Make a list of the resources each workstation computer will share. In general, peer networking has a lot of these shared resources (such as printers, scanners, shared modems, and so on); client/server networks will have fewer shared resources. No matter whether you've elected to use client/server or peer, add these resources into your diagram (see Figure 9.3).

FIGURE 9.3
The third stage of the logical network diagram, showing the shared resources.

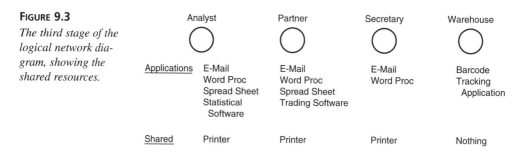

4. If the system will participate in a network-wide security scheme, note which group of users has login access to the various pieces of the system (see Figure 9.4). For example, business desktop users can log in to the file server, warehouse supervisors can log into the transaction server, administrators can log in to anything anywhere. This step helps ensure that you provide the correct levels of security.

FIGURE **9.4**

The fourth stage of the logical network diagram, showing security concerns mapped.

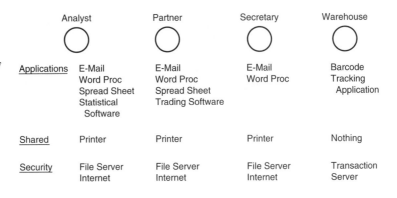

	Analyst	Partner	Secretary	Warehouse
Applications	E-Mail Word Proc Spread Sheet Statistical Software	E-Mail Word Proc Spread Sheet Trading Software	E-Mail Word Proc	Barcode Tracking Application
Shared	Printer	Printer	Printer	Nothing
Security	File Server Internet	File Server Internet	File Server Internet	Transaction Server

5. Add the workstation operating system to the bottom of the list (see Figure 9.5). The OS is usually something like MS-DOS, Windows of some stripe, OS/2, or Macintosh. Although Unix can be used as a client, outside of academic computing centers and high-end engineering workstations, it is (sadly) not common as a workstation OS. If you have more than one workstation OS, ensure that you have more than one computer drawn—each workstation OS should be shown on a separate machine.

FIGURE **9.5**

The fifth stage of the logical network diagram, showing the operating system for workstations.

	Analyst	Partner	Secretary	Warehouse
Applications	E-Mail Word Proc Spread Sheet Statistical Software	E-Mail Word Proc Spread Sheet Trading Software	E-Mail Word Proc	Barcode Tracking Application
Shared	Printer	Printer	Printer	Nothing
Security	File Server Internet	File Server Internet	File Server Internet	Transaction Server
OS	Windows NT Workstation	OS/2	Windows 95	MS-DOS

6. Add the quantity of each type of workstation to the bottom of the list (see Figure 9.6).

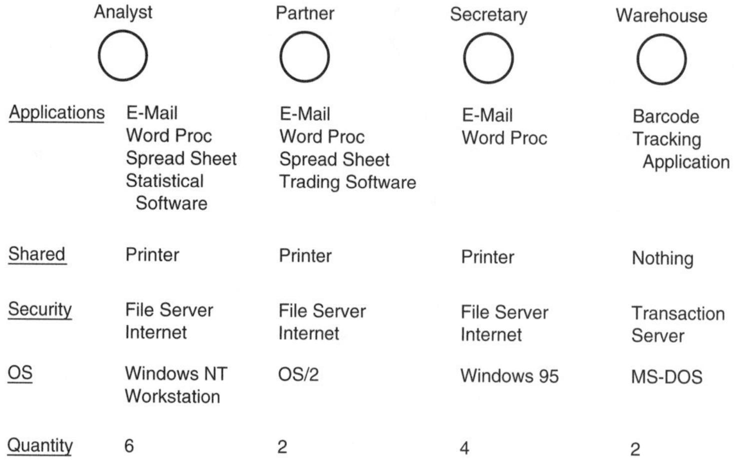

FIGURE 9.6

The sixth stage of the logical network diagram, showing the quantities of each type of workstation.

	Analyst	Partner	Secretary	Warehouse
	○	○	○	○
Applications	E-Mail Word Proc Spread Sheet Statistical Software	E-Mail Word Proc Spread Sheet Trading Software	E-Mail Word Proc	Barcode Tracking Application
Shared	Printer	Printer	Printer	Nothing
Security	File Server Internet	File Server Internet	File Server Internet	Transaction Server
OS	Windows NT Workstation	OS/2	Windows 95	MS-DOS
Quantity	6	2	4	2

Now your workstations are quantified. If you are going to build a client/server network and will require one or more servers, add the servers in at the bottom of the diagram and list the applications and resources each server provides to the network. If you are building a WAN and have to incorporate routers and so forth to hook the LANs together, draw the routers in at the side (see Figure 9.7).

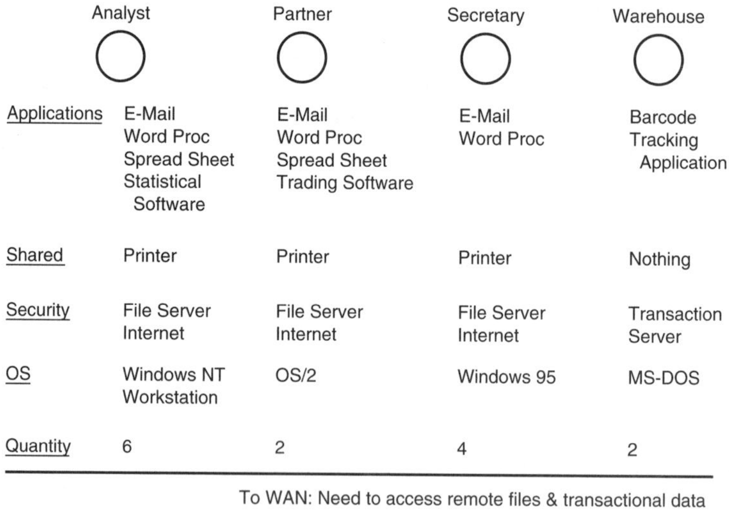

FIGURE 9.7

The logical network diagram, showing a method for indicating WAN or MAN connections.

	Analyst	Partner	Secretary	Warehouse
	○	○	○	○
Applications	E-Mail Word Proc Spread Sheet Statistical Software	E-Mail Word Proc Spread Sheet Trading Software	E-Mail Word Proc	Barcode Tracking Application
Shared	Printer	Printer	Printer	Nothing
Security	File Server Internet	File Server Internet	File Server Internet	Transaction Server
OS	Windows NT Workstation	OS/2	Windows 95	MS-DOS
Quantity	6	2	4	2

To WAN: Need to access remote files & transactional data

Now comes the fun part. Draw lines from each workstation type to each system to which that workstation type requires access. In other words, if an accounting PC requires file storage resources on a file server, select a colored marker, draw a line between the two systems, and write the name of the resource the workstation client will use. If a workstation has a shared printer, ensure that other systems that have to use it are connected to it using lines of a different color than the first. If a router provides connectivity between the network and the workstations, but must first route data through a server, draw that full path as well in yet another color.

Make certain that each connection documents the network protocols that will carry the traffic. For example, a great deal of Microsoft networking is done using NetBEUI; NetWare uses IPX; Internet-standards-compliant networks use TCP/IP. Many networks use a single protocol, but it is entirely possible for multiple protocols to run side by side on a network (that situation is just not very efficient). If you're not certain which protocol a particular service will use, put a question mark next to its connection line and make a note to find out as soon as possible which protocols will work there. Remember: Finding out what you don't know is almost as important as finding out what you *do* know.

When you're done, you've got...abstract string art! Actually, you have created a web of dependencies you can use to determine which computers need access to which resources (see Figure 9.8). Copy what you've done on the whiteboard into your notebook for future reference.

FIGURE 9.8

An example of a finished logical network diagram.

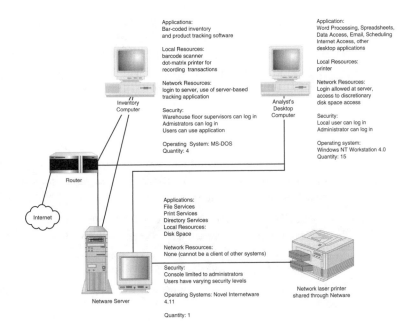

Once you have determined the various resources that have to be shared (which was probably rendered much simpler by drawing it than by trying to create a comprehensive list), you're ready for the next great task: drawing the physical network.

Drawing the Physical Network Diagram

Drawing the physical network really isn't as hard as it sounds. If you already know which clients have to be connected to specific resources and which topology you'll be using, you're halfway there.

1. Start by drawing the physical center of your network (see Figure 9.9).

FIGURE 9.9

The center of the network: the hub or switch.

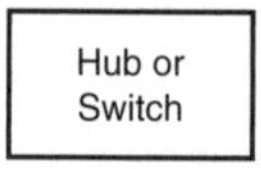

```
+----------+
| Hub or   |
| Switch   |
+----------+
```

If you're using a star configuration (such as Ethernet, Token Ring, or FDDI), the center of your network is the concentrator: a hub, MAU, or switch of some sort. If your network needs only one hub, draw a box and label it as the hub.

If, on the other hand, you will have a lot of users sharing an Ethernet collision domain or Token-Ring segment, you may want to consider adding a switch to segment the network. As you may recall from Hour 3, "Getting Data from Here to There: How Computers Share Data," switches segment networks by reducing the size of the Ethernet collision domain or Token-Ring segment to one segment per port instead of the one-segment-per-whole-hub model that *shared-media* hubs and MAUs use.

In any case, if your network is large and you're trying to fit more than 20 or 30 users on a single hub or set of *stackable hubs* (multiple hubs that can be connected to create one collision domain or segment), consider using a switch. If workstations have to access the network without being slowed down by network traffic, a switch is an appropriate solution.

A switch doesn't have to be large to help you segment your network. An 8- or 10-port switch can be adequate to segment a couple of hubs if it is set up correctly. And because you're *drawing* the network, you're at the ideal stage to consider whether or not you want to segment your network—and how you want to set it up. If you have decided that you need segmentation, draw a box and label it the switch. This is the center of your network.

2. Draw as many boxes as you will have shared media hubs. (Keep in mind that hubs are measured by the number of ports they have; an 8-port hub supports eight workstations, 16 ports support 16 workstations, and so forth.) For performance reasons,

it's a good idea to divide the network into single hubs with no more than 16 ports per segment. Connect lines between the switch and the segments; each of these lines represents a *crossover cable*, or a specially made cable that can be used to connect concentrators together (see Figure 9.10).

FIGURE 9.10

The hub/switch at the center of the network connected to additional hubs. If your network has only one hub, this step is superfluous.

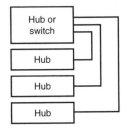

3. Draw the servers and mark them as connected directly to the switch (see Figure 9.11). A server connected directly to a switch offers compelling advantages in terms of performance at the workstation because the server has a direct connection to the port to which the workstation is connected. This holds true even if a workstation is connected through a hub connected to a switch port; the collision domain of individual hubs are usually fairly small, so there isn't much competition for bandwidth.

FIGURE 9.11

Adding servers to the hub/switch diagram.

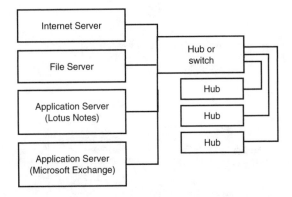

4. Refer to the drawing of the logical network and do some analysis. Look at which workstations require access to which servers and try to group them together.

> If you have a group of users who do not require a great deal of network bandwidth (such as the people who use the barcode or inventory tracking applications mentioned earlier), you can often group them together on a shared hub plugged into a switch port—that will be adequate bandwidth for them. Users who require significant network bandwidth (analysts, financial people, and graphic artists, for example) should be connected in small groups of less than 10 to a shared hub; a better scenario for power users (as these folks are called) is to directly allocate a switch port for each power user if possible.

5. Once you analyze the relative bandwidth requirements of your users, you're ready to start figuring out which class of user has to connect to which device.

   Take the time to think about this. If users don't have sufficient bandwidth initially, they will have network problems and consequently lose faith in the network. It's important to roll out systems that work for the users, otherwise the network has no credibility. Figure 9.12 provides an example.

FIGURE 9.12

The physical network drawing.

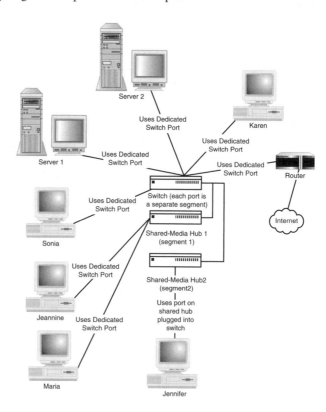

9

Now that you've drawn your network both logically and physically, you have a body of work you can use to see whether or not what you've done makes sense. One of the benefits of working graphically is that you can begin to see how your users are grouped based on common access. If you begin seeing patterns in how users work and you're using a switch, you may elect to extend the pattern and formalize it. For example, all accountants need to have access to the inventory data, so the user group called Accountants is granted that right globally.

Virtual LANs

Additionally, you may have the opportunity to configure your switch in a way to ensure that users have the bandwidth they require; that system administrators can readily control adds, moves, and changes; and best of all, that helps security.

The miraculous configuration that allows these three things is called a VLAN, or Virtual LAN. A VLAN means that a switch has the capability to create several LANs set up in such a fashion that the ports on a specific VLAN can only see each other.

Suppose that you have eight ports in a switch and have eight computers connected to the switch (one computer on each port). The switch can logically support up to four VLANs, because 8 (the number of ports) divided by 2 (the smallest number of computers that can make up a network) equals 4. Suppose that you decide to create four VLANs. Port 1 can be logically set up to see the computer on port 6, and none of the others. Port 2 might see only port 3, and port 4 might connect only to port 8. Ports 5 and 7 would make up the last VLAN (see Figure 9.13).

FIGURE 9.13

A VLAN config-uration.

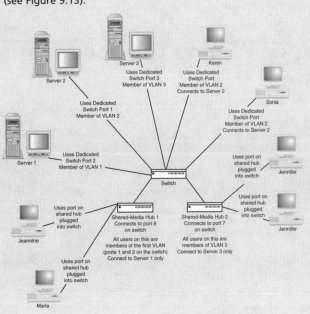

VLANs offer these benefits: performance, manageability, and security. The price for a switch that can create VLANs is not significantly more expensive than switches that cannot provide this flexibility. The benefits of using VLANs are becoming more apparent as network administrators try to support more types of users. For example, you don't want your receptionist to have access to the same network resources as your CFO or financial analysts; VLANs provide a way of logically ensuring that the receptionist can't even see the resources that the CFO and analysts use. By the same token, VLANs are useful for connecting remote access server devices. A VLAN connected to a remote access server device limits a dial-in user to a specific designated set of resources, so that even if the remote access server's security is cracked, a cracker still can't do much damage or find much information.

Once you have made any changes to your network drawings based on any patterns you've discovered (such as to segment or not to segment your network), you're ready to start drawing the workstations and connecting them to the appropriate network device (a hub or switch port). When you do this, make note of how many of each type of computer are connecting to each port; that way, you can ensure that you connect only as many workstations to each hub as each hub has ports.

Once this process is done, you'll have a set of drawings that provide you with connection-oriented data you might otherwise have missed. These drawings will enable you to quantify the number of hub and switch ports you'll need for your network.

Step 5: Writing the Specification and Getting Others' Input

Once you've gotten this far, you have enough data to write a document that includes the following:

- The organizational purpose of the network
- The specifics of the network's use (which users do which tasks)
- The quantity of both users and computers
- Whether or not the network will be centralized or decentralized
- The network topology you plan to use

You also have a pair of diagrams that portray the logical and physical connections required by the network. Pat yourself on the back—you deserve it. You've created the basis for an initial specification document, which enumerates all the preceding points and includes the diagrams.

Once you created the specification document, you're ready to meet with other users to look over the plans and ensure that all the bases are covered.

> If you want your diagrams to look cleaner than hand-drawn diagrams, several manufacturers provide software that simplifies the process of drawing networks. All the diagrams in this book were created using Visio Pro. ClickNet and NetDraw are other quality packages that accomplish the same goal.

9

Writing the Specification Document

Now is the time to actually write your specification for the network. The specification document should take into account all the points in the preceding section and list, quite specifically, the various uses of the network. Specifications do not have to be long, but they must be complete and clear; as English teachers are prone to say, "It should be as long as it needs to be—but no longer."

The purpose of a specification document is twofold: to limit the scope of the network design and to provide a reference document for network administrators.

A good specification document helps limit the insidious process called *scope creep* (a process in which the scope of a job creeps bigger and bigger while the job is in progress), in which a plan accretes additional tasks as it is executed. This is why it's so important to get buy-in from other users. If other users keep demanding new features ("Let's just add this one new feature, it's not much, it won't slow things down"), the network may never be built. However, if the network builder can point to the specification document and ask whether the feature is included, he may be able to build the base network before beginning to add additional features.

The other purpose of a specification document is to ensure that the network builder and subsequent network administrators have a reference guide to the underlying design of the network. It's surprising how easy it is to forget the basic specs of a network if you're not confronted with them every day. The specification document provides a reference for the details that can easily be forgotten.

The specification document should include, at the very least, the following information:

- Why are you building the network?
- What will the network be used for?
- How many people and computers will the network have?

- Will the network be peer or client/server?
- Will the network be Ethernet, Token Ring, or FDDI?

Note that the answers to these questions are the same things you knew when you started this section. If you can, include in the specification document some of the following as well:

- What applications will each computer type run?
- What access rights will each user have?
- How will the network's center (the hubs and switches) be organized?
- What are the planned administrative user IDs and passwords?

Anything that concerns the network that has been planned or can be standardized is fair game for this document. Add it so that you'll have something to refer to when the going gets confusing. The more detailed the specification document is, the more useful it will be.

> I personally recommend Ethernet as the best topology for building a first
> network. It's remarkably forgiving, and it uses about the least expensive
> hardware available. In general, I've tried hard not to editorialize in this
> book, but Ethernet 10BASE-T is far and away the best topology for a person
> building a first network.

Writing a specification should be done over the course of a few days. Review it frequently to ensure that it contains the depth of information you require, and try to avoid using buzzwords. As much as acronyms can ease discourse for people who are conversant with them, they do very little except increase technophobia in users who don't know what they mean. And that's important because, once you're done writing the specification, it's going to be reviewed by users, among others.

Meeting with Other Users

Once the spec is written, convene a working group of the people whose work will be affected by the network. This group will probably include a couple users, managers, and senior-level people, as well as a technology consultant or in-house IS (if either of these positions exist). Before the meeting, let the attendees know that you want to discuss the design of the network with them to get their input. If possible, provide each attendee with a copy of the spec before the meeting so that everyone can review it beforehand. Also, set a specific (but realistic) length for the meeting. If attendees don't know how long the meeting will last, they're more likely to bow out.

When the meeting convenes, have either a whiteboard or your easel pad available. Briefly recap what is in the specification document and then open the floor for questions and answers. Make certain that users know they're not there to provide technical assistance (if that's not their mètier). Instead, reassure them that your purpose is to ensure that they get what they need out of the network. As users speak, take notes; if they notice a shortcoming, take note and ask what might remedy the situation.

Once this meeting is done, revise your specification in light of the discussion. Give revised copies of the specification to the attendees and get them to provide approval of the specification as articulated in that document. Getting concerned parties to sign off on a specification can save you untold hours of grief later in the process by inhibiting scope creep.

9

Step 6: Specifying Hardware

Until this point, the network-planning process has dealt entirely with use and software application issues. The reason for this is an old piece of computer-network-design wisdom that says, "It's wise to first figure out what software you need and then figure out what hardware platform you need to support that software." At this point, you know what the network needs to do—but you haven't begun looking at hardware products…at least, not specifically.

> This book does not recommend specific hardware, but it does make the assumption that you will be using Intel-compatible personal computers and industry-standard networking hardware (probably Ethernet 10BASE-T) for most of your network. The goal of the following sections is to help you use the specification you have written as a guide to specify the hardware on which you will build your network.

Selecting Hardware

Networking hardware typically comes in two configurations: the latest and greatest hub/switch/chassis that costs the world, or yesterday's technology—reliable but well back from the cutting edge. If the network you are building is small and not slated to expand, the latter is acceptable; it will provide basic connectivity and adequate performance. If your network is expanding, try to get as much capacity as possible because doing so buys you breathing space. Because networking technology changes so rapidly, purchasing excess capacity is often the only way to get a full, useful life span out of equipment. It's not a terribly palatable decision to make, but unfortunately it's the dirty little secret of networking hardware capacity planning.

The following list provides a baseline for the physical part of your network. This list doesn't provide specific recommendations because hardware changes so rapidly. But it does tell you the features you're likely to find useful.

- **Network Interface Cards**. For each computer, you need at least one network card. NICs can cost as little as $50 or as much as $300. Make certain that your network cards are the correct topology; even though Token-Ring cards have the same network-cable connector as Ethernet 10BASE-T cards, Ethernet cards won't work on Token-Ring networks, and vice versa.

- **Concentrators** (MAUs, hubs, and switches). Once you know how many computers will be on your network, you know how many ports you need. Once you know how many ports you require, it's a matter of determining whether they will be switched or shared media, as detailed (in the abstract) in the specification you've already created.

- **Wiring**. If you're using a star-configuration network, you'll have to run cables from the wiring closet in which the hubs are stored to each workstation's location. Ensure that you use at least Category 5 or better twisted-pair wire; even at twice the price of the lower cable certifications such as Category 3, it's cheap because it has a longer useful life span. If you're using a bus-configuration network, you'll have to run coaxial cable serially between workstations. If you decide to install the cable yourself, remember to handle it gently, regardless of whether it's coax or twisted pair. Treating the wire gently (that is, not crimping or breaking it) helps ensure that you'll get a better connection. A better solution, if your organization has the finances, is to hire someone who runs cable for a living. Electricians are often stellar cable installers because they run so many cables through walls and other inaccessible locations.

If your organization is not for profit, such as a public school or public library, you may be able to arrange assistance at very little or no cost. Each October for the past two years, there has been a national event called NetDay. People from the local community come together to help local schools and libraries get wired. In some states, materials have been donated by (very) generous corporations; in others, local volunteers pitch in time, labor, and a few dollars a head to help get their local public institutions online. Check around! It's a great opportunity to do something worthwhile. In addition, a lot of the people who volunteer their time are professional networkers, system administrators, and so forth—you can learn a lot by attending!

- **Workstation computers**. Once you have specified your network cards, hubs, and cables, you're ready to spec out your computers. Refer to the specification you wrote to determine which users need powerful workstations and which ones can use lower-end systems, and specify them. Because hardware changes so rapidly, it's pointless to create a fixed specification here, but as of 2000, the fastest chips are reaching 1 gigahertz speeds, so workstations in the 600 to 850 Mhz range are fine for now. Don't consider this recommendation to be a standard; see what the market is offering. What constitutes a powerful PC changes incredibly fast, so do research to find out what's current.

- **Server computers**. By the same token, overbuild your servers. Get as powerful a machine as you can afford and add as much memory as possible. No matter what your application, the power and memory you provide will be used in six months or less, and will be tight in a year or so. Figure out your server's disk-space requirements (a good minimum is 100M per user; more is always better) and then double it if possible. Don't worry; the disk space will be used—probably sooner than you expect.

- **Management features**. When you purchase your hardware, ensure that it can support the *SNMP* or *RMON* network-management standard. Even if you don't use the management features immediately, as your network grows, SNMP and RMON capability can extend the useful life of a piece of equipment by ensuring that it can be managed as part of a greater network.

- **Other features**. Likewise, try to find networking hardware that can support advanced features like VLANs. Having the capability is crucial because it ensures that you have options. The more options your hardware has, the more it prevents your networking hardware from becoming quickly obsolete.

Finding all the hardware you have specified can be a chore, particularly if you're not familiar with the market and the major manufacturers. At this point, a consultant, *Value Added Reseller* (*VAR*; a consultant or consulting firm that sells service as well as computer hardware and software), or hardware reseller who also handles configuration, design, and management tasks can be a great help. Because you already know basically what you want (hubs, switches, cabling, and so on), and the number of ports on each, a VAR can help you by providing several possible product options. A good VAR can offer tremendous assistance when you are selecting hardware and software, but make sure that the VAR is looking at the particular requirements for your network so that you don't get a cookie-cutter, one-size-fits-all network. Ensure that the VAR knows your criteria; that will help them make better decisions for you.

Step 7: Building the Network

Once you've settled on the hardware, you're ready to begin building the network. The next hour describes the various rationales behind selecting specific pieces for your network (which you can review when you write the specification document described in this chapter). Hour 11, "Physically Assembling a Network," gets into actually building the network.

Questionnaire/Checklist

The following sections list some of the questions you might ask during informational interviews. Look through these sections and create some questions of your own. Remember that your goal is to figure out how people do what they do so that you can ensure that your network helps them do their jobs. That's why it's important for you to ask questions relevant to your *own* business rather than sticking to a script.

Meeting with Senior Management

1. What is the organization's core business?
2. How would the senior executive like to change and improve business processes?

Meeting with Rank-and-File Employees

1. Document the employees' job tasks: What do they have to accomplish?
2. Get feedback—a "wants" list.

Distilling Core Issues from Interviews

1. What do users and management want?
2. Get buy-in at this stage with a second interview.

Quantifying the Network

1. Did your users buy into your description of the issues to be addressed?
2. How many users will your network have?
3. Why will your users be using the network?
4. Will your network consist of one computer per user, or will one computer service many users?
5. How many computers will your network have?

Determining Applications and Rightsizing the Workstation

1. Does the system do one preset function or does it require user interactivity?

2. How much raw power (processor plus memory) does the system require?

3. Does the system require multimedia capabilities?

4. Will the system be used by multiple users at one console?

5. Will the network include laptops that have to connect to the network?

Deciding Whether to Centralize

1. Is your network larger than 15 users?

2. Will your network be client/server?

3. Will you have an onsite consultant or in-house IS department to manage the network?

4. Will your desktops be standardized?

5. Do your files require backup?

6. Will you institute file-level and directory-level security on your network?

Summary

In this hour, you examined the process by which your network is designed. In the next several hours, you'll work through some of the specific parts of designing your network, including selecting the network hardware type, the network operating system, and the network protocol.

Q&A

Q Why is it important to identify the desired use of a network at the outset of the design process?

A Doing so ensures that the network is built to serve the organization's needs.

Q Why is it important to determine the computers on which network tasks will run?

A By determining the location of a given process, you help build a list of criteria that can determine the configuration of your network.

Q Why is a public examination and discussion of network plans useful?

A A public examination allows you to measure the function of the network in relation to users' needs and to ensure that the planned network can accomplish the functions outlined earlier in the process.

HOUR **10**

How to Select Hardware and Software for Your Network

One of my former employers once asked a Value Added Reseller (VAR) for a recommendation for a particular piece of equipment. Instead of a single recommendation, my boss received a spreadsheet detailing several options with associated analysis and a generic assessment of the situations in which each option would be appropriate. Needless to say, it wasn't what he wanted.

After being disappointed with the VAR, he turned to me and asked which, if any, of the VAR's solutions represented a *right* solution. In response to the puzzled look I gave him, he countered with the following speech:

"For any given need, there are a lot of possible solutions. The trick is not finding a complete solution or a properly priced solution; instead, it's about finding the right solution. The right solution is a combination of price, features, and so forth, but it also has to do with knowing our needs and making certain that a given solution addresses our needs in proportion, where the cost is less important than correct function. So given those parameters, what do we do here?"

Given the particular focus he'd outlined, it wasn't difficult to provide him with an appropriate answer. All I had to do was look at our needs more closely and define them with an eye toward solving our business problems, while making the solution cost effective.

In the same fashion, this chapter is about making the right decisions for your network. If you're building a two-computer home-office LAN, you don't need the same equipment as a fully staffed office or a national organization. And naturally, your criteria are different. In the last several hours, you've learned the process by which a network is designed. In this hour, the focus is on the criteria used to select the hardware and software from the perspectives of appropriateness and cost:

- Selecting a topology
- Selecting the network type (peer or client/server)
- Selecting the OS and NOS
- Selecting the protocol

Along with this information, this hour presents a very brief primer in how to assemble the physical network pieces and a basic list of what you'll need for each configuration. This chapter is designed to help you begin the process of network design—so that you can make the right decisions from the start.

Selecting a Topology

The reasoning behind the selection of a particular network topology takes into account several factors:

- Overall network size
- Potential network expansion
- Required bandwidth
- Cost

Selection of a topology is not a light matter; it determines a great many of the limits and parameters for your network. The topology you select also has a very material effect on several other factors: the reliability of your network and the ease of network growth. The goal of topology selection should be to provide the maximum possible reliability and redundancy with the greatest possible ease of expansion.

Ethernet 10BASE-2

It used to be a truism that if you were going to have a two- or three-user network, the easiest thing to do was to build an Ethernet 10BASE-2 network. As we've noted before, a 10BASE-2 network won't scale up to an enterprise network due to the inherent fragility of its design. Consequently, we don't recommend that you use it. Even with the maturity of its hardware and *device drivers*, it's a topology that's been superseded by other, newer forms of Ethernet.

Future Proofing Your 10BASE-2 Network

If you already have a network that includes 10BASE-2, then the smart thing to do is to migrate away from it. How do you do that? Future-proofing!

First, when you get network cards, don't add any that have a 10BASE-2 interface. Instead, get cards that have a 10BASE-T interface. The 10BASE-T interface looks like a phone jack with eight connectors (also called an RJ-45 jack) instead of the four connectors that the regular phone jack has (also called an RJ-11 jack). Then get a media converter, which is a device that can connect multiple topologies together, and use that to connect the new 10BASE-T part of your network to the old 10BASE-2. Of course, it's only necessary to do this if you're going to mix 10BASE-2 and 10BASE-T on the same network.

10BASE-2 is not advisable for networks that have a lot of users. As was stressed in previous hours, the serial nature of the connections in 10BASE-2 makes it inherently less reliable than the hub-and-spoke configuration of star networks.

Installing Network Cards

Begin by reading the instructions enclosed with your network card. Most current network cards are soft set; this means that the computer resources they use can be configured with software. That software is probably included on the floppy disk you got with the network card.

In the rare case that you've purchased used network cards, chances are that you will have to change some *jumpers* on the cards before you can get them to work. A jumper is a very small piece of plastic (less than 1/8 inch on a side) with a conductive metal strip inside and is used to make electrical connections on the card, like a switch. Jumpers fit on pairs of gold pins that run in parallel on various parts of the card. They are said to be closed, or on, when a jumper connects two pins; they are open, or off, when they are not connected. Fortunately, most new cards don't require jumpers and can be configured entirely through software.

Jumpers are typically used to set two things: the *Input/Output* (*I/O*) address the card uses to talk to the computer system and the *interrupt request* (*IRQ*) the card uses to get the computer's attention when it has data to pass (often, however, the IRQ is set using the network card's setup software rather than with a physical jumper).

Input/Output (I/O) addresses for network cards generally range from about 200h (decimal 512) to about 380h (decimal 896). 200h is a hexadecimal (base 16) number. In base 16, the place values are 1 for the leftmost column, 16 for the next column, and 256 for the third column from the left. For the hexadecimal number 200, there is a 2 in the third column, which means 2 sets of 256, or 512 in decimal. For the hexadecimal number 380, there is a 3 in the third column, which means 3 sets of 256, or 768; there is an 8 in the second column which means 8 sets of 16, or 128; 768 plus 128 equals 896 in decimal.

We use base 16 because 16 is a factor of 2 (which is what binary arithmetic is based on), making it an attractive way to depict binary numbers. Rather than typing 10011011 in binary, you can type 9B in hex (that's 155 in decimal notation). Hex is very economical for depicting large numbers.

Interrupt Request (IRQ)

When a device such as a network card or a video card has to get the full attention of the computer system, it uses something called an IRQ. An IRQ, or Interrupt Request, is just that: a request that the system stop whatever else it's doing at the moment and give its attention to the device requesting attention. You'll often wind up fiddling with IRQs when you're installing cards in Intel-compatible systems, even if the card is Plug and Play, or self-configuring, so it's wise to know about them.

There are 15 IRQs in most Intel-compatible computers, of which six or seven are generally available for add-in devices such as network cards and SCSI controllers (refer to Hour 3, "Getting Data from Here to There: How Computers Share Data," for more about SCSI devices). IRQs 2 and 9 are called cascading IRQs, and control access to IRQs 9 through 15; try to avoid using these two if possible (using either might disable access to IRQs 9 through 15).

In the interest of ensuring your success, Table 10.1 provides a list of the commonly used IRQs and memory addresses.

TABLE 10.1 Common Intel-Compatible IRQ Settings

IRQ #	Function
0	Reserved for use by the operating system (system timer).
1	Reserved for use by the operating system (keyboard controller).
2	Used to access IRQ 9 and above. Use only as a last resort.
3	Used for COM2 communications serial port (often built into the motherboard).
4	Used for COM1 communications serial port (often built into the motherboard).
5	Usually unused and available.
6	Reserved for use by the operating system (floppy drive controller).
7	Used for the printer port (also called LPT1).
8	Reserved for use by the operating system (system clock).
9	Usually available, but use as a last resort. Refer to IRQ 2.
10	Usually available.
11	Usually available.
12	Often used for bus mice (as opposed to serial mice, which connect to COM ports).
13	Often unused and available.
14	Usually used for Primary IDE disk drive controllers.
15	Reserved for use by secondary IDE controllers.

The important thing to remember when you install a network card is to try not to use the memory address or IRQ that other cards or the motherboard are using. If you do, the card will not work. Fortunately, the advent of true plug and play often means that configuring cards is significantly less difficult than this description—often, Windows 98/Me (and sometimes Windows 2000) will accurately detect and install your card.

I/O addresses

I/O addresses are counted in hex. Some of the most commonly used I/O addresses are listed in Table 10.2. This list doesn't apply everywhere, however; check your own settings (in DOS, this information is usually found in the CONFIG.SYS file; in Windows 95, go to Control Panel, select System, and look in Device Manager).

TABLE 10.2 Commonly Used I/O Addresses

Device	Memory Address
COM1 (first serial port)	03E8
COM2 (second serial port)	02E8
LPT1 (printer port)	0378
IDE Hard Drive Controllers	170 or 1F0
Sound cards	220 and 330

Most network cards use addresses outside the commonly used list of addresses. But watch out! Some network cards may use memory address 0360. Although this address doesn't seem to conflict with anything, unfortunately, sometimes the software device driver takes up too much space. When this happens, the software device driver can take from 0360 all the way to 0380 in memory, which conflicts with the printer port at 0378. And if you can't print, that's a problem. So watch out for memory address or IRQ conflicts if you have to jumper-set your cards.

Usually, you use the software driver floppy disk that came in the package with the network card. In many cases, configuring the network card is a simple matter of running a utility at a DOS command prompt. However, if you select a popular card such as an NE2000-compatible card, many operating systems have software that works with the cards as part of the OS's installation package.

Once the card is set, you're ready to begin networking, as covered in subsequent hours.

10BASE-T

Of all the network topologies available, 10BASE-T may be the most versatile for everyday networking. It is widely available, scales beautifully, is simple to install and maintain, and is extremely reliable. There is also a plethora of manufacturers who make network cards for everything from Intel-compatible desktop systems to Macintoshes to laptops—you can find a 10BASE-T Ethernet card for almost any system.

Additionally, 10BASE-T cabling offers an upgrade path. If you use the proper type of wire or cabling (called 568A or B and described in this section), the network can support 100BASE-T networks. This upgrade path is part of what makes 10BASE-T a solid choice for a network topology. And since you can chain 10BASE-T hubs together (remember that hubs are necessary), it's possible to increase the size of a network relatively simply.

Actually, it's not strictly true that a network of only two computers running 10BASE-T need a hub. If there are only two computers on a 10BASE-T network, they can connect using a special RJ-45-ended cable called a crossover cable. Crossover cables are designed to enable hubs to connect to one another, but they can be used to join two 10BASE-T computers as well. However, omitting the hub in a two-computer 10BASE-T network is not advisable—how will you add a third computer without a hub? And never doubt that the third computer will make an appearance eventually. A crossover cable is wired as follows, with RJ-45 plugs:

Pin 1 connects to pin 2	Pin 5 connects to pin 5
Pin 2 connects to pin 1	Pin 6 connects to pin 3
Pin 3 connects to pin 6	Pin 7 connects to pin 7
Pin 4 connects to pin 4	Pin 8 connects to pin 8

If you anticipate that your network will grow, 10BASE-T is a great topology to start with. For one thing, it offers options for the network connection type. 10BASE-T Ethernet is the simplest Ethernet, offering both shared media (one segment per hub or collection of hubs joined by crossover cables) and switching technology (recall from Hour 2, "The Benefits of Networking," that switching uses a device that looks like a hub but works faster by creating separate network segments for each connection between computers).

In addition, 10BASE-T is a standard for network peripherals such as network printers and the new network copier/printers—almost all these devices have a 10BASE-T port. Also, routers and bridges typically require a 10BASE-T connection to connect to a network. So the 10BASE-T topology is widespread and versatile.

As was provided for 10BASE-2, here's a recipe for the ingredients necessary for a 10BASE-T network:

- Two or more computers. Almost all computers can use some form of Ethernet, from laptops to desktop PCs to Unix systems and Macs.
- One 10BASE-T network card per computer.
- One hub with enough ports to connect all your computers.
- Enough patch cords to connect each network card's RJ-45 socket to the hub's RJ-45 socket. A *patch cord* is an eight-conductor cord with an RJ-45 jack at both ends. (It looks like a really fat phone cord.) Patch cords are available premade at computer stores for a couple dollars a cable. Buy premade cables; they're cheaper and guaranteed to work.

10BASE-T, unlike 10BASE-2, is a star topology, which means that everything has to connect to a concentrator—or, more correctly, a hub or switch.

Be aware that many small Ethernet hubs have a special port designed specifically to connect your hub to other hubs (or *stack* them, in the parlance). If you connect a computer to this port (usually port 1), that computer won't be able to use the network because the hub doesn't use the stacking port like the rest of the ports. The problem is that stacking ports usually don't look different from regular ports. So read the documentation on your hub to find out whether it has a port dedicated to stacking and save yourself some frustration.

Token Ring

Although Token Ring works differently from Ethernet, its physical networking is actually quite similar. If you're going to build a network inside a business in which Token Ring is already used for all or part of the network, your new network should also use it. IBM has been the most vocal champion of Token Ring, although in general it is well supported by most manufacturers.

Compared to Ethernet, Token Ring equipment is expensive. From a speed perspective, Token Ring is also a bit out of the mainstream: It supports two modes, 4 megabits per second and 16 megabits per second. If you're building or adding to a Token Ring network, use the 16 megabits-per-second mode; 4 megabits per second is just too slow for good networking.

Token Ring also suffers from compatibility issues. Unlike finding Ethernet equipment, it's often difficult to find routers and network printer cards that connect to Token Ring networks—and when the devices are available, they tend to be more expensive than their Ethernet counterparts. Token Ring has a relatively low percentage of the networking market, so technologies such as switching are only now beginning to appear in the Token Ring world.

The recipe for a Token Ring network is similar to that for an Ethernet network because the basic cabling (Category 5 wired to the 568A or 568B termination scheme, discussed a bit later on) and jacks (RJ-45) are the same. Token Ring uses the same cable termination scheme that Ethernet uses; it's called TIAA 568B. For a Token Ring network, you need the following equipment:

- Two or more computers to network;
- One Token Ring card for each computer;
- One MAU (Multistation Access Unit, or the networking term for the concentrator in a Token Ring network);
- Patch cables for each computer. If you're running cables to remote locations, you'll need a patch panel and cables to connect the panel to the MAU. A patch panel, detailed in Hour 11, "Physically Assembling a Network," is the place in a star topology where all the network wires converge and provide connections to the concentrator—in the case of Token Ring and MAU.

FDDI/ATM/100BASE-FX/1000BASE-T(Fiber-Optic Technologies)

FDDI, as a topology, is a bit strange. Optical fiber (strands of flexible glass that carry data as pulses of light rather than as electrical signals) can provide connections for a variety of topologies (ATM, FDDI, and Ethernet 100BASE-FX and 100BASE-T, aka gigabit Ethernet) using the same type of optical fiber terminated in the same way for each topology. The difference among FDDI, ATM, 100BASE-FX and gigabit Ethernet is the methodology each uses to pass data down the fiber—the configuration of the fiber itself never changes.

Optical fiber offers numerous advantages. For one thing, using optical fiber really future-proofs your network. Optical fiber can carry data at tremendously high rates of speed. ATM over fiber can run at 1.5 gigabits per second; gigabit Ethernet runs at 1 gigabit per second.

Another positive is that optical fiber doesn't have electrical impulses passing through the wire, so it's immune to electrostatic disturbances…and snooping. Because there's no electrical impulse running down a copper wire, no one can bug the line using an inductive pickup (a magnetic pickup that surrounds a cable and captures a copy of the signal). Now, this isn't likely to happen—people don't snoop with inductive testers very often. But fiber's immunity to electrostatic disturbances means that ground loops, or unwanted electrical current passing down a wire due to difference in ground potential, are a thing of the past. No ground loops = less network equipment damaged by static = lower cost and less maintenance = good.

The downsides are just as numerous, however. The cost of installing fiber is extremely high (in a recent project, the projected cost difference between wiring with standard Category 5 UTP copper wire and fiber was almost nine times as much as copper wire). Also, fiber is not something a layperson or amateur can run through walls and terminate. Fiber requires a set of specialized skills to cut and polish the end of a cable into a lens that will work with the network card and the hub; it requires another set of skills to adequately attach an end to the polished cable. Cable also must be run through special tubes (which resemble a really long shop-vac hose) so that it doesn't get broken or damaged.

However, if cost is not an issue and bandwidth and future proofing your network are core requirements, you simply can't do better than fiber. It's expensive, but it's currently the final word on high-speed networking.

To install fiber, you'll need the following ingredients:

- Know which kind of fiber you need to install—single-mode or multimode. Most fiber that you'll find now is multimode—but always check, just to be certain.
- Two or more computers to network. These days, Cisco and other vendors are offering ways to link their hubs and switches using gigabit Ethernet, and providing hubs that do the same. This is a GREAT way to increase bandwidth to your servers.
- One network card of the fiber topology you want to use (FDDI, ATM, 100BASE-FX, or gigabit Ethernet) for each computer.

- A fiber patch panel in a central location. Don't try to install or terminate fiber yourself unless you're trained to do it; hire a professional.
- A central hub (or hubs) with sufficient ports to connect all your computers.
- A good professional fiber-optic cable installer.
- Patch fiber cables to connect the computers to wall jacks and to connect the patch panel to the hubs.

> Fiber, unlike any other networking topology, has one unique danger you can easily avoid. Because fiber-optic cards and hubs pass data using pulses of laser light, don't ever stare directly into the end of a fiber-optic cable that's live on the network. If you do, you'll risk damage to your retina.

Selecting the Network Type: Client/Server or Peer to Peer

In the first several hours of this book, you were inundated with various upsides and downsides of client/server and peer networking strategies. In the next couple of pages, you will have the opportunity to see how you can quantify your decision to go with client/server or peer.

Client/Server Networking

Pure client/server networking has one basic criterion: No workstation on your network can ever use any resources on any other workstation. The whole service architecture of the network resides on one or more servers dedicated to specific tasks including file services, Internet/WAN connectivity, remote access, authentication, back-end distributed applications, and so forth. In other words, workstations connected to the network see only servers—they never see one another. A client/server network is a one-to-many scheme with the server being the one and the workstations being the many. Note that this is the model used by large commercial Web sites, such as Amazon, where the client is essentially a small graphical front end that is delivered fresh from the server each time it's opened, and a large server architecture at the back end that handles ordering and billing and authentication. No user of Amazon knows that another user is currently online—there's no interaction between users, just between the servers and the client system.

The client-server model is useful for large businesses that have to manage their computer users' computer resources efficiently. In a pure client/server environment, a great deal of the software that clients use at their workstations is stored on a server hard drive rather than on users' own hard drives. In this configuration, if a user's workstation fails, it's relatively easy to get him or her back online quickly—simply replace the computer on the desktop. When the user logs back in to the network, they will have access to the applications needed to work.

The TCP/IP-based technology of the Internet has changed the accepted definition of client/server somewhat, with the focus being on distributed applications, where a thin client (such as a Web page application running in a browser) works in tandem with a much larger server. The advantages of this model stem from the application's capability to run in a browser. Since browsers can run on Windows machines, Macs, Unix boxes, and other systems, applications can be distributed quickly and effectively. To change a Web-enabled application, only the copy at the server need be changed, since the changes will be distributed when users open the new page.

Client/server is appropriate if one or more of the following conditions apply to your situation:

- Your network is large (more than 10 or 15 computers). On a larger network, it's not wise to leave resources entirely decentralized…the next points deal with this.

- Your network requires robust security (Internet access, secure files, and so forth). Using secure firewalls, gateways, and secured servers ensures that access to network resources is controlled.

- Your network requires that data be free from the threat of accidental loss. This means taking data stored on a server and backing it up from a central location.

- Your network needs users to focus on server-based applications rather than on workstation-based applications and resources.

Peer Networking

Peer networking is based on the idea that any computer that connects to a network should be able to share its resources with any other computer. In direct contrast to client/server, peer networking is a many-to-many scheme.

The decentralized nature of peer networking means that it is inherently less organized. Peer networks that grow to more than a very few computers tend to interact by fiat and caprice rather than by design. In this respect, peer networking is similar to the Internet; there are hard-and-fast rules about basic hardware and software interaction and standards, but specific connections between computers occur in unforeseen ways. Peer networks are curious for that reason; the connections between systems tend to evolve over time until the network reaches an equilibrium. However, there is a significant amount of wasted resources while the network is finding its balance.

Peer networking is appropriate for your network if the following conditions apply:

- Your network is relatively small (fewer than 10 or 15 computers).
- Your network does not require robust security regarding access to resources.
- Your network does not require that data be free from the threat of accidental loss.
- Your network needs users to focus on workstation-based applications rather than on server-based applications and resources.

Peer-to-Peer and Client/Server Networking

In more complex networks, it's possible that a user's workstation will be a client of one system and provide a service to another. Typically, this arrangement requires both client/server and peer-to-peer networking to work (or at least to work easily). An example of such a network is a Novell NetWare-based client/server network, whose clients are all Windows 95 computers. The Windows 95 computers can, with the addition of Microsoft Networking client software. See one another as members of a workgroup who can share resources with one another as well as with the NetWare server.

The addition of TCP/IP to most desktop operating systems over the last five or six years has made an enormous difference when setting up networks. Since TCP/IP is standards-based, almost every manufacturer has ensured that their products can use TCP/IP as the base protocol for their services. Consequently, it's no big deal for a system to be a client of one system while providing a service to another system. There's no need to run multiple protocols, which used to be almost required, because TCP/IP treats all systems as peers. So it's no longer necessary to install multiple protocols to support multiple network clients; instead, almost all the clients use TCP/IP.

Selecting the Workstation Operating System and Network Operating System

Once you've decided on the basic setup of your network, you have to decide which operating systems best serve your needs at the desktop and at the server. The following sections will help you make an informed choice about which OS best suits your particular needs.

Peer-to-Peer OSes

In a peer-to-peer network, there is no Network Operating System (NOS) *per se*. Instead, each user's workstation has desktop operating system software that can share resources with other computers as desired. Typically, operating systems include the capability to configure a protocol and share resources. Most peer OSes provide a relatively limited range of sharable devices, although file sharing (or shared disk space) and networked printing are relatively standard features.

The following brief sections describe a selection of peer-capable OSes. We'll look at the following OSes:

- Windows 98
- Windows NT Workstation and Windows 2000 Professional
- Linux

In Hour 4, "Computer Concepts," you learned about client operating systems. If you review the list of operating systems presented there, you'll find that many of them are capable of working in a peer-to-peer environment. Since the early 1990s, almost every client/single-user operating system has been shipped with at least a limited collection of network protocols and tools. This means that almost every client OS can be used to build a peer-to-peer network.

One confusing fact is that in a TCP/IP network, all computers are *de facto* peers. This means that any computer that has a full suite of TCP/IP utilities can interoperate with any other computer on the network. As a consequence, the characteristics and functions of a particular machine (processor speed, disk space, application services, and so on) tend to determine which machines are servers and which are workstations. This is a relative flattening of the PC-network hierarchy.

10

Microsoft Networking: Windows 98, Windows NT Workstation, Windows 2000 Professional

Windows for Workgroups was the original "do-it-yourself" network for Intel-compatible personal computers. It is designed around Microsoft's MS-DOS operating system and Windows shell. It is not preemptive, but it is capable (with some configuration) of sharing disk space, printers, and other storage media including CD-ROMs. It's been superseded by Windows 95, Windows 98, and currently Windows Millenium Edition (Windows Me) as Microsoft's consumer operating system.

Microsoft Peer Networking Concepts

Microsoft's peer networking products are based on the idea of a workgroup, or a set of computers that belong to a common group and that share resources among themselves. Microsoft peer networking is actually quite versatile, and can include computers running

Windows for Workgroups (now obsolete), Windows 95, Windows 98, Windows Me, Windows NT Workstation, and Windows 2000. Additionally, on a given physical network, multiple workgroups can coexist. For example, if you have three salespeople, they can all be members of the SALES workgroup; the members of your accounting department can be members of the ACCOUNTS workgroup. Of course, there is a common administrative user with accounts on all machines in all workgroups. Therefore, central administration is possible to a limited extent, but it's not an efficient administrative solution.

Windows 95/98/Me

Microsoft introduced a true 32-bit successor to Windows for Workgroups in 1995, calling it Windows 95. To date, there have been two updates: Windows 98 and Windows Millenium Edition (Me), the latter of which is the current consumer offering. Spurred by the stinging criticisms of Windows for Workgroups' network shortcomings, Microsoft designed Windows 95 to be a first-class network client, including clients for TCP/IP networks, NetWare Networks, and Microsoft networking right out of the box. Windows 98 and Me have gone further, with personal Web servers and Internet utilities included, as well. In the process, Microsoft built in a stellar peer network operating system based on its workgroup model. Windows 95, 98, and Me systems can share disk space and printers quite easily: Right-clicking (clicking with the right mouse button) any drive or printer resource icon brings up a menu that includes sharing.

Windows Me provides a good base for small peer networks. It's easy to install (Microsoft made certain of that) and its networking is much more robust than earlier Microsoft offerings. The broad range of Internet utilities available on the OS makes it a natural choice for mainstream network clients.

Windows 2000 Professional

The next step up from Windows Me is Windows 2000 Professional. Windows 2000 is a descendant of Microsoft's earlier iterations of Windows NT, which was built from the ground up to compete in the high-end desktop market. Windows 2000 Professional is a fully preemptive, reasonably secure, powerful, and robust operating system that shares a user interface with its consumer OS cousins. In this iteration of its technical-and-business desktop, Microsoft has built in an extensive suite of networking options including a Web and ftp server, and a lightweight packet sniffer. It's relatively easy to administer due to built-in remote Web-based management features. All in all, this operating system is a significant improvement on earlier versions of Windows NT.

Client/Server Network Operating Systems

If you're building a network with a sizable chunk of centralized services, one of the following client/server Network Operating Systems is for you. Where peer-to-peer networks are similar to a cooperative group of people with diverse functions but no single leader, a client/server network is similar to a hierarchy—the server is the leader, the one with all the knowledge and the resources.

The following brief sections describe a selection of network OSes, which are used in client/server networks. We'll look at the following network OSes:

- Novell NetWare
- Microsoft Windows NT Server
- UNIX

10

Novell NetWare

In the early days of PC internetworking, Ray Noorda's Novell invented NetWare. It came as a balm to early PC-networking system administrators who were used to dealing with the innumerable networking schemes that appeared in the early to mid-1980s. NetWare provided reliable, secure, and relatively simple networking; in the early years, the business world snapped up as many copies as Novell could produce.

Over the years, NetWare matured. Its focus broadened beyond the local LAN into WAN configurations. With the advent of NetWare 5 and NetWare Directory Services (NDS), Novell had a product that enabled a global network to provide its users with the same resources, no matter where on the network those users logged in. It was on a roll.

But in 1994 and 1995, two things happened that made Novell stumble badly. The first was the introduction of Microsoft's Windows NT, which Novell failed to view as serious competition. Microsoft's aggressive marketing and the ease of use of Windows NT quickly made inroads into Novell's market share.

Novell's second slip was in failing to realize that the rise in public consciousness of the Internet fundamentally changed the playing field for NOS manufacturers. Novell had used its IPX protocol for close to 15 years, and under then-Chairman Robert Frankenberg, it saw no reason to change.

Novell has at long last adapted to the Internet and open standards networking. Its current product, NetWare 5, natively uses TCP/IP.

In addition, Novell's support channels can make it difficult for end-users who have to support the product in their offices to get the support they require. Rather than provide for-fee technical support lines as other manufacturers do, Novell has always relied on a cadre of Certified NetWare Engineers (CNEs) to provide its primary product support. Unfortunately, CNE service can be quite expensive, a hindrance for smaller businesses.

In spite of Novell's difficulties, NetWare 4 and 5 are stellar network operating systems. They are fast, efficient, and tremendously reliable. The cost of NetWare is based on the number of licensed users; although the initial price may seem much more expensive than Microsoft's NT, remember that the licensing structures are different. When you purchase NetWare, your cost includes all licensed users; when you purchase NT Server, you purchase the server OS and then you have to buy the Client Access Licenses. In general, the cost evens out in the end.

NetWare is appropriate for networks in a variety of situations. If you're building a small network, NetWare is fast in comparison with Windows NT, its most direct competition. However, it's complex to install and maintain. NDS, the directory service that comes with NetWare, provides another criterion: If your network spans multiple LANs (in a WAN or MAN configuration), and you want to provide your users with resources at any company location, NetWare is the logical choice. The directory services of NetWare are stellar at ensuring secure access to resources for any user from any point on the network, from a single login. The single-login access to network resources has left Microsoft in the dust—the Active Directory wasn't released until Windows 2000, while NDS has been around for over five years.

If you want to learn more about Novell NetWare, read Hour 16, "Novell NetWare."

Microsoft Windows 2000 Server and Advanced Server

Windows NT Server, the forbear of Windows 2000, emerged out of the breakup of IBM and Microsoft's shared OS/2 initiative. Although NT Server looks like Windows 95, it is much more; it is a true multitasking, multithreaded network operating system.

Since Windows NT was introduced in 1993-4, Microsoft has weathered a storm of criticism regarding its reliability, scalability, and robustness. To be fair, some of this criticism has been deserved because some releases of Windows NT have had relatively serious flaws. However, Microsoft has persevered and continued to refine Windows NT as it passes through product cycles, up to and including the current iteration, Windows 2000 Server and Advanced Server.

In comparison with other network operating systems, Windows 2000 Server appears relatively inexpensive at first glance. A closer look shows that this is not the case; although the initial network operating system software is priced at a flat rate, it is still necessary to purchase Client Access Licenses to ensure that the system is properly licensed. The cost of Client Access Licenses brings the cost of NT Server networking into the same price arena as other network operating systems.

The release of Windows 2000 Server brought Microsoft Networking users into the age of the directory service, with the release of Active Directory. Active Directory is designed to compete in the space of Novell's NDS (the initial target) and Sun's Network Information Service (NIS), a newer rival. Windows 2000 remains backwards-compatible with older versions of NT, and will play well with others on an NT-domain based network.

Older versions of NT Server do not have a directory service. Instead, NT Servers are organized into *domains*. A domain is a group of servers bound together by common security arrangements based on trust relationships. The domain model is more complex than the NDS model and offers less flexibility; it's a newer model than NDS and lacks NDS' maturity.

One last advantage that Windows 2000 Server has over NetWare is its ease of administration. Windows 2000 Server is most appropriate for networks in which ease of administration trumps raw server bang-for-the-buck. It is an industrial-strength network operating system, just as is NetWare, but its graphical user interface makes management much simpler than is true for NetWare. Windows 2000 Server also works well for single-server networks that have to connect to the Internet because it has a suite of tools to handle networked Internet connections. It uses TCP/IP natively (Microsoft did a less-than-agile but nonetheless effective turnaround to focus on the Internet when it became apparent that the Internet would have a huge impact on the future of networking) and can be a perfectly capable Internet server, if time and care are taken to secure it adequately.

If you want to learn more about Windows NT Server, read Hour 15, "Microsoft Windows 2000 Server."

Unix and Linux

Unlike NetWare or Windows NT, Unix is not a monolithic operating system owned by a single corporation. Instead, it is represented by a plethora of manufacturers with only a few clear standouts. The most common Unixes are Sun' Microsystems' Solaris, IBM's AIX, and Hewlett-Packard's HP-UX. In the Intel-compatible Unix world, Linux, a Unix clone, has trumped the Santa Cruz Operation's SCO Unix and Novell's UNIXWare. Unix comes in many flavors, and various features and commands vary widely between versions—but in the end, it remains the most widely used high-end server operating system in the world.

However, the Unix world is fragmented by a host of issues that derive from Unix's basic design: Unix is open-ended and is available for almost any hardware platform. Unix has existed for almost 30 years, and its design has been optimized and revised and improved to the point at which it is hugely reliable.

10

Unfortunately, the availability of Unix across many different platforms has led to one significant problem that blocks its widespread adoption: Software written for one version of Unix usually does not run on other versions. This lack of compatibility has led to Unix receiving a dwindling share of the server market except at the very high end where absolute reliability is a must. Linux and the Open Source/GNU movement have ameliorated a good deal of the binary incompatibility issues by making the source code for various programs available. This means that with a copy of Linux with a C-language compiler, it's possible to compile—that is, translate from source code to machine instructions—a wide variety of software.

Unix has a reputation for being difficult to master, a reputation which is almost wholly undeserved. It *is* complex—there's no doubt about that. But once the basics are assimilated (which *can* prove daunting), its raw power and versatility are seductive—probably part of the reason why Linux, the freeware Unix clone, is rapidly gaining favor in the market for servers and (gasp) even workstations.

In spite of its complexity, however, any version of Unix makes a fine file, print, and application server. Because of 30 years of refinement, the reliability of a Unix system is typically a step above that of other platforms. Unix uses the TCP/IP networking protocol natively; TCP/IP was created on and for Unix systems, and the "port-and-socket" interface that lies under TCP/IP has its fullest expression on Unix systems.

If you want to learn about more about Unix, read Hour 17, "Unix and Linux."

Selecting the Network Protocol

In the era of the Internet, where networks everywhere are focused on ensuring connectivity to that network of networks, it is surprising that some industry pundits advise neophyte networkers to avoid TCP/IP networking—which can connect a network to the Internet as well as reduce a network's dependence on a single manufacturer's products.

Such advice is dispensed with good intentions. NetWare's IPX and Microsoft's NetBEUI are largely self-configuring and are easy to use, while TCP/IP is more complex. However, in the grand scheme of things, TCP/IP is the most worthwhile choice because of its broad acceptance by the networking community. The difficulties it presents during setup are amply repaid in performance and compatibility when the system is in production. And once the person doing the configuration understands the basics of TCP/IP, it rapidly ceases to be a mystery and becomes, like Unix, a gateway to a much broader perspective on networking.

Rather than simply explaining why TCP/IP should be the network protocol of choice, the following sections briefly discuss the three protocols that make up most modern networking and provide guidelines for their appropriate use.

IPX

Internetworking Packet Exchange (IPX) is Novell's answer to TCP/IP. When Ray Noorda and his Novell crew were designing NetWare in the early 1980s, they liked the flexibility, routability, and scalability of TCP/IP, but disliked its complexity. As a result, Novell created IPX. IPX, like IP, does not care what kind of network topology it travels over, and it is not concerned with the specific route a data packet takes between point A and point B.

Unlike IP, however, IPX is self-configuring. It builds computer systems' network addresses (which, for IPX, are hexadecimal numeric) from a combination of administrator-specified server network-wire addresses and network card MAC addresses. This simplifies the process of setting up a network because once the network is physically connected, IPX can autoconfigure and begin routing data packets very quickly. Administrators do not have to install a separate network address at each computer (a feature that can save quite a bit of time). And IPX is fast.

However, IPX does have downsides…it's a broadcast-based protocol, which is to say that computers periodically announce themselves on the network. Such announcements use network bandwidth that is better used for actual data. And IPX is not part of the TCP/IP protocol suite, so it doesn't carry Internet traffic.

NetBEUI

IBM initially invented the NetBIOS protocol as a way to build small, single-segment networks. It has what is called a *flat namespace*, which is another way of saying that every computer knows about every other computer on the network. It's a broadcast-based protocol based on Server Message Block protocols.

NetBIOS/NetBEUI was designed for small LANs—and only small LANs. It can't be routed, so it cannot work in a WAN environment unless the routers are configured to bridge the network—that is, to connect the networks at OSI layer 2 (the DataLink layer) rather than OSI layer 3 (the address layer)—a very inefficient way to build a network!

NetBIOS and NetBEUI have one compelling advantage over both IPX and IP: Instead of using numeric network addresses, they use alphanumeric names (that is, names that can be written using letters of the alphabet and a limited range of punctuation). For example, if one computer on the network is named Fred and another one is named Ginger, and the computer named Fred has to send packets to the computer named Ginger, the source address (where the packets are coming from) is Fred and the destination address (where the packets are going) is Ginger. There's no need to convert the computer names from alphanumeric names to numeric names, so this type of networking is very simple.

The downside of using names is that each computer on the network must constantly remind other computers on the network of its existence. It's like a pair of dogs; even though they're in the same room, they periodically find it necessary to bark a little, just so that the other dog knows it's still there. Just as dogs barking in a confined space can get a bit loud, NetBIOS/NetBEUI broadcasts can eat up network bandwidth while they're glad-handing the rest of the computers on the network. This "chattiness" is another reason why NetBIOS and NetBEUI are best confined to small networks. Or better yet, not used at all—as we noted earlier in the chapter, most network clients now happily use TCP/IP.

TCP/IP

If there is a universal solvent for networking, TCP/IP is it. TCP/IP was, is, and will hopefully remain a set of related protocols defined by committee and adopted by consensus. It is the scale against which other protocols are measured because the completeness of the TCP/IP protocol suite is unmatched by anything else in the networking arena.

IP as a protocol does not care which route through the network a packet takes to get from point A to point B, which is why it is used for the Internet. IP has a variety of highly standardized functions that work the same no matter which hardware the protocol is running on, and it provides a very configurable network address scheme. As discussed in Hour 3, IP has two drawbacks: configuration complexity (not much ameliorated by better software) and the dwindling number of addresses in the current IP network-address scheme. Fortunately, IP version 6 (called IPng or IPv6) eliminates the network-address limitations and is beginning to be adopted as this book goes to press.

In spite of these drawbacks, TCP/IP is worth the complexity. It offers a way to connect many diverse computers running many operating systems using a single manageable, highly configurable network. In addition, TCP/IP is pretty much infinitely scalable.

The rise of the Internet has been synonymous with a sharp rise in the usage of TCP/IP. If you've dialed into the Internet, if you connect with a DSL, cable modem, T1, or however, and you're using the Internet, you're using TCP/IP. It's ubiquitous, it's standardized, and it's everywhere.

The mere fact that TCP/IP runs on almost every hardware platform available means that a TCP/IP-networked system is far less likely to bind a customer to a particular vendor's solution. Because this protocol is a well-established standard, it is entirely possible to use solutions from multiple vendors to accomplish a single goal.

Summary

In this hour, you learned some additional criteria for deciding on the topology, the network configuration, and the base network protocol. The next hour focuses on network applications and looks at the differences between open-standards-based network applications and proprietary network applications.

Q&A

Q **What are the available topologies for networking personal computers?**

A Ethernet (10BASE-2, 10BASE-T, 100BASE-T), Token Ring, and FDDI (fiber) are the topologies from which you can select a PC network.

Q **What are typical peer operating systems?**

A Peer operating systems currently available include Windows for Workgroups, OS/2, Windows 95, and Windows NT Workstation.

Q **What are the most common PC Network Operating Systems?**

A Network Operating Systems include NetWare, Windows NT, and Unix.

Q **Which protocols are commonly used on PC networks?**

A The protocols most commonly used on PC networks are TCP/IP, NetBIOS/NetBEUI, and IPX.

10

HOUR 11

Physically Assembling a Network

At this point, you've read about the theory of networks, how they work, and what some of the favored OSes are. In subsequent hours, you'll read more about network operating systems so that you can make an informed choice. This chapter is a bit of a way station, or a turning point: It's a hands-on how-to-install chapter.

You've already learned how to identify network hardware, and in this hour, you'll pull it all together and deal with how to plug the network together.

In this hour, you'll cover the following topics:

- Installing adapter cards
- Working in the wiring closet: cables, connections, and concentrators

- Connecting star topology networks: Ethernet 10BASE-T, Token Ring, ATM, and FDDI

This chapter is meant to be used as a reference. It will familiarize you with installation processes for the various bits of hardware you've read about in preceding chapters. It is not a comprehensive guide, however; it's intended to familiarize you with the process rather than provide a be-all and end-all guide to installation. With the information you'll learn in the next hour, you'll be able to do more detailed research and engage a network-cabling company with a certain measure of confidence.

Before Installation

Although computer hardware may look robust and impervious to damage, it's not. Computer and network electronics powered by electricity also can, paradoxically, be damaged by electricity. Although your computer hardware is powered by 120-volt wall current, don't assume that the motherboard or hub actually uses that much electricity. Most computers and networking equipment use 5 volts or so at the motherboard. Static electricity, which can build up to 20,000 volts or so, can wreck computer equipment by burning up the delicate wiring inside a silicon chip.

So that you don't inadvertently burn up some expensive piece of computer equipment while working on it, this section presents a few precautions you can and should take, both for your own safety and the integrity of the computer and networking equipment you're working on.

First, take precautions to prevent electrical-shock damage to yourself and the computer:

- **Wear a wrist strap when you're working on a computer.** A wrist strap is a small device that connects you (usually one of yours wrists) to the computer. This ensures that you and the computer have the same electrical potential; in layman's terms, it means that you won't be transmitting static to the computer and burning up parts while you're installing them. Wrist straps are available at computer stores for a few dollars. They're a great preventative measure—use them.

- **Always shut the computer's power off before working on it.** Sounds like common sense, but it's not. Installing an adapter card in a computer that's running is pretty well guaranteed to burn up the card, the card slot, and (very often) the motherboard.

- **Always unplug the computer before you open it to install equipment.** Again, this may seem like common sense, but surprisingly few people think of it. It's a corollary to the preceding direction, and it ensures that the power is off, which is absolutely, positively, and utterly necessary. In addition to the near-certainty that you'll damage computer equipment by working with it while it's on, you're also taking a chance on damaging yourself—electrical shocks are neither pleasant nor particularly good for your health.

Next, take precautions when you're physically opening the computer's case and installing adapter cards:

- **If you're opening the case and the top doesn't come off easily, don't force it.** Forcing computer cases can damage the box and often the delicate electronics that make the computer useful. Force is a last resort.

> In the early days of PC networking, taking the top off a case was a risky proposition. The number of cables in an IBM XT was staggering. The arrangement of ribbon cables within the case generally ensured that if the case cover was yanked off unceremoniously, you were almost guaranteed to snag a cable and probably damage it.
>
> Since those days, PC manufacturers have improved the cable routing inside computers quite a bit. In fact, most computers no longer require tools to open the case, and the components are increasingly modular, so it's no longer common for the case cover to catch on cables. Nonetheless, it pays to be cautious. I recently disassembled a computer for which the case cover was part of the cable routing—it had clips into which cables slid to route around the inside of the box. If I'd just yanked the top off, I would have torn off at least two cables. Taking the time to figure out how the top should come off saved a lot of time and aggravation—and it was a great puzzle as well!

11

- **Mark all cables and connections, if you have to disconnect anything**. This makes reassembling a disassembled computer much simpler. You can use a marker to label the cables, and you can also draw some diagrams depicting which cables connect to which devices. The best way to mark connections is the one that helps you reconnect what you disconnected.
- **When you're installing adapter cards, ensure that the adapter card and the adapter card slot have the same interface**. In other words, don't put a PCI card in an ISA slot, or vice versa. Doing so can damage the computer, the adapter card, and (more often than not) your bankbook—new parts are expensive!

Just for the record, here's a quick lesson in what adapter cards fit into which slot types:

- ISA fits into ISA, EISA, and some VESA slots. ISA cards have either 62 or 98 gold connector strips on the edge that plugs into the motherboard slot; the connector strips are divided into one set of 62 connectors and one set of 36 connectors.
- EISA cards fit only into EISA slots. EISA cards look like ISA cards with one crucial difference: They have 100 connectors divided into one set of 62 connectors and one set of 38 connectors.
- VESA cards fit only into VESA slots. VESA cards vary from computer to computer.
- PCI cards fit only into PCI slots. PCI cards are easy to distinguish from the other cards because PCI connectors are much narrower and the entire connector is smaller.

Remembering these points ensures that you won't accidentally try to force an ISA card into a PCI slot.

Learning which adapter card interface is which is simply a matter of reading the label on the adapter card's box and then looking at the edge connector (the gold-striped thing) on the bottom of the card. After you have identified a few, you're a pro; you'll identify adapter card interfaces in a snap.

- **Don't use force to fit adapter cards into slots**. This is a sure-fire way to damage the card and void the warranty. If a card doesn't fit, pull it out and look at it. Is it the correct slot interface? Is the metal strip on the back of the card (the "slot cover") in the way somehow? Close examination can often explain why a card won't fit. Sometimes it's necessary to bend the bottom of the metal strip to fit—other times, the card just has to be rocked in slowly and gently. This process can be tedious, but it prevents cracked motherboards. You'll learn more about the process of installing adapter cards in the next section, but this precaution deserves to be repeated because it's caused more equipment failures than all the static in the world.

- **Use proper tools**. It's tempting to use any old tool to work on computers because they don't seem as mechanical as (for example) a car. Nonetheless, make certain that your tools fit. Have a good Philips screwdriver and a nutdriver set, if possible. Tweezers are useful for picking up small parts. A small pair of needlenose pliers can come in handy as well. If they're magnetized, either demagnetize them (heat works) or replace them—magnetism and computers just don't go together. And, of course, to reiterate what's said above, use a wrist strap.

Working on networking equipment need not be difficult if you're careful. It's mostly a matter of developing what writer Robert Pirsig calls *mechanic's feel*: a sense of respect for the physical properties of an object and a gut-level understanding of how much force is enough. It's common sense; don't force anything unless you have no other choice.

Installing Adapter Cards

Adapter cards are inescapable, particularly in the Intel-compatible computer world. Because very few computers come with built-in networking (although this is changing), at some point, you're going to have to take a deep breath, open a computer case, and plunge inside to install a network adapter card.

This section provides a hands-on view of the process of installing an adapter card in a computer. Remember that these instructions aren't universal; computers vary widely. The basic idea is to understand the steps and adapt to what you find when you open the computer.

1. **Shut off the computer's power and disconnect the power cord**.

2. **Identify the card**. Put on a ground strap, take the adapter card out of its packaging and examine it (see Figure 11.1). What is its interface (ISA, EISA, PCI)?

FIGURE **11.1**

Determine the slot interface by looking at the edge connector— the shiny gold connectors at the base of the card.

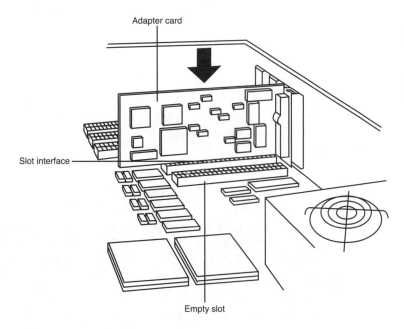

Adapter card

Slot interface

Empty slot

11

3. **Set the card (if the hardware supports it).** Look at the surface of the card. On some older cards, you may see switchblocks or jumper blocks, which are usually used to determine one or more of the adapter card's settings (I/O address, IRQ). If you see switchblocks or jumper blocks, refer to the manufacturer's documentation

to determine what settings they manage. Conversely, if you do not see jumper blocks or switchblocks, the adapter card may be plug and play or "soft-set." Figure 11.2 shows jumpers and switchblocks, which are set according to manufacturer specifications.

Soft-set cards usually require that you run installation software after physically installing the cards in the computer.

FIGURE 11.2

A jumper block and a switchblock. The jumper is a small piece of metal and plastic that makes an electrical connection like a primitive switch.

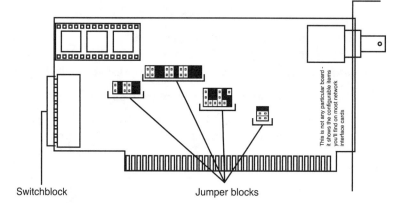

Switchblock   Jumper blocks

4. **Open the computer**. Once the card has been set (if it has jumpers or switch-blocks), rest it on its antistatic packaging (usually a bag made of silver mylar plastic). Unscrew the case cover of the computer (the screws are usually in the back) and lift off the case cover. If the case cover doesn't come off readily, don't use force; look for flanges and hidden hinges that could be preventing the case cover from coming off.

5. **Select and prepare the slot**. Select the slot in which you want to install the card and remove the slot cover—a small piece of sheet metal that covers the slot in the back of the computer when no card is installed (refer to Figure 11.1). The slot cover is usually held in with a 1/4-inch or 5/16-inch screw that often has a Philips slot as well. Save the screw after you've removed the slot cover—you'll need it to fasten the card when you're done.

6. **Install the card**. Take the card and line it up with the slot. Ensure that the sheet-metal piece that resembles the slot cover faces the outside of the computer. Once the card is lined up in the slot, gently but firmly press it into the slot. You may have to gently rock the card back and forth. When the card is fully seated in the slot, most of the connections on the bottom edge will be hidden inside the connector, and the part of the card that screws in will be level against the back of the computer's chassis. Screw the card in using the slot cover screw you removed earlier.

7. **Finish up**. Replace the case cover on the computer, screwing it back on securely. Plug in the power cord and restart the computer. You'll have to install device driver software (used to allow adapter cards and other hardware to interact with the operating system; device drivers are discussed in Hour 4, "Computer Concepts") to make it work; read the manufacturer's directions to do so.

See? Cards aren't hard to install at all. If you take a bit of time to do it correctly the first time, you can prevent the vast majority of headaches from damaged hardware. It's worth your while to look at your computer's manual and determine which slots have the same interface as the adapter card you want to install. If the computer has more than one slot with an interface that matches your adapter card's interface, use whichever slot is open—no one slot is preferable to any other.

> By the way, this procedure isn't limited to network cards. You install all adapter cards in more-or-less the same way. So once you know how to do it, you can become an installation fiend, putting cards in left and right, and wowing all your relatives (who will hail you as a computer expert and have you working on their PCs in short order).

Working on Wiring: Closets, Cables, Connections, Concentrators, and Terminators

After the network cards, wiring is in many cases the next most important part of a network. Without wires, data simply wouldn't get from there to here and back again. The next sections focus on some of the verities of wiring your network. It's basically a hands-on version of the wiring stuff you learned in Hour 5, "Network Concepts."

The Wiring Closet: Ethernet, Token Ring, ATM, and FDDI's Home Sweet Home

Most of the back end of a network should be behind locked doors. It's not because it's hazardous (it's not), but free access to data communications equipment can lead to information theft or physical theft of the equipment itself. (It's happened.)

As a result, it's a good idea to set up a wiring closet if you're building a network to serve an enterprise—whether that enterprise is a business, a town hall, a library, or whatever. (Of course, the wiring closet applies only if you're using a star topology; bus topologies typically don't have them, since they are serial by nature.) And a wiring closet doesn't have to take up a lot of space; it's perfectly acceptable for a wiring closet to simply be a centrally located closet that you can access to install electrical power and route cables. A lot of the time, the phone closet can double as a wiring closet without too much difficulty.

The basic wiring closet usually contains several items:

- **A set of 110 blocks**. A 110 block is a device, usually mounted on a wall, that has a row of RJ-45 jacks on it. Each jack is connected to a wire that runs out to a network wall jack elsewhere in the office. 110 blocks are also called patch panels (see Figure 11.3). It's possible to install and terminate your own patch panels. (It's pretty easy, in fact.) Because the wires that connect to the contacts on the back of the panel are color coded, it's difficult to make a mistake. Nonetheless, there are specialized tools involved, and it's wise to learn from someone who already knows how to do it.

FIGURE 11.3

A patch panel or a 110 block.

- **One or more concentrators**. Concentrators (hubs and switches) tend to be stored in the wiring closet for two reasons. First, they're generally pretty small—they can fit in a briefcase if an ethically-impaired person has the mind to steal one. Second, they make great listening devices; if a network card set up in a special way called promiscuous mode is plugged into the concentrator, it's possible to read every data packet passing over the network. Because this represents a huge security risk, it's best to lock the concentrators away (see Figure 11.4).

FIGURE 11.4

A typical concentrator.

- **Wiring bundles**. Because the wiring closet is where all your office network wiring converges, you'll usually have a bundle of cables connected to the 110 block. Wiring bundles represent one end of what can be an arduous task: running cables up hill, down dale, across ceilings, and down walls. If you have a lot of wiring to do, it's often better to let a professional pull and terminate your network wiring (doing so reduces the aggravation factor quite a bit).

- **Patch cords**. Patch cords are the cables that connect the 110 block to the concentrator. You need one patch cord to connect one port on the 110 block to one port on the concentrator. For Ethernet and Token Ring running on copper wire (far and away the most common type of network), this usually means a cable with an RJ-45 jack at each end (see Figure 11.5). For what it's worth, you also need a patch cord in each office to connect the computer's network card to the network wall jack.

Figure 11.5

An RJ-45 connector—a typical patch cord used for 10BASE-T and Token Ring.

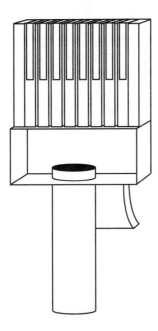

Wiring closets aren't absolutely necessary, but they do make life easier and more secure. And (for neat freaks) the best part of a wiring closet is that it keeps the messy part of the network behind closed doors.

Connecting a star or ring topology network is really easy once the wiring between the 110 block/patch panel and the jacks in offices have been installed. You simply have to plug in a patch cord between the computer's 10BASE-T network jack (it's on the network card you installed earlier) and the 10BASE-T outlet in the wall, and then ensure that the corresponding port on the patch panel is connected to the concentrator (see Figure 11.6). It's really simple, which is why it's a great design.

Figure 11.6

How computers are connected in a wiring closet/office jack situation.

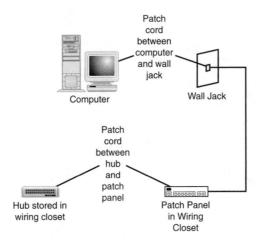

11

Summary

Thunder is good, thunder is fine; but it is lightning that does all the work.

—Mark Twain

As this statement teaches us, theory is fine and good, but practice is what allows us to hone our skills. The best way to get your networking skills into shape is to work with a bias towards action.

If you learned anything in this hour, it's that the physical hookup of a network is one of the least significant hurdles to successful networking. At the same time, in many people's eyes, this is the most daunting part of the process. In my estimation, the best way to become proficient with hardware installation is simply to do it a lot. Use old computers (they're often pretty inexpensive) and work with them. Make mistakes; you'll learn from them. And in the end, you'll be more successful.

Q&A

Q When installing adapter cards in a computer, what do you want to avoid?

A Primarily, you don't want to damage the card either by handling it too roughly or by applying static shock. Both can damage a card enough to make it wholly inoperable.

Q Why should a wiring closet be close to the center of an office space (if it's possible)?

A In Hours 3, 4, and 5, you learned that twisted-pair wire has a maximum length of 200 meters between repeaters (concentrators can function as repeaters). This means that you want to ensure that your wires are all more-or-less the same length so that none of them are too long to transmit data reliably.

HOUR 12

Network Applications

There is a cartoon that has made the rounds of the Internet a couple of times. It depicts a figure of a man and a woman in an office with all the attendant office machinery. The caption reads "We've got computers, fax machines, modems, phones, typewriters—now what can we do with this stuff to make money?"

Clearly, office equipment without a purpose is not going to accomplish any useful functions, except perhaps by accident. In the same fashion, your network needs a purpose before it can begin generating returns on your initial investment. During the next hour, you will learn about software applications that can assist you in getting full use of your network.

Some of the applications discussed in this hour are focused on accomplishing one task and one task only—group calendaring or email, for example. Other applications merely provide a framework onto which you can map your needs. Depending on the degree of function, the latter category is called either *PIMs* (*Personal Information Managers*) or *groupware*.

Both PIMs and groupware are designed to provide a framework for sharing information among multiple users; groupware typically offers a more robust, server-based solution, while PIMs often have a mechanism for sharing data that may involve nothing more complex than a shared directory on a commonly accessible hard drive.

In the next hour, you will learn about the following topics:

- What a network application is
- Why network applications are in demand
- The difference between proprietary systems and open systems

Let's begin by discussing email because it's the application that seems to drive network growth in a lot of cases.

Email

You've used postal mail; you know how it works. You write a letter, put it in an envelope, and write the address of the recipient (and your return address) on the outside. Then you put on a stamp and drop it off at the local post office. You don't really care how it gets from you to the recipient—as long as it gets there in a reasonable amount of time, that's fine.

Email works basically the same way as postal mail, only it's easier and delivery is much faster. You type your letter, select the recipient from a list (or type it in and save the name if you haven't sent email to that address before), select the priority, and send it. Your email system takes care of the return address, and the stamp is the bill you pay for your email service at the end of each month.

Email routes across your local network and the Internet without any more concern for the route it takes than a paper letter. If it gets there, great; if not, it will beat out the post office and get you a notification a lot faster that the message was undeliverable.

Email started out as a simple function of the early Unix operating systems. Essentially, email was basically an automated file-copying operation in which the file was copied from your local Unix system's hard drive onto a remote Unix system's hard drive. It was a bit of a *kludge* (pronounced "clooj"). A kludge is a term that's used to refer to solutions that work but not reliably or efficiently—a kludge is NOT a long-term solution. If you ride a bicycle and you tear a tire sidewall, lining the tire with a dollar bill to hold the tube inside the tire casing is a kludge. It works, but you don't want to bet your life on it, and it's not a long-term solution.

To get around the nonstandard and often incompatible email systems that pervaded the early Unix environment, a programmer named Eric Allman wrote a program called *sendmail*. Sendmail offers a huge range of options for sending and receiving mail. It's quite complex; properly configuring sendmail is considered quite a feat among Unix system administrators. In any case, sendmail does the following functions:

- Collects incoming mail for users on the network
- Ensures that mail is routed to the correct user
- Allows administrators to set up aliases that simplify figuring out email addresses

These three are the most basic functions of sendmail, which was and remains a hit in the networked community. In spite of its complexity, it started a trend toward email systems in which complexity was shifted to the server so that the user interface could be simpler.

Email is a lot like the telephone system; it has to be working all the time for users to have confidence in it. And if it is reliable, it will become a vital and necessary part of your work environment. Once a culture grabs hold of email and begins using it in earnest, it seldom lets go.

Uses of Email

It may at first seem silly to provide a description of the uses of email. After all, email is just mail with an electronic twist, right?

Not quite.

Email certainly can help replace interoffice memos and so forth. However, it can do a great deal more than that, both inside and outside the local network. Inside the local network, email often serves as a platform for groupware applications: Email is the *transport*, or the software that ferries data, between different computers. It's also a great way to spread news without going to the formal time and trouble of a photocopied document.

Externally, email can do additional things for you. Suppose that you have a customer list and want to keep the people on the list updated on a regular basis. Using a device called a *listserver*, you can send email to many people at once. Listservers are a curious anomaly; they provide a way to *subscribe* to or sign up for access to Internet newsgroups (ongoing multisubject and multithreaded serial discussions) and mass-mailings. Listservers are available on a variety of platforms; a properly configured listserver used within netiquette guidelines is a very useful tool for sending news to many people at once.

12

 A note on netiquette: Never put someone's email address on a listserver if they have not expressly informed you that they want to sign up for your mass mailings. Internet mass-mailings that send mail to people who are not interested in receiving it are a nuisance called *spam* by the Internet/networking community. Unsolicited email selling goods or services is also classified as spam.

Spamming is widely viewed as rude and undesirable, and typical responses to it range from angry to full-bore attacks that attempt to shut down a server. Ensure that the people on your email mass-mailings list want to be on your list—and make certain that each mass-mailing contains instructions on how to get off your mailing list. Internet junk mail is rapidly becoming an issue of major proportions for the networking community; it eats bandwidth and makes email simply another channel to shill gewgaws. At all costs, avoid contributing to the problem.

Email, in almost all its guises, is a valuable tool. If you get it right from the start, your network will have a tool that can drive demand for other networked resources.

Proprietary Mail Systems

With the advent of PC-based networking in the early-to-mid 1980s, a raft of vendors began building proprietary mail systems to operate in various PC environments. These systems, which included Lotus cc:Mail, Microsoft Mail, and various packages built around Novell's MHS (Message Handling System), often attempted to rectify what their designers saw as shortcomings in sendmail.

Proprietary email packages for PC networks are typically very easy to install and configure. However, in the main, the gain in ease of use is offset by a roughly equal decline in interoperability with other mail systems. Usually, PC-network-based proprietary mail systems from different manufacturers do not work with each other without the intercession of a mail gateway, a computer that converts mail from one proprietary format to another.

Additionally, proprietary mail systems cannot route mail directly to the Internet. To do so, they require yet another mail gateway to convert mail to *SMTP* (Simple Mail Transport Protocol) format, the section of the TCP/IP protocol suite that handles mail routing.

Most proprietary mail systems use a server-centric design. What this means is that it is efficient to use email only if you are directly connected to the network. In a server-centric design, most of the email application is stored on the server's hard drive, which means that it takes a long time to open over a remote-access connection—alternatively, it won't open at all.

As a result, proprietary email systems are generally not advisable. Although they are easy to configure and use, their drawbacks outweigh their benefits. It's usually better to select an open-standards-based email system.

Open-Standards Email

As with all things networked, the Internet Engineering Task Force (IETF) has worked out nonproprietary standards for the function of email. When you see something referring to

Internet mail standards, the IETF standards set forth in the Requests for Comments (RFC) documents are what's being referred to. Internet mail standards are surprisingly simple. As long as your network uses TCP/IP, it's possible to use Internet mail; all you need, really, is a server to run the server-side mail application software and the software to run at the client to retrieve mail from the server.

There are many different manufacturers of server and client Internet mail software. The beauty of the standards set forth by the IETF is that any client can work with any server as long as both pieces conform to the standards: SMTP for server-side work and POP3 or IMAP4 for the client side.

Server-Side Standards: Simple Mail Transport Protocol (SMTP)

The Simple Mail Transport Protocol (SMTP) is a surprisingly simple mail system that accomplishes one task superbly well: It routes mail between Internet-mail servers. SMTP is much simpler than earlier email protocols such as Unix-to-Unix Copy Program (UUCP), which demanded that a user type in the full route between his or her computer and the recipient's computer in order to send mail. With SMTP, all a user has to do is provide a username and an Internet domain name, and SMTP routes the message directly to the user's system, if it is possible.

Table 12.1 shows the difference between UUCP and SMTP mail routing.

TABLE 12.1   Comparing UUCP and SMTP

Protocol	Task	The Email Address
UUCP	User `Percy` wants to send user `Bertram` a message, and the message must route through computers `Fred`, `Ginger`, and `Tbone`.	`fred!ginger!tbone!bertram`
SMTP	User `Percy` wants to send user `Bertram` a message and all he knows is `Bertram`'s domain name. SMTP does not have to route through intermediate computers; instead, it sends mail directly to the server where the receiving user has an account.	`bertram@home.org`

As you can see, SMTP mail is much simpler to use than UUCP mail. It's fast and simple to use, and a properly configured SMTP server provides an ideal base for Internet-standards-compliant email client software such as POP3 and IMAP4, which we're (coincidentally) just about to discuss.

Client-Side Standards: POP3 and IMAP4

SMTP and UUCP handle interserver network mail. When the mail has to get from the server to the client, Post Office Protocol version 3 (POP3) and Interactive Mail Access Protocol version 4 (IMAP4) provide the services. These two protocols manage the client's interaction with the server.

Internet mail requires that two events happen when receiving mail:

- Mail must be received at the SMTP or UUCP server, where it is stored.
- A user must log in to the mail server using mail client software that is POP3- or IMAP4-compliant to retrieve the mail from the server.

POP3 and IMAP4 are client-side email protocols. Of the two, POP3 is the older email standard, and although it is very useful, IMAP4 has features that make it the more useful of the two.

In POP3-compliant mail, mail is initially received at the server. When the user logs in to the email server, mail is downloaded to the email client running on the user's desktop computer, and the copy on the server is deleted unless the user specifies otherwise. This is a useful system for passing email back and forth between the server and the client, but it works best when the client logs in with only one computer. Why? Well, with multiple machines, it's not possible to synchronize the email messages on both machines, or at least the outbound mail. Consider the following example.

Dan goes on a business trip and takes his laptop. While he is out of the office, he dials into the remote access/email server to check his POP3 email. He downloads all the mail waiting on the server into his laptop's email inbox and reads it. Some of the messages are entirely self-contained and do not refer to earlier messages; he knows what's going on with these. However, some of the messages make reference to other, earlier email messages that he received at his desktop computer at work—where they're still stored. He doesn't have a copy of them on his laptop, so he is at a disadvantage when replying to these messages. Unless he's leaving mail on his email server and only allowing one computer to delete it, his two email systems have gotten out of sync. Also, while he's on the road, if Dan wants to read a message, he must download the whole message—there's no message preview. This means that a piece of mail with a large attachment has to make the trip over the wire to his computer, even if he's connected over a phone line and doesn't want the attachment.

IMAP4, by contrast, allows a user to view all the subject lines of email when he logs in to the server—it's preview mode. In what is called disconnected mode, IMAP4 can keep copies of email on the server as well as download them to clients, which means that a remote client can access any of the email he has received.

If Dan is using an IMAP4-compliant email client, he can refer to a complete list of the previously received email messages he needs to view, and then download and read them. Because IMAP4 is supported in an increasing number of mail clients, it's recommended for networks whose users log in remotely as well as being connected to the local LAN.

Sending Files: Multipurpose Internet Mail Extensions (MIME)

In the beginning, there was Text, and Text was good enough for Email. And lo, the Lord (okay, the IETF) said, "It is not good that Text should be alone; it should also have the capability to consort with companion Files of all Types." And the IETF created MIME, and saw that it was good. And it was good.

If all email could carry were text messages, it would still be a software tool of surpassing usefulness. However, all files are not made of text-only messages. There are application binary files (programs you can run on your computer), picture files, video files, sound files, and so forth. And typically, these kinds of files cannot be carried over regular email channels.

As a result, the IETF decided to create a set of extensions for the SMTP mail standard that allowed files of many different types to be attached to email. Rather than defining all the file types and creating a new SMTP version each time a new file type came into existence, the IETF decided that they would create a system to which new file types could be added without changing the whole mail system. The IETF's standard turned out to be the MIME standard, which is used to copy files of many different types across the Internet.

As the Internet matures, many new file types will probably become available. However, MIME is open ended enough that it will support many new types of files. MIME is a useful tool; without it, the rest of the Internet-compliant email system would lose a significant portion of its utility.

12

Group Calendaring

If you've ever tried to schedule a meeting with a group of busy people who live out of their filofaxes, you know how hard it can be to find a time when every member of a group is available. You've also probably scheduled things and left phone messages or notes taped to desks asking someone to RSVP about a meeting. The process of scheduling is terrible…it is inefficient and it wastes everyone's time while they try to shuffle their schedules to be able to meet.

Fast-forward to the year 2000. If you're using a network, you have an opportunity no one has ever had before: You can use a network calendaring software package to schedule meetings directly from your computer!

Imagine this: You get a call from a client who wants you to come out and meet with him. However, he wants you to have a technical representative from your company with you as well. Instead of telling your client you'll get back to him about a time, you fire up the network calendaring software on your computer, specify that you want to create a meeting with you and your technical rep, and let the software find the next available time. You check the tech rep's calendar to ensure that she really is available on the date and time the computer suggested, and suggest that time to your client. If the proposed meeting time is good for your client, you're on. So you send a message to your technical representative that places the appointment into her calendar and sends her a notification message.

If this example seems like heaven to you, you'll be pleased to learn that it's possible with current technology. A host of great network scheduling software packages are available, and almost all of them offer a tremendous amount of flexibility. As a package, however, they all share one downside: They're all nonstandard, and no one group calendaring system interacts with any other group calendaring system. This is because there is no IETF standard that defines network calendar interoperability.

> In the last edition of this book, we mentioned several proposed calendaring standards: iCal, ICAP, SSTP, and others. Unfortunately, none of these have come to pass, and calendars are still proprietary.
>
> Eventually, the IETF will ratify one or more of these protocols for scheduling, and manufacturers will adopt it more widely.

Networked Contact Management

Contact management is an art that most of us never get particularly good at. Just think of the collections of business cards, notes, phone numbers, addresses, email addresses, and the like that the average person collects. If there were an efficient way to store all that stuff in one place so that it would be easy to search, that would provide real value. Right?

There is something that does that: contact management software. *Contact management software* is a global term used to describe a class of specialized software designed to store names, addresses, telephone numbers, and so on. Some packages move beyond phone-book-like functionality and allow users to track ongoing communications with the people and institutions stored in the database.

Used properly, contact management software can be a blessing, particularly when it's networked. For example, it provides a way for a sales force to track the most recent meeting it has had with clients; it can also schedule automatically, in some cases, a time for a next call after a preset amount of time has elapsed.

Like group calendaring, contact management software does not yet have an IETF standard, so for the most part, contact management software interoperates only with itself. This particular software has not been standardized because of the bewildering array of features falling under the contact management umbrella. For example, is a database that does nothing more than track a list of names and addresses considered contact management? Or does contact management start when you can track your phone calls, meetings, and correspondence? Should it be integrated with your email and calendaring applications? Should it be shared, private…or both? These questions have not yet been answered, and probably won't be answered for several years. However, a variety of packages exist that manage lists of contacts and allow various degrees of tracking, management, and reminders.

Commonly, contact management software must be able to store and retrieve information using a variety of criteria (a person's name, address, the company where he or she works, and so forth). Ideally, a shared contact management system should have additional user-defined fields (perhaps *client type*, or *most recent contact date*) that serve to more effectively narrow the search. Many packages offer this kind of flexibility, but until the IETF generates a standard, expect to spend a significant amount of time learning one or more groupware or PIM packages.

A Sampler of Network-Based Software

Because the preceding descriptions of email, calendaring, and contact management software are necessarily general, I decided to list several current examples of each genre. These packages are as compliant with standards as is possible, given the current state of the IETF's standards-writing process. Deployed in a network environment, these software products can provide value immediately. When calendaring and contact management are standardized, will the packages I list here change to adhere to the standard? No one knows; for nonstandardized products, that's a gamble you have to be willing to take. Of the products listed here, most will probably standardize as soon as calendar and contact standards are available.

Microsoft Outlook

When Microsoft built its Exchange mail/groupware server product, the company decided to create a fully integrated client, or a client in which email, calendaring, and contact management occur in the same interface. The first Microsoft product to realize this goal is Outlook, which is a Microsoft Exchange client. Microsoft, bucking the industry-standard PIM label, calls Outlook a *Desktop Information Manager*, or *DIM*. Current versions of Outlook support all mail protocols (POP3, IMAP4) including Microsoft's Exchange-based mail systems, and offer a variety of groupware applications which may be downloaded from the Microsoft Web site. Since its introduction, Outlook has become a fairly powerful mail client, and its groupware features have steadily gotten stronger. Unfortunately, Microsoft, being intent on leveraging *active content* including Web pages and programs embedded in emails, has repeatedly fallen prey to *macro viruses* which (for instance) send copies of infected messages to everyone in an Outlook user's contact list.

Outlook is closely linked with Microsoft's Office 2000 desktop productivity suite. In a special folder called the Journal, in fact, Outlook logs all documents generated in Office 2000 for future reference. The software has very few drawbacks; unfortunately, it's a first version, and it has not yet been optimized for speed as much as it will be in the future (see Figure 12.1).

FIGURE 12.1

A Microsoft Outlook screen.

A Few Others

Other products that fit into the PIM/groupware category include Symantec's popular ACT! product, Commence Corporation's Commence, and GoldMine. All have varying degrees of email integration, and all can share contact information. Each has its own proprietary scheduler, which for the most part does not interact with that of other systems.

Summary

In this hour, you learned something about the basic network applications that begin to extend your users' reach past the desktop. You also had the chance to learn about some of the products in this category.

Q&A

Q What is the difference between regular productivity applications (such as a word processor) and network applications?

A A network application leverages the network to enable users to communicate and collaborate with each other.

Q Why are Internet/TCP/IP-standard applications more desirable than applications that use proprietary communications protocols?

A TCP/IP is a vendor-independent standard; applications that adhere to it can work with other TCP/IP applications. By contrast, proprietary systems require expensive gateways to communicate with other systems; without a gateway, proprietary systems may not be able to communicate with other systems at all.

12

HOUR 13

Connecting to the Internet: Email and Web Sources

Over the course of the last several years, the Internet has become a measure for how well-networked a person is. At trade shows, attendees and exhibitors alike no longer want each others' phone numbers; instead, they vie for Internet email addresses. Vendors no longer offer to send product literature; instead, they direct potential customers to their Web pages, which contain complete brochures. Lots of billboards have Web addresses. And file updates for many products are available for download over the Internet. The Internet is inescapable. And email, once the dominant reason for wanting to connect to the Internet, has been eclipsed by World Wide Web access as the reason for most users to connect.

With all this fuss, it's natural to wonder how your network can be made to connect to the Internet. Once you're connected, the world is at your finger-tips. But before you can connect to the Internet, you have to sit down and figure out what your Internet-connectivity requirements actually are. Think about what bandwidth you require—do you need a high-bandwidth connection, or will something less suffice? Your network may not require anything more than Internet email access, which is a relatively simple proposition. On the other hand, you may be called on to provide World Wide Web access or FTP access to your users. As with any other business or organizational challenge, the connection you need depends on the tasks you have to achieve.

Generally, your choices range from simple low-end connections using plain phone lines (typically used for only one user—but there are a few exceptions) to high-end digital phone lines for providing World Wide Web access, file transfer, and whatever else the Internet has to offer.

Deciding which connection is appropriate can be a tribulation; the number of solutions for any given situation far exceeds the amount of time you have to investigate all of them. In the next hour, you'll get a primer on the minimum level of connectivity required to accomplish various Internet connectivity tasks such as sending email or using a Web browser.

Here's what you can expect to learn in this hour:

- The requirements to use Internet mail
- The various types of Internet connections
- The requirements for providing interactive Internet connections

Internet Email

The first and foremost Internet connection most users require is (surprisingly) not access to the World Wide Web. Instead, it's email. There's an irresistible seductiveness about the capability to send messages nearly instantaneously to anyone on earth who has an Internet mail address. Once a person has email, it's pretty rare that they'll abandon it outright; it's an exceptionally powerful tool. One could also argue that email has roused letter-writing from an fading art to a widespread skill. You can use Internet email to answer clients' informational queries, to chat with friends, to provide a personal touch to your business transactions, to pass along news—the possibilities are endless. This is referred to by some accountancy types as "making a good business case," which is to say it can be used to do work. They're right; in a world in which the fastest customer service is barely fast enough, email can be used as a tool to decrease response time and increase client satisfaction.

Before you can decide on the best method to route mail to the Internet, you must know and understand the various tasks that have to be accomplished between the time your user sends email and the time it gets to the Internet proper:

- **Email must be addressed properly**. If you are sending email from a POP3 or IMAP4 mail system, your mail has to have only the user's Internet email address added (`foo@bar.com`).

- **Email must have a connection to the Internet from where messages can be sent and received.** This connection can use any media, from wireless networks to regular phone lines, switched digital phone lines, or a full-time 24/7/365 dedicated Internet connection over a T1 or 56K digital frame relay phone line. One of the best things about TCP/IP-standard software is that it can run over almost any media; the software really doesn't care.

- **You must send and receive mail from a recognized domain.** If you get your email from a commercial provider, such as Juno or America Online, your email address is usually something like `joe@aol.com` or `joe@juno.com` (both email addresses are fictitious to the best of my knowledge). Essentially, you're sending mail through a remote server. If, on the other hand, your network is connected to the Internet with a permanent connection (T1, 56K, DSL, or cable modem), you can host your own domain, or have your own Internet domain name, such as `ourplace.com`. Sometimes, your email or Internet service provider will handle acquiring and maintaining your domain name on their servers; this is called *hosting a domain*.

Unless all three of these criteria are met, Internet mail cannot work properly. The following pages provide a pair of alternatives for Internet mail configurations, starting with the less expensive option.

Dial-Up Internet Mail

The simplest and easiest way to get Internet email is to use a dial-up email service. Not coincidentally, it's also the least expensive. If you subscribe to an online service, such as America Online, CompuServe, or an *Internet service provider* (also called an ISP, such as AT&T, the various Regional Bell Operating Companies, and a lot of small, local firms, all of whom sell connections to the Internet), you're already familiar with the basic model for this type of service: Using a modem, the computer dials into an online service and sends and collects messages. However, dial-up providers are (by and large) single-user solutions—they can't connect an entire network to the Internet. It is possible to use modems to provide Internet mail to a whole network, but it isn't advisable, since it's so slow. The ubiquity of T1s, DSL, and cable modems are much faster and much easier to configure.

13

In Figure 13.1, the workstations Fred, Ginger, and Beth send mail to each other using the mail server connected to their local network. But when they send messages to Bertram, the mail has to travel across the Internet. The local mail server recognizes that the address isn't for a user on the local network. Because the message isn't meant for a local user, the mail server forwards the mail to Bertram's mail server. Bertram can then get his mail from his own server.

The standard method for moving mail between servers is called *Simple Mail Transfer Protocol*, or *SMTP*. The standard SMTP software (used by just about every mailserver with clout) is called *sendmail*. Sendmail runs on Unix (although it's been ported to a variety of other operating systems) and manages the sending and receiving options for a large percentage of the Internet. Sendmail isn't the only message transfer agent software; lots of other manufacturers have written their own variations on the theme. But sendmail, for all its complexity, is far and away the best mailserver software on the planet (in the author's opinion).

FIGURE 13.1

Routing Internet email through an ISP.

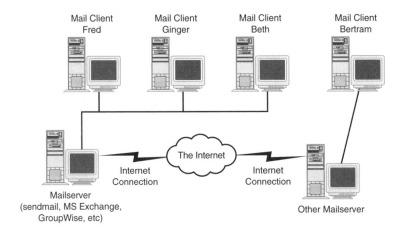

A dial-up connection using a modem requires that both sides of the connection be capable of using Point-to-Point Protocol (PPP), which is the part of the TCP/IP protocol stack that runs over standard dial-up phone lines. Typically, the ISP has a pool of IP addresses that it assigns on-the-fly to each caller as he or she dials in. When a user uses dial-up phone lines to connect to an ISP, it does not have a fixed IP address. Instead, it is assigned a different address each time it connects to the ISP (see Figure 13.2). This uses a member of the TCP/IP protocol suite called *Dynamic Host Configuration Protocol*, or *DHCP*. DHCP is a protocol used by a wide variety of network administrators to automate distribution of IP addresses to users. ISPs use DHCP to assign IP addresses because it allows them to have a pool of addresses that they can assign on-the-fly to whomever dials in.

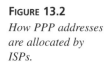

FIGURE 13.2

How PPP addresses are allocated by ISPs.

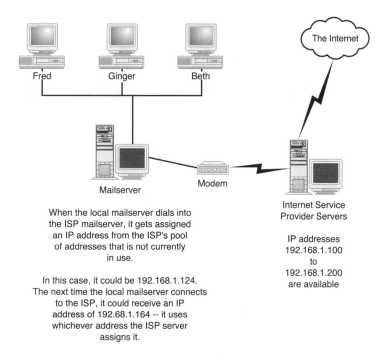

Mailserver

Modem

When the local mailserver dials into the ISP mailserver, it gets assigned an IP address from the ISP's pool of addresses that is not currently in use.

In this case, it could be 192.168.1.124. The next time the local mailserver connects to the ISP, it could receive an IP address of 192.68.1.164 -- it uses whichever address the ISP server assigns it.

Internet Service Provider Servers

IP addresses
192.168.1.100
to
192.168.1.200
are available

If the email address on a message isn't good—that is, if the user sending the mail mistyped the address, or if the email server's name-server can't match the domain name (everything to the right of the @ in an email address) to an IP address—the Internet service provider's mail server will send the user an "undeliverable mail" message so that the user knows the mail didn't get through.

This process, believe it or not, is universal. No matter what method you use to connect to an Internet mail server, the process remains the same. What varies are the speeds and the protocols.

Dedicated-Connection Internet Mail

Typically, the term *dedicated Internet connection* is used to describe a connection to the Internet that uses a high-speed digital phone line, such as a T1 or 56K. You'll also hear T1 circuits referred to as *PVCs*, or *Permanent Virtual Circuits*, if they're frame relay.

In a dedicated connection over a high-speed digital phone line (which is the most common form of digital connection), email is exchanged between servers running Simple Mail Transfer Protocol (SMTP), the part of the TCP/IP protocol stack that handles mail routing between servers. End-users who send and receive mail from servers use the POP3 protocol. POP3, the third iteration of POP, the most common user-to-server mail protocol currently in use.

13

As you've already learned, there are a variety of ways to connect a network to the Internet, ranging from dial-up to dedicated connections. The following sections describe these types of connections in greater detail.

Understanding High-Speed Internet Connections

Sometimes, a dial-up connection just won't do. If more than four users are clamoring to be connected to the Internet so that they can all use their Web browsers simultaneously, it's probably a good idea to start looking into digital phone lines, such as the aforementioned T1 or 56K frame relay link, rather than trying to provide them access over standard phone lines. Alternatively, if you have to connect a school or library to the Internet, you don't have much choice; the system has to be up and functioning, and a lot of users need to have access to it, so you need a high-speed phone line.

High-speed data networking has acquired a mystique entirely out of proportion to how difficult it is to configure and maintain. It's true that ordering them requires some time and attention, and it's also true that some are expensive, but they're not as complex as nuclear physics and they don't cost as much as anything Cartier. In fact, DSL and cable modems provide tremendous speed at very fair prices.

To get a high-speed data network line into your space, you have to call your local telephone company and order it. If you're dealing with an ISP, however, you may not have to do the ordering yourself; ISPs have got the art of ordering (or provisioning, in the telephone-company parlance) well mastered. They also control the topology (in this case, *topology* refers to the type of connection—a T1 or 56K frame relay line, or a DSL or cable modem). Once you've settled on a price for the ISP's service and the price of the connection (often rolled into one price that you pay the ISP), the ISP orders the line from your local telephone (or cable) company. This generally means that you'll get a call out of the blue several weeks later from a telco or cable installer to schedule installation of your new connection. The average lead time for a digital service line is about six to eight weeks in many parts of the United States; in large part, this delay can be attributed to a huge backlog of digital phone service that has to be installed. The phone companies and cable companies make up the backbone of the Internet; as the Internet has grown, the telcos and cable companies have found themselves scurrying to keep up with customer orders for new digital service. For what it's worth, DSL/cable modem/T1 installation is a nice secure career right now—there just aren't enough qualified installers!

After the line is installed, the installer generally ties it into your existing telephone wiring and installs a device of some sort that allows the digital phone line to connect to your local network. If it's a T1 or 56K, sometimes the phone company will install a Channel Service Unit/Data Service Unit (CSU/DSU) that will then connect to a router; in other cases, the network's router may have CSU/DSU capabilities built in. In the case of DSL and cable modems, the installer will generally put a small device on the network with one connection to your local network and another connection to the ISP's media (a DSL line or a cable connection).

In networks using T1s, the DSU/CSU just connects the digital phone line to the router. The router is what takes care of sending and receiving packets from outside the local network. Remember the example from earlier in the hour with the computer that used IP forwarding? Well, instead of using a computer to forward packets, digital lines use routers to send packets to the outside world. Same thing.

A router basically does very little except use the Exterior Gateway Protocol (yet another member of the TCP/IP protocol suite that was discussed in Hour 3, "Getting Data from Here to There: How Computers Share Data") to forward packets into the network that are meant for computers inside the network, and to forward packets from the internal network to the outside world. Usually, the router has one port that connects to the DSU/CSU, and one port that connects to the 10BASE-T hub of an Ethernet network. The IP address of the router is also the same IP address given to each workstation computer on the network as the default gateway to the Internet.

In addition to the hardware, try to get a Class C IP address, or a subset of a Class C address. The easiest way to pass messages between workstations and the Internet is if both operate using TCP/IP addresses. Depending on the size of your network, you can assign a fixed IP address (also called *static addressing*) to each system on the network, or you can use Dynamic Host Configuration Protocol (DHCP) to assign IP addresses to internal network computers each time they connect to the network. It doesn't matter how small your network is—DHCP is one of the great inventions of the last decade. It effectively preempts about ninety percent of "I can't connect to the network" problems from a hardware and IP addressing perspective and is well worth investigating further.

Digital Internet connections are wonderful. They offer unparalleled speed and access to Internet resources. However, they (and any other line that offers a fixed IP address) are a potential security hole on your network. And security holes in computers, like unlocked doors, are an invitation to less-than-honest people.

Firewalls

You may be convinced that the vast majority of Internet users are basically good (or harmless, which is more important) people. And your perception would be correct; only a tiny proportion of Internet users deliberately break into networks where they're not authorized to be.

13

Remember, however, that there are something like 100 million Internet users worldwide. One percent of that is 1 million; one-tenth of one percent is 100,000. So, percentage-wise, there aren't a lot of crackers. But even so, there are more than you might think. Whatever the percentage of crackers, that minority is responsible for a lot of misery in the form of stolen information, stolen credit card numbers, misused systems, and public embarrassment for individuals and businesses whose computers have been misused. You must protect your network if you use high-speed dedicated connections, even if you don't think you have anything to lose. It's just good sense. You wouldn't leave the doors of your business unlocked outside of business hours, and you don't leave your cash registers hanging open during business hours; by the same logic, secure your network.

To protect your network, you need a *firewall*. A firewall is a computer that essentially authenticates, or verifies the logins, of anyone who tries to enter your network through your Internet connection. Firewalls come in a variety of shapes and sizes, but it's usually a good idea to make the firewall part of a very small, separate network that sits between the router and your internal network. Almost always, firewalls have two (or more) network cards. You'll see why in the next paragraph.

Small networks that are situated between the Internet and the internal network are called (variously) *sandboxes* or *demilitarized zones (DMZs)*. DMZs/sandboxes are essentially separate networks with their own hubs or switches that route packets from the router through the separate concentrator to the first card in the firewall. The firewall then checks the packets to find out whether or not they are authorized to use the internal network. If they can't be authenticated, the firewall discards them. If they can be authenticated, the packets are allowed through the firewall and out the second network card, which is connected to the internal network.

Firewalls are not cheap. But if you're going to build a network that connects to the Internet using digital phone lines, you really need to find one, install it, and keep it up to date.

In Figure 13.3, incoming data passes through the DSU/CSU to the router, which routes through the first network card in the firewall. If the firewall authenticates the packets, the packets pass out of the firewall's second network card and into the internal network.

Firewalls come in all shapes and sizes. Some firewalls, such as Raptor's Eagle product and CheckPoint's Firewall1, or some of the Linux-based firewalls, are software that run on a *hardened* version of an operating system. A *hardened operating system* is an operating system where as many security holes as possible are closed. The firewall software then uses the hardened operating system as a platform from which to authenticate (or not) the network. Such firewalls are effective, and one of their advantages is that they can periodically be updated to protect against new *exploits* (or a means of circumventing security).

FIGURE 13.3

A diagram of a digital-phone-line connected system with a firewall/ proxy server.

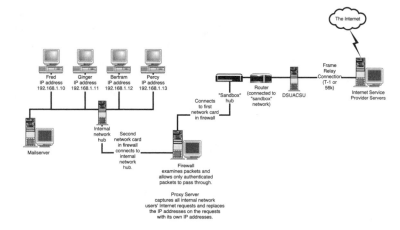

Another class of firewalls is dedicated firewall devices, such as Cisco's PIX. These are devices that look very much like routers; typically they're one or two rack-spaces high and are in a rack with your hubs, switches, and routers rather than on a bench in a server farm. These devices are designed from the ground up for security, so by default most access is denied until it's specifically enabled. Readers of T.H. White's *The Book of Merlin* may recall the ants' maxim: *"everything not expressly forbidden is prohibited,"* which pretty neatly describes the situation here. Rather than booting from a disk and having an operating system that can be hacked, this type of firewall boots from flash-memory and boot PROM chips, which are much more difficult for an attacker to modify. Dedicated firewall devices, like their software-based counterparts, *can* be updated period-ically, so the purchase of one of these devices doesn't automatically mean a limited fea-ture set in the future.

Proxy Servers

Firewalls are all well and good, but a firewall by itself can still leave you open for trou-ble. Why? If your internal network runs TCP/IP, each computer has a unique address. And without getting into the subject too deeply, those internal IP addresses can offer the discerning and skilled cracker an opportunity to get into unauthorized areas of the net-work.

How do you avoid allowing users' TCP/IP messages and requests from advertising their IP addresses? With proxy servers, of course. A proxy server is a rather ingenious method of preventing internal IP numbers from being visible to the outside world without deny-ing your users access to any of their beloved Internet resources.

How does a proxy server work? Well, you configure each user's TCP/IP software (on his or her desktop or laptop computer) to look for a proxy server at a specific IP address.

13

When the user clicks a link in a Web browser, such as Netscape or Explorer, for example, the data packets sent to that Web site don't route directly through the firewall and out to the Internet. Instead, the proxy server captures the internal computer's request to show a Web page. Then the proxy server takes note of the IP address of the computer on the internal network and sends a request for the same resources the internal user made—but the request is coming from the proxy server's IP address, not the internal user's IP address. When answering data packets (in this example, the Web page) come in over the Internet, the proxy server collects them and forwards them to the IP address of the network user who originated the request.

As a result, to any observer outside the network, all requests for resources (Web pages, FTP files, whatever) seem to come from only one computer. This is terribly frustrating for malicious users, but it should be some source of comfort for people trying to protect their networks.

Lots of firewalls offer this service; it's called *Network Address Translation*, or NAT for short. So in many cases, the firewall and proxy are on one box.

Protocol Translation

There are other things that you can do to tie your network into the Internet. If you don't want to run TCP/IP on your internal network—and that is a possibility if (for instance) you're running NetWare (which uses IPX) and don't want another protocol on your network)—and your users are clamoring for Internet access, you have another option: protocol translation.

Protocol translation is a tool that, used correctly, can ease an administrator's mind. It's not a panacea, however; if you're planning on hosting a Web site or building an *intranet* (an internal network that uses Internet standards), protocol translation won't work. You have to run TCP/IP inside the network (or at least inside the DMZ) to do these things.

If, on the other hand, all you need to do is provide simple, reasonably secure Net access to your users, protocol translation can be a boon. Essentially, it takes the IPX you run inside the network and translates it into IP. Protocol translation is also quite secure; because there's only one machine on a network that runs TCP/IP, all the IP requests seem to come from that machine. (Protocol translation is essentially proxy service with a translation at the address layer, or OSI layer 3.) Plus, even if a cracker *did* manage to get inside the protocol translator system, all the cracker would find would be a collection of IPX addresses, which bear very little relationship to IP addresses. Hopefully, the malicious user would get confused and discouraged. Since telnet and other TCP/IP services don't run over IPX, a cracker would be limited to the protocol-translating server—hardly rich pickings.

Both Microsoft and Novell now offer proxy server and protocol translator packages with their flagship products; both are simple to configure and use. While protocol translation is a good solution, in the final analysis, it's a workaround, and probably not the best way to handle Internet access to the internal network. A better solution is to stick with TCP/IP standard—install TCP/IP as well as a good firewall and pay attention to the network.

Summary

In this hour, you learned quite a bit about various ways you can connect to the Internet. Although this discussion has been necessarily general, it does provide a foundation for your decision-making process. Use the following worksheet to help determine what you need.

Worksheet

1. Which of the following Internet services do your users need?

    ___ Internet mail

    ___ World Wide Web access

    ___ FTP access

    ___ Telnet access

    If all you need is Internet mail, consider getting a dial-up mail gateway. It's the least expensive option and is usually quite reliable (even if it is not blazingly fast).

    If you need Web, FTP, and Telnet access, on the other hand, your range of options is considerably broader: from a shared dial-up connection to a full T1 or faster. What you choose depends on your needs and your pocketbook. Dial-up access is usually pretty cheap; digital service, such as T1s, cost upwards of $2,000 per month.

2. How many users do you have?

    ___ 2–10 (shared dial-up)

    ___ 10–50 (56K, low-end fractional T1, or dial-up ISDN)

    ___ 50–100 (high-end or full T1 or dial-up ISDN)

    ___ more than 100 (Full T1 or faster)

    These are just guidelines for determining which service can provide optimum performance for a given number of users. These recommendations are not absolute.

13

3. What is your annual budget (if you don't have one, what are you willing to spend annually) for Internet services?

___ $500 (typical cost of dial-up connection)

___ $4,000 (typical 56K cost)

___ $9,000 (low-end fractional T1 line)

___ $15,000 and above (full T1 or faster)

Q&A

Q What is the primary method for establishing dial-up connections to the Internet, and what advantages does it have over other methods?

A The primary method for establishing dial-up connections is Point-to-Point Protocol (PPP). Although PPP is (for the most part) restricted to the speed of a single modem (currently less than 53 kilobits per second, at the fastest), it nonetheless offers a host of benefits:

- PPP operates over standard phone lines, so it can work from almost any location that has a phone.

- PPP's use of regular phone lines means that it provides inexpensive Internet access compared to other connection methods (such as T1s).

- PPP can be used over ISDN lines, which makes it versatile. A connection that uses regular lines can sometimes be upgraded to ISDN with the installation of an ISDN line and some new ISDN hardware.

- Some PPP software allows multiple PPP lines to be aggregated, or connected together to increase bandwidth (a rather esoteric benefit).

Q How do you figure out the various speeds of a fractional T1?

A All the fractional speeds of a T1 circuit are multiples of 128K (for example, 128K, 256K, 384K, and so on until you reach the 1.544 megabit-per-second data rate that is the fastest speed of a T1). Internet service providers generally offer many of these speeds: 128K, 256K, 5112K, and full T1 are the most common increments.

PART IV

Network Operating Systems

Hour

HOUR **14**

Microsoft Windows Peer Networking

Microsoft Windows Networking

Although it's true that there are many different network products in the marketplace, it's also true that Microsoft has, since the early 1990s, done a stellar job ensuring that networking was available to most users of its Windows software. Although it's true that early versions of Windows for Workgroups were neither terribly fast nor terribly reliable, the networking built into the Windows shell—and later Windows 95, 98, Me and Windows NT operating systems—is both fast and reliable. It's also absurdly easy to configure.

In this hour, you will learn about the following topics:

- Various Microsoft Windows network software products
- Protocol selection for a Windows network
- Configuring a network on each system: NetBEUI and TCP/IP

Windows Operating Systems

When Microsoft introduced Windows for Workgroups in the early 1990s, it knew that the product had to satisfy two markets to succeed. The first was the corporate market, which had found that Windows 3.x left a great deal to be desired in terms of its capability to function in a network setting. The second was the emerging small-network market, the small offices, libraries, and yes, even the home networks of computer users eager to share files and printers.

To say that Microsoft succeeded beyond its wildest dreams would be incorrect. Although the company sold a lot of copies of Windows for Workgroups, it also took some well-deserved flak for the shortcomings of the product. People complained that it didn't multi-task very well, that it fundamentally relied on single-tasking MS-DOS, and that it had a non-intuitive interface to network resources. Last, networkers didn't like the fact that running more than one protocol on Windows for Workgroups was a recipe for disaster—the system expended so much memory in the process of networking that there wasn't much memory left for applications.

Not everyone, however, was upset by the shortcomings of Windows for Workgroups. The only protocol included with Windows for Workgroups was NetBEUI, so third-party vendors were able to sell various other protocols (mostly NetWare IPX and TCP/IP) to users for whom NetBEUI's single-segment-networking wasn't a viable option. Although this represented an additional expense for large corporate networkers whose networks relied on TCP/IP, in the long run, the arrangement turned out to be good for PC buyers.

During this period, firms such as FTP Software, Hummingbird, and others entered the PC software market in earnest. Their entry into the market revealed a shift in the attitude of corporate networking toward personal computers: Because they could run TCP/IP and connect to already-existing corporate resources, they were to be treated as acceptable (but not great) corporate citizens.

For more information on these two protocols, refer to "Network Protocols" in Hour 3, "Getting Data from Here to There: How Computers Share Data."

Although Windows for Workgroups had its shortcomings, it set a precedent: All future Microsoft operating system products would be networkable. In a world of poorly connected PC operating systems, this was both a revelation and a revolution.

Windows 95, 98, and Me

Windows for Workgroups was superseded in late 1995 by Windows 95, Microsoft's first attempt at a 32-bit consumer operating system. Windows 95's networking components were a great deal more comprehensive than those of Windows for Workgroups. Windows

95 included NetBEUI, the flat namespace, nonroutable protocol that Microsoft used for very small networks, an IPX-compatible protocol for use with Novell NetWare networks, and a surprisingly capable IP stack. Because networking consumers had expressed a desire to simplify dial-up networking, Microsoft included a capable (and relatively simple-to-configure) dial-up networking client (as discussed in greater depth in Hour 7, "Remote Networking"). Windows 95, intended to be all things to most people, rapidly found broad acceptance among PC manufacturers who sold it on desktop computer systems.

In 1998, Microsoft released a new operating system called Windows 98 that built on the capabilities of Windows 95. Given Microsoft's sudden and intense focus on Internet-capable products, it had a desktop that was intimately tied to Internet and other TCP/IP resources, and new software like Peer Web Server, which enabled anyone with Windows 98 on their PC to host Web pages. It also had better power management and better over-all stability than Windows 95, and it consequently sold like hotcakes.

The latest iteration in this family is Windows Me. Released in September 2000, it is related to Windows 98 as 98 was to 95—an update with some new features, better net-working, some minor changes.

Windows NT Workstation and Windows 2000 Professional

In 1993, between the launch of Windows for Workgroups and Windows 95, Microsoft released its enterprise 32-bit operating system, Windows NT, with surprisingly little fan-fare. It's understandable; Windows NT 3.1, the initial version of Microsoft's enterprise-level operating system, was not as capable as users would have liked. It was big and slow, and it did not run 16-bit applications (which made up the vast bulk of the Windows software market at that time) particularly well. Worst of all, it did not network well at all—there was very little software to allow it to tie into other computers.

About a year and a half after the release of Windows NT 3.1, however, Microsoft released Windows NT 3.5. NT 3.5 was not simply a minor upgrade; it was a fundamental rewrite of NT with a variety of options added that made it network friendly right out of the box. Microsoft had also, in the interim, firmed up its networking strategy, in the process dividing NT into two operating systems: Windows NT Server, which was capa-ble of managing domains, or logical collections of computers, in much the same fashion as a NetWare or Unix server; and Windows NT Workstation, which had no less connec-tivity than its server-oriented sibling but had the additional opportunity to participate in workgroups, Microsoft's term for peer resource sharing.

14

Windows NT Workstation continued to evolve to version 4.0, which shares a common interface with Windows 95 and 98. Windows NT Workstation 4.0 could connect to a variety of networks, as can its other Windows siblings, and it offers much greater stability because each application (including a great deal of the networking software) runs in *separate memory spaces*—which (ideally) ensures that no application can grab memory that other applications (or the operating system) are using.

The latest iteration in this branch of Microsoft's family tree is Windows 2000 Professional. Windows 2000 Professional is a desktop operating system that Microsoft markets to businesses rather than home users. Its appearance is closer to Windows 98 than Windows NT 4.0, and the networking configuration tools have changed quite radically for the better—it's much easier to configure now. In addition, it's also possible to make a lot of network changes without rebooting the system, a practice for which Windows NT was notorious.

In a *workgroup* (that is, a Windows network without a Windows NT or 2000 Server managing the whole network) configuration, any member of this family of operating systems can connect to each other, assuming that the correct parameters are in place. The next section acquaints you with Windows workgroup networking concepts.

Basic Windows Networking Concepts

Basic Windows networking is quite simple. There are three simple concepts to understand that go a long way toward explaining Microsoft networking: sharing, arbitrary sharing, and workgroups. There are some other concepts that you'll need to learn about, such as Windows 2000 Server domains and Active Directory, but we'll deal with those in the next chapter. This is about networking with Windows at the desktop level.

Sharing

The first major concept in Microsoft networking is sharing. When you were a kid, you probably had some object that others coveted…and that you jealously clutched, fearful of losing. Adults, who understood the social milieu better than your childhood self, probably suggested that you allow another child to use your object of desire, saying, "share—be nice." A lot of the time, you tried to put conditions on the use of the shared object, conditions that were usually completely disregarded or complained about until you were convinced to remove the restriction.

With Windows networking, you're in the same position again. Your drive space and printers are your precious objects; in Windows peer networking, you share them so that other users can access them. But this is where it gets better than being a kid: You get to set conditions for use, such as which users are allowed to access resources and when they are allowed to use them, and other users have to go along with it. *Nyaah nyaah*!

Sharing represents a huge simplification of resource sharing. It's a useful way to ensure that other users on a network can have access to a given workstation's file and print resources. Its only downside is that when an NT Server isn't involved, it's arbitrary and high maintenance. Consequently, the printer and file-sharing described here is not for use in large enterprise networks; this is how resources are shared in a smaller group of computers that may or may not have a server.

Arbitrary Sharing

The second of the three concepts is that sharing is *arbitrary*. If you share a whole drive or a folder on your local drive, any authorized user can connect to it and assign it a drive letter (for example, h:\) on his or her workstation. Likewise with printers: If you share a printer, any other user with access rights can connect to it and print to it.

However, each workstation that has access to your file and print resources has to decide to connect to them. This means that if user Beth at computer BETH shares her local hard drive and printer as BETHC and BETHPRNT, it's possible that user Alice on computer ALICE will map (or assign) J:\ as the drive letter she uses to access Beth's C drive (see Figure 14.1). By the same token, user Barbara on computer BARBARA may want to call Beth's C drive Q:\. This doesn't present a problem until users start working on more than one computer (Beth's C drive is J:\ on one user's computer and Q:\ on another). If the users don't know which drive letters are assigned to which machines (in other words, if you don't enforce at least some degree of standardization), this is a recipe for chaos.

FIGURE 14.1

Beth's computer is shared as BETHC *and* BETHPRNT, *but Alice calls* BETHC J:\ *and Barbara calls it* Q:\. BETHPRNT *is likewise renamed.*

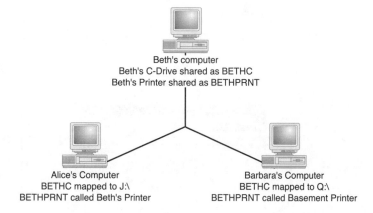

Beth's computer
Beth's C-Drive shared as BETHC
Beth's Printer shared as BETHPRNT

Alice's Computer
BETHC mapped to J:\
BETHPRNT called Beth's Printer

Barbara's Computer
BETHC mapped to Q:\
BETHPRNT called Basement Printer

14

Likewise, any authorized user can connect to a given shared printer. However, the authorized user can call the printer anything he or she wants: Beth's printer, shared as BETHPRNT, could be called Beth's Printer on Alice's machine and My Printer on Barbara's computer. Once again, this doesn't cause problems until users start using more than one machine. Then they get confused because the resources on one machine aren't in the same locations as the resources on the computer the user normally uses. This calls up another shortcoming of Microsoft networking: inconsistent naming of resources on remote systems. It's something that Microsoft would do well to change, in the author's opinion.

Workgroups

The third concept of Windows peer networking is (drum roll...may I have the envelope, please?) *workgroups*. Windows for Workgroups was not named arbitrarily; it was named after the atomic unit of network organization in Microsoft's initial take of the networking world. In Windows terms, a workgroup is a group of computers that share a common workgroup name. Workgroups don't enforce security or provide any particular resource other than making the network easier for users to browse—it doesn't provide any particular networking function other than user-level organization. More than one workgroup can exist on a given physical network; in fact, an almost unlimited number of workgroups can exist. Every computer can have its own workgroup—though the utility of doing so is questionable.

If your network will be divided between a sales staff and a technical staff, you might divide your network into two workgroups. One, called SALES, connects your sales staff together; the other, called TECH, ties your technical users together. If a user from either group needs a resource on a machine in the other workgroup, that user can connect to it, but most of the time he or she is working within his or her own workgroup. This kind of networking provides a user-level logical segmentation of the network, and can help make resources easier for users to find.

Figure 14.2 shows a workgroup as it shows up in the Network Neighborhood window in Windows. Note that the computer names are all dissimilar; they all, however, belong to the same workgroup.

FIGURE **14.2**

A Windows Network Neighborhood screen showing a work-group.

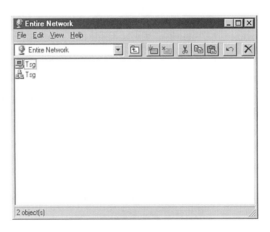

Protocol Selection for Windows Networks

In line with the recommendations made in other parts of this book, you'll find that anything that complies with open standards (which in this case means TCP/IP) is preferable to proprietary networking. Consequently, for most applications, Windows peer network should use TCP/IP as the default protocol.

However, there are reasons why you might not want to use TCP/IP. If you're building a small network that won't ever connect to the Internet, there's no reason for you to use TCP/IP. That doesn't happen very often; most networks will eventually get connected to the Internet one way or another. So TCP/IP is the protocol to select if a choice is available. TCP/IP is, as we've said earlier in the book, scalable, efficient, and heavily standardized, and thus in almost all networking situations it is the best available choice.

But just so you know about the alternatives: NetBEUI, Microsoft's small-network protocol of choice, makes Windows networking fairly simple. As long as each workstation is running the NetBEUI protocol, is correctly connected to a network (from a physical perspective), and has a unique name (for example, you can't have two computers named CLEVE in the same network), you're going to network successfully. Unlike TCP/IP, NetBEUI doesn't identify computers with a number; everything is done by names—which, by some obscure quirk, humans more readily grasp than numbers (imagine that!). So you can have a workgroup called BICYCLE that connects workstations called MOUNTAIN, ROADIE, FRED, and DOWNHILL...and never have to worry about network connectivity.

Unfortunately, NetBEUI's chief downfall is that it's not *scalable*, meaning that the network doesn't have the capability to grow. For example, if a network has 10 users and grows to 100 users, will the current network architecture continue to work well? If the answer is yes, the system is scalable; if not, it is not scalable. You can use it on one network, in one location, but you can't create a WAN using it. And because the Internet runs TCP/IP rather than NetBEUI, you can't connect to the Internet using NetBEUI. Figure 14.3 shows the connections and limitations of NetBEUI.

Now that you understand these Microsoft networking basics, the next hour shows you how to configure protocols and share resources on Windows 2000 Server. These discussions will include a certain amount of technical jargon in dealing with TCP/IP. You'll learn terms that you'll face in real life when you configure your own network.

14

FIGURE 14.3

A NetBEUI work-group has no IP addresses, no muss, no fuss—but no Internet connection, either.

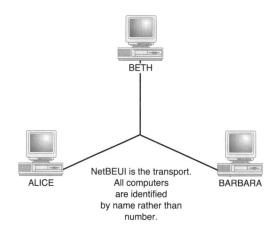

BETH

NetBEUI is the transport.
All computers
are identified
by name rather than
number.

ALICE

BARBARA

Summary

In this hour, you got a basic look at Microsoft Windows networking. It's probably the simplest network in this book because it's essentially a group of computers in a decentralized configuration that can grow by accretion...up to a point.

As you've probably noticed, peer networking, even when it's this easy, offers plenty of potential for chaos. That's why we build client/server networks. The next several hours focus on client/server technologies, starting with Windows 2000 Server, that offer some central organization—and a way to hold back the chaos.

Q&A

Q What are the circumstances under which NetBEUI is an appropriate protocol choice for a Windows peer network? TCP/IP?

A NetBEUI is appropriate for the following conditions:

- The network is very small (10 to 15 computers) and will not be divided into multiple segments (because NetBEUI can't be routed, only bridged).
- The network does not have to connect to the Internet.

By contrast, TCP/IP is appropriate for the following conditions:

- The network must be divided into multiple segments. TCP/IP is appropriate because it can be subnetted (a single TCP class A, B, or C address can be broken into smaller sets of addresses) and because TCP/IP can be routed.
- The network has to connect to the Internet.
- The network administrator has the time to set up a TCP/IP network.

Q **Which user of a Windows share (that is, a shared resource such as a disk or printer) determines the drive letter or printer name?**

A The client. Even though each share is given a name at the host computer, the client selects a drive letter for client resources. This is why drive letters in a peer-to-peer network don't have to be the same for each computer; each computer in a peer-to-peer network selects its own drive letters for a given share.

Likewise, a client computer connects to a printer (for example, //BETH/BETHPRNT) but can rename it Beth's downstairs printer when it appears on the desktop or in a list of printers.

14

HOUR **15**

Microsoft Windows 2000 Server

Now that you've had a taste of Microsoft networking, it's time to move on to the next level: basic client/server Microsoft networking. Because we've already dealt with Windows networking without servers, the logical next step is to examine Windows 2000 Server, Microsoft's client/server network operating system.

In this hour, you'll learn about the following:

- Windows 2000 Server
- Microsoft Windows 2000 Server concepts
- How to provide shared resources to your 2000 Server users
- How to configure the network for multiple client types

About Windows 2000 Server

When Microsoft released Windows NT version 3.5, they elected to separate Windows NT Workstation 3.5 from the NT Advanced Server product and marketed them separately as Windows NT Workstation and Windows 2000 Server. Over time, Windows NT Workstation has evolved into Windows 2000 Professional, targeted at the desktop, and Windows 2000 Server has evolved into Windows 2000 Advanced Server.

Windows 2000 Professional is fundamentally intended for use on the desktop of a workstation computer. Windows 2000 Advanced Server, by contrast, is packaged with many utilities that enable it to administer and manage a network much better than Windows 2000 Professional.

Windows 2000 Server is by all accounts a robust, easy-to-manage operating system. Its graphical user interface is similar to Windows 98 and Me, which eases the learning curve. The similarity of the interface to Microsoft's other offerings makes installation and most configuration tasks relatively simple.

At this point, Windows 2000 is a relatively mature product. It's got a new name and a modified interface, but it's still built on the Windows NT code that Microsoft has been working on since 1993. It's still got some shortcomings (it doesn't scale as well as Unix, it lacks a real-time disk defragmenter, it's got a few security issues, and so on) but all in all, it's a reasonable server operating system. Microsoft has a long history of aggressively tackling tough markets and beating the competition, and there's little doubt that they'll continue to take this tack with Windows 2000 Server.

Windows 2000 Server can use the same variety of network protocols as Windows 2000 Professional. The chief difference between 2000 Professional and 2000 Server's networking capabilities is that the latter doesn't use the workgroup configurations we discussed in the previous chapter. Instead, it groups computers using an organizational scheme Microsoft calls *domains*. Later in this hour, you learn how domains differ from workgroups, as well as a variety of other Windows 2000 Server concepts.

The next few pages briefly describe some basic Windows 2000 Server concepts. After that, we'll progress to discussions of domains, security, server roles, and server applications.

Windows 2000 Server's File Systems

Microsoft built its Windows NT and Windows NT-derived products, such as Windows 2000 Professional, from a clean sheet. As a result, NT has a wide variety of options, including options for two file systems. Windows NT can use one or both of two local file systems (ways of organizing the local hard drives), which offers a great deal of flexibility. Because selecting the file system you want to use is part of the installation routine, you should know what these file systems are:

- **File Allocation Table (FAT)**. FAT is a legacy from MS-DOS and Windows 95. It supports filenames that must follow a strict pattern of eight characters or less, followed by a period, followed by a three-letter extension (such as README.TXT). This has changed somewhat, as has the file system in Windows 2000; if you use a FAT file system, it's called FAT32 and it supports long filenames, although it lacks the security of NTFS.

- **NT File System (NTFS)**. In an attempt to gain the advantages of IBM's OS/2 High Performance File System (HPFS) with additional capabilities, Microsoft designed its own file system for NT/2000 and called it (naturally) NT File System. NTFS allows long filenames (up to 254 characters) and can work with Windows 95, OS/2, UNIX/NFS, and AppleShare for Macintosh computers. Windows 2000 really is designed to work with anything.

Windows 2000 Server Networking Basics

Microsoft Windows 2000 (and in fact, all Microsoft networking products) communicates using Server Message Block (SMB), a protocol for requesting remote resources. SMB is part of the structure that underlies NetBIOS Extended User Interface (NetBEUI), NetBIOS's younger, far more capable sibling. NetBEUI also includes NetBIOS Frames (NBF), the protocol that handles the OSI layer 4 tasks (the TCP in TCP/IP). SMB is pretty much the "core" protocol of Windows 2000 Server in the same way that NetWare Core Protocol (NCP) is the core of NetWare—you don't see a lot about either protocol (most of the attention is paid to protocols such as IPX, NetBEUI, and TCP/IP instead), but they're there.

Windows 2000 Server Concepts

As noted earlier, Windows 2000 Server is a remarkably robust operating system with a myriad of capabilities. It's easy to learn and administer, and because of its large suite of graphical utilities, even neophytes can figure it out pretty quickly. Nonetheless, a bit of familiarization with some basic Windows 2000 Server concepts will shorten and flatten the learning curve even further.

To have a basic understanding of Windows 2000 Server, you have to assimilate a few concepts. First is the difference between Microsoft workgroups (the backbone of Microsoft's peer networking strategy) and domains (the backbone of Microsoft's client/server strategy). Understanding these differences will help you get a practical understanding of the methods Microsoft uses to structure a centralized network.

Next, you'll learn how the operating system's user logon security works. It's not enough to know that there is logon security; knowing how it works can aid you in understanding (and ultimately, debugging) the overall security scheme.

Once you understand how security works, we'll talk about how Microsoft network sharing works in Windows 2000 Server. Sharing is a good follow-up to logon security because once a user is logged into a 2000 Server system, you'll want to ensure that they have the proper access to the resources available to them.

After you've been through these three items, we'll steer a course toward 2000 Server's various roles. Each Windows 2000 Server can work with other 2000 Server systems to build redundancy; knowing how it works simplifies the process of setting up the network for maximum speed and reliability.

After reading about all these topics, you'll want to know what you can use your Windows 2000 Server for (other than file and print resources), so we'll discuss Microsoft's BackOffice integrated server applications in some detail.

The Differences Between Workgroups and Domains

Unlike Windows NT Workstation, profiled in the last hour, Windows 2000 Server cannot participate in workgroups. Instead, Windows 2000 Server systems work through an organization scheme based on *domains*. The domains are comprised of servers that authenticate users and manage shared network resources, as well as work through *trust relationships* with other servers and workstations of various types (generally Windows clients of one sort or another, although Linux and Unix can participate if they have the SAMBA package installed). If the term *trust relationship* means nothing to you at this point, don't worry. It will be explained in the next section.

Compare the concept of a domain to the workgroup model presented in Hour 14, "Microsoft Windows Peer Networking," where each computer had its own security architecture. The domain model offers some clear advantages:

- Centralized security
- Standardized access to resources
- Easier adds, moves, and changes because of centralized resources

When a Windows for Workgroups, Windows 95, or Windows 2000 Professional client logs into a Windows 2000 Server, the server authenticates the client's login; that is, it verifies that the client is who it says it is. If the login attempt is successful, the server may then admit the user to the domain and provide access to domain resources, or it may run a *login script* (which is a text file that has a list of commands and is stored on the server). This arrangement means that each user's security settings for the entire network are stored on the server, rather than distributed in dribs and drabs across all the workstations on the network.

Microsoft Windows 2000 domains are autonomous organizations of computers. Although the maximum size of a domain can be 40,000 or so, most organizations won't lump that many users into a single domain. Instead, they'll follow a more economical path and use trust relationships to tie multiple domains together. The next section discusses trust relationships.

Windows 2000 Server Domains Versus Internet Domain Name System Domains

Although Windows 2000 Server computers control domains, don't make the mistake of confusing a Windows 2000 Server domain with an Internet domain or Internet domain name. Windows 2000 domains are hierarchical organizations of computers that enable multiple systems to communicate in a secure fashion. In other words, NT domain lists are like guest lists—they ensure that only the people who belong at the party actually get in.

Internet domains and domain names are another kettle of fish altogether. An Internet domain name is a name associated with a particular IP address, both of which are issued by the central Internet naming authority (Network Solutions, Herndon, VA) and a few other new domain registration authorities. Internet domain names are what *Domain Name Servers* (DNS) work with—a DNS receives a request for a particular resource by name (for example, www.microsoft.com) and returns the IP address associated with that name (in other words, www.microsoft.com = 207.58.156.16, among other IP addresses).

Domains are broken up into several Top-Level Domains (TLDs). A TLD is the .com, .edu, .mil, .gov, and so forth at the end of a domain name. Then there are specific domain names: microsoft.com, intel.com, apple.com. Anything after that is a specific machine. Users with email accounts on specific domains are sometimes described by where their account is in the domain (for example, erica@wherever.com).

Trust Relationships Between Windows 2000 Server Domains

What is a trust relationship? For NT domains, a trust relationship is a link between any two Windows 2000 Server domains. Trust relationships govern administration, access, and security across the two domains.

It's important to know that trust relationships function between two domains and between two domains only; there's no central domain-of-domain administration (contrast this with NetWare Directory Services, described in the next chapter, which does centralize network administration).

In other words, if domain A trusts domain B, and domain B trusts domain C, domain A does not necessarily trust domain C. This means that as a network grows, the number of trust relationships grows exponentially. For a two-domain network, there can be one trust relationship; three domains mean six relationships; and four domains mean sixteen relationships.

Fortunately, Microsoft has realized that its domain model doesn't scale as well as some of the alternatives, such as Novell's NetWare Directory Service (NDS), the open-standard Lightweight Directory Access Protocol (another chunk of TCP/IP), and Sun Microsystem's Network Information System (NIS). As a result, Microsoft has created the Active Directory, a network-wide administration tool designed to compete with Novell's NDS.

Trust relationships as they apply to domains work in only one direction. That means that if your SALES domain trusts your TECHNICAL domain, your TECHNICAL domain doesn't necessarily have to reciprocate by trusting SALES. By the same token, trust relationships exist between two and only two domains at any given time. If SALES trusts TECHNICAL, and TECHNICAL trusts ACCOUNTING, that does not mean that SALES trusts ACCOUNTING. Unless there is an *explicit* trust relationship between two computers, there is no trust relationship at all—there are no implicit trust relationships.

To make defining trust relationships manageable, Microsoft has provided for four basic organizations of trust relationships: single domain, master domain, multiple master domain, and multiple trust.

Single Domain Model

The Single Domain model is quite simple. It's good for up to 10,000 users and allows fully centralized management of all user and security accounts. *Local groups*, or groups with certain rights and privileges that users get through membership in the group, are defined only once for the entire domain. Because everything in this model is part of one domain, there are no trust relationships with other domains to manage. This arrangement is simple and appropriate for 99% of small business and small-organizational networks.

Master Domain Model

If you want to logically segment your organization a bit more (for security purposes, usually), the Master Domain model becomes ideal (see Figure 15.1). In the Master Domain model, there are many domains, all of which trust a single master domain. The master domain, however, trusts none of the other domains. This, like the Single Domain model, preserves central administration but also provides for security segmentation and more importantly, expandability.

Multiple Master Domain Model

For really large organizations, Microsoft recommends the Multiple Master Domain model (see Figure 15.2). In this model, there are several master domains, all of which trust each other. None of the master domains, however, trusts any of their subdomains; subdomains remain hierarchically beneath the master domains. In the Multiple Master Domain model, management becomes decentralized; each master domain is responsible for the administration of its immediate subdomains. There is no enterprise-wide domain management tool.

FIGURE 15.1

A Master Domain model.

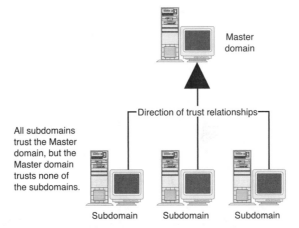

Master domain

Direction of trust relationships

All subdomains trust the Master domain, but the Master domain trusts none of the subdomains.

Subdomain   Subdomain   Subdomain

FIGURE 15.2

A Multiple Master Domain model.

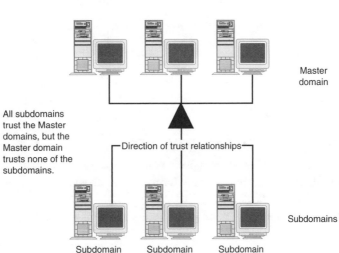

Master domain

All subdomains trust the Master domains, but the Master domain trusts none of the subdomains.

Direction of trust relationships

Subdomains

Subdomain   Subdomain   Subdomain

Multiple Trust Model

Last (and least recommended by Microsoft) is the Multiple Trust model (see Figure 15.3). In the Multiple Trust model, all domains trust all other domains to create a web of trust relationships. This model rapidly becomes unmanageable as it grows larger because it's essentially a peer-to-peer relationship among domains. It also completely decentralizes administration, which undercuts the purpose of domain hierarchies.

Another reason why the Multiple Trust model isn't recommended is because of its relative lack of security. It's a great network if you can trust all your users all the time and can closely control access to the network—but it's difficult to secure from the outside.

FIGURE 15.3

Note how the Multiple Trust model resembles peer networking on a grand scale: Every domain server is connected to every other domain without a hierarchy.

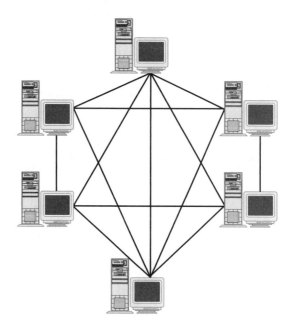

User Logon Security

Domains exist for one purpose: to ensure that users can reliably access the resources they need. But users come in many forms ranging from the local network user with relatively few rights to the administrative user with rights to almost every resource on the network. Each user must have appropriate access given his or her job requirements. How can users be managed efficiently?

Windows 2000 answers this question through the use of *user groups*. User groups are a class of Windows 2000 domain users grouped together for simplified administration.

15

Groups are created and managed in Windows 2000's User Manager for Domains application. Users can have specific privileges assigned and specific resources made available as the result of membership in a user group. For example, user group ACCOUNTING might have access to the system's accounting files and applications. Users not in the ACCOUNTING user group would not have access to those resources.

There are two varieties of user groups: *local groups* that can contain user security information derived from multiple domains and servers but that can only access resources within their domain boundaries, and *global groups* that can be assigned rights in the local domain or in any trusting domain.

So far, so good. By placing a user in either a local or a global group that has predefined rights, the process of ensuring that a user's rights can be quickly configured is assured. Now, how does the NT Server check that the user's ID is correct when the user has to access network resources?

It's actually pretty simple. When you log on to a computer running Windows (of any stripe), you log on to your local computer first. When you use network resources (a shared drive on a server in the domain, for example), you're actually logging into the domain to use that specific resource.

NT Server Roles

For users to log on to the domain, they have to have something to log on to. NT Servers fill that role by acting as either a Primary Domain Controller (PDC) or a Backup Domain Controller (BDC), either of which can authenticate a user into the domain's resources.

A Primary Domain Controller is a computer running NT Server that runs software called the Netlogon Service. The Netlogon Service is network security software that allows the user to log on to the local NT domain once and subsequently access all the resources he or she is allowed within the domain.

A Backup Domain Controller is similar to a Primary Domain Controller, except that it does not actively authenticate users when they log on to the domain. Instead, the user and security information from the Primary Domain Controller is automatically replicated to the Backup Domain Controller(s). In the event that a Primary Domain Controller computer fails, a Backup Domain Controller can be *promoted* to a Primary Domain Controller and take over running the network's security space.

Primary Domain Controller computers handle the management of trust relationships for all interdomain communications. This is why it is extremely important, if you have an NT Server network that participates in trust relationships with other domains, for you to have a backup computer built as a BDC. If the PDC fails, the BDC still has a record of your local domain's security and domain trust relationships.

Sharing

Sharing resources in Windows 2000 Server is accomplished in much the same way as sharing resources in any other version of Windows. The difference with NT Server is that there are many more security options available. The three basic Windows share settings are No Access, Full Access, and Access via Password. Windows 2000 Server expands on these settings to bring a baseline of No Access, Read, Change, and Full Control when you share a drive in My Computer or Windows 2000 Explorer.

No Access is the same everywhere—at least, you might think so. No Access means no access. Only a domain administrator can undo No Access permission—and then only if the No Access permission wasn't imposed on the domain administrator as well as everyone else.

Read means read-only access. Change is read-write access. Full Control is read-write access with the capability to change the file access permissions on any resource on the computer.

Be aware that permissions for a share specify the maximum possible access (by any user) that a network client can have for the shared resource. If you use NTFS as the file system on the server's data drive, you can also set file and directory permissions. In contrast to share permissions, file and directory permissions represent the maximum access a user is allowed—meaning that an administrator can't accidentally lock himself or herself out of a directory.

In addition to the four basic security permissions defined through shares, there are a host of other rights that can be defined through NT's User Manager for Domains application.

By using the share-level security, the file-and-directory-level security, and the user rights policies, it's possible to secure NT quite well. Sharing isn't just about accessing resources; sharing files is part of an overall security plan, which we'll discuss in detail in Hour 19, "Security."

NT Server Applications

A couple of years ago, a customer walked into a car dealership because he was interested in purchasing a popular sports-utility vehicle. He'd reviewed the pricing and had decided that this particular sports-utility vehicle was the best value, partially because it had a very low price.

He sat down with a salesperson and casually mentioned how much he liked the price he'd seen for the vehicle. The car salesperson, a kindly, gray-haired older fellow (yes, they *do* exist), clucked and shook his head ruefully as he worked up a base price that was $4,000 over the customer's initial price.

The customer was shocked. "Why does this cost so much?" he demanded. "The MSRP is much lower than this."

The salesperson noted that the base truck, which the customer was interested in, came without a roof, a radio, a rug, or a rear seat. It was truly stripped down, too much so to make it useful in the New England climate where the customer lived. To provide the customer with use out of the vehicle, the salesperson had added these items—which we normally assume come with the car—into the package, and the price had risen accordingly.

Many Network Operating Systems are sold a lot like the sports-utility vehicle in the preceding example. Although they're touted as universal solutions right out of the box, in reality, they can't do much right out of the box except provide file and print services. Although those are valuable, those services are not really enough to build a network around. In addition to file and print services, you need at least mail services; database and network management services are other pieces that help make networks more useful. In many cases, getting all these applications means running several servers and purchasing a raft of application software.

In an attempt to preempt the market, Microsoft has created an all-in-one server package called BackOffice that provides most of the administrative functions a network requires. It consists of the following:

- **Exchange Server**, a groupware and messaging server that can handle Internet-compliant email.
- **SQL Server**, a database management system that's quite robust.
- **Systems Management Server (SMS)**, a network-management package that enables administrators to install software and provide remote technical support to users.
- **Systems Network Architecture Server (SNA Server)**, which enables Windows 2000 to connect to IBM midrange and mainframe computers.
- **Internet Information Server (IIS)**, which turns an NT Server into an Internet server for the World Wide Web, FTP, Gopher, and other services.

In addition to the servers bundled in BackOffice, NT Server also comes with a complete set of TCP/IP tools. Windows 2000 Server, right out of the box without any third-party software, can be a Domain Name Server for the Internet, a Dynamic Host Configuration Protocol Server that assigns client workstations their IP addresses, or a PPP Dial-In Server through the use of Remote Access Services, NT's built-in remote/dial-up networking services.

If, on the other hand, all you require from NT Server is file and print services (often the most pressing needs an organization has), NT Server can adequately fulfill those requirements right out of the box.

Is it possible to run all these services on one computer? Absolutely. If you're going to do that, make certain that you have the fastest computer you can purchase with as much memory as you can afford. As of the beginning of 2001, that means a processor that's a gigahertz or thereabouts, 128MB to 256MB of memory, and 30GB of disk space.

Microsoft's BackOffice strategy offers users a lot of value for a relatively low price. The cost, which varies slightly from reseller to reseller, is significantly less than the cost of the servers purchased separately.

Other Computers with Which Windows 2000 Server Can Network

Windows 2000's designers realized very early on that Windows 2000 would not be the only network operating system in the world, whether they liked it or not. In addition to NT, there existed NetWare, Banyan VINES, IBM LAN Manager, TCP/IP networking, and others. In response to the market, NT's designers decided to make NT as network-capable as possible right out of the box. Although this plan was a convenience to its users, it was also a stroke of marketing genius: A connectable Windows 2000 Server allowed Microsoft to gain entry to market segments to which they previously had no access—things like the midrange market (IBM AS/400s and small mainframes) and totally non-Microsoft environments.

With the addition of SNA server from Microsoft, Windows 2000 Server was capable of handling mainframe data. In addition, there are several third-party companies that make software to allow NT Server (or, in some cases NT Workstation) to connect to Sun Microsystem's Network File System (NFS), a remarkably versatile way to *mount* (connect to) remote drives.

15

Connecting to Remote Hard Drives

A computer sharing its hard-disk resources is only the beginning of the file-sharing process. Once disk space is made available to other computers, those computers must be capable of *mounting* the drive, or make it appear as though the remote drive is just another local drive. From a PC-based standpoint, this means that if you connect to a server drive, you simply have a new drive called f:\ or h:\, or whatever drive letter you assign to it.

For the mounting process to work, the server and the client must be running software that can communicate with each other correctly. In Windows-based networks, the capability to mount remote drives on Windows machines is built into the Microsoft networking clients; for Windows 95 and NT, the capability to mount NetWare drives is provided by Microsoft's NetWare clients.

However, if you have to be able to mount drives across a WAN, it's possible that you'll need to be able to mount drives on a wide variety of systems, some of which won't or can't run Windows. The solution in these cases—which are surprisingly common—is to install NFS Server or client software on the computers that will be sharing or accessing resources. NFS, developed by Sun Microsystems, is a *de facto* standard for mounting remote drives; it's considered part of the TCP/IP protocol suite and has received wide acceptance among TCP/IP networking users. You'll find support for NFS in almost all Unix distributions, and Microsoft has an option pack that allows Windows NT 4.0 and Windows 2000 to use nfs.

Another option is Samba, a piece of software designed to allow Unix computers to connect to Microsoft networking computers running the Server Message Block protocol that forms the basis of Microsoft networking. Samba is remarkably efficient, and it allows shared Unix drives to mount in a Microsoft network and shared Microsoft drives to mount in a Unix environment. Additionally, Samba is freeware and can be downloaded from the Internet. Samba is commonly included on Linux (a Unix clone) CDs and is available for a variety of other versions of Unix as well.

Here is the list of clients that Windows 2000 Server can support right out of the box:

- MS-DOS
- Windows for Workgroups 3.x
- Windows 95/98/Me
- Windows NT Workstation
- Windows 2000 Professional
- Macintosh clients

Summary

In this hour, you learned about NT Server—how it organizes itself into domains and workgroups, and how it interacts with other systems. The next hour presents Novell NetWare in the same way.

Q&A

Q If you had to administer a series of domains from one domain, how would you set up the trust relationships?

A Each domain to be administered would trust one single domain (perhaps named `Administration` or something similar), but the `Administration` domain would not trust any of the administered domains.

Q To build a fail-safe system for user logins, how many servers do you need in a single Windows 2000 Server domain?

A Two. First, you require a Primary Domain Controller to authenticate logins, and then you need a Backup Domain Controller to swap in if the Primary Domain Controller fails.

Q What are a few of the advantages of domains over workgroups?

A There's quite a list of advantages, but here are the primary ones:

- Centralized administration of user accounts
- Centralized management of domain resources (drives, printers, and so on)
- Strong increase in security
- A great deal of control over the amount of access to shared resources

HOUR **16**

Novell NetWare

Until Microsoft introduced Windows NT, Novell NetWare was just about the most popular and, until recently, the most common network operating system for Intel-compatible personal computers. There are good reasons for Novell's early success, and unfortunate reasons why Novell is currently suffering at the hands of Microsoft server-side technologies.

With respect to NetWare's success, Ray Noorda of Novell was in the right place at the right time with the right product—early versions of NetWare were released in the early-to-mid-1980s just as corporate personal computing was beginning to flower. NetWare, in contrast to Microsoft's early PC-NET product, was secure, reliable, and (in comparison to anything else then on the market) blazingly fast. It was based on a routable protocol (IPX) that was significantly easier to configure than IP, which meant that it opened the doors to multisite networking for personal computers—what we now call a WAN. Combined with Novell's NetWare Directory Services, a global directory of all users, computers, printers, and whatever else could connect to Novell, NetWare became the corporate networking darling; the adage ran that you couldn't get fired for buying it.

In this hour, you'll learn about the following topics:

- Novell NetWare concepts
- How to provide shared resources to your users in Novell NetWare
- How to configure the network for multiple client types

Advantages of a NetWare Network

Having been around as long as it has, NetWare has some significant upsides. In many cases, its only rival is Unix, which is the great-granddaddy of all network operating systems. Although NetWare can be a bear to install, configure, and tune, it has some great features:

- Speed and scalability
- Long filenames
- Built-in hierarchical organization
- Reliability

Speed and Scalability

The core of NetWare is surprisingly efficient. It keeps in memory a record of all files stored on it; as a result, it can access and serve files to users blazingly fast. For a small network, the speed with which a server can deliver files to users isn't critical because the server is usually not highly stressed. However, NetWare continues to deliver great performance as the number of client users increases.

The trade press continues to test NetWare and Intranetware products; in a significant percentage of the tests, NetWare is the fastest PC-based file and print server. It also has tremendous scalability; one NetWare server can handle far more clients than almost any other PC-based NOS.

Long Filenames

In response to OS/2, Windows 95, Windows 2000, and Macintosh computers, NetWare also has support for long filenames. To use long filenames, however, special software (called OS2.NAM, LONG.NAM, or MAC.NAM) must be loaded to support the *name space*, or the special area on the disk that stores long filenames. Long-filename support must be loaded before the operating system begins to access NetWare partitions with long-filename support, but once it's loaded, NetWare can support filenames up to 31 characters.

This is more significant than it sounds. Even though some operating systems can save 255-character filenames, 31 characters are sufficient to name most files both descriptively and uniquely. For example, the filename `Chapter 13 files from JimC.doc` is more descriptive and easier to understand than CH13FLJC.DOC. Additionally, the long file-name is more likely to be unique, so there's less of a possibility of accidentally overwriting the file CH13FLJC.DOC with another file of the same name.

Built-In Hierarchical Organization

NetWare 5.x comes with a built-in system for building, organizing, and managing hierarchical networks. This system, called *NetWare Directory Services* (*NDS*), is capable of handling the network-organizational needs of a global organization as well as the single-server local network. NDS is Novell's method for organizing all the elements of an enterprise network. In an NDS network, a single logon provides access to the same resources, no matter where on the network the user logs on. NDS is relatively complex; a full discussion of how it works is outside the scope of this book. However, if you have to build a network across multiple sites, later versions and NDS provide a powerful enabling tool.

Novell's per-server scalability is the stuff of legend, but even a single server has limits. When Novell designed NetWare 4.x, the company realized that the flat-file single-server log on limit that NetWare 3.x effectively imposed needed revision. The result of Novell's effort was NDS. In NDS, everything—every user, every computer, every printer, every server, every site—is an object that can be managed. It's a great solution and is what is sustaining Novell in the market versus Unix and Windows 2000 Server's encroachment on its territory. As a matter of fact, Novell has released NDS software for Unix, IBM's OS/390 mainframe operating system, and every flavor of Windows. Of course, with the release of Windows 2000, Microsoft has its Active Directory, which duplicates many of NDS' functions.

Reliability

NetWare has been in existence since the early 1980s. As a result, Novell has largely worked out the bugs within the operating system. Even NetWare 4.x, a total rewrite of NetWare introduced in the mid-1990s, was remarkably stable in its first release. Subsequent releases have brought even more stability to this NOS.

It is not uncommon to see properly configured NetWare servers that have been running for months (or, in some cases, years) without a reboot. NetWare has a high tolerance for errors and can often manage a problem without *ABENDing*, or crashing.

Among all the major NOS manufacturers, Novell stands alone in its approach to updating its server software. The company periodically releases complete software patches to fix recently discovered bugs, and it's possible in many cases to load only the patch modules that your server requires instead of loading a whole set of patches. Only Unix used to offer this functionality, and while Microsoft does make some individual patches available, they generally recommend loading a *service pack*, or collection of patches, en masse. Novell's Web site, www.novell.com, enables the user to research and download software quite easily—and there's a wealth of information available there, as well.

Disadvantages of a NetWare Network

In some ways, Novell has unfortunately been a victim of its own success. In its push to become the one perfect enterprise Intel-computer network operating system—which, in many ways, it is—the company concentrated on its core strengths (file and print services) at the expense of its application services and ease of administration.

Here is a list of the downsides of NetWare; each is discussed in the following sections:

- Expensive to administer
- Weak application services
- Difficult to administer

Expensive to Administer

As NetWare eclipsed all other PC-based Network Operating Systems, Novell focused on the large-corporate marketplace to the detriment of its smaller customers, denying those customers reasonably priced direct access to Novell's technical support system. Since 1989, instead of going directly to Novell with a problem, customers, no matter how small, have had to engage the services of a Certified NetWare Engineer (CNE). CNEs are professionals trained in NetWare configuration, design, and troubleshooting. CNE service is relatively expensive; it's not uncommon to see $150 hourly charges for it.

Weak Application Services Support

NetWare was designed to function primarily as a file and print server. However, since NetWare was designed, the requirements for servers have expanded tremendously. In the early days of networking, sharing files and printers was sufficient. With the increased power of personal computers, however, servers have begun to run applications formerly performed on mainframes or minicomputers. Such services include database management and network management. Although Novell has made a valiant effort to break into the application server market, it currently plays a distant third to Unix and Windows 2000. Novell's NetWare Application Launcher is making inroads as a software distribution system and has revitalized use of NetWare on some networks.

Difficult to Administer

Last, and probably most problematic for neophyte networkers, NetWare is relatively difficult to administer. Unlike Windows 2000, NetWare doesn't have a graphical interface at the server console. Although a graphical interface isn't absolutely necessary, it does make administrative tasks easier to accomplish.

Novell has addressed this fault by writing Netadmin and NWAdmin, two graphical NetWare management utilities that run under DOS and Windows, respectively. These utilities go a long way toward easing the pain of administering NetWare servers, but they still don't run at the server console itself.

NetWare Basics

16

In the next few pages, you'll learn about several concepts that are central to an understanding of NetWare.

When you purchase a car, you don't just walk into any old dealership and announce, "I want a car." More likely, you do a great deal of research and find out which models have the features and options you require. The next few pages are like a car product brochure in that sense—they provide a very basic list of NetWare features, options, and models. And you won't have to read the blue book to find out what it's worth.

In the next sections, you'll learn the following:

- NetWare 3.x versus later versions of NetWare
- About user logon security
- What NetWare can network (interoperate) with

The Differences Between NetWare 3.x and 4.x

NetWare 3.x—particularly NetWare 3.11 and 3.12—was a great network operating system. It was reliable, relatively simple to administer, and very fast. Unfortunately, adding servers to the network was a pain; each server had to be separately administered. As a result, the poor, beleaguered network-administration community welcomed with open arms the introduction of NetWare 4.x and NDS, which allowed centralized administration of all servers and resources from any point on the network.

There are several key differences between NetWare 3.x and later versions of NetWare that extend well beyond the administration material just pointed out. The following sections describe in general terms the following differences between NetWare 3.x and later versions:

- NetWare Directory Services versus the Bindery
- Memory use (and memory recovery)
- Better enterprise support
- Multitasking capability
- Single logon

NetWare Directory Services Versus the Bindery

Every network operating system needs a way to track its users, resources, and configuration. In NetWare, the mechanism for accomplishing these tasks is either the Bindery (in version 3.x and earlier) or NetWare Directory Services (in later versions).

The Bindery is essentially a database that stores user IDs and passwords, information about the computer's physical resources such as disk space, memory, various peripherals such as disk drive controllers and network cards, and information about the operating configuration of the machine.

In contrast to NetWare 3.x's Bindery, later versions make use of NetWare Directory Services (NDS). NDS is a marked contrast to NetWare 3.x's Bindery, incorporating many improvements and a variety of new features that both simplify installation and ease server administration.

NetWare Directory Service is a relational hierarchical database that records much the same information as NetWare 3.x's Bindery. However, in contrast to the Bindery, NDS offers the ability to replicate a directory of resources from server to server and a hierarchical method of organizing large networks. These two improvements, as minor as they sound, are the source of much of the value of later versions of NetWare as well as much of the confusion that surrounds it.

NDS works by organizing certain standardized items into a *tree* structure. By organizing all the parts of the network, NDS offers a way to organize your local network as well as large organizations that span the globe. It's the most scalable directory service available, and Novell, in spite of its financial and marketing woes, is rapidly ensuring that it will be available for other operating systems, including Sun's Solaris and Microsoft's Windows NT.

Memory Use and Memory Recovery

There are two differences between the way NetWare 3.x uses memory and the way later versions use memory. The first is that since NetWare 4.x, the operating system can automatically locate and use more than 16 megabytes of memory without configuration; the second (and rather more arcane) difference is that later versions fix a memory leak that was endemic to NetWare 3.x.

NetWare 4.x and 5.x circumvent the 16M memory-configuration requirement, making it much easier to install. When SERVER.EXE loads in 4.x and later, it does a quick hardware check and figures out how much memory it has available. Memory configuration and management are therefore much easier with newer iterations of NetWare than with NetWare 3.x, and much simpler for a neophyte to work with.

The other difference between NetWare 3.x and 4.x/5.x memory usage is that newer versions fix a small but significant waste of memory in NetWare 3.x. When a software application uses memory, it is supposed to take what it needs from the operating system and return it to the operating system once it's done—sort of like a lending library. However, sometimes it doesn't work this way, as every librarian knows; sometimes people just don't bring back books. Likewise, some applications—or worse, the operating system—doesn't give back memory once it's done with it. If it's accidental, it's called a *memory leak*; if this process happens deliberately, as the result of a consciously designed operating system process, it's a problem. Over time, a memory leak slowly reduces the amount of memory the computer thinks is unused; eventually, the amount of memory the operating system believes it has is so low that the server crashes or locks up and has to be restarted. Fortunately, Novell fixed this with NetWare 4.x and as a result, the entire system is more stable.

Better Enterprise Support

Imagine having all your data stored on one computer. Now imagine what would happen if that computer crashed completely and took all your data with it. It's not a pleasant thought!! Large corporations feel the same way about their data as you feel about yours.

In NetWare 3.x, the data stored on a NetWare server was stored on one server and on one server only—unless an administrator stopped all databases, disconnected all but the administrative user, and manually copied the data from one computer to another. With more recent versions, by contrast, data can be *replicated* (a fancy computer-industry term for copied) from one computer to another in real time. This means that multiple copies of data can be running simultaneously. If one server goes down, another server can basically pick up the slack and continue serving users. In fact, third-party software manufacturers, such as Vinca, make software that enables one server to *fail over* to another server transparently—the users won't even know the first server has failed.

Failover is an alternative to fault tolerance. Fault-tolerant systems can manage partial component failure without completely crashing, while highly available systems generally require two or more systems that take over functions when one of the two of them fails.

In a NetWare failover system, there are two (or occasionally more) servers, all with identical copies of a master server's drives and resources. If the master server fails, the backup server takes over dynamically and users never see the difference (except for a small and brief slowdown).

Such failover capacity is usually not necessary for smaller networks. However, for large networks, such as those used by banks, credit-card issuers, insurance companies, and other transaction-oriented institutions, it's very useful. And it should be a comfort to you as the user to know that this is the case (it's why your ATM seldom fails to work properly).

> **Networks and the Bottom Line**
>
> Failover capability and redundancy are (surprisingly) a comfort to line executives as well as network administrators. Over the last several years, line executives (that is, those executives with financial responsibility—hence "line" from "the bottom line") have become aware that computer networking and information systems are closely woven into their companies' overall value and health. They didn't come to this conclusion out of any sudden desire to ensure their companies' technical prowess; instead, they focused on it for the same reason they focus on everything: Problems with their information systems and networks can affect their bottom lines.
>
> Networks that offer better enterprise support have a direct effect on the bottom line. Keep that in mind as you design and build your network—it's more important than ever to do it right.

Multitasking

One of the simplest but most effective differences between NetWare 3.x and its successors is the multitasking scheme. As you may recall, multitasking involves the capability of a computer to accomplish more than one task simultaneously.

NetWare 3.x multitasks, and does so very well, but unfortunately, it doesn't shield one program (such as a backup program) from accidentally overwriting, and hence crashing, the memory used by another running program. This is not to say that NetWare 3.x is in any way unreliable, however; it is remarkably well behaved. However, subsequent versions of the operating system allow the programs to run in what is called the *protected mode* of an Intel processor. This essentially means that each program runs in its own memory space, and that none of the applications can even see one another unless their communications are mediated through the operating system. As a result, 4.x and later versions are much more stable when running lots of *NetWare Loadable Module* (*NLM*) programs than is NetWare 3.x.

Single Logon

The last difference between NetWare 3.x and later versions—or at any rate, the last difference to be dealt with in this book—is based on the increased enterprise support introduced in later versions. It's a single logon: No matter where on the network you log on, you have the same resources available to you. This is a direct extension of NetWare Directory Services and was hailed as a major advance when it was introduced.

With NetWare's single logon feature, an administrator can log on from home, from his or her desk at work, from anywhere, and be able to administer the network. Likewise, a user can access his or her file and print resources regardless of location.

In an era when increasing numbers of workers are required to take to the road or work from home, NetWare's single logon feature has become a boon to networkers everywhere. By providing better network connectivity to a wider range of locations and users, NetWare works better for the network user, and it satisfies many provisions of the Americans with Disabilities Act.

How NetWare Works

16

Are you one of those people who leap out of bed in the morning with a song on your lips, or do you need a couple of cups of coffee to get you started? Although your answer doesn't directly pertain to NetWare, it does offer a great way to illustrate how NetWare servers start up.

Unlike DOS, OS/2, or Windows 2000, NetWare doesn't use a FAT, HPFS, or NTFS file system for its drives. Instead, it uses Novell's proprietary NetWare File System. Although the NetWare File System, with its relatively large partitions, long filename support, and large number of file attributes, may seem relatively mundane today, such was not always the case.

When NetWare was first introduced, MS-DOS was at version 3.3. DOS 3.3 wasn't a bad operating system, but it had some fundamental limitations that were infuriating. Most notable among its limitations was a maximum disk partition size of 32 megabytes. Even in the mid-1980s when a 100 megabyte hard drive cost several thousand dollars, the 32 megabyte partition size was tremendously frustrating. NetWare allowed administrators concerned about the 32 megabyte limitation to circumvent it by creating large disk partitions on a NetWare server and requiring that users install applications and stored files on the NetWare server's hard drive.

From the perspective of network administrators, this was great. It allowed them to centralize and manage PC-based networks in much the same fashion as they managed their mainframe and midrange computer networks. In fact, during the 1980s, network centralization got to the point at which there was a trend toward diskless workstations (essentially a personal computer without a hard drive that booted up a copy of an operating system stored on a NetWare server). These computers are like our (hypothetical) morning person: They wake up, see the light, and they're good to go; they don't need coffee.

For what it's worth, diskless workstations boot using the good offices of a special chip called a *boot PROM* (*Programmable Read-Only Memory*) chip inserted in a socket in the network interface card inside the computer. The boot PROM enables the computer to log on toon to the network just sufficiently to get a copy of a workstation operating system (such as DOS, or else a Unix X Windows client) from the server and boot it on the workstation). Note the similarities between the diskless workstation of 10 years ago and the diskless Network Computers and NetPCs being touted today by Oracle and Microsoft, respectively—it just proves that there's nothing new under the sun.

What does this have to do with how NetWare servers start up? Well, NetWare partitions aren't *bootable*—that is, the computer can't recognize the disk format and boot from it natively because NetWare partitions don't have any of the various files and so forth that a computer requires to start reading from the hard drive. Instead, NetWare requires that its startup files be stored on a DOS partition, from which it can boot. In this respect, NetWare is a lot like people who need coffee to get started in the morning.

When a NetWare server starts up, it begins by booting a small (usually 100 megabyte or smaller) DOS partition. The DOS partition is like a shot of espresso; because it's bootable, the server can lumber to its feet, rub its eyes, and get on with the process of waking up. Usually, the DOS partition has a directory on it called something like NWSERVER; in this directory are all the files that NetWare requires to start. The DOS partition's startup files (CONFIG.SYS and AUTOEXEC.BAT) have instructions to run the files that start the NetWare server…and next thing you know, the server is up and running, its drives mounted, its network cards humming along, and users logging on.

NetWare Interoperability

Have you ever lost the gas cap for your car? If you have, you're not alone; plenty of people do it every year. When they need a new one, do they have to go to their dealership to special-order a new gas cap? Usually, no. Gas caps are standardized—the same cap that fits a Toyota fits a Cadillac. (Although neither manufacturer will admit it—they want you to buy their brand. "Here, try this. It's made of unobtanium…it's so rare that you can't get any of it anywhere.") It's good that all the major auto manufacturers adhere to a standard for gas caps. Doing so makes gas caps, an easily lost item, easier to find, which increases overall customer satisfaction as well as safety.

In the same fashion, NetWare is a sort of personal computer networking standard. Almost every operating system can hook up with NetWare in one way or another. Although Novell's fortunes may have waned, no one can fairly accuse the company of having skimped on the creation of connectivity utilities.

NetWare can interoperate with everything from old single-tasking DOS to some of the most sophisticated versions of Unix available. From a user's perspective, it's ideal—it means that data can be accessed by almost anyone, almost irrespective of platform. If a Mac user saves a file to a NetWare server disk volume, that file can be shared with DOS users, Windows 95 users, or whoever—as long as there's a compatible file format.

Windows 95, 98, and Me

Unlike DOS, Windows 95 and its newer siblings do not have to use a workstation shell provided by Novell. Microsoft, recognizing the popularity of NetWare, provided a NetWare client in Windows 95 and all of its subsequent versions that is quite easy to set up and it works very well. Unlike many of the other current NetWare clients, Microsoft's Windows 95/98/Me NetWare client can work with NetWare Directory Services and it can execute NetWare logon scripts. This makes Windows 95 a very good NetWare client.

Alternatively, Novell has released (and continues, in the excellent fashion of the company, to improve on) its own Windows 95/98/Me NetWare client. For most users, it's not especially different from the Microsoft client. However, for administrators, Novell's Windows client can be a necessity because without it, one cannot run the NWAdmin utility that manages NDS-capable versions of NetWare.

If you want to install either NetWare client, open Windows 95's Control Panel application, open the Networks applet, click the Add button, and select Protocols (or Clients) from the menu that pops up. You are offered a selection of protocols from a variety of manufacturers (use the Microsoft NWLink IPX/SPX-Compatible Protocol) and clients. Once the protocols and clients are added (in that order), you have to reboot the computer. When the computer comes back up, you can log on toon to the NetWare server.

Networking Windows 95, 98, or Me to NetWare servers is about as simple as client/server networking gets. Once the NetWare client software and the IPX protocol are installed, the workstation can connect to the server without difficulty.

Windows 2000 Professional

In the preceding hour, you learned that Microsoft offers a Windows NT and 2000 Server–based feature called the Gateway Service for NetWare that enables a Windows NT or 2000 Server to allow clients that don't run IPX to connect to a NetWare server. That's like a Mack truck—a big, heavy, robust piece of software designed to carry a big load.

Windows 2000 Professional, the workstation version of Windows 2000, offers a similar networking utility called the Client Service for NetWare that enables 2000 Professional workstations to connect to NetWare networks as clients. The Client Service for NetWare is like a sports car in comparison to 2000 Server's Gateway Service: It's small, fast, and not designed to carry a server's load of traffic.

16

> **Windows NT and 2000 Version Numbers and Service Packs**
>
> When installing networking software on Microsoft servers, there is one caveat that does not apply to Windows 95/98/Me: Know the version of your Windows NT operating system.
>
> Sounds dumb. The version number is right there on the package, right?
>
> Uh-uh. NT, like its older counterpart, Unix, is a huge operating system made of millions of lines of code (that's a lot, even by Microsoft standards). As you might guess, anything with five million lines of code is going to have some imperfections...or what the average person in the street might uncharitably call a *bug*.
>
> Microsoft recognizes this, and in an attempt to stay ahead of the computer bugs that plague so many operating systems, the company release special bug-fix updates for Windows NT every five or six months called *service packs*.
>
> What do service packs have to do with installing networking software? Plenty. If you install a service pack to bring your Windows NT Workstation (or, for that matter, your Windows NT Server) system up to the most current bug-fix release, and then modify network software settings on the Windows NT system, you may have to reinstall the service pack after you've rebooted the computer. This process can screw up your connection to a NetWare server or any other networking you're running. Be sure that you know the parameters of your NetWare connection before you begin working with Windows 2000 systems.

Windows 2000's built-in NetWare clients from Windows NT version 4 and later are NDS-aware, so it's possible to fit Windows NT systems into the grand directory scheme of NDS and manage everything. In fact, in December 1997, Novell released NDS for Windows NT, so Windows NT (and now 2000) can be a directory-controlling system as well as a NetWare server. NDS for Windows NT requires that the Novell NT-NetWare client be installed on the Windows NT system serving as an NDS server, but it's part of the installation process—relatively painless and very fast.

OS/2

OS/2, IBM's client operating system, networks with NetWare quite well. Its best networking feature is that each application can have its own network session, which means that you can log on with more than one username! This feature can be really useful, particularly if you're a system administrator. OS/2 is sort of a sports sedan; it has enough power to do anything you need, and it has a few tricks up its sleeve that'll surprise you when you need additional stuff.

Although setting up OS/2 to interact with any other operating system is a complex process, the complexity can be worth it—as just mentioned, you can have two or more entirely separate logons to a single NetWare server on the same computer running OS/2.

If you're planning to use OS/2 as a client operating system, you'll need networking software. The software is available from www.ibm.com or www.novell.com.

Protocol Selection

Some years ago, a friend of mine was traveling outside the United States with friends who spoke the local language, which my friend did not speak. To communicate anything with the locals, he had to ask one of his linguistically gifted friends to translate what he wanted to say into the local patois. Needless to say, this put a damper on communications; it slowed some down (when he wanted to order another drink in a restaurant, for example) and cut others out entirely (he didn't want to try to meet women by using an interpreter).

Translation is almost always a slow process, even when it's a straightforward one-to-one task, because it adds a layer of complexity and a layer of tasks to a process. When it happens with language, it's simply frustrating; when it happens with computers, it has the potential to be a nightmare.

NetWare suffers the effects of translation, albeit on a minor scale. When running NetWare, there are two available protocols: IPX (the native tongue) and NetWare/IP (a translated non-native tongue at best). When Novell developed the IPX protocol, it designed it in a way that made (and makes) translating it to TCP/IP relatively straightforward. As a result, NetWare does not natively use TCP/IP, although it can communicate using TCP/IP (in fact, it can do so quite well). However, many applications require the SPX part of the IPX protocol suite and consequently won't run when NetWare is running only TCP/IP. As a result, NetWare encapsulates IPX packets inside TCP/IP packets to provide necessary services to some applications.

Packet encapsulation is a process akin to taking a letter, sealing it in an envelope, addressing that envelope, and then placing the first, sealed envelope into a second envelope addressed in a different language. It's not really efficient, and it wastes materials and time. Unfortunately, that's often the only way to accomplish something, so packet encapsulation happens.

For a long time, TCP/IP was difficult at best with NetWare (even its Intranetware product didn't natively use IP). Consequently, the best choice was to use IPX unless you had a pressing need for IP. Because IPX-IP translation is relatively simple (Novell includes an IPX-IP translator in its current product, and there are a raft of third-party protocol translators available from MCS, Cisco, and others), it's possible to provide Internet connectivity to your local network without actually having to run IP natively on each desktop. If you're not hosting a Web site, IPX with protocol translation is a good choice. Besides its ease of installation, it offers one additional benefit that is too seldom mentioned: a relatively high degree of security. Because most crackers run IP, they can get to the system

16

that does protocol translation, but because the crackers don't run IPX, they generally can't get inside the network to do any mischief.

Of course, we now live in the age of the Internet, and you may have users on your network who demand IP networking. In that case, if the business case is there, bind IP to the network cards in the NetWare server, add a good strong firewall, and keep an eye on security. IP works beautifully with NetWare 5.

NetWare Clients and NDS: Who's on First?

If you've ever dealt with the new release of a product, you're sure to understand the networking community's confusion when NetWare 4 was released. All too often, with new products, old familiar stuff changes (just think of New Coke and the fracas that caused). NetWare 4 and NDS were like New Coke—when it was introduced, its NetWare Directory Service feature (which you'll recall is a global directory of everything that NetWare connects to) confused people who knew and trusted NetWare 3.x. Consequently, a lot of people were disoriented by the new requirements and overall differences created by NDS.

The worst part of the change for a lot of administrators was the change to NDS-aware clients. Right after the release of NetWare 4.x, it was difficult to find clients that worked with NDS. And the list of which clients are (and aren't) capable of working with NDS is a bit obscure. Table 16.1 lists the various clients and whether or not they work with NDS.

TABLE 16.1 Client Compatibility with NDS

Operating System	Vendor	Client	NDS Aware?
MS-DOS/ Windows 3.x	Novell	VLM client (included with NetWare 4)	Yes
	Novell	IPX/NETX client	No (requires SET BINDERY CONTEXT= %NetWare Context Variable% set in AUTOEXEC.NCF to be able to see the later versions server)
Windows 95/98/Me	Microsoft	IPX/SPX-compatible protocol/client for NetWare networks	No (recent releases a new support for NDS service, however)
	Novell	Client32 for Windows 95	Yes

TABLE 16.1   continued

Operating System	Vendor	Client	NDS Aware?
Windows NT 3.51	Microsoft		No (requires `SET BINDERY CONTEXT=%NetWare ContextVariable%` set in `AUTOEXEC.NCF` to be able to see the laterversions server)
	Novell	Client32 for Windows NT (with NWAdmin software included)	Yes
Windows NT 4.0 and 2000	Microsoft	NWLink IPX/SPX-compatible protocol/ client service for NetWare	Yes (can load in either or Bindery mode)
	Novell	Client32 for Windows NT (with NWAdmin software included)	Yes

16

Summary

In this hour, you had an opportunity to learn about Novell NetWare: what it is, how it works, and which other operating systems interact with it. The next hour takes a look at the old workhorse of network operating systems: Unix.

Q&A

Q What are the differences between NetWare 3.x and 4.x?

A NetWare 3.x uses the Bindery to store user and group information; later versions use NDS.

NetWare 3.x is essentially a single-server solution—there's no easy way to log on to multiple servers except through the use of the ATTACH command. By contrast, later versions offer a single logon to all network resources, local or remote.

Because later versions have protected-mode memory, it's better at protecting applications from overwriting one another's memory spaces.

Q Why is NetWare attractive to networkers?

A Initially, NetWare was attractive to networkers because it was the only really viable Network Operating System that ran on IBM-compatible PCs. Over time, improvements in speed and reliability made it a corporate standard, and Novell's support for their product made it a "safe" buy.

Q What are a few of NetWare's most compelling upsides?

A Speed and scalability. NetWare is just plain fast compared to just about any other PC-based Network Operating System. Also, NetWare can scale to service more users on expanding networks extremely well.

Q What is NetWare's biggest downside?

A The lack of a graphical shell at the server itself. The management console for NetWare, NWAdmin, must run on a client system.

HOUR 17

Unix and Linux

With the increase in internetworking, Unix, it seems, is everywhere. If you watch TV or have read the computer trade press at all, you've seen a lot about Unix:

- Sun Microsystems runs TV ads stating that their Unix is the best performing Internet server.

- Linux, a freeware Unix clone, is the most popular operating system among hobbyists.

- Silicon Graphics' high-end graphics systems render their movie magic on Unix systems.

- Huge numbers of banks and other institutions that run mission-critical applications run—and bet—their businesses on Unix systems.

- IBM puts kiosk ads for their high-end AIX Unix servers in consumer shopping areas to get them into the public consciousness.

All these examples, and more stories like them, constitute a staggering endorsement of Unix as an enterprise-capable file, print, and application server. Unix is widely regarded by the system administration staffs of many companies large and small as the ne plus ultra Network Operating System,

and no engineering firm would dream of putting anything but a Unix workstation at their
design engineers' desks. And they're arguably making the correct decision because
Windows NT and NetWare can't even begin to approach the flexibility, power, configurability, maturity, and overall feature set of Unix.

Yet for regular computer users, including a great deal of PC networkers, Unix remains
shrouded in mystery and suspicion. The most common attitude toward Unix is that no
matter how fast, efficient, useful, or otherwise good it is, it's too complex for mere mortals. As a result, it's rarely used in small networks, which is a shame. Fortunately, Linux
(Finnish coder Linux Torvalds' open source operating system) has made great inroads in
the PC world, and has increased the number of users who have access to Unix and Unix-
like operating systems.

Does this endorsement mean that Unix isn't complex? No—it is. Does it mean that it
doesn't have a steep learning curve? No—it does. But in spite of the difficulty of learning Unix's cryptic command-line syntax and the difference between its windowing system and the interfaces of the common Microsoft and Apple systems, it's well worth
learning. A well-configured Unix system can do something no other operating system
can do: It can be all things to all people. Right out of the box, Unix is a natural for
TCP/IP networking because TCP/IP is built in at the very base of Unix. Unix is capable
of hooking up to NetWare networks, and it can interoperate with Windows NT. Unix
can provide terminal sessions for many users, and it can provide security and routing
services.

But what is Unix? This chapter will teach you. In this hour, you learn about the
following:

- History of Unix
- Some basic Unix concepts

The History of Unix

Unix started out as a joke—or at any rate, as a bit of a put-on.

In the late 1960s, AT&T Bell Laboratories started work on a *multiuser operating system*,
an operating system that could support more than one user session at a time, called
Multics. Programmers made fun of it; it was large, slow, and unwieldy, built by rules
generated by management committees. Multics wasn't extensible, either; the resources
that came with the system represented the total sum of resources available to the system.

In an attempt to show up the Multics programming team, several ardent AT&T Bell Labs
programmers set out to build a small, fast multiuser operating system that would be easily extensible and would encourage users to modify the system to suit their needs. When

the dust settled, they had created exactly what they set out to create, and in a poke at the Multics crew, they named their operating system Unix. (Unix, implying one, versus Multics, implying many—get it?) The first systems ran on Digital PDP-7 servers, which would be considered laughably underpowered by today's standards, but it was a starting point.

Growing Pains

Initially, Unix was considered a sort of hacker's paradise. (We use the term hacker in this book to mean a clever problem-solver or good coder. A person who unlawfully breaks into others' computer systems is a cracker.) People didn't really think it was enterprise-class software. After all, it was small, it was highly modular—it was possible to add operating system modules on the fly—and it hadn't been written in the typical plan-it-to-death corporate fashion. But it caught on just the same because it was small and cheap. Educational institutions and engineering businesses got on the bandwagon simply because Unix could run on computers with less power than the high-end systems that ran operating systems such as IBM's VM or Digital's VMS. It made sense for people without deep pockets; they could get mainframe power for microcomputer prices.

Spreading the Word

AT&T sent out copies of Unix very inexpensively during the formative years of Unix. At first, it ran on a relatively limited selection of machines, and in spite of its extreme usefulness, this might have led it to wind up on the sidelines as time passed. But in the mid-1970s, an event happened that saved Unix from the dust heap: It was rewritten from the ground up in the C programming language. C is a *portable* language—that is, code written in C can be modified and recompiled to run on different types of computer hardware. The ultimate result of this was that Unix became available for multiple machine types; every distribution of Unix included the *source code*, or the C language code; that source code could be *recompiled*, or translated into computer code, that could run on almost any platform.

The C programming language, or "C", is a high-level computer language developed by Brian Kernighan and Dennis Ritchie at Bell Labs. The C language enables programmers to write code that can be compiled to run on different types of computers. C programming is widely regarded as a cross between an art and a science. A compiler is a program that takes computer source code (which is plain text, just what you see in Windows Notepad or the DOS Edit program) and translates it into machine language, which is a string of instructions that the computer can execute.

C has a reputation for being ferociously difficult, but it's not really that hard. If one takes the time to learn the basics and to ensure that the syntax of the computer code is correct, it's possible to write small, elegant programs that do just exactly what you want.

In recent years, C has been superseded by C++, a newer and somewhat more streamlined version of C with additional capabilities.

Compilers are synonymous with Unix; almost every Unix package comes with at least a C compiler. Many versions of Unix now also come with C++ compilers. The C compiler is a necessity on many of these systems to build the kernel of the operating system.

Following is an example of the source code for a very simple C program:

```
#include stdio.h
main()
{
 printf("Hello, World\n");
}
```

This program, when run though a C compiler and executed, simply prints out the words *Hello, World*. This is usually the first program that a C programmer learns.

The Great Schism

In the mid-1970s, another momentous event occurred in the history of Unix. Ken Thompson, one of the original Unix programmers (as well as a coauthor of the C programming language—the book, *The C Programming Language*, written with Brian Kernighan, is still the definitive text for learning C), went on sabbatical to the University of California at Berkeley, where he met graduate student Bill Joy. Joy was fascinated with Unix, and he wrote an editor program (a program used to edit text) called *vi* that is still one of the most common text editors used in Unix systems. Shortly afterward, in early 1978, Joy released the first non-AT&T Unix; it was called *Berkeley Software Distribution (BSD)*.

To date, all variations of Unix stem from one or the other of these two initial distributions of Unix. Even Unix clones, such as Linus Torvald's Linux freeware operating system, adhere closely to the standards set forth by the AT&T and BSD Unixes.

Several years later, BSD released another very important addition to the rapidly growing group of Unix tools: a *port* of the TCP/IP protocol. A port is the process of recompiling C language source code into versions that can run on different computers. (For example, you can port the Hello, World program to a Macintosh by compiling it with a Macintosh compiler, and then port it to an IBM-compatible computer using an IBM-compatible compiler.) This BSD release was important because TCP/IP was the language of the ARPAnet, the precursor to the Internet. Since then, TCP/IP and selected TCP/IP utilities have become standard issue on Unix systems.

Over the years, AT&T and BSD went their own separate ways with their *command-line syntax*, or the rules about how commands are typed at the command prompts. However, over the last five or six years, the varieties of Unix have begun to use similar syntax; it's no longer easy to tell whether a particular variant of Unix was derived from AT&T or BSD. The coming-together of the Unix tribes has been driven by two factors: First, users wanted a command-line syntax consistent from Unix system to Unix system, and second, Microsoft launched an assault with Windows NT, their flagship OS, that could not be ignored.

Unix Under Attack

In spite of the fact that Windows NT has cut hugely into Unix-system revenues, it may turn out to be the best thing that ever happened to the Unix world. Ever since AT&T began licensing Unix to commercial developers, the Unix field has been wide-open. Unix ceased to be *binary compatible* (meaning that applications that ran on one variant of Unix would not run on other variants). Third-party developers wrote very little software specifically for Unix systems because to be reasonably profitable, an application would have to be ported to 10 or 15 of the most popular Unix systems. Unfortunately, this helped keep Unix, which is not user hostile (despite its reputation), out of the consumer and business markets.

Fortunately, the threat of Windows NT—which, for all its shortcomings (its youth, scalability concerns, and reliability concerns), remains a single-vendor OS, and therefore a strong point of focus for software developers—has spurred Unix vendors to do what all the Open Systems forums have been unable to do over the last 10 years: Agree that a common Unix platform is extremely important for Unix's survival. So the Unix vendors have begun to rally toward a common standard for Unix systems—which is ironic because the term interoperability, or the capability of computer systems to work together and communicate properly, is best defined by invoking the name of Unix. Even with the disparate varieties of Unix, interopererability between Unix systems on a networking level is extraordinary. Unix can interoperate at a network level with anything that can run TCP/IP, and many systems that can't. A computer running HP-UX (Hewlett-Packard's Unix) can nfs-mount disks from a Sun Solaris system, which in turn might be handling the Network Information Service information for a network that includes IBM's AIX, Red Hat Linux, and SCO Unix and UnixWare. And the syntax for the basic commands between systems is sufficiently similar to enable a user who knows one system to use another system—and to figure out how to use it if they *don't* know how. Unix is chock-full of online documentation called *man pages*. *Man* is short for *manual*, and if you type *man* and a command name (like *man ls*), the manual page for the ls ("list," similar to DOS/Windows "dir") command will pop up and tell you how to use the command.

Unix Woes

The Unix vendor community, however, is not solely to blame for Unix's commercial woes. In the early 1990s, AT&T decided that it didn't want to be in the Unix software business any longer and sold the trademark and licensing rights to Novell (the same Novell that makes NetWare). Novell planned to position its Unix variant (called UnixWare) as the scalable big brother to NetWare, and to use it for certain mission-critical applications. Unfortunately, Novell had acquired WordPerfect, Borland's Quattro Pro spreadsheet, and several other applications products at the same time they acquired Unix Systems Laboratories. In the bottom-line bashing that sometimes follows a major acquisition, Novell founder Ray Noorda was forced out; his position as CEO of Novell was taken over by Robert Frankenberg. During Frankenberg's tenure, the applications business was sold off (to Corel Corporation) and the rights to Unix were sold to the Santa Cruz Operation, or SCO, a company which creates SCO OpenServer and OpenDesktop, some of the most popular Intel-compatible Unix products. And in mid-2000, SCO sold the rights to UnixWare to Caldera, a company founded by Ray Noorda, late of Novell and rightfully famous for Caldera OpenLinux, a version of Linux bundled with many productivity tools.

As licensing rights to Unix were getting bounced around from company to company, many potential customers began to view Unix as a failing business proposition (patently untrue) and opted instead for other, "more secure," operating systems—most notably Windows NT. NT was in the right place at the right time and has successfully taken away a great deal of Unix business. In fact, in 1997, Windows NT shipped more copies than all Unixes combined. This trend has slowed with the advent of Linux, but at base, Unix still needs to make up ground it lost to NT.

The Future of Unix: Still on Solid Ground

The ascent of Windows NT does not mean that Unix is in any way dead. Unix is far more scalable, more reliable, and more battle tested than any version of NT. After all, NT has been out only since the early 1990s—Unix has been around since 1969. Unix can handle larger amounts of disk space and is significantly faster than any operating system that operates in its market sector.

It's easily modified, and it has a variety of tools, such as scripting languages—perl, tcl/tk, and shell scripts—that enable users to write *shell scripts* (short programs to auto-mate tasks). Its X Windows graphical user interface offers an easy-to-use graphical interface on the operating system as well as the capability to distribute processing according to an organization's needs. And the Common Desktop Environment (CDE), used by many commercial Unixes, means that the desktop will look the same whether the OS beneath it is HP-UX, AIX, Solaris, or what-have-you.

In addition, the rise of Linux has extended the reach and availability of Unix-like systems to people who might never otherwise have had access to this type of operating system due to cost constraints.

The current uses for Unix are manifold. On the low end, Linux—a freeware, primarily Intel-compatible version of Unix—is used as a powerful, capable, and very inexpensive Web and mail server by many organizations. At the next level, Unix is used to run workstation computers—typically, SunMicrosystem's SunOS or Solaris running on a Sun-compatible SPARC box, Silicon Graphics' INDY machines, IBM's AIX running on RS/6000s, or Hewlett-Packard's HP-UX running on PA-RISC. Some of these machines aren't used as servers; instead, they're programming workstations or engineering workstations. They also do graphics exceptionally well—workstation computers from Silicon Graphics were used to do the computer-graphics sequences in the movie, *Terminator 2*.

At the high end are multiprocessing servers that support banking systems, huge e-commerce sites, public safety data systems, and other mission-critical applications. These systems run the same operating systems listed above; typically the only difference between a workstation and server Unix system is raw horsepower and input/output capability, usually abbreviated i/o. These Unix servers can support hundreds or thousands of simultaneous users, and have 16 or more processors and gigabytes of RAM. The disk space these behemoths control is truly staggering—some systems control close to a terabyte of disk space. They're almost mainframes, but instead of running a proprietary mainframe operating system, they run Unix.

In the nearly 30 years since its birth, Unix has acquired a dizzying array of services and capabilities. It can run on almost any processor, and can be scaled up to run high-end banking systems—or scaled down far enough to operate a microcontroller in a factory machine. Its versatility allows it to exist at almost every level of almost every type of business, and its flexibility allows it to accomplish almost any task. It's the preferred operating system for a lot of Internet servers because the Internet grew up on Unix—it's a natural.

Basic Unix Concepts

OK, now you know the history of Unix. Let's start looking at it a little more closely, from a technical perspective. You've read several times about Unix's power, but what about Unix makes it that powerful?

Everything Is a File

Here goes. The first, and probably the hardest-to-grasp concept, is that in Unix, *everything is a file*. Everything in Unix—whether it's a hard drive, a serial port, or a text file—is a file. And what can you do with files? You can read and write to them. So it is with

Unix—when you write to a hard drive, the software sees it as writing to a special kind of file called a *block device* since it reads disk blocks at a time. If it read single characters at a time, it would be a *character device*.

Standard Input and Output

Second, Unix has *standard input and output*, which more often gets called *redirection*. OK, you say…it has monitors, keyboards, and printers? Nope. Standard input and output, from a Unix perspective, means that you can chain programs together and stream the output from one file into the input of the next program in the chain. For instance, there's a command in Unix to list all of the programs (in Unix, they're called *processes*) called *ps*. If you type *ps* at a Unix command-line terminal, it will tell you which processes are running. But if you're at a command line screen, you're often limited to the 25 lines that the screen has, so the output of the *ps* command will scroll across your screen way too fast for you to read. But you can redirect the output of the *ps* command to a command called *more*, which displays only one screen of data at a time, by typing *ps | more*. This would give you the output of the *ps* command, but only display it one screen at a time, while you used the spacebar to scroll through all the pages of output. The "|" symbol is called a *pipe* because, in this case, it "pipes" data from the output of one command into the input of the next.

In most operating systems, you have to do a significant amount of programming to be able to filter or modify the contents of a file. In Unix, however, this isn't the case. Unix is basically a kernel, the very center of the operating system; a series of small, modular programs with very focused purposes can be run on the fly. Using standard input (the keyboard or a file), standard output (the screen), and pipes (represented by the "|" character), it is possible to pass data between programs and accomplish a variety of complex tasks right from the command line.

Pipes are neat, but they don't do everything that you need for redirection. Let's say that you want to take the output of a particular *ps* command and put it into a file so you can read it in a text editor and print it. You could, at that point, type *ps > /tmp/ps-output*. What this would do is take the output of the *ps* command and redirect it into a file in the /tmp directory called ps-output (this filename is ad-hoc; you can name a file whatever you want to!). Literally, this command would be read "run a ps command and redirect the output of it to the file /tmp/ps-output." Pretty simple, no? What happens if you want to create a log file that just keeps having new information tacked onto the end of the file? Simple. Instead of using >, you use >> instead to make the command *ps >> /tmp/ps-output*. If you read THIS command literally, you'd get the following: "run a ps command and put the output into the /tmp/ps-output file. If there is an existing /tmp/ps-output file, don't overwrite it; instead, append the new output to the end of the existing /tmp/ps-output file".

There are other forms of redirection, but these are the ones that people use at the command line all the time.

Hierarchical File System

The third Unix concept is that *every file on a Unix system is mounted in a hierarchical file system—EVERYTHING.* In the Windows world, the root of each drive is a letter that denotes a physical disk, such as C:\ or D:\. If a disk is full, it's full, and there's no way to extend the file system on that disk onto other disks. By contrast, Unix has a file system that starts with a slash " / " and is called the *root file system.* This logically includes the whole world (of the system). Disk drives are resources mounted within subdirectories of the root file system, and consequently all the disk space available within a system is theoretically available to any file system. And unlike Windows where the physical disk is irrevocably tied to each file system, Unix allows file systems to use available disk space, whether there's one disk or fifty in the system. This makes Unix file systems greatly extensible—in many Unixes, you can increase the size of file systems as you require. Since more than one file system can span more than one disk, the concept of file system becomes independent of the concept of physical disk. In this way, Unix makes efficient and extraordinarily flexible use of disk space in ways that Windows systems don't and can't.

It's difficult to cite a particular directory hierarchy as definitive for Unix, but there are some fairly common standards. Table 17.1 shows a list of standard Unix file systems and their uses:

TABLE 17.1   The Organization of a Typical Unix File System

/	The root of the file system. This is the logical base for every other file system on the computer. The root file system usually contains the /dev directory, where devices such as hard drives and serial port (also called *ttys*, short for *teletypes*) are stored; the /etc directory, where password and group files are stored; and /bin, where system binaries are stored.
/usr	/usr is used for a variety of software available to users. Often, files in /usr/bin won't be "real" files, but will be special links to files stored in the /bin directory in the root file system. IBM installs a great deal of system software, such as compilers, under the /usr directory.
/var	/var is used for accounting and other *var*iable items such as log files. /var/adm/logs or /var/logs is where many system log files are stored by default.
/opt	/opt is not used by every Unix system. It's used for *opt*ional software. HP-UX uses /opt to store things like the C and COBOL compilers.

TABLE 17.1   continued

/home	/home is where users get to put their stuff. If you're a user on a Unix system, you'll have a *home directory* that matches your logon name—for instance, Joe Smith might log on as *jsmith* and his home directory would be */home/jsmith*. In every user's home directory is a file called *.profile* which runs when the user logs on. The *.profile* file sets environments, starts menus, and does a variety of other things, since the user can modify it to do whatever they want on logon.
/tmp	The /tmp file system is where stuff that doesn't have a place to go gets stored. On many systems, it's flushed when the system boots up, so it's not necessarily a good idea to store anything of real value there.

Shell Scripts: Make Your Own Programs

The fourth important Unix concept is that *almost anything can be a fully functioning program, even if it's just a shell script*. Scripting languages are programming languages built into many operating systems. A shell script is essentially just a text file with a variety of Unix commands chained together in order, and it's set up so that the system reads the file and runs the commands in it. Shell scripts are like very powerful DOS/Windows batch files. In Unix, it is possible to build shell scripts from commands that are usually issued at the command line. For example, you can list the contents of a directory and then copy that list into a file with a one-line shell script. All you have to do is start a new file in vi (a text editor) and type the following line:

```
ls -l  > dirlist.txt
```

If we read this as a command in English, it would read "list files in the current directory (ls –l) and redirect the output of that command from the screen into a file called dirlist.txt (> dirlist.txt)."

After typing this line, you save the file as (for example) *dl* and make the file executable by using the *chmod +x* command. Just like that, you've created a shell script. Then, any time you want to write the contents of a directory to file, you simply type dl, or preface it with a ./ (which appends the current directory onto the PATH, which is basically a list of directories the operating system searches when it looks for the command you've just typed).

It's possible to write whole programs in scripting languages, or as shell scripts and have them work as part of the operating system. It's not uncommon to have shell scripts managing things, such as auditing security and printing reports for administrators, or automating system backups. Just because these shell scripts are written by system administrators instead of commercial programmers doesn't necessarily make their scripts inferior—in many cases, a custom-written shell script is better adapted to the particular system than any commercial software.

There are a lot of Unix scripting languages. Practical Extraction and Reporting Language (perl) is commonly used in situations where standard shell scripts can't efficiently accomplish the task at hand. Perl has some features of more advanced programming languages, such as C.

Other scripting languages include Eiffel as well as Tool Command Language and the ToolKit. The last two are referred to as tcl/tk and are used to build graphical applications…from scripts!!

Clearly the power of scripting languages to customize Unix to do what you require is extraordinary…and we've only just scratched the surface.

Interoperability and Open Standards

The fifth Unix concept is one of which we've harped on throughout this book—interoperability and adherence to Open Systems standards. Because Unix systems adhere to the open standards published by the Internet Engineering Task Force (IETF), they can interact with one another without significant problems. A Unix from one vendor can interoperate with a Unix from another vendor at the standards level without fear that one vendor's interface won't work with another vendor's interface. This is why things such as Web services and Internet email are so often entrusted to Unix or Linux systems; they adhere to the standards that have been agreed upon by committee and therefore can work together easily. This reduces cost and makes Unix a much more predictable system than highly proprietary operating systems.

Unix as a Network Operating System

Selecting Unix for a local network—or even a first network—is not necessarily a bad choice. The software with which it is possible to build a small local network is relatively low cost (Linux is available as a free download on the Web or on CD-ROM for about $30; FreeBSD, a version of BSD Unix that's free of copyright restrictions, is also available for $30 or so on CD-ROM) and provides a fine introduction to Unix and Unix-style systems. Although Unix is not user-hostile, neither is it simple; you'll need a book specifically dedicated to Unix, Linux, or FreeBSD to get the server running. If you use it, you'll learn a great deal and wind up with a system that is fast, reliable, and (typically) less prone to user-created problems than almost any of the other operating systems described in this book.

Unix makes a great network operating system. It's got great file services via nfs, it's the best Webserver in the world (the freeware Apache Webserver running on Linux is used by more Webservers than any other Webserver software in the world), the *sendmail* email program is the world standard for exchanging email between servers, and there are a host of other services that Unix can provide. It's worth the learning curve.

17

The Specs: A Close Look at Unix

At the beginning of the hour, we asked the question "What is Unix?" Here's one answer: Unix is a preemptive multitasking operating system that can support multiple users through two methods: through terminal screens (the famous "green screen") where the processing is done at the Unix server (the user sees only the screen on his or her desktop computer), and through TCP/IP networking over Ethernet, FDDI, Token Ring, or some other network topology.

The following sections describe the types of access to Unix systems: terminals and networked connections. This is some heavy going, but it's worth the work. After you've finished reading these sections, you'll understand how Unix interacts with people.

Terminals

Unix supports some user interaction through *terminals*. A terminal is essentially a dumb system that has no local processing; it's similar to a monitor with just enough intelligence to know how to display stuff on the screen.

Unix talks to terminals and controls access through a series of programs that all have the letters *tty* in them, which is short for *teletype*. For instance, *tty0* is the Unix system's name for the first terminal in the list (Unix starts counting at 0), and in many systems, it's the default administration console (also called */dev/console*). Over the years, many manufacturers have made "dumb" terminals that can be used with Unix systems; the most common was made by Digital Equipment Corporation and was called the VT100, although IBM, Hewlett-Packard, and Wyse are also found periodically.

When a terminal connects to a Unix system, it is (often) connecting by way of a serial port (also called a *COM port* on an Intel-compatible PC, and a *tty port* in Unix parlance), as opposed to a network connection. Typically, in this scenario, the Unix system does all the processing and the terminal only displays the data onscreen, passing keystrokes and mouse movements back to the server.

Sometimes, command-line terminal sessions can be run across a network, and the sessions are known to the Unix server as *pseudoterminals* or *ptys* instead of *ttys*. Either way, they function in the same fashion—they just pass keystrokes back and forth, and all the processing is done at the server end of the connection.

Command-line terminals are primarily used for two things: administrative consoles for the Unix system, and for non-graphical applications (as opposed to a Windows system, which uses a Graphical User Interface to interact with the user). Because terminals are primarily used to key and retrieve data, they have no local storage; the extent of their connection to peripherals is usually a printer, and sometimes not even that.

The next step up from a dumb terminal is an *X terminal*, so called because it runs the X Window system. Typically, an X terminal is a graphical terminal with a small amount of local RAM, a high-resolution full-color graphical screen, and a mouse (and sometimes, hard drives). X terminals offer significant benefits in some environments; although they don't do their own processing locally, they do have a bit of local processing and can handle all of their own graphics. For many years, graphical X terminals formed the mainstay of the engineering computer workshop because they offered great performance (by late 1980s standards) on CAD applications and were cheaper than putting a workstation on everyone's desk. X terminals are generally not connected to the Unix system with a serial cable as are terminals; X terminals usually use an Ethernet connection of some type.

Terminals are useful tools; even within an X Windows interface, an xterm (x terminal session) is often on the desktop—it's like having a command-line MS-DOS window in Windows 2000. Sometimes the command line is just the simplest way to get things done.

17

On the whole, the use of remote terminal hardware of either type (dumb or X) is fading for a couple of reasons.

The first is that there is a lot of terminal emulation software available for PCs and Macs that enable users to work on a Unix system from their local PCs; in fact, many applications simply dispense with a direct connection to the Unix system and use *socket connections*. This is where an application on the PC client passes data on specific TCP/IP connections to the Unix server, which responds in kind so the user doesn't know what kind of a system is interacting with his or her desktop software.

The second is that the cost of local workstations is going way down due to Linux and less-expensive powerful Intel-based computers. It's more efficient for some companies to provide (for example) engineers with a Linux workstation or less-expensive AIX, HP-UX, or Solaris workstation than an X terminal. Why? Well, for one, the use of individual workstations provides each user with a greater volume of dedicated computer power than a session on a larger computer. Then there's redundancy: If the server goes down, users may be able to continue working. There are downsides to putting workstations at each desktop, but they're downsides that exist in any distributed network—cost of licensing software at each workstation, cost of maintenance for workstations, and so forth. This is part of the reason why Linux is making such great inroads: It provides the user more power and flexibility while running on less-powerful hardware and keeping costs relatively low.

Things That Go Together: Networking and Unix

In the late 1980s and early 1990s, networking burst open and all of a sudden, anyone who could network, did. Ethernet, long a mainstay of Unix business environments, was suddenly everywhere—and when it showed up, everyone wanted to be able to run TCP/IP and network with existing Unix systems. Users wanted to be able to access their terminal applications over the network because it was faster and more reliable. To accomplish this, a new class of software appeared on PCs: terminal emulator software. Terminal emulators offered people with PCs the capability to connect to Unix systems using Ethernet networking. It worked, but it wasn't good enough; it was slow and it offered only a limited range of features.

Over time, vendors became aware that servers in the PC world were doing more than simply running specific applications for users. Servers were acting as file repositories, print servers, communications servers, and the like. PC users wanted to have the same type of client/server connections to Unix systems that they had with their NetWare servers. But initially, there was no way to mount a Unix drive on a PC system—that is, there was no way that a PC could see a Unix system as another network drive letter.

Remote File Systems: nfs

Files don't exist in a vacuum on a network. They need to be shared to be useful. Sun Microsystems realized that the marketplace needed a way to allow PC users to see Unix-server hard drives as network hard drives. Consequently they ported their Network File System (nfs) software to personal computers. nfs has long been a mainstay of the Unix world, since it enables Unix systems to gain access to files on remote systems as if they were stored locally.

PC-nfs provided the facility for remote computers to see a Unix disk volume in their own file system—whether the volume was seen as another drive letter (as in Windows) or as another directory in the local file system (as in Unix). When using nfs, a PC simply sees a Unix system's hard drive as another network drive.

nfs offered a great way to share Unix file resources with personal computers. PC-nfs was a smash hit from the beginning. It enabled Unix systems to work with a variety of other computers as though the Unix system was local. It could work in the local network or across the wide area link—it solved a lot of problems.

Currently, the market has expanded, and there are a number of vendors (Hummingbird, WRQ, and others) who offer nfs connectivity in their Unix host connectivity packages. Even Microsoft has gotten into the act with their *Unix Services for Windows NT* package.

Other Remote File Systems: afs, dfs, and Samba

Sometimes, however, nfs didn't serve all the needs of users quite right. Two responses to nfs were Andrew File System (afs) and distributed file system (dfs). Both offered a slightly different range of features than nfs. To get into the differences, however, would be delving into esoterica.

Windows machines, however, were still outside the range of most remote file systems, except for PC-nfs. To remedy this situation, a new product called Samba was written in the early 1990s. Samba is a Unix implementation of Microsoft's Server Message Block protocol (SMB, hence "samba"), which you may recall from the discussion on protocols in Hour 3, "Getting Data from Here to There: How Computers Share Data."

Samba enables Unix to share its resources just as if they were shared from a Windows machine. It's easy to use; like a great deal of Unix software, it's available at no charge from a variety of sites on the Internet and has already been compiled for a huge number of different Unix versions. In fact, using Samba, Linux systems can function as Windows NT Domain servers (although they don't yet work with Windows 2000's Active Directory).

Long Filenames, Case-Sensitive Names, and Switches

Unlike DOS, Unix allows long filenames, typically 32 characters. For those of us who don't like to be forced to interpret DOS's truncated 8.3 filenames, Unix offers long filename support and has from the very beginning.

In addition to long filenames, Unix also has case-sensitive names and switches. For example, the file `Marks_Legal_files_1997` is *not* the same as `marks_legal_files_1997`; Unix won't find the first filename if you type the second filename. This is both good and bad. On the good side, file naming in Unix is rigorous and ensures filename uniqueness. However, it can be extremely frustrating if you're not expecting it. Novice users often forget that Unix is case-sensitive and are exasperated when they type a filename in lowercase that is actually in upper- and lowercase, and it doesn't work.

Graphical User Interfaces

Unix started out with a purely command-line interface. To multitask, users had to start a program with certain command-line switches that made one program run in the background (such as appending an ampersand (&) to the end of the command) while the user worked on another application in the foreground. This approach worked—that is, as long as the user was a computer science major at a major university and could remember all the commands to switch between programs. However, the rank and file found this approach wearisome. The complexity of the commands wore on users and made them want a better way to run multiple programs.

The introduction of X Window was intended to remedy this situation. In an X Window session, data runs in resizable windows onscreen; if you've used a Windows PC or a Macintosh, you've seen such windows. Initially, X was a character-based environment; it looked like DOS with lines and arrows. However, with the introduction of more powerful computers and video cards, X took on a look that is familiar to any Mac or Windows user: 3D menus, proportional fonts, scalable windows and WYSIWYG (what you see is what you get) graphics. Actually, X didn't take on the graphical user interface; instead, programmers wrote programs called *window managers* to handle the graphical appearance of the screens. Common window managers include (but aren't limited to) Motif, Open Look, and CDE; each has its own style and conventions.

Protocol Selection

The choice of network protocols for Unix is simple. Although Unix can run SMB protocol stuff, internetwork with Windows, and can use IPX to interact with NetWare, its native protocol is TCP/IP. TCP/IP was basically written for Unix, so the two go hand in hand and are a near-perfect fit.

Most Unix systems have extensive TCP/IP implementations; it's a given for most Unix systems that you'll have IP and all the underlying functionality—mail, news, DNS servers, DHCP server, SNMP, RMON, and so on. Configuration for Unix TCP/IP can be difficult because many common versions of Unix have only command-line interfaces to configure system parameters such as the network address.

Summary

In spite of Unix's complexity, it is a viable operating system that scales better, works faster, and is more reliable than any comparable midrange OS available. Learning Unix is a lifelong task; one headhunter says she's learned to hire candidates who say, "I've worked with Unix," rather than "I know Unix." From her perspective, and the technical hiring managers she deals with, the latter statement is presumptuous.

If you've got the time to invest in learning Unix and building a Unix server, Linux is the best first choice, hands down. It's essentially freeware and is available from companies such as Red Hat, Caldera, Slackware, and Yggdrasil. The cost of the OS is usually less than $100; in some cases, you can download it at no charge from various sites on the Internet. This is a worthwhile pursuit because the server you build will be one of the most capable systems you'll ever use—it will be able to do almost anything you require.

Q&A

Q Why is Unix used in so many mission-critical applications?

A Unix is used in mission-critical applications for several reasons:

- It has been around for almost 30 years and is battle tested.
- It's easily customizable to suit a particular enterprise's needs.
- It's tremendously fast in comparison with other operating systems that can operate on a given computer.

Q What are some of Unix's weaknesses?

A Unix has three primary weaknesses:

- A fragmented market caused by many versions of Unix that can't run common software.
- The complexity of its command-line interface.
- Its unfamiliarity to most computer users.

Q What are some of Unix's strengths?

A Unix has many strengths, among them these:

- Speed
- Reliability
- Rich feature sets
- Huge amounts of useful software in most releases

17

PART V

Introduction to Network Administration

Hour

HOUR 18

The Network Administrator

What is a network administrator?

From a purely functional perspective, it's the person responsible for ensuring the health and well-being of a network. He or she has to be able to install and configure hardware and software and ensure that the infrastructure of the network is sound.

In a large corporation, that's an apt, general description of a network administrator's duties. However, the vast majority of network administrators don't work in large companies. They work in small to mid-sized enterprises where they wear a multitude of hats. It's not uncommon for a network administrator to bear responsibility for almost all aspects of technology—whether they're computer-related or not. All too often, this is because many people have become administrators simply because they have a knack for computers and technology.

This chapter is an attempt to ensure that network administrators have an appropriate understanding of the basic tasks essential to the successful management of a network. But even if you're not interested in becoming a network administrator, the maintenance of a network is central to its very existence. The next few hours not only describe the duties of the network administrator, they will also deepen your understanding of networking in general.

Managing a network is not a homogenous job. Instead, it's a melange of several different jobs:

- Architect
- Detail-oriented record keeper
- Troubleshooter
- Facilitator
- Coach
- Teacher
- Therapist

This isn't a complete list, either. Network administration accretes new tasks like the bottom of a boat accretes barnacles—they're a natural outgrowth of a vigorous and growing environment. So don't take what's in this chapter as a complete list of the tasks of successful network administration; instead, look at the information here as a baseline. Depending on your environment, you'll find your job is diverse enough to prevent boredom—as well as reinventing and stretching your knowledge on a daily basis.

Here is a list of what you will learn in this hour:

- The importance of keeping system log files
- Data storage for a secure network
- About system maintenance—how to do it right
- Design practices
- User account design and management
- Network resource-item naming conventions
- Distribution of functions and redundancy
- Backup plans
- Security design
- Disaster recovery

Planning and Installing a Network

Because you've gotten to this section of the book, you undoubtedly have a good understanding of how a network should be designed. This is good—but it's quite a stretch getting from knowing how the pieces fit together to actually planning and installing a network. Planning and installing require organizational skills in addition to technical skills. This section discusses how to plan a network installation as well as how to carry out a network implementation (in which your plan is put to the test). You will also find a few notes to help you get through the inevitable glitches during installation.

As a network administrator, you typically have only a finite role in space planning; that's where managers and architects have their say in the process. If the space as designed isn't suitable, don't be afraid to speak up, but don't expect to be given free rein, either. Your job really begins when you specify considerations, such as the number of network wires each space (cubicle, office) will have.

As covered in earlier hours, the main tasks involved in any network planning remain the same: plan, design, implement, and tune. The specific things you typically have to do during network design and installation are the same things you've learned about in this book so far:

- **Basic knowledge of networking.** The first few hours of this book discussed the basics of networking. This stuff is the staple of networking knowledge: topologies, protocols, nomenclature, and the like. This phase of the networking process is where you learn how the whole thing fits together.

- **Know the design of your network.** If you designed your network, you'll understand how the pieces fit together logically and physically. This is very useful when solving network administration problems because the designer can rapidly identify potential points of failure.

- **Understand how the pieces fit together.** This knowledge comes from knowing the design of the network: understanding how data is supposed to flow inside the network. This understanding eases network software troubleshooting.

- **Make the pieces work together.** This is where the preceding three items come together in one concrete—and occasionally terrifying—ordeal.

When viewed in this light, network planning and building looks pretty simple and, in some ways, it is. During network planning, the network administrator's job is to create an internally consistent plan for the network so that in theory, the network will work. During the time the network is being built and thereafter, the network administrator's job is to ensure that the network does work. To do the former, it's necessary to understand networking in the abstract; to do the latter, you need a knowledge of abstract concepts plus the ability to work with concrete reality.

The Planning Checklist

Here's a checklist of what the network planner has to think about. This is a generic list; make sure that you take your own circumstances into account and add and subtract items as you require them.

- **Designing the logical network.** How does stuff need to work together? Refer to Hour 10, "How to Select Hardware and Software for Your Network," for this information.

- **Designing the physical network.** How are you going to bring the logical design into the real world? Refer to Hour 10.

- **Which protocols are you going to run?** Refer to Hour 3, "Getting Data from Here to There: How Computers Share Data," and see whether you can decide.

- **When you're running network wire, how much are you running?** Look at the building plans and decide whether you can get it from point A to point B without violating the fire code or the Category 5 standards. Refer to Hour 5, "Network Concepts," for more information on this.

- **What software will your users run?** Have you planned to license it? Refer to Hour 4, "Computer Concepts," for more on this.

- **Will all the hardware and software you've planned for the network interoperate?** Remember to plan for interoperability…and test it. Refer to Hour 9, "Designing Your Network," for details.

- **Have you ensured that there will be enough power for your equipment?** This isn't a concern for networks with only a few computers, but if your plans call for many computers clustered in one space, make certain that you have enough electricity to power them all.

Figuring out power demands is easy: On the back of each piece of computer equipment is a label that tells how much current (in milliamps) the piece draws. As long as the sum total of the electricity needed by equipment plugged into an electrical outlet doesn't exceed the number of amps that outlet is rated for, everything works fine. Go over that limit, and *pop!* you'll be in the circuit breakers every 10 minutes. So, carefully inventory the power requirements of the equipment slated for your network and create a spreadsheet; figure out how many amps are required, and what voltages your hardware requires. Ensure that there's enough in total to allow for fifty percent expansion at the junction box and ensure that each space has sufficient power to operate the equipment planned for it.

There are obviously other issues to deal with when planning networks, but they're situational and thereby tactical. The issues outlined here are strategic (that is, global) and are almost universal.

The Installation Checklist

During installation, you have to ensure that all your *I*s are dotted and your *T*s are crossed. Obviously, you've done the groundwork outlined in the preceding section if you're ready to do the installation, but here is a checklist of installation-specific issues:

- **Have you made a plan for the installation?** In other words, do you have a list of tasks to be accomplished? Here's a sample list:
    - Install servers in a locked room with some sort of uninterruptible power supply (UPS).
    - Install hubs in locked wiring closet.
    - Connect hubs/switches/routers to wiring; connect servers to wall wiring; configure hubs or switches or routers as required (or do ahead of time if possible).
    - Test power to servers to verify correct voltage, and then power up servers.
    - Attempt to connect to the server with a known functional workstation computer to ensure that the server's networking is functional. If you can't make a connection, test for troubleshooting.
    - Install production workstations and test for connection to the network.
    - Connect functioning internal network to external networking equipment (for WANs, the Internet, and so on).
- **Are you certain that the cable has been installed, terminated, and (most importantly) tested?** Most reputable cabling installers provide you with a list of cables installed and the results of cable tests. (Cable is tested with special pieces of equipment called, not surprisingly, *cable testers*; they measure the speed and overall length of cables. They're cool. They're also very expensive; cheap cable testers are $5000 or more.) It's important that you have your cable installed and tested ("certified" is another common term) before you start plugging anything in.
- **Do you have enough patch cords (if you're installing a 10BASE-T, Token Ring, FDDI, or ATM network)?** Are they rated at the correct level? If they're fiber, are they the correct type (multimode or single-mode)?
- **Can you identify which patch panel ports in the wiring closet go to which locations in the office?** If not, identify them and create a map and number both the patch panel and field ends of each wire. Identifying these ports beforehand makes connecting equipment much simpler because you don't have to run down wires.

18

- **When you're installing computers, did you install your server first and ensure that other computers can connect to it through the wiring you've had installed?** It's important to get the server running properly first because if it's not running properly, troubleshooting is twice as hard. A good trick is to take one workstation and connect it directly to the server with a crossover cable (if you're using 10BASE-T); if you can connect, chances are good that the server works okay.

- **If you have external access through digital phone lines (a WAN or an Internet connection), have you ensured that the CSU/DSU and router work?** By getting this done first, you can test your Internet connection as each computer is installed on the network.

- **As you install your network, are you securing the computers?** Servers should be in locked rooms or closets; wiring should likewise be in locked spaces. Computers and peripherals should ideally be secured with a cable lock because this precaution makes the equipment harder to steal.

As you work through your installation process, realize that you will doubtless have issues unique to your situation. The most important thing you can do before an installation is to outline the objectives—that way, you can try to plan for what *could* go wrong.

Administering a Network

Like any other worthwhile pursuit, networking does not just happen; it requires maintenance. In the same way that a field of grass has to be trimmed and reseeded from time to time if it is to be a good playing field, a network requires an administrator to manage users, security concerns, backup, and a host of other tasks that come under the network administration aegis.

Most network administration falls under one of the following heads, which are discussed individually in following sections:

- Logs
  - Machine-generated logs
  - Human-generated logs
- Data storage
- Maintenance
- Design and expansion
- User account design and maintenance

- Set up and administration of naming conventions
- Distribution of functions
- Backup planning
- Security design
- Disaster recovery

Of course, as with almost every other list in this book, the preceding list doesn't cover every possible situation. Instead, it presents a base skill-set for the network administrator. Once you've mastered these skills, it's likely that your network will run smoothly and users will trust it.

Keeping Logs

In the context of a network, logs are not big, wooden, branchless things you see floating down the river if you live in Maine. Instead, system logs are the record of what you and the computer have done to each other. (Actually, if you kept a log file that listed what the computer did to you, you'd have to add things such as "made me tear my thinning hair out," and "kept me up all night because of a missing comma.")

So, what is a log? A log is a record of events. In most cases, the computer can record its own log files, but it's a good idea to keep a handwritten text file log as well so that there is a record of a problem and the solution.

The importance of log files cannot be overstated. Here's a real-world example: If you're having a mysterious system crash at 2:00 in the morning every Friday, you can consult your system log and look for the events that precede the crash. The log is very likely to assist you in identifying the cause of the crash. Believe it or not, the log is sometimes more useful than staying up to watch the system crash; you can't always see what's going on with the machine.

The cause of the system crash, for example, might be that your backup software kicks in at 2:00 a.m. every day, but for some reason, when it starts on Friday, the system crashes. Why? Perhaps early on Friday mornings your system does disk defragmentation that overlaps the backup. That *could* be the cause of a crash...and it would be right there in the log.

Log files also prevent charges of negligence from sticking. If you have a complete log of all system events and all recent changes made to the system, you've limited your organization's liability because there's evidence of proper maintenance and due diligence.

18

Logs are invaluable when they record logons. If you're trying to secure your network, keeping a good record of logons is an absolute necessity. If you use a logon-recording log file, you can determine who has accessed the system and when they accessed it. Watching this kind of a log can track patterns of use that can spur investigation when they don't seem right.

In any case, logs are an important and necessary part of your network administration. Like a sailing ship's log book, your computer's log is your record of what you've done and what the machine has done.

Generally, there are two kinds of logs: electronic (machine generated) and paper (human generated).

Machine-Generated Logs

Electronic logs are text files that reside on your server. They're usually generated automatically by an operating system or application, and in most cases are accessible only by the administrator. If you're running a Windows 2000, NetWare, or Unix system, the operating system generates log files for you on the fly; for other operating systems, there are fewer logging options.

System log files have a variety of purposes and uses. The first, and probably the most common, is troubleshooting. If your system keeps a log file that tracks all the errors, running programs, and other events that occur on that particular machine, you have a head start on solving problems once they emerge. If you can open up a log file you can see what's happened. In Windows 2000, the Event Viewer is your default log; in Unix, `/var/adm/syslog/syslog.log`; NetWare uses `SYSTEM.LOG`.

Very often, system logs can provide a level of minutiae that goes all the way down to the memory-address level. Such detail may not be meaningful to you at first glance; it's arcane and, without the capability to decode hexadecimal addresses on the fly, may seem rather pointless. However, even apparently arcane data is useful when debugging crashes. Take the time to compare the memory and crash-related data recorded in the log; if you find common information, even if you don't know what it means, you can begin to formulate hypotheses about the cause of crashes.

Electronic log files are not limited to tracking system events. Windows 2000's *Performance Monitor,* Novell NetWare's *CONLOG* and *MONITOR* utilities, and Unix *top* can also track network packets and help you determine the causes of network outages. When a computer is set up to read all the packets passing around a network for diagnostic reasons, the process is called *packet tracing* or *packet sniffing*. A packet trace (the name of the text file that results from packet tracing) can indicate a variety of ills on a network, from poor configuration to too much traffic and more. In a marked contrast to standard log files, which are relatively dynamic (that is, they prune off older parts of the file as more data comes in, allowing the system log files to remain more-or-less the same size), packet traces tend to represent a snapshot of network activity.

Human-Generated Logs

Electronic logs allow you to track what happened to a system from a software perspective; as an administrator, you'll also want to keep a paper log of adds, moves, and changes to the system. This log can be paper (it's easy to keep a date book and fill it up with the events of the day), but it's just as easy—and more searchable—if you create a log file in a database or (better still) a personal information manager (PIM) database. As long as you print the data every so often and back up the file to tape or floppy disks, your data will be safe—and it will be searchable. I keep my system log file in Microsoft Outlook; however, any PIM with outlining capabilities and a to-do list will work just fine.

> Because your log file contains proprietary information and other data that applies to your environment, it should be secured. More on this in Hour 19, "Security."

18

The file is broken into the following sections:

- **Daily/Weekly/Monthly/Annual Tasks.** This section lists all the various things the system administrator has to do and their frequency.

- **Network.** This section lists all the specifications of the network, ranging from TCP/IP address allocation by machine to a diagram of network segmentation.

- **Hardware.** This section lists in excruciating detail the components of all the computers, switches, hubs, routers, network printers, non-networked printers, and whatever other devices are on the network. This is where serial numbers, part numbers, and version numbers of various pieces of hardware are recorded.

- **Software.** This section lists the licensed software for the network, the license numbers, information about installing software, and information about the location of software installation disks.

- **Network and Systems Restart Instructions.** Even if you're the administrator, and the human-generated log file is secured with a password (and it should be), ensure that someone else (an administrator, an officer of the company, whoever) has the password to unlock the file. That way, these instructions can be made available if the network goes down catastrophically (because of a power failure, a natural disaster, or what-have-you) and the network administrator is not available. This section of the file generically deals with how to restart the systems that provide network services, not the network per se. Following the directions in this section of the file should be relatively simple; make certain that every keystroke is entered and clearly marked—and don't forget to tell the reader to press the Enter key after typing a command.

- **User Information.** This section is an exhaustive list of the resources to which each user has access as well as all the users' passwords. In this section, you should list all the NetWare and NT Server security groups to which each user belongs as well as any custom file access; list all the printers to which each user can print; and last, list all of each user's passwords. Keep this list up to date; knowing what resources your users have access to is very important because it can prevent a user from inadvertently having access to sensitive files. Keeping the password list up-to-date is also important because it ensures that administrative staff (including personnel) has access to users' files when such access is required.

- **Online Services.** Typically, companies have several online-service accounts, some of which are shared among users. Keep lists of passwords, phone numbers, circuit numbers for frame relay lines, and the phone numbers to contact in the event of an online service failure. Keeping all of this information in a log ensures that the information isn't written down and lost. This list should also include information such as the name and configuration of your Internet service provider because the ISP qualifies as an online service.

- **Premises Security.** Computers are a favorite item for thieves to steal because they are, like automobiles, easily partitioned and sold as parts. As a result, you should ensure that you are involved in premises security if your firm is small enough; make certain that door codes into office spaces and particularly into computer rooms are stored here so that you know what they are—and can test that they work. Refer to Hour 19 for more information.

- **System Maintenance Checklist.** No system continues to run smoothly without regular maintenance. However, regular scheduled maintenance isn't really possible until you know what tasks your maintenance consists of. This section of the log file should be a checklist for each system's maintenance—and it goes beyond hardware. Maintenance involves checking a computer's configuration and ensuring that it is up to current software revision levels. Hour 20, "Upgrades," discusses this in a bit more depth.

- **Software Protocols, Conventions, and Rules.** This section deals with how the system should work. It defines what the network standards are (this is a copy of your network design), what the basic conventions for use are, and the rules, including password lengths, the allowable age for passwords, standard user access, and what constitutes trespassing access to resources.

One of the most useful things about machine-generated logs is that everything that happens to the network is logged by time and date. This is more important than it sounds. Although the maintenance logs don't make terrifically exciting reading (they're a great way to put yourself to sleep), they also provide you with a list of what you've done and what you've fixed. So if you run into a knotty problem that you fixed a year ago, and for which you only dimly remember the solution, you can refer to your log. It will enable you to respond much faster when you have a crisis on your hands.

Human Logs Versus Machine Logs

Of the two sorts of log files, the human-generated log is often more useful to the network administrator. Why? Because it accretes information fairly quickly and incorporates necessary elements of the machine-generated log files. An administrator can use his or her log files to track trends and to look for patterns—in short, to generate useful data from a perusal of the machine-generated log file.

Don't construe this observation as belittling machine-generated logs; they're necessary. However, they just give you data, not information; in that, they are similar to the Gross National Product number of the United States, which Bobby Kennedy said "tells you everything except why you would want to live in America." The logs generated by the administrator become a history of the network, and consequently provide a powerful way of ensuring that the network can be managed by anyone with the proper operating system skills—not just by the person who has memorized how the network works and what is supposed to be connected to what.

Data Storage

When you're building a network, particularly a client/server network, there are certain tacit assumptions that are never quite revealed to end users. First and foremost among these tacit assumptions is the following: If we can store data in a central location, we're less likely to lose it.

Although management may clearly understand the reasons for putting in a network—increased productivity, data security, better access to customer data—the users typically flounder around in the dark. They're the people who actually use the network, and all too often, they simply have no clue why they've been told to store their data in one place and to do various tasks.

Without getting into dark mutterings and conspiracy theories regarding the purpose of a network, it's necessary to explain up-front to your users that part of the purpose of the network is to ensure that all their data is stored in a central location. Stress that the control end users give up by not having the data stored on their local hard drives is more than made up for by the data security gained through a centralized backup system. And if you can make only one rule for your network users (and there are several others, listed at the end of this chapter), make it this one:

Work locally, save remotely.

This means that users' applications are installed on their local workstations' hard drives, so that's where they do their work. On the other hand, announce that their data is always to be saved to a remote server's hard disk; ensure that your users know where they should save their files, and whether the files are to be read-write, read-only, or totally inaccessible to other users.

This rule must be absolutely iron clad. No files should be saved locally; even the most sensitive files can be stored on a server if the server's security is correctly configured.

> Server security has become a high-profile issue in the age of the Internet. It seems that every other week there's news about another flaw in network security; a casual watcher can be forgiven for thinking that network security is not secure at all.
>
> However, that's not the case. To paraphrase Mark Twain, "rumors of cracking have been greatly exaggerated." Properly configured, with up-to-date patches and physically secured, servers provide reasonable security. This is not to say that they can't be cracked; anything can be broken into, given enough time. However, most systems aren't under the constant, unrelenting, brute-force attacks that eventually wear down a system, and properly configured systems are resistant to attacks.
>
> If a senior executive insists that his or her files are too sensitive to be stored on a server, it's worth your while to argue your case with them. If a server is connected to the Internet, the data stored on that server is indeed somewhat vulnerable, but a well-secured server in a small local LAN not connected to anything in the outside world is not very vulnerable. File-sensitivity arguments are often more closely related to lack of knowledge (and hence, distrust) than to actual security problems.

If a user insists on saving files locally, ask them to save to the network, citing the reasons above, focusing primarily on data security and backup. If the user refuses or doesn't begin to do so after a few reasonable requests, go over the user's head; remember, if a user's data is destroyed and can't be reconstructed, their supervisor will feel the heat, too. Data is too important to lose because of ill-trained users.

Maintaining a Network

About 10 years ago, a friend of mine saved a good deal of money to purchase a car he really wanted. Finally, after scrimping for a year (he was in grad school) he purchased the car. He was delighted about it, driving it endlessly and showing it to everyone he knew.

In spite of his liking for the car, about six months after he bought it, the bloom was clearly off the rose; the car was breaking down day and night, the engine was making noises, and the suspension was rattling.

He complained endlessly about the lack of reliability of his car, which he claimed he had been led to expect would be a paragon of automotive virtue. Finally, someone asked him what he'd done to take care of it. An embarrassed silence ensued. Apparently he hadn't realized that maintenance went beyond filling the tank with gas.

Networks work a lot like the car in this example. Systems do not run by installation alone, any more than cars run eternally once purchased. They require maintenance. As with a car, network maintenance should be done at scheduled intervals, with anomalous problems dealt with as they arise.

Most modern operating systems come with limited software utilities so that they can diagnose themselves. Microsoft operating systems come with the ScanDisk utility, which you can run each time the system boots; Unix, Windows 2000, NetWare, and other high-end operating systems are also largely self-checking; each comes with utilities to manage the system.

If your operating system supports it, a copy of a third-party computer utilities program such as Symantec's Norton Utilities is very useful. Such third-party software adds function, such as the capability to *defragment* a disk (that is, to rearrange the files on a disk so that each file is all in one spot on the disk rather than spread out in a variety of locations). Ensure that you have a licensed copy of the utility for each computer on which you install the software. Software piracy is not a game; there are substantial fines (and, in fact, jail sentences) that can result from not lawfully licensing software.

Last, make a maintenance list and schedule—and stick to it (see Figure 18.1). Nothing is worse than dealing with systems that have become problematic because of deferred maintenance. Remember that a network that is unreliable rapidly loses credibility with its users—which means that they won't use it. Hour 21, "Network Admin Tips and Tricks," deals with scheduled maintenance in a bit more depth.

18

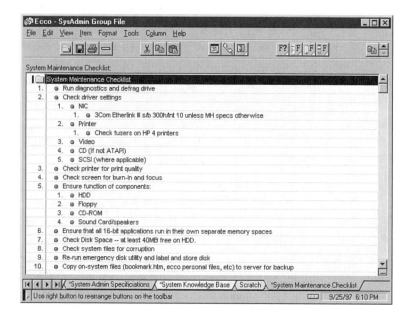

FIGURE **18.1**

A typical system maintenance checklist.

Design and Expansion

Hour 9 discussed design best practices; however, there are a few things to keep in mind once you've built your network and are beginning to administer it. The following sections cover these additional points

Never Select a Quick-Fix, Closed-Ended Solution

All too often, quick fixes to expand a network are implemented without thought for the long-term implications—and in the long term, the solution turns out to be a dead end that requires more money to be spent to accomplish the same goal.

Never assume that the network can support more users using a scaled-up version of the current architecture. It's tempting to assume that if you are using Ethernet hubs chained together by crossover cables, you can keep adding capacity almost infinitely. Unfortunately, this is not the case; a collision domain runs out of steam after it reaches 48 to 64 ports, more or less. When you hit these kinds of port numbers, it's time to start segmenting the network with an Ethernet switch or better yet, replacing all of the hubs with switches—multiple segments ensure that your network can expand further and retain reasonable performance. The lesson here? Even if you designed your network with an eye toward open standards, see whether there are alternatives that enable you to grow your network sensibly and not by rote.

Always ensure interoperability and backwards compatibility. It's great if you are given a budget to purchase superb equipment—it will make your users happy with speedy performance. However, before you buy, make certain that the various pieces work together. If, for example, you're combining switches made by different manufacturers, get a representative from each company to meet with you and each other to ensure that their products will work together. It's a no-brainer: If the parts don't work together, you don't have a network. The lesson here is to check for connectivity—revise your plans if you can't get it or if your vendors treat each other acrimoniously.

User Account Design and Maintenance

User accounts are the lifeblood of your network.

Don't believe that? Think about it: Your users are your internal customers. Without users, you may as well not have a network—it's not going to do anything. Even huge scientific-foundation networks with only two or three users require those users to justify their cost; without users, a network is an expensive pile of sand and wire.

As a result, you must ensure that your users have access to the resources they require. As a first step, you can ensure your users have access by implementing server-based security and by checking in with users to make certain that they're getting what they need to do their jobs.

The second, and more difficult, part of the equation is ensuring that your users take care of their own account responsibilities. This statement usually refers to passwords. Most of the time, users want a password they can keep for their entire tenure with the company. This is understandable; it's human nature to want things to be as simple as they can be. However, as a system administrator, you must discourage this practice. Keeping passwords for the long term is attractive to users but is simply not a good idea. It is too easy for crackers to break into a network using a password a user has never changed; it is more difficult for a cracker to break into a network where the passwords are changed on a regular basis.

Usually, users are reasonable if you ask them politely to change their passwords every so often. However, there is always that single user who simply does not want to change a password. Initially, it's your responsibility as the network administrator to speak to that user and attempt to convince him or her that changing the password is a good idea. If the user still won't change the password, no matter how much you plead your case, it's time to elevate the matter to a supervisor. Unfortunately, this approach makes for ill will but secure networks—and clearly, the latter is important.

18

Ideally, passwords should be changed every two weeks or so; however, it is likely that you will not see passwords changed much more often than once a month. If you can get your users to change their passwords once a month, you will be doing fine (unless you are in the government or some other very secure environment).

For more information about user account security, refer to Hour 19, which discusses security in some depth.

Naming Conventions

In any network, it is commented that names are assigned to various network resources. Why? Because people remember names much more readily than they remember numbers; as a result, it makes sense to ensure that network resources are named to simplify locating those resources on the network.

If your company's name is Acme, for example, you may want to name your file servers Acme 1, Acme 2, and so forth. It also makes sense to standardize the format for user IDs and workstation names. For example, if you have a user named Joe Smith, his login ID might be jsmith, and his Internet email address might be jsmith@acme.com; his desktop workstation might be JSMITH1 on the network.

How did we arrive at these name? The algorithm is simple and obvious: User IDs are nothing more than the first initial and full last name of the user; email addresses simply paste the user's network username onto the email server's address. Network computer names are defined using the same name as the user ID with a number appended: a 1 might be used for desktop workstations, 2 might indicate a laptop, 3 might mean something else.

You will also have printers and other resources to name. A good practice is to provide a short descriptive name with a number (for example, ACCT0001, ACCT0002, PROD0001, and so on). When you provide a printer resource with a name, always put a physical label on the printer with that printer's network name so that users won't be confused when they're printing.

Most important, however, is to decide on your naming criteria (those criteria can follow the preceding guidelines or adhere to a standard you design for yourself) and then codify and adhere to that standard (see Figure 18.2). If a network grows without standard names—or with cute names selected by the administrator while he or she is reading Tolkien—you'll wind up with a network full of meaningless names such as FRODO, BILBO, and of course SMAUG. Looking at these names, no user can determine that FRODO is a mail server, BILBO is a firewall, and SMAUG is a router. But if you give these devices less colorful names such as MAIL, FW, and RTR1, you'll have a much better chance of finding what you need.

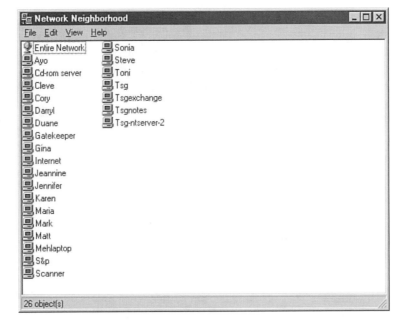

FIGURE 18.2

A Windows NT Network Neighborhood with a view of the computer names in a small workgroup. They're not entirely standardized, but the listing makes sense!

18

Distribution of Functions

There is an old saying about keeping one's eggs all in one basket. Presumably, if the basket is dropped, all the eggs are lost. In the same fashion, ideally, no single machine on a network should be allowed to take on so many functions that its loss represents a critical event. In practice, that's not how it works; servers do take on a hefty amount of the value of the network because so many times the servers are the central repository for files and for network print resources.

Some Practical Advice for Distribution

If you can, distribute functions among multiple computer systems, and do it from the start. Given shrinking budgets and increased workloads, managers often try to tell network administrators to make do with existing machines. This arrangement is less than desirable because it means that computers are overloaded. It's wise to begin by distributing functions and continuing to keep them distributed as time goes on. If you can set up a second system to be the network's print server, for example, do so. Likewise, if you can set up a computer to be a firewall, do so. The same with shared CD-ROMs. Although it's possible to do everything with one machine, it's best to create several smaller servers to take on the ancillary functions of the file server and let the file server do what it does best—big amounts of input/output (I/O).

Initially, your network may be too small to do this; if you have only two or three computers in a peer configuration, distributed functions are sort of overkill. However, as your network grows, it's possible to find uses for your older computers as servers for various and sundry network tasks. In fact, you can often continue using equipment that's well past its complete depreciation: In some situations, small Internet mail servers run on 386-level computers without much memory and do just fine.

The Honorable Tautology: Redundant Systems

In larger environments, distributed function takes on a different spin; it deals with *redundancy*. As a rule, the more you rely on a particular server system, the more redundant that server should be. If your server has all your data on it and you can't afford to lose the data, mirror the hard drives—that is, add a second hard drive, identical to the first, and ensure that all the data written to the first drive is also written to the second drive. Then watch the drives; if one fails, all your data is still on the other, and all you have to do is replace the failed drive to be mirrored again.

For systems that must be fail safe, there are redundant power supplies, redundant motherboards, and even (using failover systems such as IBM's HACMP for AIX, HP's MC/ServiceGuard, Digital's TruCluster, Vinca's Standby Server, and Microsoft's clustering systems) wholly redundant servers. If one server blows up, the other server picks up where the first left off. Clearly, as redundancy increases, so does cost...but that's an inimical fact of networking.

Try to see how little you can allow your file server to do. File servers are great; it's wonderful to be able to run your whole network on one—but the more applications they run at any given time, the more likely they are to crash. By contrast, if you distribute the load across several machines, you're less likely to have a network-crippling crash.

Backup Planning

You may recall Aesop's fable about the grasshopper and the ant. During the summer, the ant worked his skinny butt off to put food away while the grasshopper hung out in the sun and sang. When the weather got cold, the ant had food for the winter but the grasshopper had none. Granted, the grasshopper was more fun to hang out with, but you'd trust the ant with your 401(k) portfolio.

Backup is a lot like being an ant. It's easy to assume that you'll never have a network crash or lose data, but as your network increases in size and complexity, that assumption becomes increasingly unlikely. It's much wiser to assume that you will have a crash at some point, and to prepare adequately for it.

The Basics of Backing Up

A lot of neophyte networkers shy away from tape backup because they think it's compli-cated. I'm here to dispel that belief. If backup were difficult or complicated, I wouldn't be doing it—I'm as lazy as they come and I hate fighting with complex stuff (okay, I like it, but that doesn't mean I want it all the time). Backup is actually pretty simple—it's basically a process of figuring out the following:

- How much data you have to back up
- How often you want to back up
- Whether or not backing up your data requires dealing with open files and ensuring consistent data sets
- What kind of media you want to store your backed-up data on
- What kind of backup scheme you want to use

For what it's worth, the first three items determine the choice of the fourth, and the fifth item is pretty much predetermined. Suppose that you have a server with 20 gigabytes of disk space. You want to back up everything on it because it's all very valuable, and you want to capture changes on a daily basis. As a result, you are pretty well limited to using magnetic tape for backups because the largest-capacity removable disk (Iomega's Jaz drive) is only 2 gigabytes, and to back up a 20 gigabyte drive, you'd have to change disks ten times—not fun. You don't want to wait around all night while the system backs up. So you select magnetic tape, probably Digital Audio Tape (DAT) or Digital Linear Tape (DLT), the two most common backup tape formats. DAT (in the form DDS3) can support up to 12 gigabytes of data raw, and up to 24 gigabytes of compressed data, and DLT allows you to store up to 70 gigabytes per tape. The tradeoff is that DLT is much more expensive than DAT.

The Grandfather-Father-Son Scheme

Once you've determined what kind of backup media you're using, you have to have a system to ensure that you capture all the data you need to back up. The easiest backup scheme is the Grandfather-Father-Son scheme. Basically, the Grandfather-Father-Son scheme sets up a sequence of tapes ensuring proper tape rotation, so you won't lose data.

How do you do it? First, label four tapes (or tape sets, if you're using a tape changer that uses more than one tape per day) *Monday*, *Tuesday*, *Wednesday*, and *Thursday*. Then take four more tapes or tape sets and label them *Friday 1*, *Friday 2*, *Friday 3*, and *Friday 4*. Once you've done this, you've created all your repeating tapes. The remainder of the tapes are labeled *Friday 5*. The Friday 5 tapes are your archive tapes; you use each one only once (at the very end of the cycle) and then archive it. This approach ensures that every five weeks, you have an archive tape.

18

Next, you have to configure your backup software. Typically, the easiest way to back up is a differential backup. In differential backups, the Friday tape is a full backup, and each successive tape (Monday through Thursday) captures all the changes since the last Friday full backup tape. With differential backups, you only need two tapes to restore a crashed server: the last Friday full backup and the most recent weekday tape. Most commercial backup software can be configured to do differential backups.

Once your software is configured for differential backup (it's seldom hard to configure), you have to start rotating the tapes. Here's how that works:

	MONDAY	TUESDAY	WEDNESDAY	THURSDAY	FRIDAY
First Week:					
Tape name	Monday	Tuesday	Wednesday	Thursday	Friday 1
Second Week:					
Tape name	Monday	Tuesday	Wednesday	Thursday	Friday 2
Third Week:					
Tape name	Monday	Tuesday	Wednesday	Thursday	Friday 3
Fourth Week:					
Tape name	Monday	Tuesday	Wednesday	Thursday	Friday 4
Fifth Week:					
Tape name	Monday	Tuesday	Wednesday	Thursday	Friday 5

Each fifth Friday tape is the Grandfather; Friday tapes 1 through 4 are the Father tapes; and the Monday through Thursday tapes are the Sons. Every Friday tape except the Friday 5 tape is reused in each five-week period; Monday through Thursday tapes are reused each week.

See? It is pretty simple. It just requires some time to set it up and understand it. Then it usually runs pretty simply. One caveat: Make sure that you change tapes according to the schedule. If you don't, you'll have incomplete backups and be asking for trouble. Also, store all your Friday 5 (archive) tapes off-site as part of disaster recovery.

There are other kinds of backup as well, and they're often best run manually. For many operating systems, it's possible to make a bootable tape of the operating system that can be used to recover from an operating system crash. If the OS disks are mirrored, it's unlikely that disk failure alone will lose data, but it's better to be prepared. For IBM's AIX, there's the *mksysb* command, and Hewlett-Packard offers *mkrecovery* for HP-UX. Crashed Windows NT and 2000 systems can sometimes be revived with a copy of an Emergency Disk, which with an install disk can fix a system. There are doubtless other such utilities, but these are a place to start.

Security Design

Network security is a thorny issue; it's paradoxical, in fact. Networks are designed to share information; that's their very purpose. On the other hand, they have to be secured because there's always information on them that ought be kept private. Given writer Bruce Sterling's adage that information wants to be free, how do you control the flow of information so that it's secure?

To begin with, you start by doing the following:

- Design security into the very base of your network. In other words, try to ensure that you're doing things such as putting servers, wiring closets, and other security-sensitive computers behind locked doors, and ensuring that there are no password-free logins to the network. Thinking this way isn't natural; it's a little bit paranoid, in fact. But it helps close security loopholes before they become problems.
- Create security logs to track all users' comings and goings.
- Build a firewall if you're connected to the Internet—and then keep it updated.
- Ensure that your users change their passwords regularly. Also let your users know that writing their current passwords on sticky notes attached to the bottoms of their keyboards (or other such location) is grounds for immediate dismissal.
- Monitor file-copy operations at the server, and flag writes to floppy and other removable-media drives for auditing.
- Monitor Web use and ensure that no user is sending files out that can compromise your system.
- Physically secure all computers and provide key-only or pass-coded door access to the server room.
- Keep an inventory of the hardware and software you own, complete with serial numbers.

In short, become aware of who does what. You don't have to become an omnipotent watcher to do this, and neither need you be dour about it. But you *do* have to do all these things; if you don't, you're opening yourself and your company up to terrible financial risks. Given that a single person with a computer can cause untold harm to a company's computers, you must prevent all charges of negligence. Not doing so can kill your company. No fooling.

Make sure that you read Hour 19 for more advice about security issues.

18

Disaster Recovery

To the medieval church, *disaster* was a literal interpretation of the Latin *dis aster* or bad star, an omen that ill events could be linked to celestial events. Of course, those medieval people were wrong; it was their political systems that were really screwing them up, not the stars. Now, however, with low-voltage microprocessors populating the earth, disasters can strike from the sky (but again, not from the stars): lightning can do a perfectly good job of melting down a network. So can the sun, for what it's worth: Solar flares can overload power grids and burn up your precious network. So can floods, fire, and (presumably) famine. If the four horsemen of the apocalypse show up at your business location one day, what will you do to retrieve your data once they're gone?

If you haven't thought about an answer to that question, you're not alone. A surprising number of networks have no disaster recovery plan in place. From a potential-liability-for-negligence perspective, this is a biggie, guaranteed to win in the courtroom.

How do you prepare for disaster? Every situation is different, of course, but here's a list to provide you with a starting point for planning:

- Do you have recent backups stored off site?
- Do you have any backup computers off site?
- Could you build a server that would service your users out of spare parts?
- Does your company have provisions for alternative space if the current space is damaged?
- Do you know enough to set up a new server by yourself?
- If you rely on data phone lines, do you have a plan that will reprovision your lines quickly in an alternate location?

These are only a few of the many questions you have to ask yourself. Think about what your company needs from its network, and try to figure out how it's possible to satisfy those needs in a disaster situation. Then codify those answers and put them in the files while you begin to implement the solutions—doing so is a great defense.

Summary

In this hour, you learned about best practices as they apply to network administration. The next hour deals with security. We'll skip the Q&A section this hour and give you the summary information in the form of (read these next words in a baritone voice) *the System Administrator's Commandments:*

I. Keep two types of logs—machine generated and human generated—and pay attention to them. Keep the latter up to date.

II. Keep a maintenance log and ensure that you follow it religiously. No kidding. Also, always have a paper copy or offsite backup of this maintenance log because it's supremely important.

III. Ensure that your users always log off at the end of the workday or if they're going to be away from their desks for a while.

IV. Work locally, save remotely.

V. Don't use quick fixes that don't scale unless you have no other alternative.

VI. Make your users change their passwords regularly and keep their passwords secure.

VII. Create a standard naming system for network resources and stick to it.

VIII. Try to distribute server functions across several systems as much as possible.

IX. Make and keep a comprehensive backup scheme.

X. Work up an explicit security scheme and disseminate it to all users. Require a signed affidavit that the users have read and understand the security policy.

XI. Create a disaster recovery plan and keep it on file.

18

HOUR 19

Security

You don't leave your keys in the car when you go into the supermarket, do you?

You don't leave your bicycle just sitting outside the cafe where you hang out, right?

You don't leave your house unlocked all the time, right?

You don't go down dark alleys in the bad part of town, do you?

I didn't think so.

Most people are pretty sensible, and in our current material-goods-obsessed culture, good sense often means ensuring that the possessions you own are safely secured. It's a sad fact that if you leave something lying around, sooner or later, someone will steal it.

Like everything else, networks have to be secured. There are two kinds of things to secure: the physical pieces and more importantly, the data stored on them. Finding ways to secure both of these items is as important as anything you will learn in this book. As a result, in this hour, you will learn about the following:

- Why network security is important
- Potential network security risks
- Common nontechnical types of attacks
- Common technical attacks
- Setting up defenses

Why Network Security Is Important

Here's a scenario: A person drives a convertible car to a mall on a wonderful sunny day and parks it, with the top down, in the middle of the parking garage. In the car, the car's owner leaves a cellular phone, a briefcase in the trunk containing a laptop, and perhaps one or more high-tech toys. As well, the owner leaves a spare key magnetically clipped under a bumper. It's foolish, and it's almost certainly negligent.

While the owner is in the mall, along comes another person with a less-than-honorable record of respecting other people's property. Said person sees all the stuff in the car and begins to covet it. So he hunts around until he finds the key the owner conveniently hid, hops in, and drives away.

When the rightful owner of the car discovers it's gone, he is aghast. Everything he needed was in the car. Fortunately, the police track the car (it had one of those radio-tracking systems that are so popular these days) and locate the vehicle. In the final analysis, nothing was stolen; the car, phone, laptop, and spare key are returned, much to the owner's relief, and the individual who took the vehicle is arrested and held pending trial.

When the case gets to court, the defense put forth by the accused runs through the following syllogism:

- The owner was negligent in leaving the car almost completely unguarded and provided a hidden key to enable access to it.
- Taking unguarded out-in-the-open stuff is not necessarily criminal.
- Therefore, taking unguarded stuff is not criminal because of the owner's negligence.

Also, the defendant was young; the defense team argues that this car theft was "youthful exuberance." Finally, the accused's defense team rises and follows with these arguments:

- The accused returned (albeit under duress) the property of the owner.
- Consequently, no property was actually permanently taken from the car's owner.
- Therefore, the accused's acts are not criminal behavior.

Here's the kicker: The court buys the accused's arguments and the accused walks out of court free to go and steal another unguarded car.

Sound far-fetched? It is if you're talking about real physical property like cars. But in the early days of computer security, this was all too often the model for criminal cases revolving around data security and unauthorized break-ins. All too often, defense attorneys for *crackers* (people who acquired unauthorized access to computer systems) turned the tables on the companies whose systems had been cracked, arguing that "the victims had it coming because they had no security in place." More to the point, many crackers claim that since all they do is utilize services provided by machines (albeit without authorized access), and since copies of computer files are identical to the master copies of files, they've caused no one any harm.

The problem is that computer security is inherently something of an oxymoron, particularly when networks enter the picture. Computers operate by running program code, and program code is almost always insecure in one way or another. It's inevitable that at some point or another, someone will find a security flaw in one or more operating systems or network devices and exploit it. Unfortunately, crackers, and many people critical of the Internet, tend to confuse inevitability with correctness, which is a red herring—if your neighbor's house is unlocked, it doesn't provide a legal pretext to wander in and look at things to remind him that his security's lax. The same holds for a network. The oft-repeated mantra that "Information wants to be free" is a red herring—the ease of digital copying does not provide tacit permission to freely redistribute proprietary information.

In spite of the relative difficulty of adequately securing a network in the age of the Internet, it's necessary to do the best job you can. The issue is not simply loss of data or sabotage, but charges of negligence. For a business entity, gaining a reputation for negligence can have a direct effect on the bottom line and provide a pretext for shareholder lawsuits.

The age of the perpetrators in computer crimes (often young teenage males, but not always; see Katie Hafner and John Markoff's *Cyberpunk!* to learn about the diverse body of crackers) often paved the way for undeserved leniency. Perpetrators of computer break-ins often threw themselves on the mercy of the courts, claiming that at their tender age, they could not have known that what they were doing was wrong, or that lax security at the sites they invaded provided tacit consent to their entry into unauthorized networks. And the courts bought it.

The argument that the material was returned and therefore there was no theft was common in early cracker trials. What the courts missed—and didn't get, in fact, until very recently—was the fact that the fungibility of computer data makes it fundamentally

19

different from other types of intellectual property, such as books and confidential papers. With books and confidential papers, the criminal needs a photocopier to make duplicates, and usually the duplicates are easy to spot because copied originals often have imperfections and artifacts indicating that they were photocopied. It is impossible, however, to tell an original disk file from a digital copy; part of being digital is a precision in copying that far surpasses anything in the physical world. (Remember the discussion of checksums from Hour 3, "Getting Data from Here to There: How Computers Share Data"? Other file attributes such as date, time of creation, time of modification, and so forth, make it possible to cleverly "forge" a believable copy of a file.)

A cracker could certainly "return" files that they had stolen from an organization's computers, but that in itself provides no evidence of any sort to indicate whether or not the files were copied elsewhere. In the event of theft of electronic files, the assumption of the court must be that theft of files represents significant economic damage and loss of competitiveness unless the defendant can prove that they did *not* forward the stolen files to other agents. However, this assertion will probably not stand up to a court challenge because it almost directly violates the Constitutional provision that places the burden of proof in a criminal case on the state, not on the defendant. In any case, stolen digital files are a Pandora's box: Once out, no one can be certain that they have been entirely regathered.

Although no amount of negligence provides legitimate reasons for a third party to steal data, neither does that absolve system administrators of the responsibility to secure their networks. In this hour, you learn what the risks are, what the potential attacks are, and how to limit them. As you read this chapter, keep in mind that security is a process, not a destination. You will never create a network that's entirely secure; however, you *can* continue to work toward closing up holes as more and newer holes are discovered. And don't take what's in this chapter as the whole of network security—there are a lot of excellent books encompassing thousands of pages that address network and Internet security issues.

Potential Network Security Risks

Here's a list of common network security risks; we'll discuss each in greater depth in the coming pages. Right now, just be familiar with the terms so that you can identify them as risks:

- The ease of replication of digital data
- Nonaudited networks
- Non-firewalled Internet-connected networks

- Viruses
- Various TCP/IP attacks
- Social engineering
- Unaware users
- Unsecured computers
- Unsecured (unbacked-up) data
- Nonmalicious attacks
- Malicious attacks

The Ease of Replication of Digital Data

You know that it's easy to simply replicate digital data bit-for-bit and never have anyone the wiser. Essentially, that's because data is encoded on the hard drive (or other storage media) in bits, or patterns of 1s and 0s. Any file stored as bits on a computer's hard drive has its data stored as 1s and 0s, plus a few additional pieces of information about the file: the date the file was created or last modified, the size of the file, and the name of the file. All these things are copied when a file is copied from one system to another; insofar as the computer is concerned, all a file-copy operation consists of is a disk read (or, at the other end, a disk write) of a stream of digital data. It doesn't matter whether the computer at the receiving end can even decode the pattern of bits and read it; as long as the pattern of bits and bytes are copied correctly, the data is intact and can be read.

Because digital data is stored as bit patterns only, there cannot be any difference in the bit patterns of a legitimate and a pirated copy of a file. Because the computer copies only the bit pattern of the file, it simply reads the file; there is no change to the original bit pattern itself, so copying has no effect on the original file. How, then, does an administrator know when his or her system is under file-theft attack?

The answer, in short, is that the system administrator *doesn't* know—particularly when the network is not well-secured and audited.

Nonaudited Networks

Given the inexact capability to track the copying of digital data, the only way to track the comings and goings of data on your network is by *auditing*. Now, it's probable that the only experience you've ever had with the word *audit* is still ringing with unpleasant memories of an IRS agent asking you probing and unflattering questions about your personal finances. If that's the case, hold that thought; it's appropriate.

Most network operating systems have some form of audit mechanism. NetWare has the Accounting module, Windows NT has its Security log, Unix also has /var/adm/wtmp,

19

/var/adm/syslog, and other logs, but none of them are worth anything unless they're used and regularly reviewed. An unused security log is almost as bad as no security log; you learn as much from both.

Consider the following: If someone breaks into your system and you have a security log of the event, you have a much better chance in a court of law than if you had no evidence of a break-in. All a cracker has to do is wipe and overwrite the files on his or her hard drive, and it's possible that you'll have no case for lack of evidence. Not good.

As a result, one of the best things you can do is start security-auditing all the connections to your network. It's not difficult. Start keeping a security log that audits all the comings and goings of your network and then read it. If you find that there's activity or files in the home directories of users who have never logged in, that's a sign of illicit activity. If file sizes of critical files (sendmail.exe, telnet, top, and so forth are examples on a Unix system) change, that's another tipoff.

One way to verify that your system has been modified is to do the following. Right after initial staging, do a dir (on Unix, an ls –l) and capture the files and filesizes and modification dates of as much of the system as possible, and store it on media that's offline. Then, when you suspect tampering, do another dir identical to the first and verify file sizes. Some files *will* change size, like logs. But executable files shouldn't change, and differences need investigation.

Non-Firewall Internet-Connected Networks

If your network is connected to the Internet with a digital phone line, you have a finite set of options:

- Connect with no security and hope that no one notices you're there.
- Connect only a limited network to the Internet and make users move to special Internet-connected computers to get access to the Internet.
- Secure your network connection to the Internet.

Surprisingly, many companies who connect to the Internet select the first or second options. Essentially, this is a lot like leaving your front door unlocked and not checking to see who's wandering in and out. It offers a cracker what amounts to carte blanche within the confines of your network; if there's no security and no auditing, a cracker can waltz in and out of your network without you even being aware of it.

How can a network administrator secure access to their network? With a firewall. But what is a firewall? Essentially, it's a computer that sits between your internal network and the Internet. All packets passing in and out of your network have to pass through the firewall; if these packets can't be *authenticated*, they can't get through. It's that simple.

Authentication is essentially the process of ensuring, as much as possible, that logons and messages from a user (such as a password or email) originate from an authorized source.

Passwords have long been used in an attempt to ensure that users' accounts remain secure. However, passwords have limitations. They can be procured by various means (for example, by *shoulder-surfing* or *dumpster-diving*, as described in the following sections) and can be put to use by unauthorized users.

The next level of authentication beyond simple passwords is *access tokens*. Access tokens are small devices that range from magnetic cards to small calculator-like tools. These devices are used in conjunction with a password; neither a password nor a token can gain network access by itself.

The last and most secure method of authentication is *biometrics*, the use of users' bodily measurements to ensure that users are who they claim they are. Biometrics are nearly foolproof.

So install a firewall and ensure that it's properly configured. Stay up-to-date on developments in security. If the firewall has new patches to enable it to protect against newly discovered attacks, install them.

Viruses

Another danger to your network is viruses. A *virus* is a piece of computer code that attaches itself to a file ("infects" the file) and replicates itself without regard for the data or the system on which it's operating.

Viruses come in several varieties. The most common used to be *boot sector viruses*, which infect the boot sector of a hard drive or floppy disk. They were popular before networks became ubiquitous because floppy disks were at that time the medium of data exchange. *EXE viruses*, which infect program files, and *macro viruses*, which can infect any software that uses a built-in macro language (Microsoft Word is the primary target of these attacks, although Excel and 1-2-3 are also potentially open to attack), still exist. These first three have been largely eclipsed by viruses encapsulated in HTML (Web page) code, which arrive in emails and which, on an HTML-compliant email system, can execute and cause problems similar to the Windows Outlook Melissa virus. The effect may be as minimal as a mild annoyance (messages displayed onscreen) to data corruption or outright data deletion.

Viruses can enter the system in several ways: through an infected floppy disk (for years, this was the most common method of passing viruses around) and, more recently, by receiving files over the Internet.

19

When a virus infects your system, it typically doesn't run rampant right away. If it did, you would notice it and eradicate it before it did much damage. Typically, a boot-sector or EXE virus lies low for a while; you may not even know you have a virus. EXE viruses typically lodge in memory and infect each new EXE file as it is run.

Macro viruses are another story. They come into your network by way of infected files used by applications that have macro languages (Microsoft Word and Excel are examples of such applications). When the documents are opened, the macro virus infects the application's main template file (in Word's case, the file is called NORMAL.DOT). Thereafter, every other document opened in word is infected with the macro virus. Macro viruses can be quite difficult to eradicate because there are so many of them and they have many varieties, and because they infect files as they open them—this can be a problem.

Email-based macro viruses are also on the rise. Some email programs are susceptible to viruses that propagate themselves by hijacking the address book and sending a copy of an infected message to each user in the address list. Some email programs display Web pages with active content that can do damage.

Antivirus software is available in a variety of configurations ranging from desktop file scanning to server-based file scanning to firewall-based file scanning. It's wise to have as many file scanners as possible between the user and their files (whether the files come from the Internet or the local network); although there's a slight performance degradation involved with virus scanning, time spent cleaning out virus-infected systems is time well spent. Typically, virus software vendors have a method where the software install on each computer can be automated and maintained successfully with minimal input from the user.

Various TCP/IP Attacks

As we have noted *ad nauseam*, TCP/IP is the protocol used by the Internet to transmit data. However, TCP/IP was designed to provide reasonable connectivity; it wasn't designed with security in mind. Because of this, crackers have found a host of technical tricks that either make an end-run around security or else crash the system completely. The next sections briefly detail a few of these kinds of attacks.

Before detailing the attacks, however, it's wise to know that there are two basic types of attack. The first is the *denial-of-service attack*; the purpose of such an attack is to disable a server computer entirely. The other type of attack is the *stealth attack*, and its purpose is to gain access to a computer system to which a user would otherwise not have access. We'll discuss the denial-of-service attacks first.

Denial of Service 1: The SYN Flood

When TCP/IP connections are established, they begin with a request from the client system to the server system. The request must be acknowledged by the server system if the connection is to complete. Each separate connection must be acknowledged before the connection can take place.

Of course, responding to a request for a connection takes some server resources: a bit of memory and a small slice of processor time. Ordinarily, the amount of processor time a system uses to respond to TCP/IP connection requests isn't significant. However, of late, a popular attack (often directed against Internet service providers, or ISPs) called a *SYN flood*, after the SYN message used to request connections in IP networks, has been making the rounds.

In a SYN flood attack, a cracker sends a huge number of connection requests to a server computer; usually, the connection requests don't have IP return addresses, so the computer sending the attack is difficult to identify. The ultimate result of a SYN flood/denial of service attack is a server that is so busy responding to connection requests that it can't do anything else. The server either crashes or is useless.

If you're getting attacked by a SYN flood, run snoop, tcpdump, or any other packet sniffer you have. Apparently, one out of every several hundred SYN requests sent in this manner has an Internet Control Message Protocol (ICMP, more commonly known through the name of the application that uses it, Ping) message tucked into it. The ping message contains the source IP address of the computer system where the attack is originating. This can enable you to retaliate and (hopefully) shut down the attacking computer.

This isn't a universal panacea. Some SYN floods *don't* have the ping message, but it's certainly worth a try if you're being attacked.

19

Fortunately, the SYN flood attack has largely been patched in most operating systems. If you get a fresh copy of an operating system, however, it's wise to check with your vendor to see whether there are patches for various Internet-related potential security problems.

Denial of Service 2: The Ping of Death

As mentioned earlier, TCP/IP was and remains focused on flexibility and adaptability. Sometimes, however, this flexibility works to the advantage of the irresponsible yahoos who populate the fringes of the computer world. The *ping of death* denial-of-service attack is one such example of the flexibility of the Internet Protocol being used for malicious ends.

In a ping of death attack, a malicious user sends an Internet Control Message Protocol (ping) message and modifies the size of the packet so that it is larger than the legal size for a ping packet (the maximum legal size is 65536 octets or bytes). When a host computer receives the illegal packet, *bang!* down it goes. The system under attack can freeze, require a reboot, or crash completely. It's an annoying attack, and it's juvenile. Fortunately, as soon as this type of attack became publicized, vendors began issuing patches to fix the ICMP part of servers' TCP/IP protocol software; most recent systems aren't as vulnerable to the ping of death as older unpatched systems.

Ping is the application name for an application that uses the *Internet Control Message Protocol*. The application is called *ping* because that's what it does. It's like sonar: It sends out a packet and waits for a response. If there is no response, the computer is unavailable.

A ping message is a useful tool to determine whether or not another computer is available and how long it takes to respond. Here's an example of a ping listing:

```
C:\WINDOWS> ping 199.0.65.2
Reply from 199.0.65.2: bytes=32 time =263ms TTL=249
Reply from 199.0.65.2: bytes=32 time =177ms TTL=249
Reply from 199.0.65.2: bytes=32 time =205ms TTL=249
Reply from 199.0.65.2: bytes=32 time =188ms TTL=249
```

In a normal environment, system administrators use ping to determine whether a particular machine is available. It's a useful command; it's small and quite elegant in its simplicity. However, when turned to dark-lantern uses, it becomes a nightmare that can crash a whole system.

As you do with SYN floods, ensure that your operating systems are patched against the ping of death attack if your network will connect to the Internet.

Denial of Service 3: Email Spoofing

Email spoofing is an attack that is fully as juvenile as any of the preceding methods. In email spoofing (actually, in all TCP/IP-related spoofing attacks), the sender forges a return address on the packets sent out of his or her computer. What this means from an email perspective is that a malicious user can (for example) subscribe an unwitting user to ten thousand USENET newsgroups without the user knowing. When the user begins receiving messages through his or her server, the server is quickly overwhelmed and crashes.

Although email spoofing is listed here as the last denial-of-service attack, it is also a stealth security attack. Think about it: If you received an email from your boss's email address asking for a password so that he could do something while you were out of the office, would you think twice about replying? If a cracker had changed the header of his or her own email to reflect your boss's email address before sending the message, you could wind up sending the password to someone who ought not have it. This is not uncommon; in fact, it's tremendously common.

Denial of Service 4: Spammed to Death

Spam, or unsolicited commercial email, is the plague of the Internet. In general, spammers (or commercial emailers) do two things to deny service. First, they *relay* their email through insecure mailservers attached to the Web. This means that they send a message with a whole lot of email addresses on it to a server that isn't secured, and the server will forward the mail to someone else, with a return address on the relaying server. This does several things: It eats processor power on the relaying server, and it makes recipients of mail block all email from the relaying server. This means that legitimate users of the unsecured email server may have their mail refused by other mailservers as spam.

The second thing that spammers do is send thousands of copies of emails to users. Sometimes this is done in a deliberate attempt to overload an email server or a user's email, and sometimes it's just sloppy attempts at relaying (see previous paragraph). Either way, this denies service to the legitimate users of a mail server.

Stealth Attack 1: IP Spoofing

As you'll recall from earlier chapters, all TCP packets have a packet header that contains the source address and the destination address for each packet. In an IP spoofing attack, a cracker monitors the data flow in and out of a network until they discover the IP address of a system inside the firewall. Once the cracker has that address, they can begin to pass data in and out of the network as if it were being sent to the internal IP address. This is not good.

For this attack to work, however, there must be a couple of other pieces in place.

First, the router that connects the network to the Internet must be configured to allow access to the internal network from the Internet using internal IP addresses. In other words, this attack requires that your router allow access to the internal network by machines that have addresses usually reserved for the internal network.

Second, the server on the internal network must have predictable connection numbers (also called sequence numbers). A *connection number* is just that: a number the server assigns to determine the connection for which a particular packet is used. In some systems (particularly those based on certain variants of Unix), this number is surprisingly predictable because the server assigns connection numbers based on a known increment.

Third, the machine being attacked must have special trust relationships with other computers on the network. Unfortunately, like the first two items in this list, the privileges needed with special trust relationships are common.

Although it sounds as though these three conditions might make IP spoofing more of a hurdle than some of the other attacks, that is not the case. The three preconditions required for IP spoofing exist all over the place.

Stealth Attack 2: Brute-Force Password Hacking

Although brute-force password hacking is far and away the most common form of attack on a network, it may be satisfying to you to know that it's generally slow, requires hard work, and is unproductive much of the time. Brute-force password hacking generally requires only one thing: A server that won't disconnect after a fixed number of unsuccessful login attempts. Even if a server *does* disconnect after a certain number of failed attempts, it's possible to simply keep trying, or automate the process.

Brute-force password hacking is pretty simple. Essentially, the cracker uses an electronic dictionary to keep trying different passwords for a known login name. It's a tedious process; if there's any auditing being done on the network, the stealth attack is usually picked up in no time, which makes cracking the password all the more difficult.

Nonetheless, password hacking is an effective way to eventually gain some access to a remote network. It's common, it works, and there's not much you can do about it except make your users change their passwords regularly, per the best practices stressed throughout this book.

> Ideally, passwords should be changed every two weeks. However, if you can get your users to buy into changing their passwords once a month, you'll be lucky unless higher management has seen the light and actively supports your security efforts. You'll find that the effort you put into getting such a policy into effect can have a marked effect on security, especially if your business works with sensitive data.

Stealth Attack 3: Attack of the Script Kiddies

It's bad enough having a network cracked by someone who knows what they're doing. It's worse when the user or users who have broken into the system really don't know what they're doing. The rise of Internet sites dedicated to breaking into systems has led to a rash of script kiddies, or people who download more-or-less canned software (shell scripts/executables) and use them to attack various systems. In many cases, the scripts are quite sophisticated, but the users aren't; they leave traces where they shouldn't.

The first order of business when using scripts is to gain control of the system in one fashion or another. There are scripts that can (for example) send a piece of mail to a mail server in a way that will create an error called a buffer overrun. Ordinarily, this would result in an error and life would go on. However, mail services are usually run by administrative users on systems, and in some cases the buffer overrun can be used to execute instructions as the administrative user on the attacked system—at which point the cracker has control of the system.

Other scripts can change out a wide variety of files so that the cracker's manipulations won't be noticed. This is annoying, and it's difficult to fix short of shutting down and restaging the server.

Common uses for compromised servers include using the compromised server as a place to store files, to chat using illicit copies of Internet Relay Chat (IRC), or (most alarmingly) to launch attacks on other servers.

Stealth Attack 4: Email Relaying

Note that email relaying isn't just a denial-of-service attack; it's also a stealth attack. One of the most common security exploits stems from the use of an unsecured site and an unsecured Unix sendmail server. If a Unix system is used as a mail server, it will have an interface to the Internet, one way or another. If the sendmail interface is older than version 8, it's possible for a spammer (or junk emailer), to use that mail server to *relay* their mail, making it appear that the mail originated at the hijacked server.

This can eat up server resources and slow down the speed of a high-speed Internet connection to a crawl as spammers relay thousands of pieces of mail through a compromised server. It can also create other problems for legitimate users of the email server, since there are sites that blacklist known spamming sites. If a user on a compromised email server wants to send email to a person whose site is using a blacklist filter, the first user's mail may be refused. Such events can cause a serious loss of face for a business.

Nontechnical Attacks

Just because a computer system is a technological marvel doesn't mean that the only way to get access to it is through technical means. Keep in mind that when the goal is the acquisition of a legitimate password, anything that gets that password is fair game for unauthorized users.

The following sections describe some of the most common security holes and attacks on the nontechnical side of the house. Please don't mistake this for a complete list; new tricks are invented all the time, and we haven't seen the end of them yet.

19

Social Engineering

All the previously listed potential security holes have assumed that an attacker has some technical competence. However, with networks as with anything else, there's more than one way to skin a cat. If a cracker can't get access to your network using any of the technical techniques just described, they will resort to what crackers call *social engineering*. Social engineering is, quite simply, getting sensitive information about user IDs and passwords by playing on human nature.

Here's an example of social engineering at work:

> A system administrator at a business datacenter site receives a call from a young woman who purports to be executive X's secretary. She tells the operator that executive X has forgotten his password; would he please get it for her? The system administrator, having some common sense, offers to call her back at the office to give her the password; however, he says, he won't release it to her over the phone. She asks if she can put him on hold for a second; he agrees. When she gets back on the line, she sounds resigned and tells him that it's fine if she has to wait for him to call her back—the executive wants his password right now, but if the system administrator wants to wait and verify the call, that's his business. He'll be the one who takes heat from the executive.

> The system administrator, now a bit flustered, weighs the possibility of problems caused by an irate executive with other possible outcomes and hands over the password. *Click!* goes the line, and the password has been social engineered into a cracker's hands.

Social engineering was used to great effect during the late 1970s and early 1980s when people were still largely unfamiliar with computers. However, in the last decade or so, people and organizations have become more aware of the possibility of social engineering as a security hole. These days, an executive who asked his secretary to secure his password would likely be laughed at and thought incompetent, and a system administrator who gave out the password out of fear of retribution would be out of work. It's become widely recognized in all but the most Byzantine and dysfunctional organizations that part of a system administrator's job is to ensure security whether the users like it or not.

The Case of the Clueless User, or The Sticky Note on the Bottom of the Keyboard

You can have the best security infrastructure in the free world, but if your users aren't aware of it and don't think about it, you might as well not have any security at all. One of the most common ways for someone to gain unauthorized use of a network is to get a job cleaning the offices of the organization whose network they want to crack. After hours, as the cracker cleans the offices, they can look for sticky notes stuck to the sides of computers, under keyboards, in pen drawers, and so on. In many cases, it's more than likely that the cracker will find sticky notes with passwords on them. In fact, the most common places to find sticky notes with passwords scrawled on them are somewhere at a secretarial desk and, yep, you guessed it: the executive suite, whose network accounts typically have significantly more rights than the executive user requires.

If you want to build a secure network, you have to make and enforce rules that maintain that security. Passwords should *never* be written down, and they should be changed frequently (two weeks is a good password life). Make a rule to that effect, and make the penalties severe for continued misbehavior. If a user has a habit of writing down passwords where they can potentially be read, that user should be disciplined. Continued misbehavior should result in dismissal, particularly in companies where data is sensitive.

Passwords should always be at least eight characters long, and they should be alphanumeric. 2b|!2b (to be or not to be) is a good password, though it's short; take a common word and mix it with another common word and then substitute numbers for some letters, and you'll be on the right track. The word *scooterpie* becomes *5c00t3rp13*. *I don't know!* becomes *1_D0ntKn0w!*

Users usually don't buy into this initially. They have to be trained. Once they've been trained in the policy regarding passwords and security, they should be required to sign a copy of the policy with a statement that they have read and understood it. After that, violations should come way down.

Unsecured Computers

Just as users should change passwords to ensure security, so should system administrators work toward security. In many cases, a network has firewalls, proxy servers, and other security tools, but the servers remain in an unguarded closet or back room. Although it's true that a well-secured network must include firewalls, proxy servers, on so on, it's equally true that a secure network has *physically* secured computers.

Let's go back to the preceding scenario (someone gains fraudulent access to the organization's office space by posing as a cleaner who works at night). If the server room isn't secured, the cleaners have access to the consoles of the servers…a line right into the heart of organizational data.

The rule here is to place your servers in a room that can be physically secured and locked. Even that's not perfect; someone always has a key to a room. However, the goal is to place as many hurdles as possible in front of the unauthorized user and make the cracker take his or her business elsewhere.

19

Unauthorized Remote Access Devices, or The Clueless User Redux

These days, remote access is a big business. You spend huge amounts of money ensuring that your users have remote access from all the various places they require: at home, on the road, wherever. You make that access secure, with password authentication and encryption for all dial-in users.

And then someone decides to add a copy of some sort of remote access software to his or her desktop computer in defiance of policy. The user starts the software when they go home and leaves it in a "wait" mode, so that when the user gets home, they can dial in and use the network.

From a motivational perspective, this is great behavior; it shows that the user wants to be able to access stuff when they need to, during nonwork hours. However, from a system administration perspective, unauthorized remote-access software is a disaster waiting to happen. It's a modem waiting for a call on a system that probably doesn't have auditing enabled, and it probably either has no password or a very weak password enabled. If an unauthorized user can access a system running remote-access software, they have just found the crown jewels. It's a window directly inside a network, into what a user uses: the applications, policies, and procedures of the organization, and just about anything else to which that user's account has rights.

Therefore, if a user wants remote access for whatever reason, it should be set up in such a fashion that the software's internal auditing is enabled (if the software has that feature), and the workstation's operating system should audit all events. Although doing so doesn't increase the security at the workstation, it does ensure that you have logs to audit, thereby making it much less likely that unauthorized accesses will go unnoticed.

Logged-In Computers During Off Hours

If you owned a store, you'd lock the door during the hours the store was closed, right? Otherwise, someone could get in and stuff could be stolen. In the same fashion, when your office workers leave at the end of the day, they should log out because a logged-in computer can be a boon to an unauthorized user seeking access to your network.

There are utilities for almost every network operating system that allow the system administrator to set up a user's hours of access. Use that utility. In addition, find software that logs a user off if they are away from the desk for more than a certain amount of time. The point is to leave the network as inaccessible as possible while there are no users on it.

Unsecured Data, or Backup Tapes on the Loose

If you back up your data on a regular basis, particularly if you use the Grandfather-Father-Son plan outlined in Hour 18, "The Network Administrator," you've got data lying around that can be pocketed at a moment's notice. Every full backup tape set has the potential to give your adversaries a complete copy of a file server's contents. For the typical file server, this data includes a variety of stuff, including company financials, accounting data, expense data, and correspondence. For a software company, it can mean the difference between keeping business secrets and losing them, along with the business.

The lesson in this case is simple: Between backups, secure your tapes in a locked drawer. Or better yet, store them in a locked drawer in your locked server room.

Dumpster Diving, or It Pays to Shred

The last item in this section deals with a form of attack that is no longer very common but still eminently possible. It's called *dumpster diving*, and it means rummaging through an organization's garbage in the hope of coming up with a piece of paper that contains identifiable user IDs and passwords.

This particular attack has tapered off a bit in recent years as corporations have turned away from high-speed dot-matrix printers for reports and have instead resorted to onscreen reports. Another cause for a decline is the increase in security consciousness; more companies shred their old reports than was the case until recently. This form of attack has also been criminalized as the result of arrests and prosecutions of dumpster-diving crackers.

To get around this form of attack, ensure that your users know that any sensitive data must be shredded or otherwise completely destroyed before it goes into the trashcan.

19

Malicious and Nonmalicious Attacks

Up to this point, we've discussed some of the methods people use to break into networks. What we haven't discussed is the motivation behind them. As noted at the beginning of this hour, the vast bulk of cracking is done by young males. Many of them really *are* kids who don't realize the seriousness of their actions until it's been brought home to them by an arrest. Attacks by kids can be a pain in the butt, and they can cause a significant amount of grief. But by and large, they're not doing it for profit; they're doing it for sport.

The more serious danger comes in the form of the hired gun whose job consists solely of getting into your network and getting data. This is cracking for profit; statistics printed in the trade press indicate that this part of the cracking market is increasing as access to networks gets simpler. These crackers are hard to find, hard to catch, and harder to convict. But they are out there, and if your network harbors any data that can provide significant competitive advantage to a competitor, you want to ensure that you set up your defenses to frustrate these guys as much as possible.

Setting Up Your Defenses

Given all the hazards discussed in this hour, what can you do to secure your network?

To begin with, you can make the following rules and stick to them:

- Keep and monitor security audit logs on your systems. Look for odd patterns of access: Should the junior accounting clerk be logged into the network at 2:00 a.m.? Question the entries in this log just as you would question phone calls on your business long-distance service. And keep records of questionable access that apparently checks out; it's possible that someone is working from within the organization to compromise security.

- Build your network model in such a way as to foster security. This means adding a proxy and a firewall if the network is connected to the Internet, and hooking both up to a "sandbox" network that is wholly separate from the internal physical network (see Figure 19.1).

FIGURE 19.1

A network with a firewall and a proxy server in the "sandbox" network between the internal physical network and the Internet.

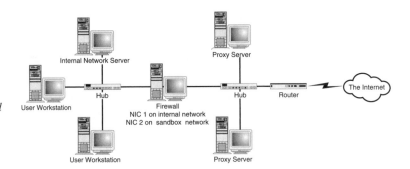

- The goal of the firewall is to deny access to those users who should not have access; the goal of the proxy server is to hide internal IP addresses to help avoid spoofing.

- Add virus-checking software to your system. Ideally, you'll have one kind of antivirus software on your firewall, another on your server, and yet another on your workstations. If you ensure that you keep your virus software up to date, you'll largely ameliorate the problems caused by viruses. It also helps to ensure that users scan any files they receive on floppies (or bring them to the IS department to be scanned).

- Make certain that your systems are patched against TCP/IP denial-of-service attacks. Most operating system vendors offer significant patches against the ping of death, SYN flood, and other attacks. Watch your vendors' Web pages for details. There are other security fixes available; research them and implement them.

- Make and enforce a password policy. With modern workstation operating systems, it's possible to ensure that users are forced to change their passwords every X number of days, where X is a number you select. Allow no blank passwords.

- Instruct your users and system administrators that they are not to give out passwords, user IDs, or other computer-security-related material over the phone unless they are absolutely certain who they are talking to. Ideally, they should demand to call back any caller who wants password, user, or network information.

- Make passwords secret; enforce this policy strictly.

- Make passwords unique, alphanumeric strings with both capital and lowercase letters.

- Physically secure your server computers. Allow only password access to server's consoles, and log all attempts to gain entry to those systems.

- Secure backup tapes in a locked area.

- Ensure that users log out of the network at the end of their workday and if they are going to be gone for more than a few minutes.

19

Summary

Remember that security is a process. You have to be vigilant, but the price of vigilance is secure data and no net loss of competitive advantage.

HOUR 20

Upgrades

And on the seventh day (or in the twentieth lesson, whatever) the network builders rested, and they looked on their creation, and saw that it was good...and it was good.

But don't kick back with a tall cool one just yet. Even the best networks exist in a constant state of change. Just when you think your network is finished, you find you have a bug-fix to install, a new upgrade to put on the computers, or a server that demands maintenance.

Most often, however, networks grow. And grow. And grow. We've spoken at length in previous hours about the need to plan for growth; the basic tenet is to strive to build things in an open-ended fashion. However, that simple statement is not really enough information. This hour focuses on the things you can do to manage the growth of your network in a way that won't drive you crazy or leave you sleep deprived.

Therefore, this hour addresses the following topics:

- Planning for network growth
- The reading prescription

- Managing hardware growth
- Managing software licensing
- Network management software
- Rules of thumb

Once your network is built, the immediate temptation is to sit back and relax. If the network is operating properly and is stable, it's certainly tempting to put your feet up on the desk and kick back.

If you get a chance to do that, good for you; network builders periodically need some slow periods to regain their sanity and redevelop a sense of perspective. Just don't expect the down time to last. Even if you're not doing end-user support (a full-time job in itself), you should be planning for the next iteration of your network.

The Inevitable Upgrade

Sam Walton, the founder of Wal-Mart, used to say that if a business wasn't growing, it was dying. Networks, for good or ill, seem to follow that pattern as well. A network that's not growing and expanding is rapidly falling into obsolescence.

Consider this: Moore's Law, coined by Intel cofounder Gordon Moore, says that the amount of computing power provided by a particular processor will double every 18 months or so. This rule has held steady now for almost twenty years, and given some recent developments, the development cycle may shrink to nine months or so. No matter what kind of computers you put on your users' desks two years ago, it's out of date now. Processors are faster, memory is cheaper, hard drives, tape drives, everything…they're all faster, bigger, and cheaper than they were when you initially built your network.

At the same time that hardware has gotten faster pursuant to Moore's Law, software has continued to evolve in ways that require more processor power, following Myrhvold's Law, named after Nathan Myrhvold, Microsoft's former Chief Technology Officer. Myrhvold's Law states that software expands to fill the available space. At first, Myrhvold's Law sounds tongue-in-cheek, but an examination of the various operating systems and applications over the last 10 or 15 years shows that it's an observation that accurately reflects reality. Think about it: Windows 3.1 and DOS 6 took about 30 megabytes, but Windows 2000 Server can easily take six hundred megabytes or more.

The Upgrade Cycle

Given that hardware and software change at such an exponential rate, it's pretty much a given that you're going to get caught in upgrade cycles. What is an upgrade cycle? It's what you get when users with the latest machines and management listen to management consultants who talk about the value of reinvestment in the business and the dangers of falling behind in a competitive marketplace. The upgrade cycle is a vicious circle; it's a privatized version of the missile gap (the nuclear competition between the USA and the USSR) of the early 1960s, and it makes almost as little sense. Computer power by itself doesn't make for competitive advantage; only well-designed, properly used computer power can enable an organization to prosper. Poorly designed networks (and there are many) can cost much more than they earn.

The upgrade cycle can be productive, although in many cases it's not. Upgrades are useful when they serve business needs, not when they follow management fads or are used as a palliative for disenchanted users.

Think about it: When a business purchases computer equipment, it doesn't do so to be cool or to have the hottest toys on the block. Instead, the business is making an investment; it's betting that the return from having purchased computers and spent money on networking will provide more of a return on investment (ROI) than (for example) taking the same money and investing it in a mutual fund. If the network is poorly designed, such that the computers aren't upgradable or whole sections of the network have to be ripped out and replaced with each successive upgrade iteration, the network is not going to be profitable; instead, it'll be a veritable sinkhole, a colossal money pit.

Designing for Sanity: Healthy Growth Plans

It's in your best interests to try to design the network so that it can be upgraded minimally when it requires upgrades. It's also in your best interests to try and temper management's enthusiasm for every upgrade; by advising moderation and testing, you can avoid unforeseen problems.

Upgrade Madness

A network administrator friend requested some assistance in upgrading her network. In spite of the fact that she had just finished installing the first version of an office productivity software suite, she was upgrading to a product that had been on the market for less than three months. What's worse, the product had some significant known bugs, with no patches for them.

When asked why she was upgrading, she explained that a senior manager had attended a breakfast meeting at which this particular office suite was being pitched. The manager had come back to the office and asked her which version they were running; when she told him, he told her to upgrade the network to the newer version because "we can't fall behind." She made a token protest (the software was new and wasn't market-proven yet, and she wanted to do a limited test before rolling it out to the entire company) but

20

was overruled. She had little choice but to go through the purchase of an upgrade site license and do the upgrade.

Several days after the upgrade was completed, it became clear that it had been a fiasco. The software basically worked but was unstable, crashing at the drop of a hat. It also didn't work with some third-party software, which significantly reduced the productivity of many users.

The executive who had ordered the upgrade then called her into his office to ask why the new application had so many problems. The network administrator reiterated the same doubts she had mentioned previously. The executive was adamant, saying that if the software hadn't crashed at the demo, it ought not crash in production.

At last, after a long and hard argument, the system administrator won the right to reinstall the older software on the systems because it was a known quantity. Since then, she hasn't done an upgrade without a trial, and she'd rather lose her job than go through the experience she went through again!

The Costs of the Upgrade Cycle: ROI

Return on Investment (ROI) is difficult to calculate for computer equipment, for a variety of reasons. For one, the use of computer equipment, either hardware or software, cannot be calculated in any sort of linear fashion; it's pointless to try to calculate the value of a memo done on a user's PC. Nonetheless, there exist a tremendous number of financial models to calculate the ROI of computing, and any one of a number of vendors can "prove" that purchasing their products can save you money.

No more likely is the Gartner Group's estimate that supporting a PC can cost upward of $10,000 a year in some environments. The benefit you get from the use of networked personal computers is not magical; networked computers provide value by doing the following:

- Working as a communications locus
- Working as a shared file space where files are easier to find than in paper files
- Working as a way to avoid buying multiples of some items by sharing a single copy of those items with multiple users

Upgrading blindly doesn't provide value; it merely provides sound and fury, which, as Shakespeare correctly said, signify nothing. Just as you began your network by planning, not by blindly purchasing a network-in-a-box kit (and they do exist), you should not do upgrades and mass changes without significant planning and testing.

Planning for Network Growth

Suppose that you're the network administrator at ACME Corp. Several years ago, a network was created at the behest of a middle-management workgroup that wanted to connect its users for email and scheduling purposes. Once the network was in, it gained popularity, and as it grew, you were hired to manage the process.

Random Growth

Unfortunately, to date, the network's growth has been sort of random. As new people have joined the firm, you have received word that a new computer was needed; with the help of the CFO, you have been selecting ever-more-powerful computers that have stayed about the same price as the pace of technology advanced. Occasionally, you have had to upgrade an older computer, but there has been no standard.

From a user's perspective, the purchase method is good, since it ensures that whoever gets the newest computer has the hottest computer on the block. However, from a management perspective, it means that you have very few standard computers; you have to maintain a large device driver library on the network server to enable you to install all the machines you have on the network.

Trying to Standardize

One day, you decide to sit down with the CFO and try to plan for sensible, orderly network growth that won't cause chaos and make your head hurt trying to remember which computer has which equipment installed in it.

As you talk, you realize that there's a finite amount you can do to plan, short of replacing every computer in the place every two or three years. You also realize that you can't tell the CFO that. So you talk about open standards, setting company software and hardware standards, and adhering to them.

However, you do have one mandate you can leverage: The powers-that-be have agreed that a standardized environment is good. Using that mandate, you can plan at least the technology half of your upgrades.

Figuring out how to do an upgrade without unduly inconveniencing users is the other half of planning for upgrades. No matter how complex the technology in your network, it is simple when you're faced with the human side of a network upgrade. Network users don't really care about upgrades; they just want the network to work. If the network doesn't work, then the network administrator's credibility is in tatters; if it does work, the network administrator is either wonderful, or invisible, or both.

20

Recommendations for Upgrades

The reasoning behind standardization is relatively obvious. A standardized network can present a greater number of users with better service than can a disparate network. However, there are some basic tenets to keep in mind when you're in the process of standardizing or doing network-wide installations.

If you're migrating data to new servers that will replace older systems, consider these suggestions:

- Plan to do the migration over a weekend, if that's possible.
- Talk to the managers of the affected departments as far ahead of time as possible, and come to a consensus on a time for the upgrade.
- The week before the upgrade, do a full backup on the affected server every night; that way, when you finally migrate the data to a new server, you'll have a record of the old server if you need it.
- After the upgrade, plan to test as many of the user accounts as possible to ensure that they can still connect to the new server. If they can't, that's a sign that something needs to be done.

If you're upgrading user workstations across the whole network, follow these suggestions:

- Talk to the users well in advance and figure out what's important to them. They may have files that must be stored locally for application reasons (Netscape Navigator's COOKIES.TXT and BOOKMARK.HTM fit into this category, as do many macro programs) that they don't want to lose.
- If possible, try to accommodate users' desires; it builds goodwill, bolsters confidence in the network, and fosters a strong sense of continuity.
- Keep a backup of the users' special files if possible.
- After the upgrade, check in with the users and ensure that they're doing all right and aren't floundering.

If you're adding back-end hardware (network switches, hubs, or whatever), follow these suggestions:

- Plan to do the installation late at night or on a weekend.
- If you're planning to use a switch to segment a network, allow extra time for the switch to "learn" the network. Although the switch "autodiscovery" process (the

process in which the switch learns all the MAC addresses on the network) doesn't usually take very long. A couple of minutes are usually more than enough time for most switches to learn the lay of the LAN on most small networks. Build in extra time just in case something's not working properly. I try to allow a couple hours for a switch installation; that usually provides enough time to debug any problems that crop up. Theoretically, a switch should go right in and get to work, but in the real world, problems happen.

- After doing something to the hubs or switches that are the center of the network, make sure that your users' workstations can connect to the resources they require. This step is always appreciated; your users will love you for it.

Planning Upgrades

Whatever the task you have to do, you should always try to share plans with your users in advance. Always disseminate a copy of your plans well in advance and get a buy-in from your users. If there's anything that can drive a user crazy, it's unreliability or inconsistency in a network setting. The truth may be that the network is neither unreliable nor inconsistent; however, if users perceive it as such, they'll respond in kind.

The Reading Prescription

During the time you are planning the upgrade of your network, your knowledge of the products that can work in the upgrade is critical. The only way to get and maintain that knowledge is to read as much as possible about the subject. This means that it's worth your while to subscribe to the trade press (a great many of the common magazines have free subscription offers for qualified readers) and it's definitely worth your while to make friends with your local bookseller. Use the magazines to learn about trends, products, and emerging technologies and standards; use books to get an in-depth look at a particular topic such as TCP/IP networking or CGI programming or Ethernet or whatever else is the topic at hand.

It's tempting to dismiss the trade press as just a hype-laden marketing machine, and indeed, there are parts of the computer trade press that fit that description. But for the most part, the large networking magazines are a valuable resource, and you'd do well to read them. You don't have to read every word; skim them and you'll certainly find items of value to you. Even if you don't understand everything at first, you'll gain something, and eventually your understanding will become more complete.

20

On the average system administrator's desk on a Monday morning, there are 15 or 20 magazines, ranging from the weekly glossy network newspapers to more esoteric material on programming or telephony. Given that almost all these magazines are 100 to 150 pages in length, that makes for close to 2,000 pages a week. Do system administrators *read* 2,000 pages each week? Absolutely not. They do, however, *skim* 2,000 pages a week looking for articles that affect what they're currently working on. And just as they did in college, they take notes on what they read (either in paper notebooks or in the system administrator's log file stored on the computer) for later reference.

It can be very wearing to read or skim this much information; it's a drenching exposure to networking. But at the same time, perusing the available information enables system administrators to ensure that they know what they need to know to successfully administer their networks.

Fortunately, the Web is a prime site for reducing your reading. The variety of tech resources for IT managers can allow a system administrator to restrict their reading to highly focused searches. If you're currently fatigued from reading too many trade magazines, check out the Web sites. They may ease your learning curve.

Managing Hardware Growth

In spite of the fact that I said earlier that hardware growth can't be truly managed (and I stand by that assertion) there are a variety of strategies that, with the support of management, can simplify the hardware growth process:

- **Set floating standards for hardware**. In other words, every two years or so, create a standard computer configuration based on the current most powerful computers, and try to stick to it for as long as possible. The benefits of this approach are twofold: First, the computers are a known quantity (if you spec a computer and discover a hardware bug, quirk, or incompatibility, you know that the remainder of the computers of that type will likely share that trait). The second benefit is cost; over two years, the cost of most computers will decline significantly, making your bottom-line staff very happy.

- **Determine whether a complete computer upgrade is required or whether an incremental upgrade is acceptable.** Given the ridiculous pace with which computers get faster, many OEM computer manufacturers and a host of third-party companies are building upgrades that range from faster processors that plug into the original processor socket to memory upgrades. It's possible that a processor upgrade and an extra shot of memory can extend the life of many an old PC by providing adequate performance at a bargain price (at least in comparison to the cost of a new computer).

- **Have a complete inventory of what's in your computers, not just the CPU serial number.** If you know what is inside the computer, you can more readily make a call about whether it's wiser to upgrade it or replace it. This inventory list also helps when a part fails; rather than taking the case apart, you can simply look up the failed part in your database and order another.

- **Never purchase proprietary products.** You've heard this statement before, but it deserves to be repeated. If you purchase a proprietary product, you're bound to that manufacturer for the entire life cycle of the product, which means that upgrades are especially expensive, if they're even possible.

- **Regularly do hardware audits with network management software that can handle the process.** If you have to do your inventory by going from computer to computer, it will never get done. However, most network management software has a hardware audit feature; used properly, this feature can help you diagnose a system on the fly.

At best, computer hardware is protean; it changes in the space of a heartbeat. By following the strategies just listed, you'll have a chance to have a manageable collection of hardware.

Managing Software Growth

In many ways, software is easier to manage than hardware. The simple reason is that companies tend to standardize on certain software; not using that software puts a user outside the loop. The larger reason is that use of software has legal ramifications that force a company to treat software more rigorously than hardware. After all, hardware is a capital asset and can be depreciated out of existence; software, even expensive software, is often expensed. It's simply written off as a cost of doing business.

With software, unlike hardware, you can do a tremendous amount of management, ranging from the setting of corporate standards to auditing the versions used. The strategies you should follow for managing software are as follows:

20

- **Site license your software if you can; if you can't, purchase enough licenses to be legal.** If you've got more then 20 or so workers using the same application, you may be able to site license software, or get a license that allows a fixed number of users at your location to simultaneously use the software. Site licenses are expensive, but their cost is generally less expensive than buying an equivalent number of standalone licenses at retail cost.

  Even if you have a very small office, license your software. It's expensive, but it's worth it. A software license entitles you to technical support and upgrades. It's also the right thing to do; although software companies do make a lot of money, they work for it. You wouldn't want to work and not get paid for your efforts; enough said.

- **Work with senior management to come up with company standards for software.** This sounds silly, but it's worth discussing. Suppose that your company has standardized on PowerPoint for presentation graphics but one user wants to use ClarisImpact because it's what they know. A company standard is a handy way to avoid the cost and complexity of putting another software package on the network. Be advised that this strategy works only when you get management support up front, and get it in written form.

- **Unauthorized software is unsupported software.** If your network serves more than 15 or 20 people, you must lay down the law here: The rule is that no user-installed software is allowed on the network. If a user installs their own software in defiance of such an edict, and the installation creates a problem, the only support you will provide is to reset the user's PC back to the original, approved configuration. Allowing unauthorized software is problematic not just because it's wrong (users do have a proclivity for installing unlicensed copies of software in a work environment) but because it raises the bar on the management hurdle to an unacceptable level.

- **Create a standard installation and stick to it if possible.** If you can install a fixed set of applications on each hard disk so that all disks match, that's good. If you have a large network, get a disk-duplicator and use it to make exact copies of hard drives. The standard install means that if a user's hard drive fails, you can install a new one, rename the computer, and be off and running relatively quickly.

- **Use a license management utility.** License management utilities ensure that you're never in violation of the terms of your software agreements. License management utilities can be a pain for users who can't get an application because it's at its license limits, but they ensure that you're in compliance. Thanks to the efforts of the Business Software Alliance (BSA) and the Software Publishers Association (PSA), noncompliance is becoming increasingly expensive. It's not uncommon to see $250,000 fines for gross and willful license violators.

- **Always buy one or two more licenses than you need.** When you consider new users, laptops, and so forth, you'll always find a use for the extra licenses.

Network Management Software

As personal computer networks have grown, it's become increasingly difficult for any single administrator to do all the myriad tasks of network administration. PC maintenance, repairs, software installations, and audits are a huge amount of work if a network manager has to do it all manually.

Fortunately, it's possible to automate most of these tasks. Over the last five to 10 years, a host of manufacturers have come out with management software that spans the enterprise. Here's a list of a few of the common names:

- Tivoli's TME
- HP's OpenView
- Sun's SunNet Manager
- Microsoft's Systems Management Server
- McAfee's Saber LAN Workstation
- Symantec's Norton Administrator for Networks

These are common products, but there are many other products on the market. Their chief purpose is to enable you to do the following tasks:

- **Software metering.** Software metering counts how many copies of a software product are running on the network and compares that number with the number of copies of legal licensed software you own.

- **Configuration management.** If you have 20 users with 20 PCs that start out identically, it's only a matter of time until the users have customized their systems so that they're beginning to malfunction. With configuration management software, you can manage the degree of control a user has over his or her desktop computer, which can mean an end to surreptitious installations of unauthorized software.

- **Electronic software distribution (ESD).** Imagine the amount of time it takes to add a software package to one computer. Now multiply that process by the number of computers you have on your network. If the prospect doesn't look palatable, you're not alone; there's enough of a demand for a method to install software remotely that software manufacturers began creating modules for their network management software to automate installations across a network. Automatic installation saves an inordinate amount of time for the network manager; it also ensures a more regular installation. The software has to be installed according to certain parameters; if it can't be installed, an error message is generated and sent to the system administrator, who can then tend to the problem manually. ESD is a useful tool and is absolutely necessary as network size increases. In some networks, it's used regularly to keep workstation software configurations in line—once every couple of months, the ESD server puts a disk image on a variety of workstations, in the process wiping them clean and reinstalling a baseline image. Users don't like it, but restaging systems from a standardized image ensures that all of the systems have the same software.

20

- **Remote management.** Imagine being able to get to a user's computer without leaving your desk and fixing a problem while on the phone. That's what remote management does: It enables a system administrator to take over a user's workstation and diagnose or work on it without actually sitting at the system's console. This is great for networks in which the buildings are far flung. ("Yep. I can see the problem from here. Let's just go into the Task Manager and kill off that hung application, and then we'll try again.") Remote management software also tends to make users think you're some kind of magician.

- **Task scheduling.** One of the things most PC-based operating systems don't have is a *batch job* scheduler. A batch job is a way of automating large numbers of tasks on an unattended server computer. The term *batch processing*, from which *batch job* is derived, comes from the old mainframe computer days when users submitted jobs that ran *en masse* in (you guessed it) batches. If you have to run a series of reports, you may be stuck doing them manually. However, many network administration packages have modules that handle scheduling of network tasks; they're usually pretty easy to set up as well.

- **Access management and tracking.** Auditing can be a difficult task even when the generation of logs is automated. Using quasi-intelligent systems, some network management software allows users to access their materials and files with relative ease until there's an abrupt break in the user's access pattern. Such patterns are then tracked for the system administrator to peruse as part of the log.

Summary

In this hour, we've looked at the options for growing an existing network. Working with open standards and setting organizational hardware and software standards are at the core of the network-growth process. Remember, too, that network management becomes increasingly important as the network grows larger—otherwise, the system administrators are overrun doing work that can easily be automated.

- Always buy more bandwidth than you think you need.
- Always try to purchase open-ended equipment.
- Settle on a corporate standard for hardware and stick to it.
- Set standards for corporate software.
- License the software you use.
- Use management software to simplify your administrative tasks.

Q&A

Q What should a system administrator faced with a software upgrade do before deploying the new software on production systems?

A The administrator should test the software in a safe, nonproduction environment where software failure will not cause major data loss or user distress.

Q What kinds of security information can an administrator find in a system log?

A Typically, a system log contains login/logout times and lists accessed files. This information is important because it enables an administrator to notice whether users are logged on at odd times and accessing files they do not usually access.

Q Which is better when setting network standards: buying industry-standard software that's not cutting edge or newer software with bells and whistles?

A In general, neither old, tried-and-true software nor new, relatively untested software is the best way to go. Instead, when standardizing on software, the trick is to find the best compromise between features and reliability.

20

HOUR 21

Network Admin Tips and Tricks

Even well-configured networks aren't perfect. Network cards can go bad, software can misbehave, and some services that make life easier just plain don't exist. But there are resources that can be put to use to add to the capabilities of a network.

This hour presents a collection of a few tricks that can provide commonly needed services on a LAN. These services are not necessarily aimed at enterprise networking; in general, businesses with enterprise networks have the resources to purchase expensive dedicated systems. Instead, these tips are aimed at the small network system administrator who has limited resources and wants to get the best use of the machines they have on the network.

In this hour, you'll have the opportunity to learn a bunch of small useful things—how to make cables, how to use common tools as diagnostic tools, how to make use of old hardware. Make notes in the margins if you have ideas and add your own. If you have useful ideas, send them to me care of MCP, and maybe we can incorporate them into the next edition of the book!

Here's what you will learn in this hour:

- Tips for making your own Ethernet and Token Ring cables
- Cheap network diagnostic tools: ping, ftp, traceroute, and Nslookup
- Inexpensive software
- Internet tricks

Making Your Own Cables

People who build networks do not always have free choice of the hardware and software that comprise their networks. In the case of many public institutions, such as schools and libraries, a lot of network equipment is donated. The people who manage libraries and schools are grateful for the donations; given the current stingy state of public finance, anything that keeps spending down is a plus.

However, the question that inevitably arises is how to tie all the wonderful stuff together once you've acquired it. A huge percentage of donated equipment is Ethernet, simply because it's the most common topology.

Equally interesting is the fact that you can pay ten or twenty dollars for a cable to connect systems to hubs. With cable costing less than a buck a foot and ends costing about fifty cents each, premade cables are expensive!

So how do we make cables? It's pretty simple. The following section explains how to make cables to the 568B standard that's used for Ethernet and Token Ring. If you buy cable ends and good-quality Category 5 cable, it's possible to make custom patch cables for less money that it would cost to purchase them.

If you've ever looked at a length of unshielded twisted-pair wire (the stuff of which Ethernet and Token Ring cables are made), you'll see four pairs of wire, in four color schemes: orange, green, blue, and brown. For each color, there's a solid color wire and a wire with white and the solid color, such as white/orange and orange.

These wires have to be terminated according to one of two methods prescribed by the EIA (an electronics regulatory group): 568A or 568B. The 568B standard is far and away more common. The reason for adhering to the 568B is that doing so ensures that a particular signal that needs to communicate between two network cards can do so properly.

It's wise to ensure that wiring is adequately terminated to these standards, since as networks evolve, this is the wiring architecture that new products will use.

Ethernet Cables

Ethernet cables use RJ-45 plugs. If you've never seen an RJ-45 plug, it looks like a modular phone plug with eight connectors instead of the four connectors that phone wires use. The recipe for making cables is

Ingredients:

- Category 5 Unshielded Twisted Pair (UTP) cable (available at computer stores and electrical supply houses).
- RJ-45 ends (you can get these at computer stores and electrical supply houses, too).
- An RJ-45 Terminating Tool. This is a tool that enables you to put the RJ-45 ends on the UTP cable. Typically, good terminating tools will work for both 8-wire and 4-wire plugs. They're expensive ($80-$100 or more), but they're worth it if you're working on lots of cables.
- Inexpensive cable continuity tester.

Start with the cable. Strip the outer insulation back about an inch, very carefully—you don't want to damage the wires inside. Notice that you have four pairs of wire inside—one is white/orange and orange, one is white/green and green, one is white/ blue and blue, and one is white brown and brown.

Separate the wires so that they line up in the following order from left to right:

1	white/orange
2	orange
3	white/green
4	blue
5	white/blue
6	green
7	white/brown
8	brown

Trim the ends off so they're all the same length. This can be done with wire cutters if you've got them, or you can use the cutter edge on your terminating tool.

Now comes the tricky part—insert all eight wires into the RJ-45 end so that they are inserted as far as possible. Then push the cable jacket up under the notch in the end.

21

Carefully insert the end in the terminating tool to its full depth and squeeze the terminating tool tight. This will crimp the end onto the cable and connect the pins on the RJ-45 jack to the wires in the cable.

Now do the other end.

Congratulations! You've just made a cable to the 568B cabling spec, the most common wiring used for networking.

If you've followed the instructions, you should be able to plug the cable you've made into a cable continuity tester and see that pin 1 at one end connects to pin 1 at the other end, all the way to pin 8. Don't get discouraged if your first cable doesn't work. Like anything else, this takes practice.

Crossover Cables

If you've got Ethernet hubs or switches to interconnect, it's necessary in many cases to use a specially-made cable called a crossover cable.

Essentially, it looks like a standard 10BASE-T patch cable except that it's wired differently. Most 10BASE-T and 100BASE-T patch cords are straight-through, which means that the colors are lined up the same at both ends.

In a crossover cable, the difference is that the wire on pin 1 at each end must connect to pin 2 at the other end, and pin 3 on each end must terminate at pin 6 at the other end. So the wiring scheme is as follows:

Pin #	End 1 color	End 2 color
1	white/orange	orange
2	orange	white/orange
3	white/green	green
4	blue	blue
5	white/blue	white/blue
6	green	white/green
7	white/brown	white/brown
8	brown	brown

This works because Ethernet only uses pins 1, 2, 3, and 6. A crossover cable connects pin 1 at one end to pin 2 at the other, and pin 3 to 6. It's useful and it's easy to make.

Cool Cheap Tools

There are a variety of tools you can use to test the function of your network, and most of them are built into your own operating system. This section lists a few of them and how to use them. Some of them aren't usually used as debugging tools at all; they're applications that can be used creatively for a purpose other than what they were designed for, where they perform a useful function other than what the designers intended. The tools we'll deal with are ping, ftp, traceroute, and nslookup. There are more, but these are basic, always-available tools to aid you in diagnosing TCP/IP problems.

ping: Is There Anybody Out There?

There comes a time on a TCP/IP network when you need to determine whether or not your computer can connect to a particular remote computer. One of the most useful and universal tools for this is the humble ping utility. ping is an application that uses Internet Control Message Protocol (ICMP), one of the foundations of TCP/IP, to determine whether or not another computer is on the network and whether or not you can reach it.

To use ping, simply type

```
ping the.remote.ip.address
```

such as

```
ping 172.16.0.12
```

This will return one of several types of value:

First, if your computer is able to connect to the computer it's pinging, it will look like the following:

```
C:\>ping 172.16.0.12
```

Pinging 172.16.0.12 with 32 bytes of data:

```
Reply from 172.16.0.12: bytes=32 time<10ms TTL=255
Reply from 172.16.0.12: bytes=32 time<10ms TTL=255
Reply from 172.16.0.12: bytes=32 time<10ms TTL=255
Reply from 172.16.0.12: bytes=32 time<10ms TTL=255
```

Ping statistics for 172.16.0.12:

```
    Packets: Sent = 4, Received = 4, Lost = 0 (0% loss),
```

Approximate round trip times in milliseconds:

```
    Minimum = 0ms, Maximum =  0ms, Average =  0ms
```

21

This means that your computer is able to send 32-character packets to the remote computer. The time it takes to send and receive a packet is 255 milliseconds. The stats on the bottom tell you if you had any errors or packet loss.

Now, if you can't connect to a particular computer, you'll get a different message:

```
C:\>ping 172.16.0.13
```

Pinging 172.16.0.13 with 32 bytes of data:

```
Request timed out.
Request timed out.
Request timed out.
Request timed out.
```

Ping statistics for 172.16.0.13:

```
    Packets: Sent = 4, Received = 0, Lost = 4 (100% loss),
```

Approximate round trip times in milliseconds:

```
    Minimum = 0ms, Maximum =  0ms, Average =  0ms
```

In this case, you're sending packets but no one's replying. Consequently, it tells you that all four packets it sent were lost. This means that the computer to which you want to connect isn't on the network—or else the computer you're using to ping isn't on the network.

ping can also be used to determine whether or not you can get to a particular network:

```
C:\>ping 156.234.84.95
```

Pinging 156.234.84.95 with 32 bytes of data:

```
Reply from 12.126.207.17: Destination host unreachable.
Reply from 12.126.207.17: Destination host unreachable.
Reply from 12.126.207.17: Destination host unreachable.
Reply from 12.126.207.17: Destination host unreachable.
```

Ping statistics for 156.234.84.95:

```
    Packets: Sent = 4, Received = 4, Lost = 0 (0% loss),
```

Approximate round trip times in milliseconds:

```
    Minimum = 0ms, Maximum =  0ms, Average =  0ms
```

The "Destination Host Unreachable" message means that your computer's default gateway doesn't know how to get to the address at the other end. So this message might mean your router needs some attention.

ping is a great, useful tool. It's the first thing a lot of system administrators use when they start trying to diagnose network problems—and you can too!

ftp: A Poor Man's Throughput Tester

ftp (or file transfer protocol) is the standard for moving files around on a TCP/IP network. That's what it's intended for, and it's what it's usually used for.

But ftp has an odd characteristic that makes it useful for system administrators. As it's transferring files across the network, it measures the throughput of the network, so you know how fast the network is running. If you can ping another computer but everything is running slo-o-owly, try to ftp a file to it.

Start with a file that's about 1 megabyte in size. That's big enough to accurately measure throughput, but small enough to not cause the network any problems. Then send or receive it from another machine (you'll need to have an ftp server on at least one of the machines to do this). If you remember in Hour 3, "Getting Data from Here to There: How Computers Share Data," we discussed TCP/IP; ftp is a member of the TCP/IP protocol suite, and an ftp server is a system containing files which other network users can download using ftp client software, which is built into almost every operating system available.

```
ftp> get telnet
200 PORT command successful.
150 Opening data connection for telnet (512338 bytes).
226 Transfer complete.
ftp: 512338 bytes received in 0.57Seconds 897.26Kbytes/sec.
```

Note that this file shows that I received a 512k file (half a megabyte) in about half a second, and then the system showed how fast the file transferred. There's a catch—the transfer speed is in bytes, which are equivalent to 8 bits each. So you have to multiply the speed by eight to get the correct measure. So

```
897.26 x 8 = a network speed of 7178.08 bits per second, or about the best usage
you'll see on a 10BASE-T network.
```

This is a use for ftp that isn't usually mentioned in teaching texts, but it's a great tool. If the network is slow, this can help quantify *how* slow.

Traceroute: How Can I Get from Here to There?

Sometimes, networks get complicated without anyone realizing it. You'll find that sometimes packets seem to be taking ten times as long as they should to get from point A to point B on your network.

21

Traceroute (or tracert on Microsoft systems) is a utility that enables you to see how your packets are being routed across the network. This is useful if you want to determine specifically which route your packets take. It's also useful if you want to see whether your packets are timing out on the network because they've gone through too many routers.

To use this utility, type

```
Tracert (or traceroute) remote-ip-address or hostname
```

Here's an example:

```
C:\>tracert mcp.com

Tracing route to mcp.com [63.69.110.193]
over a maximum of 30 hops:

  1   <10 ms   <10 ms   <10 ms   routerfrelan.anonymouscom [172.16.0.1]
  2   <10 ms   <10 ms    10 ms   12.126.207.17
  3   <10 ms   <10 ms    11 ms   gbr2-a31s1.sffca.ip.att.net [12.127.1.146]
  4   <10 ms   <10 ms    10 ms   gbr4-p70.sffca.ip.att.net [12.122.1.189]
  5    10 ms    11 ms    10 ms   gbr3-p20.la2ca.ip.att.net [12.122.2.70]
  6    10 ms    10 ms    10 ms   ggr1-p360.la2ca.ip.att.net [12.123.28.129]
  7    20 ms    20 ms    30 ms   att-gw.la.uu.net [192.205.32.126]
  8    20 ms    20 ms    30 ms   503.at-6-0-0.XR2.SAC1.ALTER.NET [152.63.53.6]
  9    20 ms    20 ms    30 ms   184.at-1-1-0.TR2.SAC1.ALTER.NET [152.63.50.142]

 10    71 ms    80 ms    80 ms   127.at-6-1-0.TR2.NYC8.ALTER.NET [152.63.6.13]
 11    70 ms    80 ms    81 ms   184.ATM7-0.XR2.EWR1.ALTER.NET [152.63.20.241]
 12    70 ms    80 ms    80 ms   192.ATM7-0.GW7.EWR1.ALTER.NET [152.63.24.209]
 13   290 ms   231 ms   230 ms   headland-media-gw.customer.ALTER.NET [157.130.19
.94]
 14    71 ms    80 ms    80 ms   63.69.110.193

Trace complete.
```

In this case, it completed the trace and I can see all of the routers (all 14 of them) between my network and mcp.com. If you get timed out, or if you get starts in place of the times, that is generally where your problem is occurring. Consequently, traceroute/tracert is useful for settling disputes with ISPs and network providers over the quality of your service.

Nslookup: What's the Number for the Name?

Sometimes, you need to use an IP address instead of a name. Other times, you don't know the IP address for the name. Nslookup (short for *name server lookup*) is a utility that can help you figure out what IP address is associated with a particular name. Here's an example:

```
/$ nslookup www.microsoft.com
Server:  rayban.tibinc.com
Address:  172.16.0.10

Non-authoritative answer:
Name:    microsoft.com
Addresses:  207.46.230.219, 207.46.130.45, 207.46.230.218
Aliases:  www.microsoft.com
```

Clearly, these four tools don't comprise a whole suite of diagnostic tools, but they come with your operating system and can give you a place to start when you're having network problems.

Inexpensive Software

Throughout this book, we have repeatedly focused on operating systems, and rightfully so. They're the core of networking. An operating system without networking installed (even if it's just a dial-up connection to the Web) is a curious and marginally useful tool, but not something that offers much utility.

However, almost all the operating system software discussed in this book is pricey. Even the least expensive commercial operating systems cost $100 or more for a single copy; it's not uncommon for sites with 25 or 50 users to spend $5,000 or more for server software. That's a lot of money for a small network, and if you don't want to spend it, you're often relegated to setting up a glorified peer network. This solution is less than desirable because it means your network is less secure and robust than it might be.

The Linux Alternative

There is an alternative to commercial network operating system software if you're willing to invest some serious time and effort. *Linux* is a freeware operating system that has been through two or three versions; it is available because of the efforts of thousands of idealistic coders led by a young Finnish coder named Linus Torvalds. Designed to run on Intel-compatible personal computers (but already extended to run on Mac PowerPC hardware and DEC Alpha systems), it's a clone of the popular Unix operating system, and it shares Unix's command-line syntax and complexity. Nonetheless, it's freeware; if you've got a high-speed Internet connection, you can download Linux. If you don't have a high-speed line, you can get a copy of Linux from one of the major distributors (Red Hat, Caldera, Slackware, Yggdrasil, and others) on a CD-ROM for about $50.

By itself, Linux can't provide resources to other PCs except by standard TCP/IP utilities (Telnet, FTP, HTTP, and so on). However, a utility called Samba enables Unix systems to share their drives with Windows-networking systems using the Microsoft SMB protocol

21

over TCP/IP. When you install Samba on a Linux system, it's possible to use Linux as a powerful, secure, and very capable server. Samba often ships with Linux distributions, but it's also widely available on the Web. Do a search and you'll find it! In fact, Samba can be used to make a Linux server part of a Windows NT or 2000 Domain. It's great software.

The downside of Linux, as with almost any freeware, is lack of support. To install and support Linux, you'll have to spend some quality time with in-depth books on the subject because there isn't a lot of reasonably priced third-party support for any version of UNIX out there. On the other hand, your investment of time in Linux can conceivably build a server system that will do almost anything you need a server to do. It can be a file server, a print server, an Internet server (handling Web (http), FTP, Telnet, dial-up networking hosting, DNS, sendmail, and other services), and almost anything else you require. Linux is even a great software-development platform. It simply takes a bit more time and energy to set up, which is the case with any Unix variant.

Of course, Linux isn't a commercial operating system per se, so most commercial software manufacturers don't recompile their software to run on it. Some software companies such as Oracle have ported their code to run on Linux, but in many cases they're the exception rather than the rule.

The GNU (Gnu's Not Unix) project, fostered by Richard Stallman in Cambridge, MA, writes and compiles a collection of software readily available at a relatively low cost that runs on almost any platform. GNU software is not free software in the sense that it costs nothing, although you may find some software without charge in GNU software archives on the Web (start at http://www.gnu.ai.mit.edu/). Instead, GNU software is free from restrictions; a user can lawfully use, modify, and pass on the software and source code as long as the original GNU license agreement is attached.

Linux isn't the only low-cost Unix clone out there. A lesser-known Unix variant called FreeBSD costs about the same as Linux. FreeBSD is basically the same as Linux, it's just not as popular. FreeBSD is a capable operating system and is another alternative.

No GNUs Are Bad GNUs

It is fair to say that a great deal of the software produced under the GNU public *copyleft* (explained in the following sidebar) is as good or better than commercially developed software. This is because a lot of eyes see each version of GNU source code and a given set of source code must be able to compile on multiple platforms; consequently the source code tends to be cleaner and freer from platform-specific code. Also, GNU software tends to be smaller and more focused than the packages released by larger manufacturers; in some cases, this can make the software easier to use.

What Is a "Copyleft"?

A copyleft is the Free Software Foundation's way of ensuring that the use of Free Software Foundation GNU software cannot in any way be restricted. The GNU copyleft (more commonly referred to as the GNU General Public License) makes this statement:

"To copyleft a program, first we copyright it; then we add distribution terms, which are a legal instrument that gives everyone the rights to use, modify, and redistribute the program's code or any program derived from it but only if the distribution terms are unchanged. Thus, the code and the freedoms become legally inseparable."

In other words, the GNU General Public License guarantees your right to use the software you have as you please. It's a unique concept; to read more about it, go to the following Web location: `http://www.gnu.ai.mit.edu/copyleft/gpl.html`.

It's worth reading about. Copylefting is a thought-provoking way to look at software distribution.

If you have a small budget but are rich in human capital and time, GNU software such as Linux can be a highly effective way for you and your organization to set up powerful servers using relatively inexpensive hardware and software. It takes a bit of extra effort on the front end—the learning curve is steep compared to that for some commercial products—but it's a great alternative.

Other GNU software has reached a level of use where it's common on commercial versions of Unix. GNU Emacs, a text editor for Unix, is the single-most popular editor on Unix systems; GNUChess is arguably one of the best machine-chess games you'll find. There are a host of other utilities, but detailing them goes into needless minutiae, so I won't. Visit the GNU Web site for more information (`http://www.gnu.ai.mit.edu/copyleft/gpl.html`).

Internet Tricks

21

If you're building a first network, chances are that it won't be too large. For a lot of small networks, it doesn't make sense to connect to the Internet using digital phone lines; they're often too expensive to make their use cost-effective for small businesses.

However, there are ways to use regular dial-up Internet accounts to tie a small network to the Internet. The performance of a dial-up line is usually acceptable for a small network; when your network grows to more than 10 or 15 people, however, you'll want to consider a digital phone service such as ISDN or frame relay T1s. When you do that, you'll have to install additional equipment (typically a router) to handle moving data between your network and the Internet. Until you do that, however, you can use a regular computer with a dial-up connection to the Internet as a sort of quasi-router.

There are several strategies for using dial-up lines to tie a small network to the Internet so that the Internet connection is available to all network users:

- IP forwarding
- IP masquerading/address translation
- Protocol translation (proxy server)
- Dial-on demand multilink PPP devices

All these methods rely on your ability to connect to an Internet Service Provider using a dial-up account; that's the first prerequisite. Once you've got that working on a single computer, you're ready to start sharing the connection.

IP Forwarding

To share any TCP/IP connection, you have to be able to enable what is called IP forwarding on the operating system of the machine connected to the Internet. IP forwarding is a technique that enables the system connected to the Internet to determine whether data packets are intended for the internal network or the external network. Most operating systems support one form or another of IP forwarding; Unix and Windows NT seem to do it best from an ease-of-use perspective.

In Unix, you have to modify several system files to enable IP forwarding to work; in Windows NT 4.0 Workstation or Server, all you have to do is select the Allow IP Forwarding option from the Properties tab of the TCP/IP Protocol (select Control Panel and then select Networks).

On Windows Me and 2000, there's a feature called Internet Connection Sharing that simplifies this whole process—so it's obvious that Microsoft is aware of the need to share slow connections.

Once you've done this, the network card of the system on which you've enabled IP forwarding becomes the default gateway for IP packets bound for points outside the local network. The computer essentially becomes a router—it connects to the network through its network card, and it routes packets out through the modem. The only real difference between this computer and a dedicated router is that dedicated routers generally connect only over digital phone lines; they don't use regular phone lines. Remember, though, if you decide to simply allow a server to forward IP packets, your network is (potentially) open to IP-based attacks. Review Hour 19, "Security," for more information.

Linux, the freeware OS mentioned earlier in this hour, also handles IP forwarding with aplomb, albeit with a bit more complexity when you're setting it up.

Next, you need to set up a scheme that allows your internal workstations to talk to the Internet. This scheme is available in a variety of forms: IP masquerading/address translation and protocol translation. Both of these approaches have their merits, as discussed in the following sections.

IP Masquerading/Address Translation

Even in the best-secured networks, the best way for a cracker to break into the network is to know the legal IP address of a computer on the internal network. Ideally, then, you should hide your internal network addresses so that your users' IP addresses aren't readily apparent to anyone outside. That's what IP masquerading, also called *address translation*, does.

A *masquerade* is what you get when you hide behind a mask; ideally, other people see the mask but can't see what's behind it. IP masquerading works by connecting one computer to an Internet service provider with any connection (from a dial-up connection to a digital phone line; the media isn't important), and assigning an Internet-legal IP address to it. It then translates the legal IP address (which can be something like 209.61.64.32) into internal network addresses (which are not Internet-legal addresses; the internal addresses generally use the range 192.168.X.X, where the X can be from 0 to 254). The rest of the Internet can see the only legal IP address; the rest of the addresses, for all practical purposes, are invisible and unreachable. Figure 21.1 shows an example of IP masquerading.

The machine doing the masquerading (I use Linux for this, but this feature is available through most Unix-based operating systems and Windows NT Server's Proxy Server) re-labels every packet going out of the network with its own IP address, so that all data packets appear to come from one machine. The masquerading server stamps inbound packets with the not-Internet-legal addresses of machines on the internal network (such as 192.168.1.50) and routes the packets to the correct machine.

21

FIGURE **21.1**

How IP masquerading works.

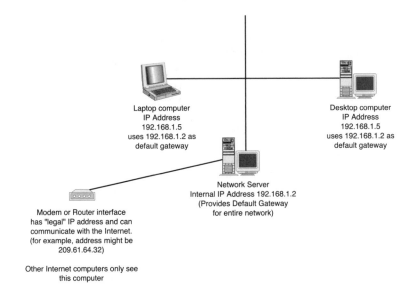

Laptop computer
IP Address
192.168.1.5
uses 192.168.1.2 as
default gateway

Desktop computer
IP Address
192.168.1.5
uses 192.168.1.2 as
default gateway

Network Server
Internal IP Address 192.168.1.2
(Provides Default Gateway
for entire network)

Modem or Router interface
has "legal" IP address and can
communicate with the Internet.
(for example, address might be
209.61.64.32)

Other Internet computers only see
this computer

IP masquerading is a remarkably secure way of connecting to the Internet at any speed. The benefit of using it when you're connecting over a phone line is that it only requires one legal IP address; the rest are reserved, not-Internet-legal addresses. Network clients don't have to know that their IP addresses aren't Internet-legal; the only operations that aren't possible from a machine on the internal network are server tasks (you can't put a Web server or an FTP server on one of the reserved IP addresses because, as far as the Internet is concerned, that number doesn't and can't exist).

Even if you're connected to the Internet at a faster speed than a dial-up connection affords, IP masquerading offers advantages. Why? In the first place, a 192.168 address (the reserved, not-Internet-legal address range specified in RFC 1597, which was mentioned in Hour 3) allows up to 65,536 computers (or *hosts*) within its address range. IP masquerading allows you to connect as many computers as you need to the Internet without worrying about whether the InterNIC (the Network Information Center, which allocates IP addresses, see www.internic.net) will allocate them to you.

Most TCP/IP client applications work with IP masquerading—that means browsers, FTP clients, and Telnet clients have no problems with this approach to security. Again, the only things that won't work are server applications—but in most cases, you won't need to put up a Web server of your own until you've established an Internet connection that's faster than dial-up.

IP masquerading is a neat trick. The reason it can save money is that it relies on TCP/IP's capability to run over any physical link. TCP/IP sees no difference between a telephone line, a radio link, and a network connection; it can run over all three.

Protocol Translation

IP masquerading/address translation is great because it allows your users to have full access to the Internet while ensuring that the rest of the Internet can't enter your internal network. It works quite well if you're running TCP/IP on your internal network. But what if you're not running TCP/IP? A lot of sites run only NetWare's IPX protocol, but their users want to get connected to the Internet. But how can they? The Internet runs on TCP/IP, period. And NetWare runs on IPX. How can these two protocols work together?

The answer is protocol translation. *Protocol translation* is a technique in which a single machine connects to the Internet (using either a dial-up line or a digital line connection) and sends and receives IP packets for the whole network, translating Internet IP into IPX that the network can understand. Protocol translation is very convenient and requires very little to work. With protocol translation, it's not necessary to install IP on each workstation; in fact, Novell's Intranetware and Microsoft's Windows NT Proxy Server can do protocol translation without any additional software at the client.

Protocol translation adds an additional layer of security to your network in comparison with IP masquerading. With IP masquerading, it's still possible (but just barely so) for a cracker to get into your internal network because your internal network runs TCP/IP. By contrast, protocol translation doesn't use IP on the internal network, so there's no way a cracker can get into the internal network if the security is tight on the protocol-translating machine.

> For security reasons, the protocol-translating computer can't have any network drives mapped on it. If they were, the addresses would be available to the outside world and defeat the purpose of whole setup.

Dial-On-Demand Routing

Imagine that you have a network of 10 or 15 users, all of whom are fairly unsophisticated about the network. If you have a dial-up or switched ISDN connection to the Internet, that connection will periodically disconnect whether you like it or not—line conditions can deteriorate, the ISP can down its server to do maintenance, your modem can experience a glitch, your ISP's modem can experience a glitch—and you're going to have to reestablish the connection.

For the most part, reconnecting a dial-up line is not terribly difficult. Much of the time, the connection is automated; once you click a Connect button in your dial-up Internet connection software, you are connected. In some rare cases, you may have to log in by

21

hand, but even that is not difficult. However, for inexperienced users, reestablishing a broken Internet connection is simply beyond their ken.

As a result, you've got two options. First is to figure out how to keep your Internet connection up and running at all times; although you can't prevent network errors, you can prevent the network from disconnecting because of inactivity. Second, and far more efficient, is to find a way to enable the network to connect to the ISP when a user requires Internet services. The former is easy to accomplish: Put a mail client on the machine connected to the Internet with a dial-up or switched ISDN line and instruct it to try to collect mail every five minutes or so. That way, the connection always has activity on it and won't "time out," or disconnect because of a lack of activity on the wire.

The second method is dial-on-demand routing. Dial-on-demand routing essentially says that whenever users request Internet services (by opening their browsers and clicking a bookmark, for example), the system interprets those messages as commands to connect to the Internet.

Dial-on-demand (DoD) routing has been implemented in Unix for many years; Windows NT finally got it for Microsoft's Steelhead upgrade to RAS; it's now called Routing and Remote Access Services. In software, DoD routing requires significant configuration to make it run right, but you generally have full control over the process. It's also less expensive than keeping a connection open all the time; if you're using long-distance phone lines or ISDN (both of which are tariffed by the minute), DoD routing can save you money.

DoD routing has also been implemented in hardware devices: Dayna, purchased by Intel in late September 1997, makes several devices that dial and connect to an ISP on demand for you. Transcend makes a two-line dial-on-demand router that effectively doubles the speed of the connection. The Transcend product is neat; it uses a standard called *multi-link PPP* that enables the bandwidth of several dial-up lines to be aggregated into one stream of packets. Products for dial-on-demand regular phone lines and ISDN routers include the Cisco 776 Access Router, the Kendrox Pacesetter, and Ramp Networks WebRamp (also available for regular phone lines). As more small networks need to connect to the Internet, these devices will become more mainstream and will provide the kind of connectivity needed to survive in today's Internet-drenched world.

Summary

The tips presented in this hour are designed to assist you in overcoming some of the hurdles that first-time networkers have to deal with. They're not all the tips you'll need, however; for more, read the trade press regularly. A host of columns deal with tips, tricks, and solutions for difficult problems. And remember your system administrator's notebook log. Over time, you'll find you've discovered some neat ways to simplify the process of networking—so share them with other people! Remember that when two merchants meet, they make a transaction and each feels that they have gotten the better of the other. But when two students meet and share information (and network administrators fit in this category because they're always learning) each goes away from the meeting with more than they brought.

21

Hour **22**

A Day in the Life

In the current computer-mad culture, system administrators are the unsung heroes. They handle the care and feeding of the networks our institutions increasingly rely on while typically remaining outside the pale insofar as involvement in the core business is concerned.

However, because you're building a network, it's probably a good idea to provide you with a realistic perspective on what it's like to work as a system or network administrator.

This hour pulls together everything you've learned in the previous chapters. This is where it all comes together.

Here's what you will learn in this hour:

- A description of a typical system administrator's day
- A list of standard tasks
- How to provide help to users and user management

A Day in the Life...

The day of a network administrator typically starts like anyone else's; you crawl out of bed and handle your morning ablutions. The difference starts midway through breakfast, when the pager goes off for the first time. A user at work has a problem (she can't print) and needs it fixed posthaste. So you break out your laptop and dial in to work to see if you can fix the problem remotely. If you can, you're "great," and the user will thank you profusely and then forget the whole thing, including the fact that you exist.

If, on the other hand, you can't solve a problem remotely, you have to hurry, since users don't like to wait for support. And rightfully so; they've usually got the core work of the business to attend to, and outrank your overhead-cost job. So you get to work as fast as possible, cruise into the user's office, and discover that she didn't select the correct printer; while she thought she wasn't printing, she sent 20 print jobs to the network printer at the other end of the building. You gently show her which printer she should select from her list so that she can print where she wants, have her print, and feel confident that she'll use the correct printer from now on.

When you get to your desk, your phone's message light is flashing one...two...three... more times. You listen to your messages and create a to-do list of users who need assistance right out of the gate, triaging them by order of seriousness, and then head out on your rounds. You're a computer doctor who makes office calls.

One user is complaining that his copy of the corporate database is locked up. You get to his desk and discover that he's caught in a transitional screen; there's a menu onscreen that he has to deal with before he can get control of the database again. You instruct him how to get through the screen and back into his application; he's happy but complains about the complexity. Oh, well. At least he's working again.

Another user is complaining that his system is blue-screening (that is, Windows NT is crashing in the famed Blue Screen of Death, or BSOD) on a regular basis. You go into his office and ask him if he's noticed anything particular: Does it happen when he presses specific keys? Is he running a specific application? He answers no to all your questions, and you can't replicate the problem. You tell him you don't know what's causing the problem and ask him to call you next time it blue-screens; he rather crossly agrees. As you turn to leave, he inserts a music CD into his CD player, and as he goes to play it, the system blue-screens. Aha! you think, this may be the event that precipitates these crashes. You reboot the system, do what the user just did, and lo and behold, the system crashes again. Now that you know the cause, it's largely a question of reinstalling the correct disk drivers. Because the system's emergency backup system-file disk is stored in your arsenal in the computer room, you get it, come back to the user's system, and use the emergency disk to check for nonoriginal files and replace them. During the system's search for nonoriginal or corrupt files, you notice that the CD-ROM disk driver has been replaced. After the fix, you test it by repeatedly putting CDs in and seeing whether they crash the system; they don't. You wish the user well and go on your way.

Your last help-desk call of the morning is to an associate whose laptop never seems to work when she's on the road. Every time you've tested it, however, it works perfectly. This time, you ask the user to show you how she tries to connect to the network remotely. You ask her to set her laptop up in a conference room so that you can see how she does what she does. You figure out what's wrong when you see her plug her network cable into a phone jack and try to dial the modem. You correct her choice of cords and make a mental note to make tags for her cables that read Network and Modem. She dials in successfully and now knows how to connect properly.

Once you have your user calls out of the way, you begin to start your daily tasks. First, you head into the computer room (which is actually the server room; everyone has a computer on his or her desk, so computer room is sort of a misnomer) and change the tape according to the backup scheme. You check your server logs right off the bat and see that someone was trying to get through the firewall last evening, using an executive's user ID but the wrong password; you call the executive whose ID was being used and ask whether he was trying to get in. No, he answers, but his kid was on the computer all night; maybe he was trying to get in. You respectfully request that the executive ask his kid to quit trying to crack the firewall; having asked that, you move on.

> For more information on making backups, refer to Hour 18, "The Network Administrator"; for more information on firewalls and security, refer to Hour 19, "Security."

You notice that your NetWare logs are full to overflowing, so you open NWAdmin on your administrative PC (refer to Hour 16, "Novell NetWare," to learn more about this utility) and archive the logs before cleaning them out. On your NT Server, you see that a variety of users have dialed into the Remote Access Server (RAS, described in Hour 7, "Remote Networking") the previous evening, and all were authenticated. Once you're done checking your logs, you change your backup tape (you're using a differential backup scheme running on NetWare) and review your to-do list. It includes the following items:

- Get a senior executive's PDA synchronized with his desktop computer
- Install a high-speed networking switch and segment the network

- Call several vendors regarding products you're interested in
- Figure out why the frame relay line connecting the network to the Internet is slow
- Write a CGI script to allow users to connect to a database over the corporate intranet
- Figure out which laptops offer the best value and submit a report to the CFO
- Provide a progress report on various initiatives to the CFO

Clearly, these things have to be prioritized; the items that affect users (the executive's PDA, the slow Internet connection) come first, followed by the networking switch, the vendor calls, and the laptop reports.

The executive's PDA is a no-brainer; you've done this before. Usually, this particular executive has either failed to plug his PDA fully into the cable connecting it to the desktop computer or else he's trying to replicate to the incorrect serial port. Today, the cause is just a loose cable; once connected, the executive's PDA is online, which he'll discover from your note when he gets back to his office.

While you're fixing the PDA cable, you call your telecommunications vendor and ask him to check the T1 digital phone circuit between her office and yours because you've noticed a really serious slowdown. She says she'll get right on it, and does; by the time you get back to your office, there's a voice mail from her saying that she found the problem and will fix it right after lunch.

You look at your watch and see that the morning hours have passed; it's noon, and lunch is due soon. You take your lunch and hunker down in your office, trying to simultaneously eat, call a vendor who's probably out to lunch, and read the trade press so that you can stay current. In the meantime, between bites of your sandwich, an analyst calls. His sound card isn't working right; at any rate, he can't play his CD and he's testy about what he calls the unreliability of the network. He wants you to come and fix it right now. So you put down your sandwich and trundle over to his office, where you find that he's been fooling with the volume settings on his desktop machine. You increase the volume and magically the sound card begins to work. He's happy. So are you. Your lunch is waiting.

On your way back to your office, you're pulled aside by the senior executive whose PDA you fixed earlier. He wants you to make time to speak to the technology committee at his kids' private school. You feel a flush of pride, and then a minor spot of panic: When will you find the time to do it? In any case, you agree and ask when the meeting will be; he answers seven-thirty the following morning. You ask what your topic will be, he gives it to you, and you start making mental notes so that you don't look like a fool in front of the technology committee.

22

During the afternoon, you finally make contact with the various vendors you tried to contact at lunch and get the information you need. At the same time, you create a multivariate scatterplot to indicate the weight of the various laptops' merits and provide a spreadsheet, a copy of the chart, and a cover memo to the CFO; you hope she'll read it and agree with your recommendations.

Toward the end of the day, you send a memo requesting that users log out of their systems when they leave. It's not a big request, but often users don't log out and backups are incomplete. By six o'clock, most of the users have filtered out of the office. You go from desk to desk and log out those workstations that are still connected to the network. Once that's done, you figure it's safe to add the switch, so you bolt it into the rack and connect a crossover cable to each separate 10BASE-T hub, removing the previous crossover cables that had linked the hubs together. Five minutes later, the switch is up and running, and performance at the end user stations is a bit better.

You change the backup tapes for the day, and lock the old ones in a drawer where they're reasonably secure.

You copy the logs on your email server (a Linux box running sendmail) and find out that there have been attempts to use your server as a relay. Fortunately, you've closed off most of the access to the server, so even a sendmail hack would be comparatively difficult.

Just before you leave, you read your mail. Most of it is advertising, which you bundle up to add to the woodstove pile at home after you've read it. You try to respond to the pieces that require that kind of attention.

Finally, you head out at about 8 p.m. You figure you got off easily today; no one threw a temper tantrum over perceived inequities in computer distribution. You head home to a well-deserved good sleep and prepare for tomorrow.

Daily Tasks

If you read through the preceding section, you understand that a system administrator has a long list of fairly mundane things to do over the course of a day. Typically, it's wise to make a list of the things you have to do on an ongoing basis (similar to *standing orders* in the military) in addition to your regular to-do list. The standing-order list usually includes things such as changing backup tapes, doing scheduled maintenance, checking log files, and doing research on various network-related topics. However, every network is different, and every network administrator has a different set of tasks. Some network administrators deal with telephone issues as well as computer networking, others deal with the whole technology infrastructure, still others deal with corporate information management. As with everything else, the tasks that become regular for you depend on the nature of the network you work on and the requirements and technical savvy of the people around you. Ideally, there should be no one-person network administration staff; a small department (two to four people) can schedule coverage around the clock.

As you make your list, ensure that you keep old records of what you've done by date. The benefits of doing so are twofold: First, you have a record of what you did and when you did it (invaluable when you're trying to remember how to fix something you worked on six months before). Second, keeping dated records provides a list you can use during yearly evaluations. It also creates a linear timeline that can help identify patterns and avoid burnout.

One of the most important things you can do, however, is to make time for yourself inasmuch as that is possible. Your effectiveness as a network or system administrator is directly related to how much you know, so even if your company doesn't pay for education, educate yourself. Read everything you can on networking and take note of things you think apply to you. If you have access to a more experienced networking professional, be shameless about learning as much as you can from him or her. Network professionals are usually quite willing to answer questions if you're polite about how you ask.

If you can, take a half hour every day and dedicate it to learning a tiny bit of programming. Even if you don't intend to program, understanding the process of coding and being familiar with the data structures full-time programmers use is a definite advantage when you're talking to tech support. In addition, being able to knock together a 10-to-15-line program to hotfix something in an emergency is a highly desirable skill, and one that can earn you your employer's loyalty.

If a headhunter calls (and one will), don't ignore him or her. If you're a qualified networking professional (which these days means you're someone who can work with various environments, regardless of certification), you're in demand. If you're not happy where you are, particularly if you're a single-person IS department (far and away the least-appreciated members of the profession), you can move and probably gain both happiness and money in the transfer.

Strategies for Supporting Users

As noted in the preceding hour, users are the bread and butter of networks. Without users, we'd all be out of work. So it's your job to keep your users happy, a job that most network administrators accept with alacrity.

22

Users, however, are not always reasonable. As a network administrator, you have certain charges laid on you, such as agreed-on network standards and behaviors; if a user calls on you to violate those basic charges, you have to be able to either say no, escalate the user's request to someone who can grant an exception to the rules, or (in rare cases) escalate the issue because you see potential security breaches or behavior that exposes the organization to liability.

- Never get angry with a user, even if they're senselessly venting on you. The user's anger may come from a variety of sources, ranging from frustration at not getting his or her work done to a wholly unrelated argument with someone else.

- Stop and listen to the user when he or she complains. It's way too easy to interrupt a user in midsentence and announce that you've got a solution to the problem. If you take the time to actually listen to a user's complaint, you may discover that the problem extends beyond the computer per se; he or she may be upset that the software won't automate certain functions.

- After you've listened to the user, take a second and think about what your most appropriate response should be. It's all fine and well for you to know that the user's TCP/IP configuration is incorrect and that changing the subnet mask will resolve the problem, but do you have to explain it? For most users, the answer is *no*; all they want is a functioning network, and they don't care what's behind it. So your response to the user should be based on a now-or-later fix: If it's a 5-to-10-minute fix, suggest that you can do it now; on the other hand, a long fix means that you have to defer the repair if the user needs the machine and can limp it along until you fix it properly.

Summary

This book has dealt pretty heavily with theory. In the end, however, theory doesn't do anything. It's practice that counts. And as a network administrator, you'll find ample opportunities to practice. You've learned a host of things that will stand you in good stead when you are in practice:

- The basics of networking theory
- The nomenclature of the hardware and software
- The basic configurations networks use
- The software networks run on
- The basics of network administration

This is not the only book you should read to be a good network administrator. Although I won't recommend specific networking titles, I can say that there is a plethora of quality, in-depth books about networking you can find at any reasonably complete library or bookstore.

Other books are useful if you're going to be a network administrator. They don't necessarily mention computers; instead, they deal with problem solving, which is the stock in trade of a good network administrator. These books can help you break out of regular thought patterns and think creatively, which is a great help when you're trying to figure out a knotty problem.

Here's a list of some of the best books I've found:

- Anything by Edward Tufte. Tufte's books—*The Visual Display of Quantitative Information; Envisioning Information; and Visual Explanations*—are *tours de force* on out-of-the-box thinking. The solutions he finds to multivariate data offer the discerning reader a powerful dose of clear thinking.
- *The C Programming Language*, by Brian Kernighan and Dennis Ritchie. Even if you don't want to become a programmer, this book opens up a great understanding of the logical processes on which computers rely.
- *Categories; Metaphysics; and Rhetoric*, by Aristotle. These titles offer rigorous methods of breaking objects of thought into their component parts. Great methodology for learning problem solving.
- *The Mythical Man-Month*, by Frederick P. Brooks. This may well be the single best treatise on the management of large-scale projects that has ever been written. Lucid, informative, thoughtful. A classic. Highly recommended.

If you find additional books of value, add them to your list. Whatever works to help you think about networking more clearly is worthwhile.

PART VI

The Future of Networking

Hour

HOUR 23

Wireless LANs

Mobility is important. Human beings like to be able to move around the office and think while staying in contact with our network. On factory and warehouse floors, we like to be able to hook into the network while out on the shop floor. Doctors in hospitals love the thought of being able to carry a live, dynamically updated patient chart around with them.

Unfortunately, wired networks can't readily provide these things. Wired networks tend to make the tacit assumption that a user works in one physical location and stays there during the course of their workday.

However, new technologies spurred by the ratification of IEEE standard 802.11 for wireless networking have recently come onto the market. Wireless networking holds a great deal of promise to connect workers who move around their workspace, such as doctors, police and fire personnel, factory workers, anyone who doesn't work in a fixed office location. Wireless networks enable people to have data where they need it, when they need it. The technologies are new and relatively expensive, but they herald a new phase of networking that's more focused on the user's needs than ever before.

Here's what you will learn in this hour:

- Why use wireless networks
- What wireless LANs are
- Why wireless LANs are attractive to networkers
- The target constituency for wireless LANs
- Whether or not wireless networking is mature enough to roll out on a production basis
- The costs of wireless networking

Why Use Wireless Networks?

For most of us, a hardwired connection between our desktop computer and the rest of the network is sufficient. Basically, all most users need is a single connection to a network; almost no one carries a computer while walking around a workspace, expecting to remain logged into a network. After all, most of us work at our desks and leave our desks only to get additional materials with which to do our jobs.

That's all fine and well for office workers, whose jobs *do* fit the preceding description. But there is a small and steadily increasing group of people who have to be able to connect to networks from a variety of locations: in multiple locations in the office, while they're on the road, and so forth. Often, the dual solution of Ethernet in the office and dial-up networking on the road is inadequate for one reason or another, and then the poor network manager has to figure out how to provide the services his or her users require, which can be quite a conundrum.

Why? The simple answer is that wireless networking is complex and not entirely standardized. It's currently a relatively obscure branch of networking. Many administrators (and, of course, users) will forgo the convenience of near-universal connectivity when confronted with the complexity inherent in wireless networking.

Recent advances in standardization (*not* technology) have leveraged wireless LAN technology with promises of interoperability between different vendors' systems. The growth of the Web stirred interest in wireless Web access. That, combined with the push for wireless-network standardization over the last several years, has led to a surge of growth in the industry. It's still not a mainstream technology, but it's just a matter of time until it will be possible to order a new computer with a wireless network adapter.

What Is Wireless Networking?

But what exactly, you ask, is wireless networking? Here are some identifying features:

- First and foremost, it's data carried over radio waves or with infrared light.

- It's a plethora of standards built around the IEEE 802.11 standards and the TCP/IP protocol. IEEE 802 standards specify the physical layer of the OSI network model. TCP/IP does not care what underlying network media it runs over; between the two, it's possible to build a network that runs over any media, ranging from coaxial cable, unshielded twisted-pair wire, glass fiber, and, of course, radio waves and infrared light.

- Wireless networks are versatile ways to transfer data. They can run over a variety of radio waves, from the infrared spectrum to cellular phone bands. The most common uses of wireless networking, and the specific connection type most suited to servicing each of them, are described in this hour.

Typically, wireless LANs are not completely wireless (although completely wireless LANs do exist). Most often, wireless LANs are built in a way similar to cellular networks, with several wireless access points connected to a standard Ethernet network. Take a look at Figure 23.1 for a common wireless LAN configuration.

23

FIGURE 23.1

A wireless network with several Ethernet access points.

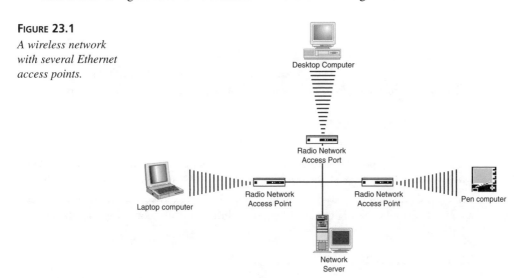

When a computer connected to the wireless LAN moves around the network, the computer senses which access point the laptop is closest to and uses that access point. The local range of spread-spectrum networks covers up to about 50,000 square feet (which isn't as big as it sounds: 50,000 square feet is a two-dimensional square about 225 feet on a side). Some manufacturers make systems that, with the use of external antennae, can transmit as much as five miles, and such systems are used by public safety personnel.

Wireless Network Applications

Different kinds of wireless networks lend themselves to different applications. A list of applications and the common wireless topologies is provided in Table 23.1.

TABLE 23.1 Some Common Wireless Networking Applications

Application	Topology
In-office	Spread spectrum connectivity; the ability to roam in the office with a laptop computer and remain connected to the LAN.
Wireless networking	Infrared LANs, radio LANs at fixed location.
Wireless networking out-of-office	Radio modems connected with VPN wireless network provider (RadioMail, Sprint, MCI, and so on)…or else it could be Ethernet over RF.

Within each of these divisions are multiple (and often competing) standards. As you can see, there's quite a bit of variance with regard to connection type; some use the laptop computers' existing infrared equipment, some use special wireless Ethernet hardware, and some use third-party service providers with still more specialized modems.

In-Office Wireless Networking Technologies

In the office, the two most common topologies are spread spectrum and infrared connections. Of the two, spread spectrum, a radio technology that uses the 902-to-928 MHz and 2.4-to-2.484 GHz Industrial, Scientific, and Medical (ISM) radio frequency (which, fortunately, requires no FCC license) is more useful for intraoffice mobile workers because it can connect all over a building. By contrast, infrared is used only for line-of-sight applications.

Spread Spectrum

Spread spectrum, the most common topology for wireless LANs, was developed for the military to guard against enemy radio frequency jamming and eavesdropping. Spread spectrum spreads the signal across a range of frequencies in the ISM bands.

Frequency Hopping Spread Spectrum

Frequency hopping spread spectrum (FHSS), the first implementation of the spread spectrum technology, hops from frequency to frequency in a set pattern. The receiver can receive frequency hopping spread spectrum data only if the sender and the receiver use the same hopping pattern (which is controlled by what is called a *hopping-sequence algorithm*). According to FCC rules, no transmitter can stay on a single band for more than 0.4 seconds within a period of 20 seconds for the 902 MHz band (30 seconds for the 2.4 GHz band). Each transmitter must also cycle through 50 to 75 radio bands before restarting the hopping-sequence algorithm. The IEEE 802.11 standard proposes limiting FHSS to the 2.4 GHz band.

Direct Sequence Spread Spectrum

The other, more recent, type of spread spectrum technology is *direct sequence spread spectrum* (DSSS), which is more commonly used in wireless LANs. In DSSS, the transmitter modifies the data with "chips," or extra data bits (a minimum of 10) inserted in the data stream. Only a receiver that knows the algorithm for the insertion of chips can decipher the code. Because of the effect of the chips, the effective throughput of DSSS is currently limited to 2 megabits per second in the 902 MHz band and 8 megabits per second—a usable speed—in the 2.4 GHz band.

Infrared Technologies

Infrared technology is typically used in a single office where the user moves around the room with a laptop. Infrared is a line-of-sight technology and is most useful for offices. Infrared is the same technology used for television remote controls; it can carry a lot of bandwidth, but because it's line-of-sight, it's easily interrupted by any visual obstruction.

Out-of-Office Wireless Network Technologies

The third topology, radio modems, is currently in a state of flux. The technology used is called Cellular Digital Packet Data (CDPD), and it enables a user to send data packets using a cellular network similar to what is used for cellphones. CDPD is still in a nascent state. CDPD is the fastest wireless networking protocol available, but even so, it's limited to a 19.2 kilobits-per-second data transmission speed—quite a bit slower than today's regular wired modems and an order of magnitude slower than an Ethernet connection. Nonetheless, the allure of being able to connect to a network without a phone jack is difficult to resist, and many corporate networkers are cautiously testing CDPD networking for their remote users.

Some new wireless networking technologies offer 4 megabits per second speeds and true network connectivity. Cisco's AirLAN offers wide range and allows multiple systems access from a single access point.

Not Built for Speed: Wireless Networking Performance Considerations

Wireless networking offers a variety of conveniences when compared to a wired network. Unfortunately, speed isn't one of them. Even the best wireless connections are only as fast as a middling LAN; the cost for the convenience of disconnected access is lower data transmission rates. Table 23.2 shows the speeds of typical data connections. For what it's worth, CDPD runs slower than either the infrared or spread spectrum topology, but because the CDPD standard is in flux, it's not included in the table.

Because of the lack of a broadly implemented industry standard, connection speeds vary from manufacturer to manufacturer, but the current consensus seems to be striving towards interoperability. Unfortunately, several manufacturers (including Proxim, AMD, Breeze Wireless, and Raytheon) each contend that their own proprietary model for wireless networking has set the standard; right now, the purchase of wireless LAN equipment is likely to bind the purchaser to one manufacturer's products.

TABLE 23.2   Various LAN Topologies and Their Speeds

	Spread Spectrum	Infrared
Frequency band	2.4 GHz	300,000 GHz
	902 MHz	
	5.7 GHz	
Maximum distance from receiver	1,000 feet	50 to 100 feet
Total coverage	<= 50,000 square feet	N/A
Wattage required	1W or less	N/A
Used in multiple rooms in same building?	Yes, with internal antennae	Yes, with several internal receivers
Speed	2 to 5 megabits per second	5 to 10 megabits per second

Why Wireless Networks Are Attractive to Networkers

Wireless LANs offer a host of upsides for networkers, particularly in larger organizations. Several major benefits are outlined here:

- **Simplifies adds, moves, and changes.** Currently, the add/move/change process in wired networks is comparatively cumbersome. You have to run network wiring out to the area in which the user will be located; if that user is outside the geographical limits of the local LAN, expensive repeaters that extend the reach of the local network are often necessary. Wired LANs, for all the freedom they give their users, are not so different from the old telegraph line; you have to be on the wire to get the signals. If you have to move your network (or part of it) elsewhere, you have to bring all the cables, wiring, and so forth along, which makes transportable wired networks quite rare.

- **Quickly deployable.** Wireless networking offers quite a contrast to the cumbersome earthbound wires of wired LANs. Wireless networks work well in situations in which the requirements state that the network must be transportable, rapidly deployable, and very reliable.

- **Offers mobility for users who don't work in a single location.** In hospitals, for example, wireless networks enable nurses to monitor patients wherever they are; there's no need to be at a fixed network. Increasingly, doctors are using wireless PDAs, such as Palm devices or Windows CE devices, to connect to patient data; more than one metropolitan hospital now provides its physicians with such technology.

Is Wireless Networking Ready for Prime Time?

Is wireless networking mature enough to roll out on a production basis? The answer depends on your needs. If you have remote users who have to get connected *now*, the answer is yes. The good news is that you can build a spread spectrum network that is reasonably reliable and can give your users the in-building mobile access they require. The downside is that the products you have to use to do it don't yet adhere to a standard; as a result, once a standard is adopted by all the manufacturers, you may have to replace your equipment.

If you have only a few users who want their laptops to connect to the internal network while they are in their offices, yes, wireless networking is an option. Instead of the spread spectrum technology, this application calls for infrared networking. Infrared technology costs less and operates on line-of-sight. As long as users don't require the ability to move from room to room while on the network, infrared is perfectly functional.

If, on the other hand, you are working with a relatively low budget and can't afford to have to abandon existing technology when a standard emerges, the answer is *no*, wireless networking is not yet ready for you. Although wireless networking has gotten less expensive, it's still too expensive to adopt if you can't afford to upgrade it in a couple of years.

The Costs of Wireless Networking

In wireless network integrations, getting the system running was the exact opposite of a regular technology upgrade. Instead of getting a sign-off from management on the purchase of the parts and then sweating to integrate them, he sweated to get management to sign off on the purchase of what they'd mandated but the installation took only a week.

On a per-computer basis, wireless LAN adapters currently cost from $250 to $500. Radio modems are about $500, and the back-end pieces from the major wireless manufacturers can easily cost $5,000 or more even for a small installation.

The trend is changing, however. Industry analysts point to the increase in interest in wireless networking and the reduction in the cost of manufacturing. They suggest that the day of the $200 wireless network adapter is not too far off.

Summary

Although the current generation of networks is solidly grounded in hard-wired connections—and likely the next generation as well—wireless networking is gaining ground as corporate IS discovers its flexibility, mobility, and reliability. Wireless networking is a trend to stay on top of; it could be the network topology of tomorrow.

HOUR 24

Where Are Networks Going from Here?

You've reached the end of the book. You know how networks work. You know how to plan and build them.

Now it's time to look at the future of networks. As networking moves into the future, we'll see an increasing amount of convergence between your network and the public Internet. The location of files will become less important and less apparent. Hopefully, the amount of time put into configuring networks will be reduced somewhat by the advent of new networking technologies, such as IPv6.

Other factors affecting networking in the future include virtual offices and the increasing degree of remote access. That's why, in this hour, we'll discuss these topics:

- The future of the virtual office
- The need to design virtual offices hand-in-hand with management
- Access types

- Managing remote users—the balance between network management and regular management responsibilities
- The dangers facing the Internet
- IPv6, the first part of the solution
- Internet II—the Internet, Part Deux

What's Behind the Mandate for the Virtual Office?

Over the last 10 or 15 years, the demand for out-of-office workers has increased tremendously. Many corporations no longer demand (or even desire, in some cases) that their sales force shows up for work at a central facility (except for prescheduled meetings). From management's perspective, this has led to some great gains: the cost of office space is significantly reduced and middle management has gone the way of the wind. In many cases, not being tied to the office has made users happy; when they work from home, they don't have to wear dress clothing and deal with office politics.

What's made all this possible? It's not just the computer; the steady downward trend in the prices of office equipment has fostered the growth of the small office and home office market. Ten years ago, purchasing a computer, a fax machine, and a second home phone line would have cost close to $10,000. Today, it's closer to $3,000.

Such trends are good news for the thousands of employers who have found that their workers require personal computers to do their jobs. The raw increases in power and connectivity over the last decade have enabled organizations to build virtual groups that communicate using phone, fax, and email and that are as effective as any group of workers toiling away in an office. Home offices also serve to keep workers happy—not a small task in a strong economy where valued employees can jump ship at the slightest provocation and not worry about finding another job.

The distributed sales force model, in which salespeople keep in touch with a central office by phoning in their orders and getting new instructions, is a sort of baseline model for the modern virtual office. Workers can work out of their homes, but increasingly, they're using the Internet (or at least a World Wide Web interface) to connect to their companies. VPNs, the Web, decentralized companies, and other business conditions are driving the development of new TCP/IP and Internet-based technologies to enable the distributed enterprise.

Organizations' desires to have their workers working out of their homes rather than central offices is driven by several conditions currently affecting the business community:

- The need for increased customer service
- The need for cost reduction
- The need to comply with the Americans with Disabilities Act
- The need to comply with environmental legislation

And the last reason is almost an afterthought: convenience.

Customer Service

Having workers, particularly sales and customer support personnel, working out of their homes allows an organization to cover a significantly larger territory than it could if it were based out of a central location in a hub-and-spoke relationship with its clients. If a worker lives and works 50 miles from an organization's central office, they can reasonably be expected to serve clients who are geographically farther away from the central office than can a worker who lives in the same town as the central office (the remote worker is sort of a sub-hub of the main hub). This arrangement allows companies to be more responsive to a wider range of customers and have better response times. It also keeps clients happier; when they don't have to wait for a company representative to drive all the way from the central office, it feels as though they're getting better service.

Cost Reduction

Office space is expensive. Even in depressed markets, commercial real estate usually costs more than industrial or (in some markets) residential real estate. Therefore, if a company can reduce the size of its central office (or better yet, get rid of it altogether), it saves a great deal of money. Combined with relatively low-cost, high-powered computers, connectivity need not suffer. Workers can meet on a regular basis at an agreed-on central location (sometimes it's as prosaic as a meeting in a restaurant once every several weeks) to ensure that they're all on the plan. This has added benefits: Employees don't have a commute, which increases employee satisfaction and does good things for the environment—less smog!

Americans with Disabilities Act

The Americans with Disabilities Act has provided companies with another impetus to virtualize their workforce. Often, mobility-impaired people find that buildings built for fully ambulatory people are hostile to them. The building may not have wheelchair ramps, or its hallways and doorways may be too narrow to accommodate wheelchairs. A building may not have Braille markers for the blind, either. If a disabled person is an office worker, it's perfectly possible to ensure that they can work by providing a means by which they can get their work done and interact with the rest of the company—it just requires that the company use technology to provide adequate and appropriate services to their remote users. Working from home enables many disabled workers to work in the field they desire. Virtual companies with work-at-home policies make that possible.

Environmental Issues

An increasing number of urban centers befouled by smog have either passed or are about to pass legislation mandating that corporate entities must establish work-from-home programs. Such programs are intended to reduce traffic congestion and smog; although these measures *are* being contested in the courts, it's a safe bet that one day in the near future some form of these laws will come into effect.

Convenience

Convenience is the last reason virtual offices are taking more of a role in American business...and for once, the convenience is a win-win situation. It affects both the corporation and the worker. From a corporate vantage point, a worker who can be relied on to work from home is a major plus; it means less supervision and better work because workers are self-motivated (they don't need the whip laid on to do their work). From a worker's perspective, working at home affords a certain flexibility and casual atmosphere that simply isn't available in most office situations.

Of course, working at home isn't for everyone. To work at home successfully, a person has to be able to stay focused on work and not be distracted by the dog, the laundry, the housework, the door-to-door salespeople, and the like. But for people who are self-motivated, working at home can be the realization of a dream.

The Future of the Virtual Office

The future of office technology is largely the future of the virtual office. At this point, we're just beginning to reach communications speeds at which working at home or in remote locations is feasible. The continued expansion of switched digital phone service into the "last mile" (the wiring between the central office and the home) will continue to improve the situation.

Computers are also getting faster, more capable, and in some ways more reliable. They're no longer "that box that sits on the table"; they've become an information appliance as integral to communications as the telephone or the fax machine. In some cases, the computer that companies ship to workers' homes is the phone and fax machine. This trend towards *convergence* (combining office equipment into a single box) will continue as computers evolve.

The support relationship between remote workers and companies will change in the coming years. Currently, if users have a problem with their computers in a home environment, they have to call the office; a tech support representative will try to talk them through a solution to the problem. The next line of defense is to dispatch a technician to fix the problem, which is often unacceptable (all too often, the tech takes too long to get out). Typically, one technician covers a fairly large geographical area consisting of about the same number of users as would be found in a centralized office space; consequently, the technician is quite overloaded. In the next couple of years, companies with far-flung workforces will hopefully realize that to provide quality technical support, the support must be relatively ubiquitous. Ultimately, this will lead to outsourced tech support—companies will hire local technical support service firms to assist its users.

Hopefully, fewer technical support calls will be needed in the future; the reliability of computers is slowly improving, and centralized technical departments may be able to perform remote management of the desktops of home workers.

24

The biggest shift, however, is well underway, and it presents a ticklish situation for both the company and the user. It's the question of the employee who does several jobs from home. Or more correctly, it's the case of a remote user who uses their own computer equipment (yes, it does happen, although it contradicts common sense) and has company data on that computer.

Because corporate loyalty has been largely destroyed (a victim of the investment community's axiomatic willingness to reward downsizing companies), it's a no-brainer to understand that workers will leave a company in a heartbeat for a better offer. Unfortunately, in the rush to the virtual office, many companies have elected to allow their workers to use personal equipment if they elect to do so, albeit without nondisclosure agreements and the like. This arrangement means that unless companies work to rebuild the loyalty shattered during the 1980s and early 1990s downsizing binges, they will be caught in a difficult situation: Workers who do not work onsite and whose loyalty to a company ends when a better offer comes along have access to corporate data which, for better or worse, is a commodity. Remember that digital data can be replicated without leaving traces; this means that a company's data is constantly at risk.

As a result, it's probable that organizations with Small Office/Home Office (SOHO) workers will create highly restrictive nondisclosure agreements and post-employment covenants (although the former will probably stand in court, the latter won't and can't). And it means that whatever corporate data is in a user's head (and there's probably more in a home user's head than in an office user's—the home user has to know more to be more self-sufficient) is up for grabs by the highest bidder.

Last, it's fair to say that more users will work at home and work at one or more jobs. There will probably always be a central job that pays the majority of the bills, but it's probable that several side jobs will also be a constant; they provide security and a way to diversify one's resume.

Designing Virtual Offices: Working with Management

Too often, the relationship between line management and technical management is at odds with respect to business goals. All too often, a mandate to do something is handed down from the executive suite without any explanation about the reasoning and the goals behind the process. As a result, misunderstandings develop, and the users are caught in the middle.

That's why it's important to get everyone on the same side of the table when you're developing a virtual workforce program. Virtual workers are pretty disconnected from the company; if they get good service and a consistent line from management and technical services, they're going to be secure. If they don't get consistent and good treatment, they're liable to draw the conclusion that their jobs are at risk. The reasoning makes sense; if you're a vestigial part of a company, and you're not being dealt with, it's safe to assume (based on recent corporate behavior) that you're likely to get the ax.

If management wants to create a virtual office, it has to come to technical services, discuss the ramifications, and learn what the available technologies can and can't do. As a matter of fact, management should also spend some time looking at the costs of building a virtual network from a technical perspective. After doing so, management will have a much better idea of the technical ramifications of its decision. If, after technical review, management is still interested, it's time to proceed. Ideally, in future years, collaborative software and ubiquitous email (that is, email that's even used by the executives themselves in their executive suites) will enable a frank, open discussion of issues before the planning and deployment of offsite worker programs—it can prevent misunderstandings from arising.

As we move into the future, management will have much better productivity tracking. Technical managers will be able to audit time on workers' systems and provide reports to regular managers. This is a significant lack in the current paradigm; workers who work out of the office have only one measure of productivity: whether or not the job gets done (which, some argue, should be the only measure). However, in the grand scheme of things, it is in the blood of commercial enterprises to want to quantify everything, and the increase in network management software will enable a greater degree of "Big-Brotherism"—worker's privacy will have to be jealously guarded against the urge to track every keystroke.

Off-site equipment management will change as outlined earlier in this hour. As computers converge with phones and fax machines, the company will have to provide a single, highly reliable information appliance to users; users will be expected to use it within certain limits. Hopefully, such appliances will mark a net increase in the ease of use and reliability of current systems.

Access Types

Hour 7, "Remote Networking," discussed some of the different methods by which remote users connect to an internal network:

- Dial-up into a central server
- ISDN dial-up
- Virtual Private Networks (VPNs)
- And a new entry—wireless access using Personal Digital Assistants (PDAs), such as the Palm VII or various wireless Windows CE devices

24

From a remote-access point of view, currently the best, most secure methods of access to a corporate network are the first two. The reason? Except for where the signal passes over the public phone network, these connections are basically secure—they don't pass through anyone else's servers.

However, dial-up systems, now the dominant form of communication between a remote user and a central network, will rapidly become the least preferable form of remote access as digital technology and local networks become more common. As of January 1998, the absolute maximum speed a modem can sustain is 53 kilobits per second—and that's on a perfect phone line. Digital technology (either ISDN phone service or local LAN connections that allow VPN-style connections at T-rate speeds over the Internet) will become the new standard in the next 5 to 10 years. With greater speed comes the capability to encrypt data in real time and authenticate multiple times during a session using *dynamic access tokens*, or smart cards that generate a new password periodically depending on the connection.

Access over the Internet (or over ISDN, for the matter) will require highly secure firewalls and strong authentication. Quality of Service (QoS) agreements with ISPs will be essential to ensure that your network always has the bandwidth it needs to allow enough remote users to dial into the network.

The advent of technologies such as Gigabit Ethernet and ATM will usher in a new era of Internet bandwidth, which will have direct ramifications on remote access. Eventually, remote access speeds will be sufficiently fast so that it will be possible to cease drawing a distinction between local access and remote access.

The Future of the Internet

The Internet is a boom town. In fewer than 10 years, it's grown from a sleepy little village into a thriving online metropolis with all the complications such rapid growth implies. And like most places that experience rapid growth, its growth is outstripping its infrastructure. As discussed in Hour 3, "Getting Data from Here to There: How Computers Share Data," the number of addresses available for Internet computers is rapidly diminishing, and there is little provision for prevention of fraud and other crimes. There's also very little provision to enable commerce.

Although you may or may not agree that the purpose of the Internet is commercial, the Internet's explosive growth has been largely fueled by businesses trying to gain a competitive edge. To remain a successful and viable network, the Internet has to change to provide secure, authenticated, easy-to-use service at both the network level (that is, the underlying software) and the user level (the browser software most users use to access Internet resources).

The following sections outline the travails that the Internet is facing and what solutions exist to ameliorate them. And this isn't a complete list; new solutions are proposed to the marketplace every day. With luck and hard work, the Internet will remain viable and grow into a universal service much like the current telephone system. Or so we hope.

The Dangers Facing the Internet

The Internet started life as a small electronic town populated by mostly academic researchers and the occasional military computer guy. Relationships and behaviors were based on a sense of shared trust; people left their electronic doors unlocked and didn't worry too much about unauthorized access.

As the ARPAnet became DARPAnet, and DARPAnet became the Internet, however, the community grew like a frontier community. And like any growing community, it suffered from several social pathologies endemic to being on the frontier. Although the great mass of people who moved in were good and honest people, curious about this new world, a few unsavory characters crept in and threatened to spoil the situation for everyone. Instead of being called outlaws, they were called *hackers* or *crackers*, and they did a great deal to disrupt the equanimity of the community. Crackers led to a dangerously paranoid attitude on the part of too many people who should have known better than to think that the Internet was a hotbed of data thieves and pornographers. Such thinking led to reactionary responses to the Internet, most of which were and are wholly inappropriate. The Internet is only a tool; like any tool, its use by humans can be either good or evil, but the tool itself is value neutral. And like any other tool, if it's abused, it will wind up regulated to a degree where freedom is compromised in the name of order.

The Shrinking IP Address Pool

As the Internet continued to grow, it ran into problems that well and truly paralleled big city development. First, it began to run out of service: The bandwidth (the width of its streets) and the number of addresses (the amount of available territory) were shrinking very fast. Through the use of reserved addresses (such as `10.X.X.X` and `192.168.X.X`) and Common InterDomain Routing (CIDR), the Internet has managed to continue growing. Even though the methods used are a bit *kludgy*, or contrived, they merely address the symptoms but not the etiology of the problem.

The Bad Part of Town

The second similarity between the Internet and big cities is the fact that the Internet has provided a medium through which pornography, gambling, and assorted scams are easier to distribute. Attempts to limit these behaviors, however, have in some ways been worse than the disease—the infamous Communications Decency Act, struck down very quickly after Congress enacted it, and the even worse Digital Millenium Copyright Act. These laws, which may be well-meaning, essentially curtail first-amendment rights in the Internet medium, and provide precedents for limiting political speech online. Ultimately, changes in the architecture of the Internet are the only means by which behavior can be regulated; the current architecture is difficult to control.

Fraud and Insecure Commerce

In addition to the red-light districts on the Net, the Internet has proven to be a fertile ground for fraudulent enterprises. Because there's really very little authentication available under the current Internet architecture, a fraudulent enterprise can seem as legitimate as any other.

A corollary to the ease of perpetrating fraud is the difficulty of ensuring true secure electronic commerce. Although the risks are vastly overrated—most common criminals can't decrypt encrypted data—it nonetheless has a damping effect on the growth of the commercial Internet.

Governmental Overreaction to Internet Hype

An initiative passed by Congress and signed into law by President Clinton—the Communications Decency Act (CDA)—is worded so vaguely that it outlaws discussion of almost any adult topic on the Internet based solely on word choice, all in the stated interest of protecting children from obscenity. It fails utterly in protecting children; instead, its function is a chilling restriction of speech.

Under the CDA, discussions about breast cancer, prostate cancer, or uterine fibroid tumors can be deemed obscene because they use the words *breast*, *prostate*, and *uterine*.

The law's backers, in a clear show of partisan unity, have clearly indicated that they believe the law should apply to information about AIDS, abortion, pregnancy, sexuality, and of course pornography, among other controversial topics. Because of the limitations of current technology, barring children from these sites also bars adults from them, but that appears to be the goal of the CDA's backers: To restrict discussion of topics they have labeled moral issues.

Fortunately, the CDA was largely overturned in Federal court. Although the CDA would certainly protect children using the Internet from obscene material, it would also undermine the near-limitless free flow of information on almost any topic for which the Internet is rightly lauded.

The Relentless Hype Factor

The last danger the Internet faces is that it is relentlessly overhyped. The Internet is cool, without a doubt. However, its importance in the grand scheme of things has been greatly overstated; consequently, users often expect too much from it. Librarians report that library patrons no longer look for information on the paper shelves; instead, they want to find information on the Internet because they've been told that that's where all the information is. Clearly, the Internet has a great deal to offer, but it doesn't have everything— and very rarely does it have the depth a researcher requires to become conversant with a subject. Remember that although the Internet is powerful and broad ranging, it is not yet H.G. Well's World Brain, where every item of information is stored. Credibility should come as hard for the Internet as it does for any other source of information; unfortunately, the Internet's delivery media (computers and the World Wide Web for most user situations) lends a gloss to the proceedings that is often undeserved.

The Internet is, as Popeye said of himself, what it is. It is a huge, largely anarchic, loosely organized repository of substance and minutiae—small nuggets of the former, huge wads of the latter. The Internet is here to stay; it is too useful to set aside. Even if we could set the Internet aside, it wouldn't be possible; once opened, Pandora's box is not easily closed. The next task facing networking professionals is to teach their users about the realities of the Internet: On the one hand, it's not all child pornographers and scam artists; on the other hand, it's not the noble repository of all the greatness the world has. It's somewhere in between, and as it matures, it will mirror humanity ever more closely, with all our human glory and human frailties.

Some Thoughts on Solutions to Some of the Internet's Nemeses

Even as the Internet suffers from broad problems—some systemic, like security, some hype-related, some constitutional problems—people are working to bring solutions to the fore. The Internet offers too much promise to abandon to the forces of mediocrity; it can change the world by making a data available to people who otherwise might never see it.

The solutions presented in the next few sections aren't the be-all and end-all, but they're a start. As time passes, the Internet will hopefully smooth out and eventually fulfill its promise.

A Solution to Cure Many Ills: IPv6

As noted earlier, the address space for the Internet is rapidly shrinking. This is true because the original designers of the Internet never envisioned a world in which personal computers would exist; they never imagined that the 4,294,967,296 (also described as 2 to the 32nd power) addresses their 32-bit address space provided for would even be close to fully used.

They also never imagined that ordinary mortals would one day come into acutely close contact with the protocols of the Internet and have the unenviable task of configuring IP addresses, subnet masks, DNS, DNCP, and the like.

And they can't have imagined a world in which palm-based computers or cell phones were connected to the Internet. Clearly, it's time for a change.

Because the Internet designers' initial network was noncommercial, they never imagined that they would need a method to ensure secure transactions. They knew that networking was fast, but they didn't realize that bandwidth would become a constraint on a massive scale to the network's growth. And because they didn't envision the growth the Internet has seen, they didn't realize that the Internet protocol had to be able to prioritize the importance of traffic for Quality of Service reasons.

Because of the shortcomings of the existing Internet Protocol, the Internet Engineering Task Force (IETF) in late 1993 issued Request for Comments 1550 (RFC 1550) titled "IP: Next Generation (IPng) White Paper Solicitation." The purpose of this RFC was to draw together the disparate ideas about what specific features various constituencies wanted in the Next Generation Internet Protocol.

In a document titled RFC 1726, "Technical Criteria for Choosing IP: The Next Generation (IPng)," the initial specifications for an improved Internet Protocol were outlined. In January 1995, RFC 1752, "The Recommendation for the IP Next Generation Protocol," was issued. Table 24.1 specifies the improvements IPv6 offers over IPv4 (the current Internet Protocol). RFC 1883 later followed with an official specification for IPv6; these specs reflect the influence of both RFC 1883 and RFC 1752.

TABLE 24.1   The Differences Between IPv4 and IPv6

	IPv4	IPv6
Address space, bits	32	128
Number of possible addresses	2^{32} or 4,294,967,296	2^{128} or 3.402823669209^{38}
		It's difficult to explain here, but the number of addresses in IPv6 is enormous. The 128-bit address space is not four times larger than IPv4's 32-bit address space; instead, it's something like a billion billion times larger. With IPv6, we won't run out of addressees for a long, long time.
Header length, bytes (also called octets)	20 octets	40 octets Note even though the address space is four times as long in IPv6, the header, which contains packet routing information, is only twice as large. This represents a very efficient use of bandwidth.
Extendable	No	Yes In this context, extendable means that options that don't have to be read each time the packet is routed are located in extension headers located after the core header information. This arrangement makes better use of bandwidth.
Encryption, Authentication, and Privacy	No	Yes; IPv6 has the built-in facility to authenticate the sender of a data packet and to encrypt the data in a packet.
Autoconfiguration	No	Yes; IPv6 has facilities to automatically configure an IP address for itself and can work with networks to receive appropriate unique network addresses.
Quality of Service capabilities	No	Yes

In addition to the differences listed in Table 24.1, IPv6 also prepares for a simple transition from IPv4 to IPv6. The requirements of RFC 1752 and RFC 1883 state that the transition from IPv4 to IPv6 must fit the following four requirements:

- It must be possible to upgrade an IPv4 network to an IPv6 network without having to do it in an all-or-nothing scenario. IPv6, therefore, must be backward compatible with IPv4.

- New IPv6-capable devices must be able to be deployed on the network without changing any of the IPv4 computers on the network.

- When IPv4 computers are upgraded to IPv6, they must be able to use their existing IPv4 addresses in an IPv6 context—no change should be needed.

- The cost of deploying IPv6 must not be excessive; very little preparation work should be required to do an IPv4-to-IPv6 upgrade.

IPv6 was intended to remedy the shortcomings of IPv4, and it has done so magnificently. Early implementations from IBM Corporation, Digital Equipment Corporation, and FTP Software provide proof of the concept. Over the next five to 10 years, IPv6 will hopefully begin to replace IPv4 implementations. Because IPv4 compatibility is included in the IPv6 specification, the upgrade can be done incrementally and should not cause any undue displacement. System administrators and network builders will be able to relax as well; IPv6 offers an autoconfiguration facility in which a network card's MAC address is built into the IPv6 address. This arrangement guarantees unique addresses and prevents address conflicts. The autodiscovery and autoconfiguration features also have an additional benefit: Workstations with IPv6 software and hardware can automatically configure themselves for the network to which they're attached.

The net benefit of IPv6 is to simplify connection to a common protocol, thus simplifying networking and creating an open, interoperable standard that regular users can use. As IPv6 becomes more widely adopted, networking will be freed from many of the current technical hurdles and will grow exponentially. Building networks will no longer be a peril-filled process with a steep learning curve.

In addition, the authentication and encryption features built into IPv6 will satisfy consumers who currently fear to do business on the Internet, and it will help enable secure electronic commerce, giving business the green light.

IPv6 isn't the fix for all ills, but it certainly offers a great deal of promise for fixing the problems of the Internet.

A Solution to the Red-Light District: Netblocking Software

In the effort to bar children from accessing certain sites, several software manufacturers have brought out software that blocks access to a list of Web sites based on either the site address (which is coded into a list that's part of the program) or the presence of contraindicated words on a given site. Software programs such as CyberPatrol and

NetNanny offer parents a way to limit children's exposure to what they may consider the insalubrious parts of the Internet. However, parents may want to examine the list of forbidden sites; some Web-blocking software shows distinct biases, blocking not only obscene sites but some political sites and certain sites critical of religious organizations. You should examine the software closely and determine whether or not you want your child to be blocked from certain sites—or whether you want to personally supervise your children until they have developed sufficient critical skills to be able to judge the value of Web sites on their own. Don't trust software to shield your children; better to discuss proper Net use with them and do some parental monitoring.

A Solution to Organizational Confusion: New Top-Level Domains

If you've looked at Internet addresses at all, you've noticed that most U.S. addresses end in three-letter abbreviations such as .com, .gov, .mil, .edu, .org, and .net, among others. These names are called Top-Level Domains (TLDs). Right now, the purpose of TLDs is relatively clear-cut, as Table 24.2 shows.

TABLE 24.2   TLDs and Their Meanings

TLD Name	Meaning
.com	Commercial entities, businesses, Web stores, and so on (for example, Microsoft.com).
.gov	U.S. federal governmental entities (for example, sba.gov, irs.gov).
.mil	U.S. military sites (for example, nic.ddn.mil).
.edu	Educational organizations; typically restricted to colleges and universities, although grade and secondary schools are also beginning to use this domain name (for example, yale.edu).
.org	Not-for-profit organizations (for example, wshu.org, npr.org).
.net	Network service providers (for example, uu.net, worldnet.att.net).

Most of these TLDs are pretty clear—you can determine what category an organization falls into by reading the TLD. But the .com domain is problematic—it's exploded since it was introduced in the early 1990s. As a result, the meaning of the .com domain has become diluted to mean any for-profit enterprise on the Web.

In an attempt to categorize the various types of entities that currently reside in the .com domain, several groups have proposed adding several new TLDs (see Table 24.3).

TABLE 24.3   Some of the Proposed TLDs to Clarify the .com Designation

TLD Name	Meaning
.firm	Firm-based businesses, such as law offices, accounting firms, investment houses (for example, paperchase.firm).
.store	Commercial entities that sell merchandise over the Web (for example, stuff.store).
.nom	Personal Web pages (for example, joesmith.nom).
.web	Activities centered around the World Wide Web (for example, surfergrrl.web).
.arts	Cultural and entertainment sites (for example, MetropolitanMuseumNY.arts; alternatively—and more likely—WoodyAllen.arts, which adds a whole new dimension to the domain).
.rec	Recreational sites (for example, beachvolleyball.rec).
.info	Information services (for example, Library.info).

These proposed TLDs would go a long way toward segmenting the current .com domain into intelligible pieces. At this time, the proposed TLDs are just that: proposed. If and when they become official, there will almost certainly be a stampede to stake claims on the choice addresses within these new domains.

Summary

The Internet is growing and changing at a rate beyond any one person's comprehension. The rise of the Java "write-once-run-anywhere" programming language and the tremendous strides made in HTML and other Web-design tools have made the Internet into far more than the small community it started out as.

Over the course of this book, the emphasis has been on theory rather than practice. The reason for this focus is quite simple: It's easy to figure out how to plug a network in and get it physically connected. The difficult part of networking is figuring out why the network works (or alternatively, doesn't work) and the causes of various problems.

I hope you will take what you learned in this book and put it to good use. My charge to you is this: Go forth and build a network. You know what you need to know by now, and you know where to find the resources to help you figure out the rest. Good luck and good networking. I wish you success.

GLOSSARY

As networking terminology changes, so do glossaries. This glossary does not claim to define everything; nothing can. However, there are Web glossaries (such as www.whatis.com) that offer frequently updated definitions of current computer and networking terms. So if you don't find it here, look on the Web...you may find it there.

10BASE-2   Ethernet networking running on coaxial cable. Also called thinnet or cheapernet, 10BASE-2 supports network segments up to 185 meters in length. It is a bus topology, and cannot withstand any interruption in any cable between two computers.

10BASE-5   Also called yellow-cable Ethernet, 10BASE-5 is similar to 10BASE-2 but uses a thicker cable. Each computer attached to a 10BASE-5 segment has a device called a transceiver that connects the computer to the network wire. 10BASE-5 is a bus topology and cannot withstand disconnections of any computers.

10BASE-T   Ethernet in a star topology. 10BASE-T uses unshielded twisted-pair wiring (UTP) with eight connectors terminated according to specific standards called TIAA 568B. Because it is a star topology, 10BASE-T is much more robust than 10BASE-2 or 10BASE-5.

56K　A digital phone line that can carry data at speeds of up to 56 kilobits per second.

adapter card　This definition applies primarily to Intel-compatible computers. An adapter card is an electronic assembly that connects to a computer through a standard interface (see card-slot interface, later in this glossary) called a card slot. Adapter cards can provide a variety of services to the computer, including video, network, modem, and other functions as required.

administration　An impossible task that involves figuring out how to keep a network running without problems all the time. Part V of this book, "Introduction to Network Administration," is dedicated to this topic.

analog　Based on waveforms rather than on binary patterns of voltage.

analog phone line　A phone line that transmits the sound of your voice as a waveform (like a radio wave). Analog phone lines are common; chances are that analog phone lines are what you have your home phone plugged into. To transmit data over an analog phone line, you must convert it from digital data to sound—that's why modems (devices that convert data to sound) make funny-sounding squawks and hisses. That's digital data being converted to sound.

application　A software program intended to accomplish a single task. For example, Microsoft Word is intended to ease document preparation.

ARPA　Advanced Research Projects Agency, the government group responsible for starting the Internet.

ASCII　American Standard Code for Information Interchange, a way that computers format 1s and 0s (binary code, which computers can understand) into the alphabet, numerals, and other characters that humans can understand.

ATM　Asynchronous Transfer Mode, a new topology for transmitting data across a network. ATM is complex but has many advantages compared to older topologies such as Ethernet and Token Ring. ATM offers Quality of Service and a standard frame (or "cell") size. ATM is rarely used on small networks because of its cost; it is most commonly used in large WAN networks.

authentication　The process of ensuring, as much as possible, that logons and messages from a user (such as a password or email) originate from an authorized source.

backbone　A series of very high-speed phone lines (ranging from 155 to 622 megabits per second—really fast!) that phone companies use to transmit high volumes of traffic. Compare this speed to that of your LAN, where data moves at 10 megabits per second, and you begin to see why it's called the backbone. New technologies are offering increased speed of over a gigabit per second, which will be useful as more people want to use the Internet.

backward compatibility   The capability of a software or hardware product to work with earlier versions of itself.

bandwidth   The measurement of the amount of data a particular medium can carry. For example, the bandwidth of the average phone line is only about 33.6 kilobits per second; the bandwidth for a T1 digital phone line is 1.544 megabits per second.

batch processing   A situation common in early mainframe environments in which many tasks were scheduled to run at a specific time late in the evening. The user never directly interacted with the computer in batch processing.

binary   Having only two states; used to describe the base 2 arithmetic that computers use. In binary notation, 1, 2, 3, 4, 5 is represented as 1, 10, 11, 100, 101. The place value of each place in binary notation doubles with each digit to the left of the decimal point, hence 16, 8, 4, 2, 1. Contrast this with decimal notation (base 10), in which each place value is equal to ten times that of the column to its right.

bit   One piece of information, represented as a 1 or a 0. To the computer, a bit is actually a difference in voltage: high voltage represents a 1, low voltage represents a 0.

bridge   A device that links different networks together so that they form a single logical network. Bridges work at layer 2 of the OSI model.

browser   A program that provides a way to view and read the documents available on the World Wide Web. Netscape Navigator and Microsoft Internet Explorer are browsers.

bus topology   A network topology in which all computers are serially connected to a length of cable. Bus networks are not terribly reliable; if one cable segment goes bad, the whole network fails. 10BASE-2 and 10BASE-5 are examples of bus networks.

byte   Eight bits (also called one octet when discussing TCP/IP). A byte is equal to one character; for example, the letter e is one byte. One byte (eight bits) can represent 256 numbers (0 to 255) in binary numerals.

C programming language   Also known as "C", a high-level computer language developed by Brian Kernighan and Dennis Ritchie at Bell Labs. The C language enables programmers to write code that can be compiled to run on different types of computers. C programming is widely regarded as a cross between an art and a science.

cable modem   A device used by cable providers to provide high-speed data access using cable as the media.

card-slot interface   The place in which adapter cards are installed in Intel-compatible personal computers. Card-slot interfaces come in several varieties: ISA, EISA, VESA (now outdated), and PCI.

CDPD   Cellular Digital Packet Data, the most common way to send data over wireless links. Most commonly, CDPD uses the 2.4GHz radio spectrum.

cheapernet   A colloquial name for 10BASE-2, so called because it is just about the least expensive type of network one can build.

checksum   A part of a packet header that ensures that the packet has not been damaged during transmission across the network. A checksum is a number calculated on-the-fly based on the size of the packet; if the checksum is incorrect, the receiving computer discards the packet and asks the originating computer to resend it.

ciphertext   The text of an encoded message. Ciphertext is not readable unless it is decrypted into plaintext. In other words, up cf ps opu up cf is an example of a ciphertext message.

CIR   Committed Information Rate, a guarantee from the provider of a digital phone line service (usually your local telephone company) that ensures the slowest data transmission speed your network will ever have. CIR is usually calculated at a fraction of the rated line speed; for example, a 128K frame relay line often has a CIR of 64K, or 50% of the bandwidth.

client   A computer that uses the resources shared by server computers.

client/server   A network in which the processing is distributed between a server and a client, each with specific roles. Also used to describe networks with dedicated servers. Opposite of peer-to-peer.

clustering   In networking, clustering is aggregating several servers so that if one of them fails, other servers seamlessly take over.

coaxial cable   A two-conductor cable with a solid center conductor and a braided outer conductor. Coaxial cable is used for 10BASE-2 networks and is similar to the cable used for cable TV.

collision   In terms of networking, what happens when two computers attempt to transmit data on the same network wire at the same time. Doing so creates a conflict; both computers sense the collision, stop transmitting, and wait a random amount of time before retransmitting.

collision domain   The group of computers that communicate on a single network wire. Each computer in a collision domain listens to every other computer in the collision domain; each computer can transmit data only when no other computer is currently transmitting.

compiler   A program that takes computer source code (which is just plain text, the same kind you see in Windows Notepad or the DOS Edit utility) and translates it into machine language, which is a string of instructions that the computer can execute. Compilers are synonymous with Unix; almost every variety of Unix is packaged with at least a C compiler. Many versions of Unix now also come with C++ compilers. Compilers exist for many languages; C is simply the most common.

concentrator   Also called a hub or MAU, a concentrator helps ensure the robustness of the network by making sure that the network can't be disconnected because of a single cable failure.

configuration management   The art (or science) of ensuring (from a central console) that user workstations have the correct hardware and software installed and that the software and hardware is set up according to consensual and preset standards.

CPU   Central Processing Unit, the microprocessor inside a computer that enables it to function. Examples of CPUs include Intel's Pentium and Pentium Pro, Motorola's PowerPC, and Digital Equipment Corporation's Alpha chips.

cracker   Someone who makes unauthorized accesses into others' computer systems, usually maliciously. Not the same as hacker.

CSMA/CD   Carrier Sense Multiple Access/Collision Detection, the means by which computers exchange data in Ethernet networks.

CSU/DSU   Channel Service Unit/Data Service Unit, a device that changes local network packets into packets that can be transmitted over a WAN.

DARPA   Defense Advanced Research Projects Agency, or ARPA after it was taken over by the military.

database   A file or collection of data structured in logical relationships. For example, the phone book is a database on paper, with names in one column and phone numbers in another column.

datagram   See packet.

decimal   The way of writing numbers we use all the time; base 10. In base 10, you count from 1 to 9 like this: 1, 2, 3, 4, 5, 6, 7, 8, 9. Contrast this with binary and hexadecimal notation.

denial-of-service attack   An attack on an Internet-connected computer that forces it to cease performing its designated function (Web serving, file serving, and so on).

device driver   Software that controls specific hardware on your computer. For example, the software that controls your mouse and keyboard is a device driver.

DHCP   Dynamic Host Configuration Protocol, a piece of the TCP/IP protocol suite that handles the automatic assignment of IP addresses to clients.

dial-on-demand   Whenever a user needs a resource on another LAN (a file, database access, whatever), the local LAN catches the request and dials the remote LAN using either garden-variety Plain Old Telephone Service (POTS) or a switched digital phone line such as Integrated Services Digital Network (ISDN).

digital   A data transmission type based on data that has been binary encoded (that is, data that has been formatted into 1s and 0s).

digital phone line   A phone line that converts the sound of your voice into digital data. Digital phone lines work better for computers than analog phone lines because computers transmit information digitally. Digital phone lines are often used for WANs in which data has to be transmitted at high speeds over long distances.

directory services   A set of tools that enable network administrators to provide users with access to certain specific resources independent of where on the network the users log in. In other words, if Tom in Marketing has access to Server1 and Server2 but no access to Server3, he can access only to Server1 and Server2 regardless of whether he logs in to the network on a computer in Marketing, Production, or Administration. As networks have grown more complex and required management of greater numbers of users, directory services have become a saving grace for network administrators trying to manage access across thousand-plus-user, multisite networks.

disk   A device that stores digital 1s and 0s (also called bits) on magnetic media such as a hard drive or floppy drive. CD-ROM drives use light rather than electrical impulses to retrieve data.

DNS   Domain Naming System, the pieces of the TCP/IP protocol suite that resolve IP addresses to names. For example, DNS resolves 192.168.1.5 to alice.library.net.

domain   A group of computers whose logon across the network is authenticated through the NT Server. Essentially, a domain takes authentication out of the hands of the individual workstations and centralizes it on the server.

DSL   Digital Subscriber Line, a means by which the phone company provides high-speed digital data services over standard two-pair copper wire.

email   Electronic mail, a way of sending text and files across a network with postal-mail-like notification.

encapsulation   The process of taking a packet of one protocol and putting another protocol's information around it. Equivalent to taking a letter, sealing it in an envelope, addressing that envelope, and then placing the first, sealed envelope into a second envelope addressed in a different language. It's not really efficient, and it wastes materials and time. Unfortunately, that's often the only way to accomplish something.

encryption key   A series of letters and numbers used to make plaintext messages into ciphertexts. An encryption key's security depends on how long it is.

error correction   The process of ensuring that data transferred across the wire is done so correctly. Typically, error correction works by using a checksum to determine whether or not data has been corrupted in transfer. The process of error correction takes a certain amount of the bandwidth of any connection. The more failure-prone the connection is, the more robust (and hence, the larger in bits) the error correction should be in relation to the entire bandwidth. In other words, a dial-up line tends to be noisy and unreliable, so error correction takes up a lot of the connection's bandwidth. By contrast, a digital connection such as a T1 is much cleaner and hence has less error correction.

Ethernet   A local area network (LAN) topology based on a method called Carrier Sense Multiple Access/Collision Detection. Ethernet comes in many varieties—the specification is available in IEEE 802.3. Other versions of Ethernet include 802.2, SNAP, and II. Ethernet is, by all accounts, the most common network topology in the world today.

fail over   The logical extension of fault tolerance. In a fail-over system, there are two (or occasionally more) servers, each with identical copies of a master server's drives and resources. If the master server fails, the backup server takes over dynamically and users never see the difference (except for a small and brief slowdown).

fault tolerance or redundancy   The capability of a computer system to shrug off failure of a device and continue operating normally. Generally, fault-tolerant devices send a message to an administrative user when a particular device fails so that the device can be replaced. Fault tolerance is often implemented by simply adding a second device (a second hard drive, network card, or whatever). Of late, however, IBM-compatible computers are beginning to use clustering for fault tolerance; that's when a whole extra machine is on standby, waiting for the first one to fail. See also clustering.

FDDI   Fiber Distributed Data Interface, a method of transmitting data across a network using lasers and pulses of light sent over a glass fiber cable rather than sending electricity over a copper wire.

fiber Optical fiber is used instead of copper wire in some networks. It looks like coaxial cable with flexible strands of glass in the center rather than copper wire.

firewall A computer that controls access to an Internet-connected network.

frame relay A method of reframing (or repacketizing) already-packetized data to allow it to be transmitted over the phone company's frame relay network.

frame type A type of packet. NetWare 2.x and 3.x used the Ethernet 802.3 packet scheme; NetWare 4.x uses more-standard Ethernet 802.2 frames. The only thing you have to know about frame types in a NetWare context is that you must run the same frame type on the client's network card as you're running on the server's network card so that they can communicate.

FTP File transfer protocol, the piece of the TCP/IP protocol suite that enables users to copy files between computers.

gateway A catchall term to describe a system that essentially bridges two systems. Gateways can pass mail, translate protocols, forward packets, and perform other tasks. A gateway's primary purpose is communication.

gateway protocols Members of the TCP/IP protocol suite that routers use to determine the best route for data packets.

groupware application A software application that allows people to use networked computers to work together. Groupware often helps increase efficiency by automating the flow of work from person to person and reducing the overall amount of paper generated by a task.

GUI Graphical user interface, a shell on a computer's operating system that graphically represents data. Windows, the MacOS interface, and UNIX's Motif are all GUIs.

hacker A much-misused term. A hacker does not break into computer systems (a cracker does that); instead, a hacker is a skilled programmer and problem solver. The sobriquet is seldom accurate if self-endowed.

hard drive A nonremovable magnetic media drive that stores data on a computer.

header The part of a packet that carries information about the source and destination of the packet, the checksum, and any other data about the packet.

hexadecimal notation Base-16 notation. In hexadecimal notation, you count from 0 to 15 like this: 0, 1, 2, 3, 4, 5, 6, 7, 8, 9, A, B, C, D, E, F.

HTML Hypertext Markup Language, a way of formatting plain text so that it can be displayed as graphical text in a browser window. HTML uses tags, or inline formatting commands, to define how things look. For example, <h1> This is a header </h1> is inter-preted by a browser as a command to format the text This is a header in the header-1 style (whatever that has been defined as).

HTTP   Hypertext Transfer Protocol, the piece of the TCP/IP protocol suite used to transmit World Wide Web documents across the Internet.

hub   A colloquial term for Ethernet concentrators.

I/O or throughput   Generally, a loose measure of the speed at which a particular piece of hardware can move data. A fast processor, for example, is said to have better I/O than a slow one. I/O is most commonly applied to devices that have to actually move information: hard drives that have to read and write information to and from their drive platters and network cards that have to send and retrieve data from the network.

IDE   Integrated Drive Electronics, a way of attaching hard drives to computers using logic built into the hard drive rather than using a third-party device.

IMAP   Interactive Mail Access Protocol, a new piece of the TCP/IP protocol suite that handles the transmission of mail between server and client. IMAP largely supplants POP; its current revision is IMAP4.

infrared   The light spectrum just shorter than red; invisible to human eyes. Infrared is often used for line-of-sight data transmission in wireless networks.

Internet   The global network of networks now used for everything from email to elec-tronic commerce to research.

interoperability   The capability of two products to operate together, ideally according to open standards such as the TCP/IP protocol.

IP   Internet Protocol, the part of the TCP/IP protocol responsible for providing address-ing and routing services to packets. IP ensures that packets are addressed properly.

IP address   A sequence of numbers associated with a network adapter's MAC address. It is 32 bits long and is divided into four 1-byte strings that have values ranging from 0 to 255. Example: 209.61.64.1.

IPX   Internetworking Packet Exchange, the part of Novell NetWare's IPX/SPX protocol responsible for addressing and routing.

ISDN   Integrated Services Digital Network, a switched digital phone service that in its Basic Rate Interface (BRI) can carry up to 128 kilobits per second of data; in its Primary Rate Interface (PRI), it can be as fast as 1.5 megabits per second. ISDN is very useful for connecting remote users who have high-speed network requirements.

ISP   Internet service provider, a company that provides connections to the Internet. The connections can range from dial-up to frame relay, depending on the ISP and the connection speed desired.

Java   A programming language invented by Sun Microsystems that enables programmers to write software that can run on any platform using a Java Virtual Machine developed for that platform.

jumper   A very small piece of plastic (less than $\frac{1}{8}$ inch on a side) with a conductive metal strip inside it. Jumpers are used (like switches) to make electrical connections on a card.

LAN   Local area network, a group of computers in a local area tied together without any routers between them. All computers are connected to the same set of hubs or switches in a LAN, and all network resources are "local," running at the full speed of the network.

Linux   A freeware Unix-like operating system developed by Linus Torvalds and a host of Internet programmers. Linux is free, fast, and astonishingly stable. If you have to learn Unix, Linux is a great place to start.

logical segment   A network configuration in which a single network segment is simulated through the use of devices called concentrators.

login script   A text file stored on the server that has a list of commands. When a user logs in, the server reads the text file, executes the commands included in it, and often maps drives and connects network printers on-the-fly for each user. Typical login scripts can include lines that don't do anything except let the user know that he or she is being logged in; the login script can also include commands such as net use which establish network connections to other computers.

MAC address   Media Access Control address, a 6-byte (48-bit) address unique to each and every network card, represented in hexadecimal notation.

MAN   Metropolitan Area Network, a group of LANs in a relatively small geographical area joined by digital phone lines or by other technologies such as microwave radio.

MAU   Multistation Access Unit, IBM's name for a Token Ring concentrator.

memory   The chips that provide a place for the computer to store the 1s and 0s it needs to do computations. Memory chips are fast—an order of magnitude faster than virtual memory.

modem   Short for modulate-demodulate. A device used to convert digital signals into analog tones that can be transmitted over the telephone network.

multitasking   In operating systems, the capability to divide computer time among two or more running programs simultaneously.

NDS   NetWare Directory Services, a set of standards for organizing enterprise networks. Proprietary to Novell, but available on many systems. Very powerful for organizing and logically segmenting networks.

NetBEUI   NetBIOS Extended User Interface, an extension of NetBIOS that includes the capability to frame packets (NetBEUI Frame, or NBF) among other extended features. NetBEUI is a common implementation of NetBIOS.

NetBIOS   Network Basic I/O System, a small, nonroutable protocol developed by IBM for small PC networks.

NetWare   Novell's network operating system. Powerful and extremely scalable. Quite complex to administer but very fast.

network   Any conglomeration of parts working together in a predictable order. In computer terms, a group of computers connected by a common topology that enables data to be transmitted.

network adapter   An adapter card installed in a computer that allows it to communicate on a network.

NFS   Network File System, Sun Microsystems' standard way of allowing a computer to access the files on another computer's hard drive as though the files were part of the local file system.

NIC   Network Interface Card, also called network adapters; an add-in card that plugs into a computer and enables it to communicate on a network. NICs are usually ATM, Ethernet (of one variety or another), Token Ring, or FDDI.

NLM   NetWare Loadable Module, a program that can execute natively on a NetWare server. Most NLMs can be loaded and unloaded on-the-fly. They control a great many NetWare functions, from the protocols it uses (IPX.NLM and SPX.NLM) to backup and administration (MONITOR.NLM).

NOS   Network Operating System, software that allows a computer to perform certain network-centric tasks such as authenticating users, handling file security, and providing connections to network resources. Windows NT Server, Unix, and NetWare are NOSes. Part IV of this book, "Network Operating Systems," is dedicated to this topic.

octet   The "official" name for a byte (eight bits, or eight digital 1s and 0s).

open standards   Hardware and software standards that are not proprietary to any given manufacturer. TCP/IP and Ethernet are both open standards.

operating system   The software on a computer that enables the user to communicate with the hardware and get tasks done. Windows 95, Windows NT Workstation, OS/2, and Unix are all operating systems.

optical fiber   The medium used by fiber-optic networks. Most networks use either coaxial cable or UTP.

OSI model   Open Systems Interconnect Model, a reference model that details seven layers of functionality for networks. The OSI model offers an ideal way to understand the theory of networking.

OSPF   Open Shortest Path First, a routing protocol that uses what's called a link-state algorithm. Link-state algorithms look at the available routes a data packet can take to its destination and decide the best route. OSPF does not have a maximum hop count as RIP does.

packet   Also called a datagram; information placed inside a "wrapper" called the header. Packets contain headers (which handle addressing), error correction, checksums, and (eventually) the data sent across the network.

packet header   See header.

packet-switching   A technology in which binary data is divided into small packages that handle error correction and address information to transmit data across a physical medium such as cable.

PC card   A credit-card-sized electronic device that slides into a slot on the side of a laptop. PC cards can be almost anything, but they are usually network adapters and modems.

peer-to-peer   A network built without a central server. In a peer network, all computers can be both servers and clients as required. Generally unmanageable, but useful for small networks.

plaintext   The text of a message in human-readable format. In other words, to be or not to be is an example of a plaintext message.

Plug and Play   Adapter card hardware for which I/O addresses and IRQs are set through software rather than through hardware jumpers of some sort.

POP   Post Office Protocol, the TCP/IP standard for mail transmission between server and client. POP3 is the current version.

porting   The process of recompiling C language source code into versions that can run on different computers.

POTS   Plain Old Telephone Service, the regular old Ma Bell dial tone used for voice and modems.

PPP   Point-to-Point Protocol, the part of the TCP/IP protocol suite used to connect computers across switched telephone lines—either regular phone service (POTS) or switched digital service (ISDN).

programming languages   Standardized ways of creating instructions for computers. Common programming languages include C, Fortran, Java, Smalltalk, COBOL, APL, and others.

protocol   An agreed-on standard. In networking terms, a protocol is used to address and ensure delivery of packets across a network.

protocol translator   A device that can translate between two network protocols. Typically, protocol translators translate NetWare IPX to TCP/IP so that users on an IPX network can access the Internet or IP resources.

proxy server   A server that hides internal network IP addresses from the Internet by making requests for the internal clients.

QoS   Quality of Service; in packet data, QoS is very similar to QoS in regular mail. In regular mail, you have a choice of services—first class, second class, third class, bulk mail, overnight, and so forth. When you send an overnight letter, it receives priority over first-class mail, so it gets to its destination first. A few bits of data in a packet of data indicate the QoS required for that data. QoS is an evolving standard and will hopefully be common on all platforms and topologies within the next few years.

RAID   Redundant Array of Inexpensive Disks, a method of ensuring data security, ranging from simple disk mirroring with two disks (RAID 1) to striping all data across three or more disks (RAID 5).

redundancy or fault tolerance   The capability of a computer system to shrug off the failure of a device and continue operating normally. Generally, redundant devices send a message to an administrative user when a particular device fails so that the device can be replaced. Redundancy is often implemented by simply adding a second device (a second hard drive, network card, or whatever). Of late, however, IBM-compatible computers are beginning to use clustering for redundancy (when a whole extra machine is on standby, waiting for the first one to fail).

repeater   A device that enables networks to communicate reasonably well. A repeater amplifies and cleans up digital signals and forward them on towards their destination.

RIP   Routing Information Protocol, a protocol that works by counting the number of times a packet has been moved toward its destination. Each new routing is called a hop, and the maximum hop count is usually set to 16. In RIP, if a packet is routed more than 16 times, it's discarded.

RMON   Remote Monitoring, the part of the TCP/IP protocol suite that handles network management and network data collection. RMON is much more efficient than its older sibling, SNMP.

router   A device or (optionally) software that routes packets toward their destinations. Routers must be connected to at least two networks. They decide how to send data based on network conditions.

routing tables   A database of routes between networks that routers carry in their memory. In general, the smaller the routing table, the faster the router.

RPC   Remote Procedure Call, a method used on client/server networks for communicating between processes (applications) running on different computers. RPC is sometimes used to distribute work across a network according to appropriateness. For example, a server running a database might handle searches locally, while queries are generated at the client computer.

scalable   The measure of a system's capability to grow. It is not quantifiable; unfortunately, there is no standard against which to compare a particular system. As a result, scalability is relative. For example, if a network has 10 users and grows to 100, will the current network architecture continue to work well? If the answer is yes, the system is scalable; if the answer is no, the system is not scalable.

scope creep   A process in which the scope of a job grows while the job is in process. Scope creep is the bane of project managers; it almost guarantees that a given project will be over budget and late.

scripting language   A limited programming language built into many operating systems.

SCSI   Small Computer Serial Interface, pronounced "scuzzy;" a method for connecting a variety of peripherals to a computer. SCSI devices include hard drives, CD-ROM drives, scanners, and so on.

separate memory spaces   In Windows NT (versions 3.5x to 4.x), it is possible to run 16-bit applications (that is, older Windows applications) in their own memory space. This means that if and when these applications misbehave, they theoretically can't crash other applications.

server   A computer on a network that shares a specific resource (file, print, applications) with other computers.

share   Microsoft's method for allowing computers to access other computers' drives and printers as though those resources were local.

shell   The interactive user interface in an operating system or network operating system. The shell takes the user's commands either at the command line (the DOS C-prompt, for example) or through a graphical user interface (the Windows interface, for example) and passes them to the operating system or network operating system.

shell script   In Unix, a text file containing operating system commands. When the name of the shell script is typed at a command line, the series of commands in the file runs. DOS has a pale shadow of shell scripting called batch files. Batch files do much the same thing, but because DOS can do only one thing at a time, batch files are of limited use.

SLIP   Serial Line Internet Protocol, an older standard, part of the TCP/IP protocol suite used to connect computers over phone lines. Superseded by PPP.

slot interface   See card-slot interface.

SMTP   Simple Mail Transmission Protocol, the TCP/IP standard for Internet mail. SMTP exchanges mail between servers; contrast this with POP, which transmits mail between a server and a client.

Sneaker Net   How files got moved before networks—usually with floppy disks and a bit of shoe leather or sneaker rubber (hence the name).

SNMP   Simple Network Management Protocol, the piece of the TCP/IP protocol suite that deals with the transmission of network information for system administration and management. SNMP is not as efficient as its younger sibling, RMON.

soft-set   See Plug and Play.

SOHO   Small Office/Home Office, a term used to describe the increasingly decentralized office market. SOHO devices typically support from one to four users instead of many users.

source code   The text files written by programmers that are fed into compilers; the compilers output executable files that the computer can understand so that programs can run.

star topology   A network topology in which all connections pass through a central device called a concentrator. 10BASE-T, Token Ring, FDDI, and ATM all use star topologies.

striping   The process by which a RAID drive controller card writes data to multiple disks.

subnet   A way of dividing TCP/IP networks into smaller pieces for management or security purposes. Subnets are bridged by routers.

subnet mask   The portion of an IP address that defines the network, as opposed to identifying a particular computer. For example, a computer with an IP address of 192.168.1.5 might have a subnet mask of 255.255.255.0. The portion of the address that reads 192.168.1 is the network address, and the .5 is the address of the specific machine on that network. The subnet mask explains that the first three numbers in a dotted-decimal address (for example, 192.168.1) are the network and that the last number denotes a specific computer on that network.

switching   A technology in which each connection between two computers has a dedicated channel available to only those two computers at any given time.

T1   A digital phone line that can carry data at speeds of up to 1.544 megabits per second.

tag   In HTML, a formatting device. A tag starts with a formatting command between two angle brackets (<HEADING 1>) and ends with the same command preceded by a slash (</HEADING 1>).

TCP   Transmission Control Protocol, the part of the TCP/IP protocol suite that ensures reliable delivery of packets to their destinations.

TCP/IP   Transmission Control Protocol/Internet Protocol, a catchall term to describe the multifaceted protocol suite on which the Internet runs. TCP/IP is also an open standard; it is not owned by or proprietary to any company. Anyone can create an implementation of the TCP/IP protocol if they want to do so.

thinnet   Yet another colloquial name for 10BASE-2 Ethernet.

throughput or I/O   Generally, a loose measure of the speed at which a particular piece of hardware can move data. A fast processor, for example, is said to have better throughput than a slow one. Throughput is most commonly used to describe devices that have to actually move information: hard drives that have to read and write information to and from their drive platters and network cards that have to send and retrieve data from the network.

Token Ring—A topology that exchanges data between computers by token passing rather than CSMA/CD.

topology   In networking terms, a topology is nothing more than the arrangement of a network. The term can refer to the physical layout of the network (which is where 10BASE-2, 10BASE-T, and fiber come into the arrangement) or the logical layout of the network.

transceiver   The part of the network adapter card that manages sending and receiving data packets from the network wire.

tunneling protocol   A protocol that ensures that data passing over a company's Virtual Private Network is secure. Tunneling is similar to putting a letter/envelope addressed to a non-local company mailstop in another, larger envelope that uses postal mail to send it to another company location. When the mail gets to the nonlocal company mailstop, the mail clerks take it out of the large envelope and send it on to the person to whom it's addressed.

UDP   User Datagram Protocol, the part of the TCP/IP protocol suite that handles "unreliable" delivery of packets. In other words, UDP handles the delivery of packets over links that aren't always available.

Unix   An operating system developed by Bell Labs during the late 1960s and early 1970s. Arguably the best OS for mission-critical applications because of almost 30 years of refinement. Common Unix vendors are Sun Microsystems and Santa Cruz Operation (SCO).

user group   In Windows NT domains, a class of domain users grouped together for simplified administration. Groups are created and managed in the Windows NT User Manager for Domains application. Users can have specific privileges assigned and specific resources made available as the result of their membership in a user group. For example, user group Accounting might have access to the system's accounting files and applications. Users not in the Accounting user group do not have access to those resources.

UTP   Unshielded twisted-pair wire, a cable with four pairs of wires (blue, orange, green, and brown) used for Ethernet and Token Ring network wiring.

VAR   Value Added Reseller, a reseller who also handles integration and project management tasks.

virtual memory   Space on a disk dedicated to providing memory space when the capacity of physical memory chips has been exceeded.

VLAN   Virtual Local Area Network, a network that appears to be a small LAN to its users but which is actually a logical construct. Users can be local or distributed across several sites; connectivity is provided by various software packages.

VPN   Virtual Private Network, a network established over a carrier's digital phone lines (such as AT&T or Sprint lines) and dedicated solely to connecting several specific client sites. Used to implement WANs by using the Internet to create a quasi-private network.

WAN   Wide area network, a network composed of two or more LANs connected by phone lines (generally digital phone lines) and routed between segments.

Windows 95   Microsoft's client operating system.

Windows NT   Microsoft's enterprise operating system. Fully preemptive and reliable.

winsock   A set of files, usually centered around a file called Winsock.dll, that Windows uses to interact with TCP/IP.

WWW   World Wide Web, the resources that can be accessed on the Internet using HTTP, often published in HTML.

yellow-cable Ethernet   Another term for 10BASE-5 ("thicknet") Ethernet.

INDEX

R

X - Y - Z

Other Related Titles